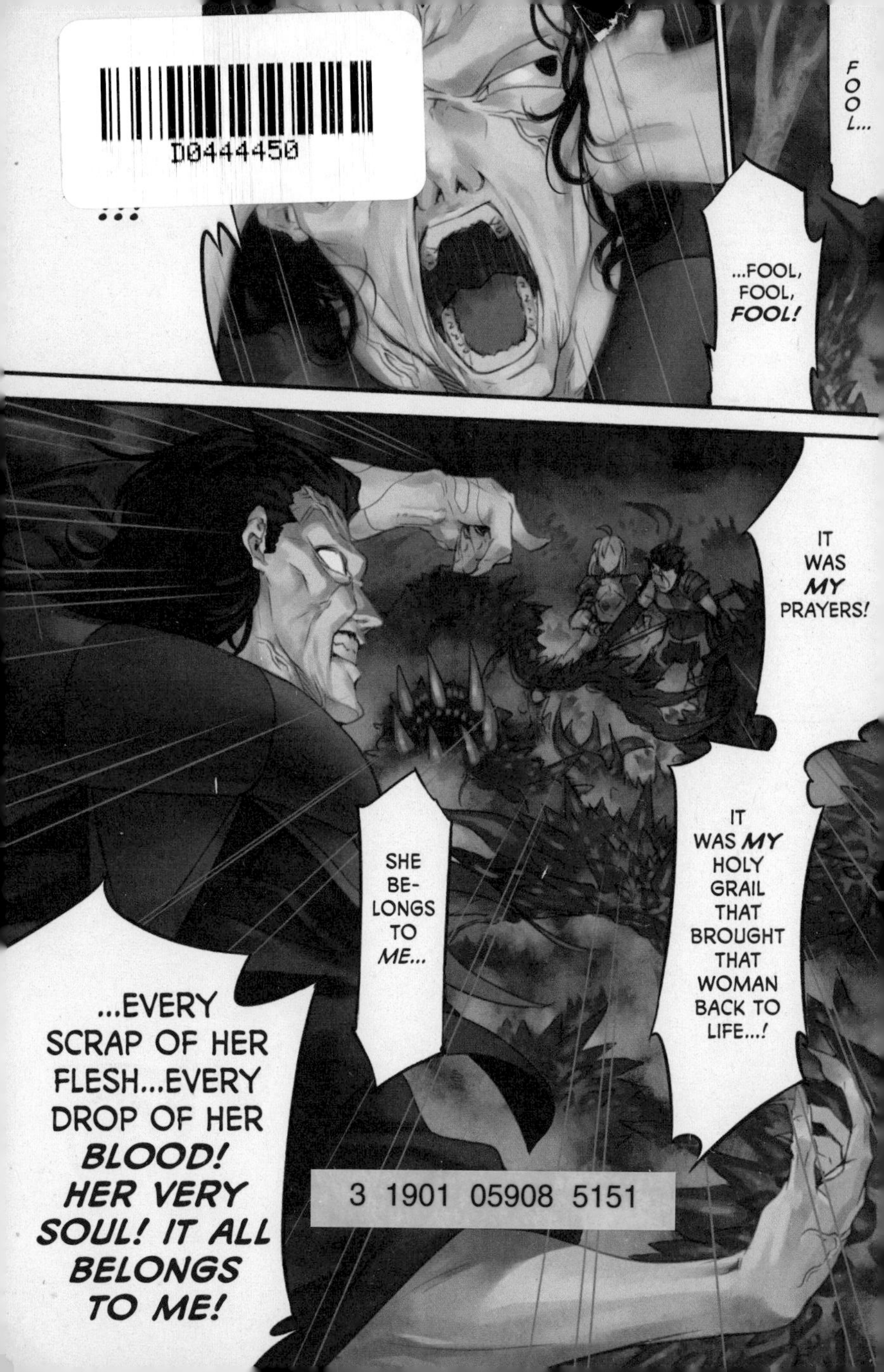
FOOL...
...FOOL, FOOL, FOOL!
IT WAS MY PRAYERS!
IT WAS MY HOLY GRAIL THAT BROUGHT THAT WOMAN BACK TO LIFE...!
SHE BELONGS TO ME...
...EVERY SCRAP OF HER FLESH...EVERY DROP OF HER BLOOD! HER VERY SOUL! IT ALL BELONGS TO ME!

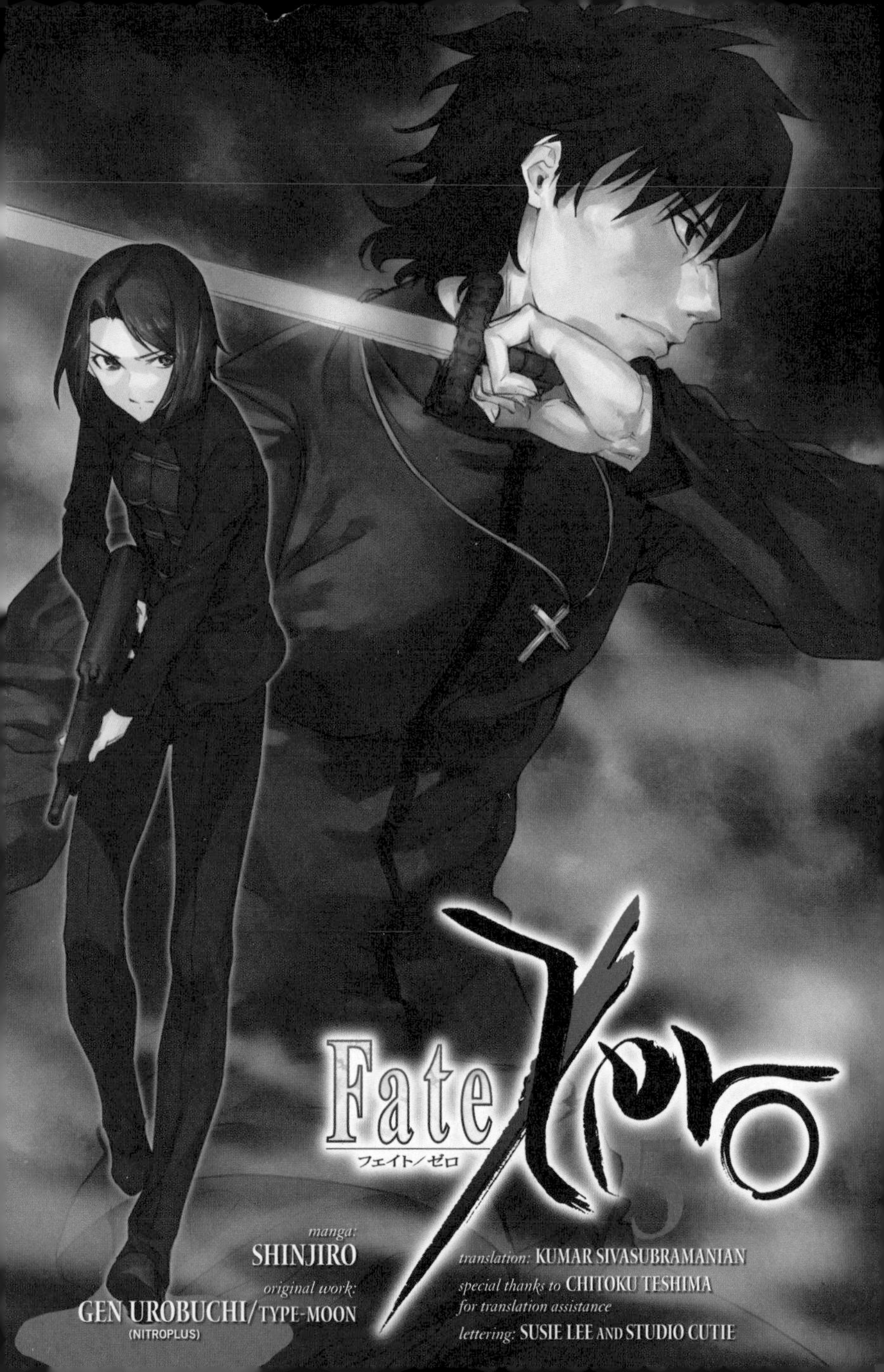
Fate Zero
フェイト/ゼロ

manga: **SHINJIRO**

original work: **GEN UROBUCHI/TYPE-MOON**
(NITROPLUS)

translation: **KUMAR SIVASUBRAMANIAN**

special thanks to **CHITOKU TESHIMA** *for translation assistance*

lettering: **SUSIE LEE AND STUDIO CUTIE**

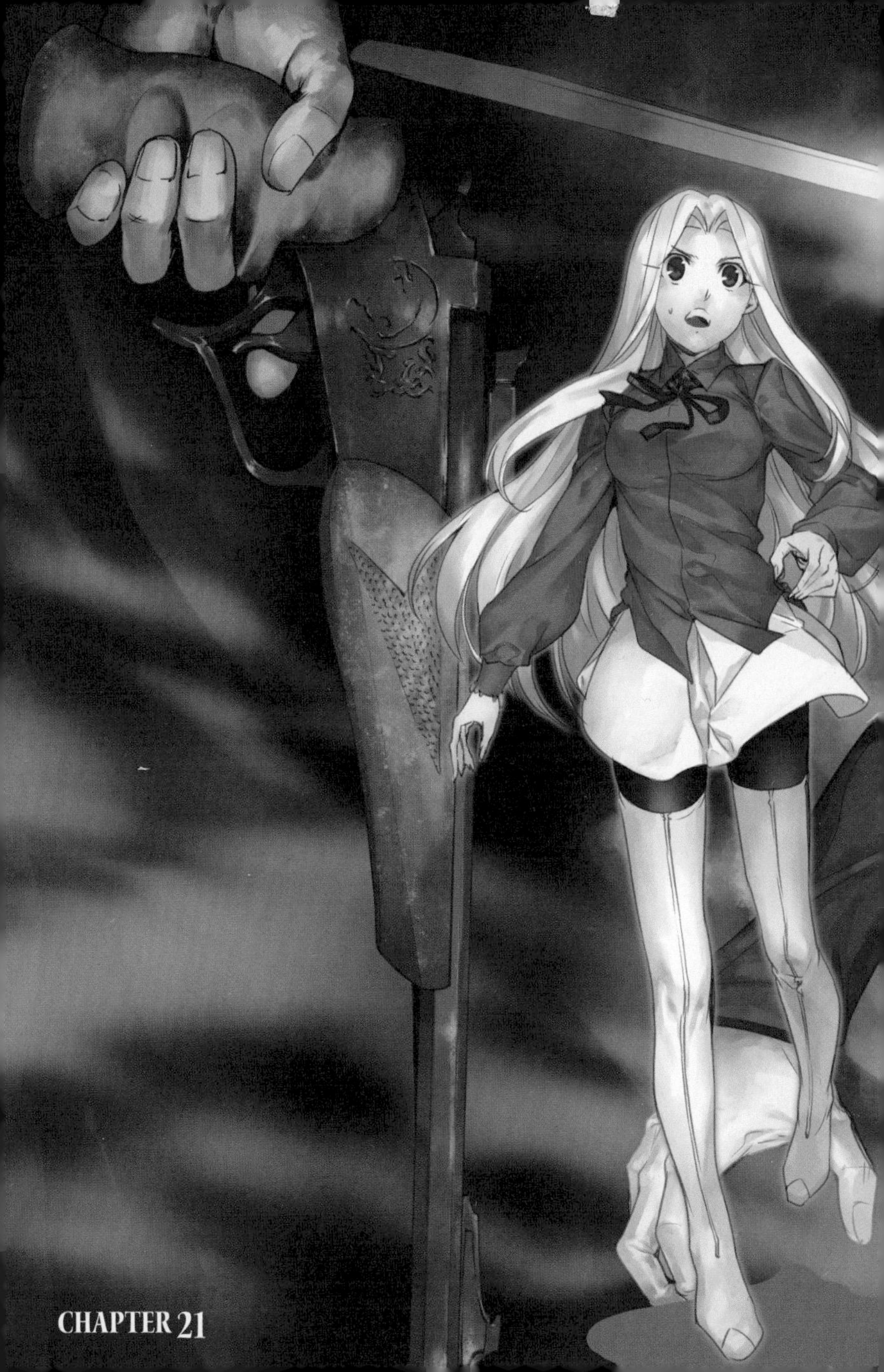

CHAPTER 21

Fate Zero

フェイト／ゼロ

5

Contents

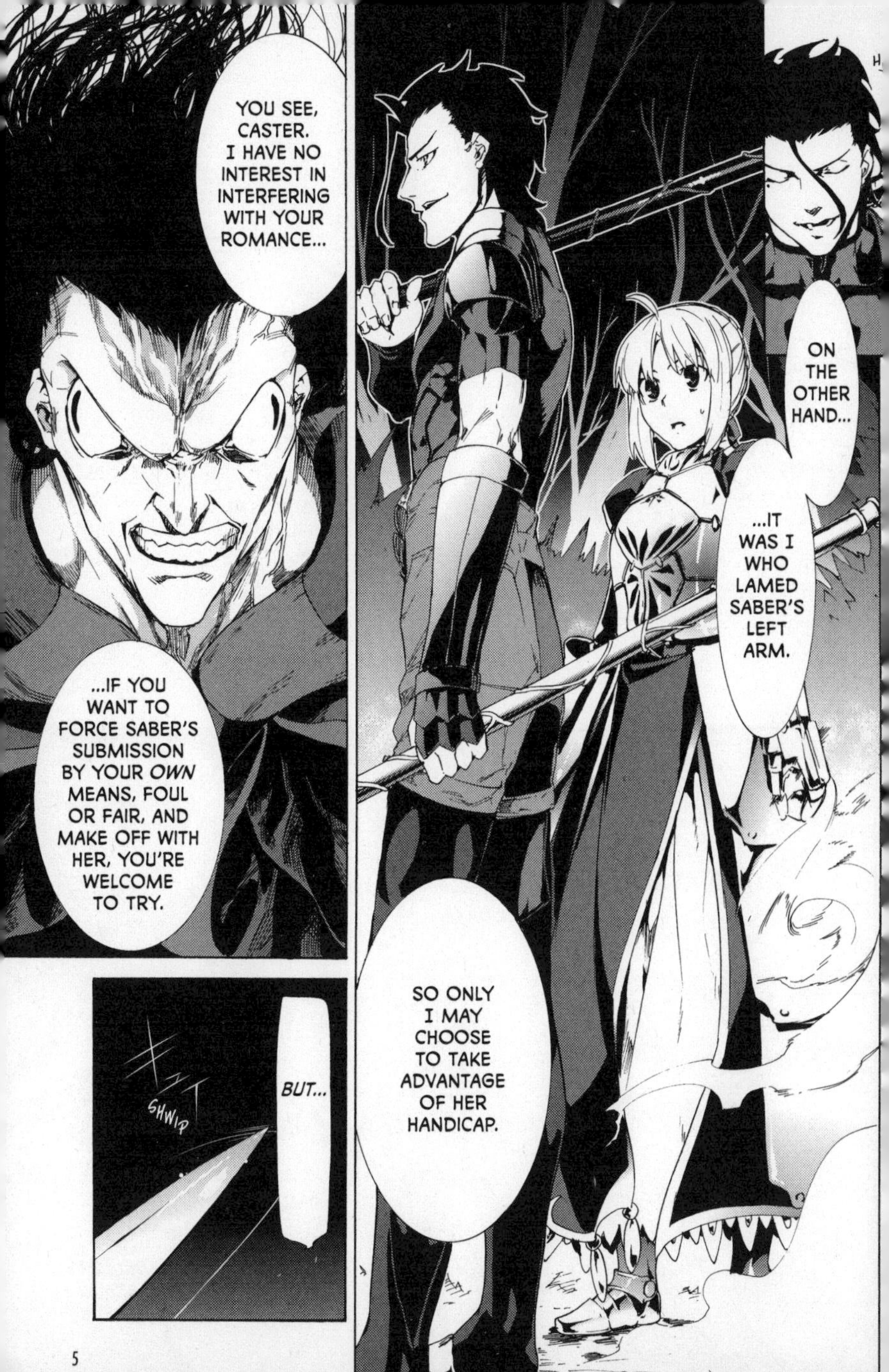
YOU SEE, CASTER. I HAVE NO INTEREST IN INTERFERING WITH YOUR ROMANCE...
...IF YOU WANT TO FORCE SABER'S SUBMISSION BY YOUR *OWN* MEANS, FOUL OR FAIR, AND MAKE OFF WITH HER, YOU'RE WELCOME TO TRY.
BUT...
SHWIP
ON THE OTHER HAND...
...IT WAS I WHO LAMED SABER'S LEFT ARM.
SO ONLY I MAY CHOOSE TO TAKE ADVANTAGE OF HER HANDICAP.

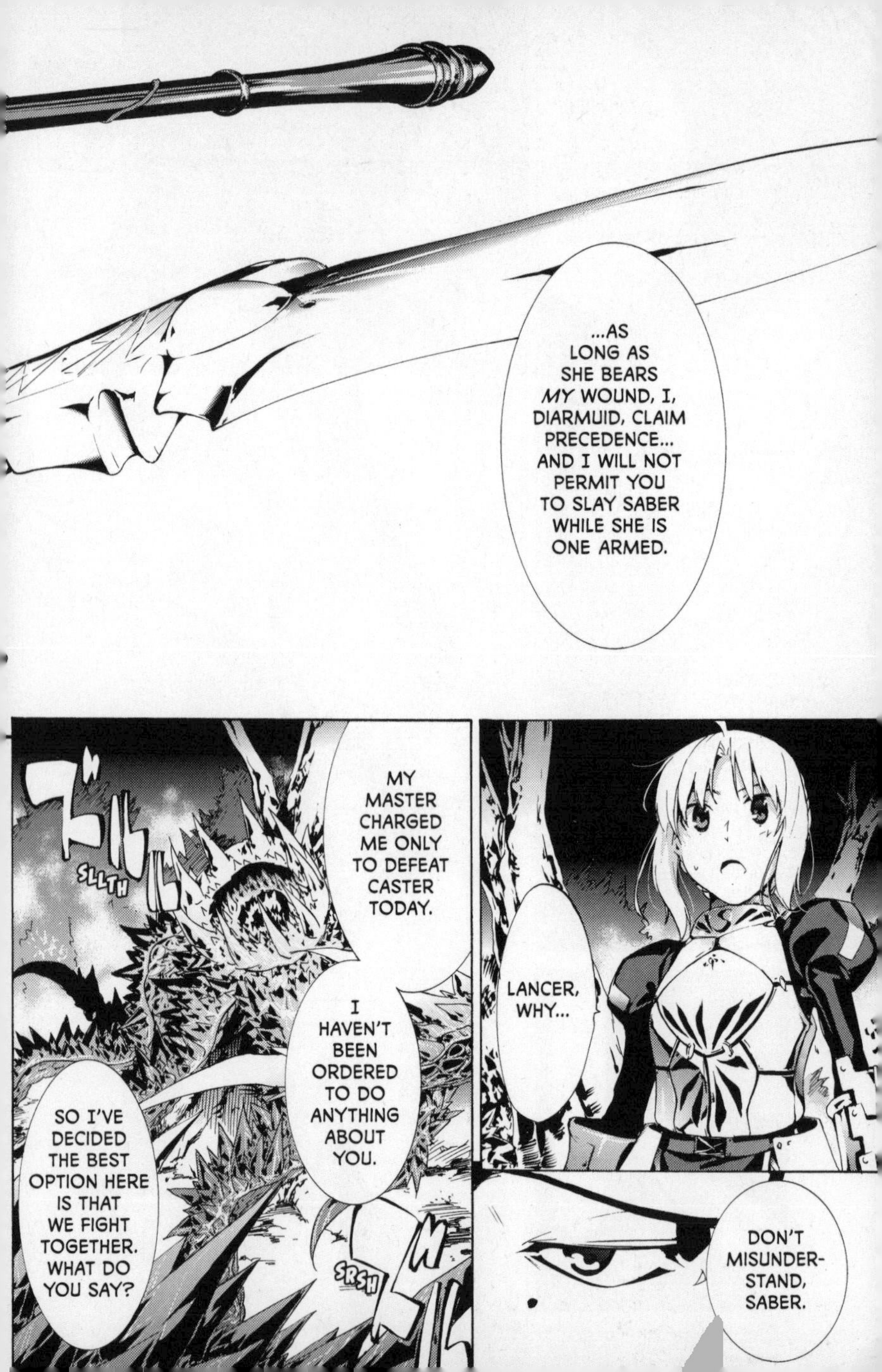
...AS LONG AS SHE BEARS *MY* WOUND, I, DIARMUID, CLAIM PRECEDENCE... AND I WILL NOT PERMIT YOU TO SLAY SABER WHILE SHE IS ONE ARMED.
LANCER, WHY...
DON'T MISUNDER-STAND, SABER.
MY MASTER CHARGED ME ONLY TO DEFEAT CASTER TODAY.
SLLTH
I HAVEN'T BEEN ORDERED TO DO ANYTHING ABOUT YOU.
SO I'VE DECIDED THE BEST OPTION HERE IS THAT WE FIGHT TOGETHER. WHAT DO YOU SAY?
SRSH

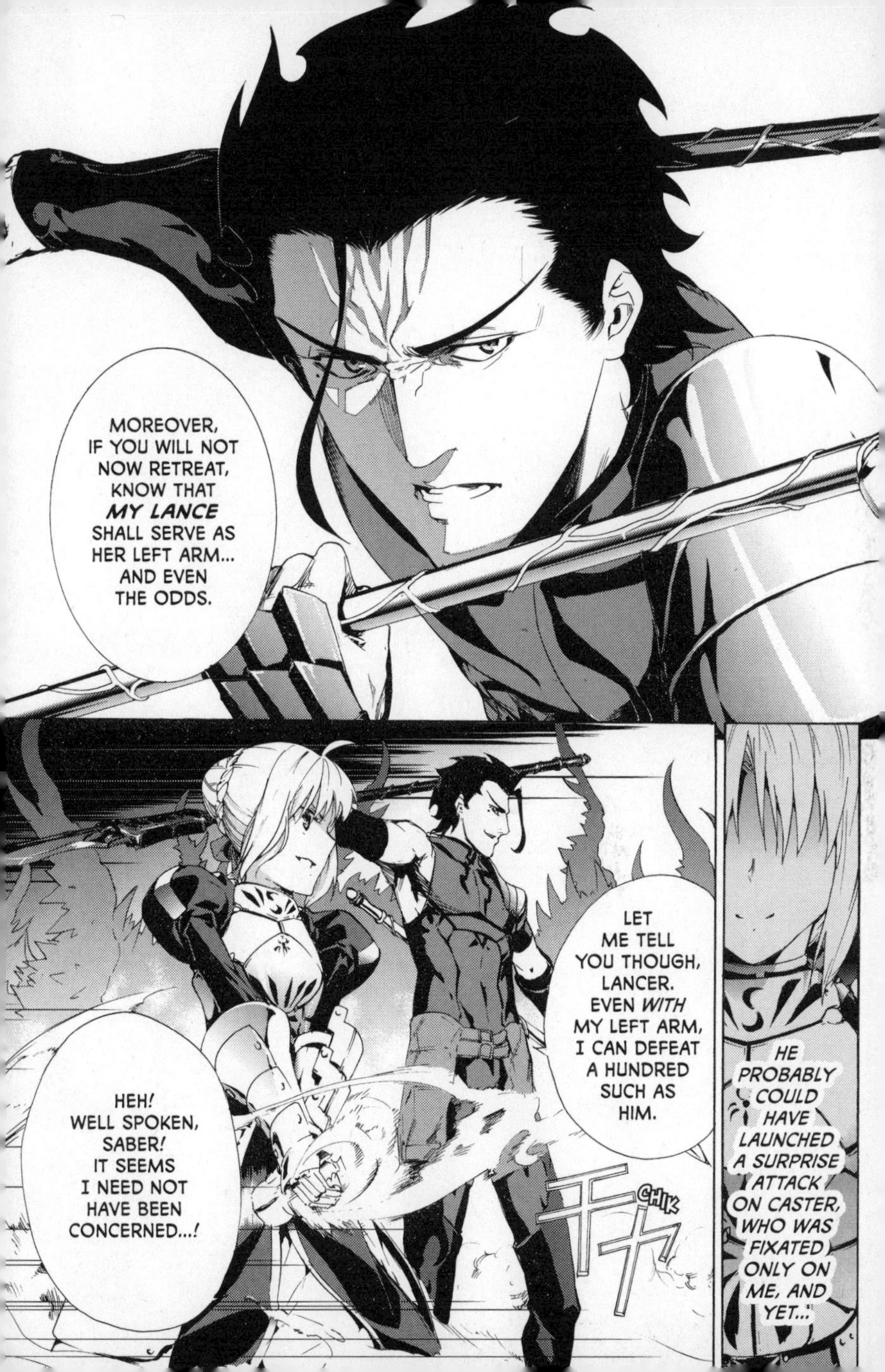
MOREOVER, IF YOU WILL NOT NOW RETREAT, KNOW THAT *MY LANCE* SHALL SERVE AS HER LEFT ARM... AND EVEN THE ODDS.
HE PROBABLY COULD HAVE LAUNCHED A SURPRISE ATTACK ON CASTER, WHO WAS FIXATED ONLY ON ME, AND YET...
LET ME TELL YOU THOUGH, LANCER. EVEN *WITH* MY LEFT ARM, I CAN DEFEAT A HUNDRED SUCH AS HIM.
HEH! WELL SPOKEN, SABER! IT SEEMS I NEED NOT HAVE BEEN CONCERNED...!
CHIK

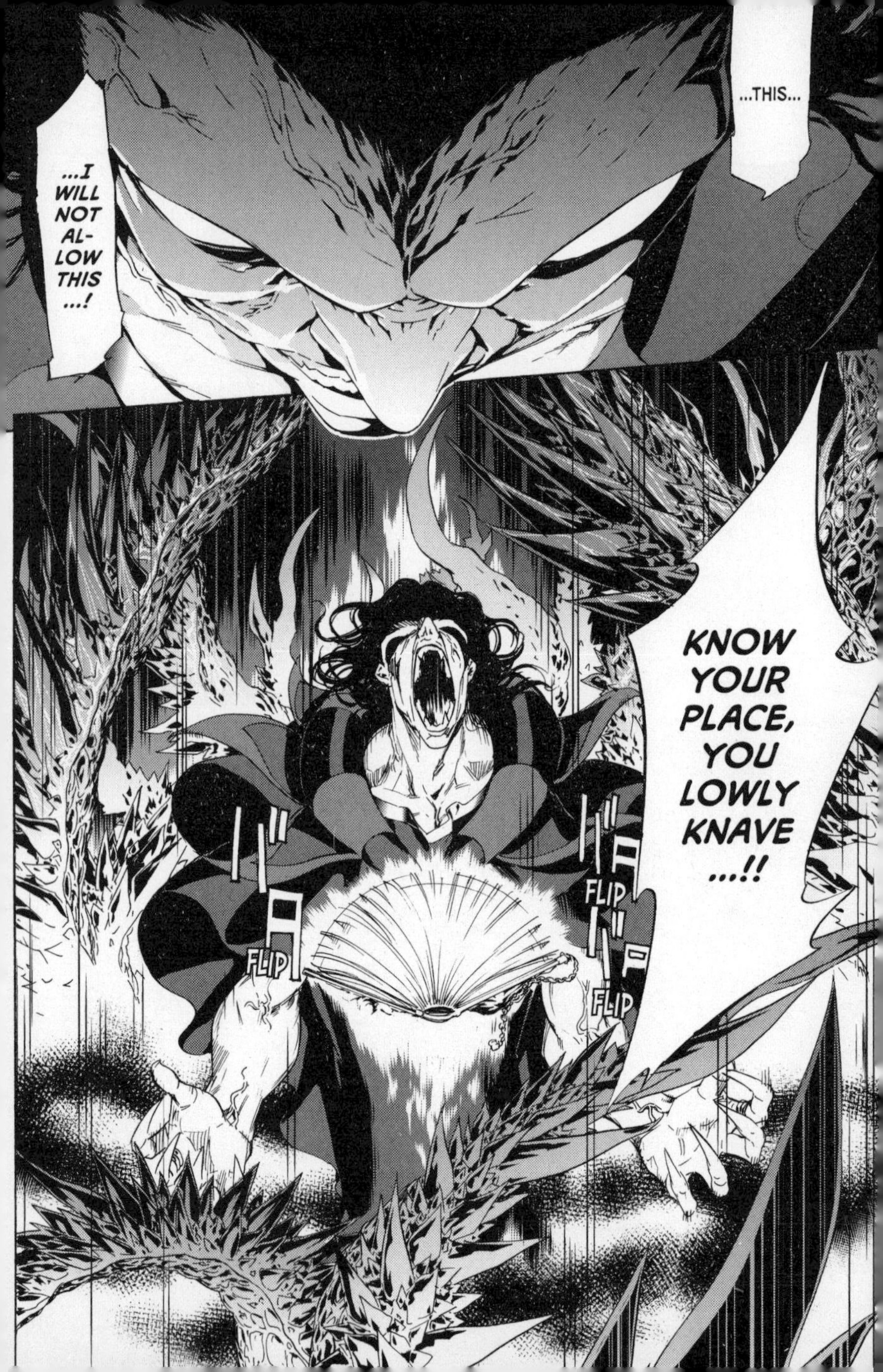
...THIS...
...I WILL NOT AL-LOW THIS ...!
KNOW YOUR PLACE, YOU LOWLY KNAVE ...!!
FLIP
FLIP
FLIP

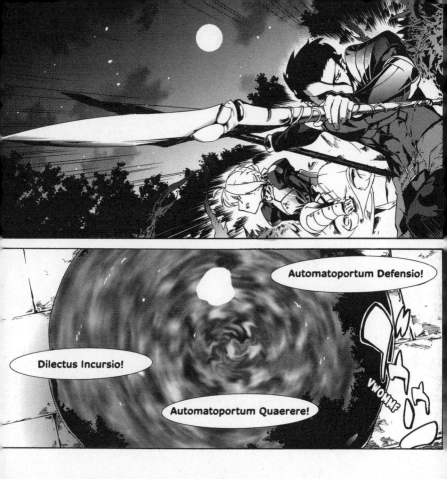

Automatoportum Defensio!

Dilectus Incursio!

Automatoportum Quaerere!

VWOMMF

SCALP!

SLASH!

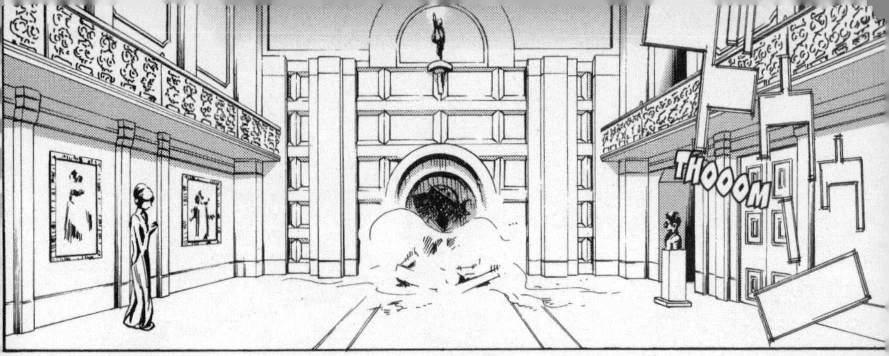
THOOOM
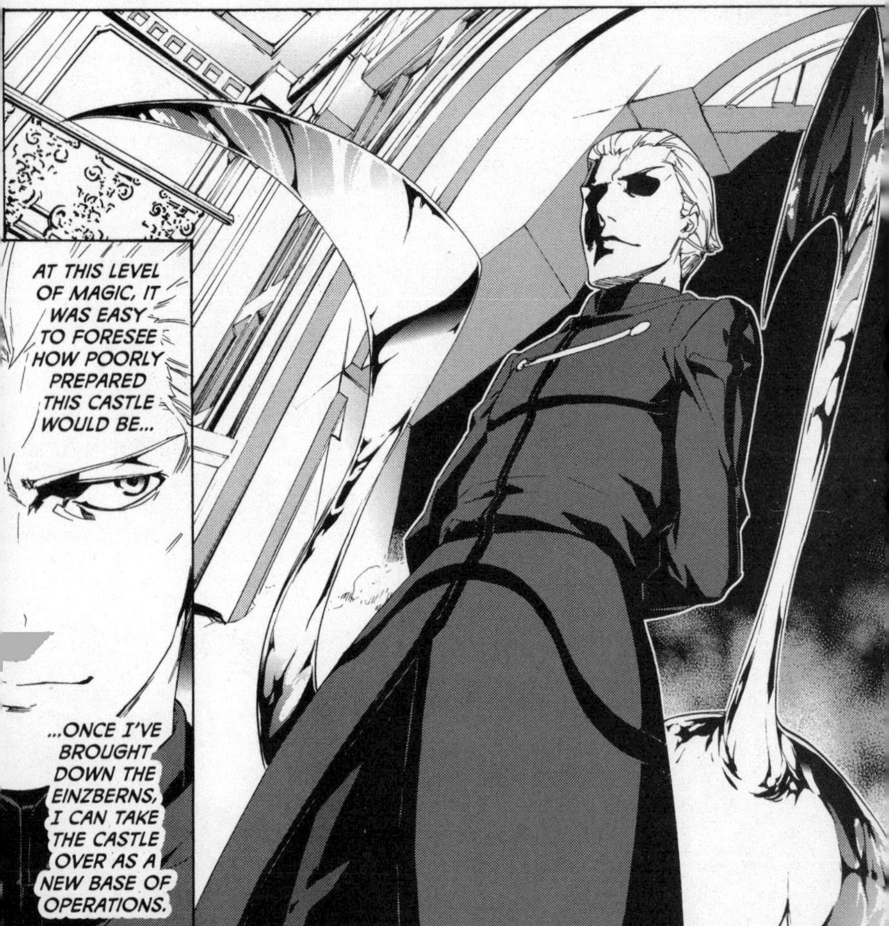
AT THIS LEVEL OF MAGIC, IT WAS EASY TO FORESEE HOW POORLY PREPARED THIS CASTLE WOULD BE...
...ONCE I'VE BROUGHT DOWN THE EINZBERNS, I CAN TAKE THE CASTLE OVER AS A NEW BASE OF OPERATIONS.

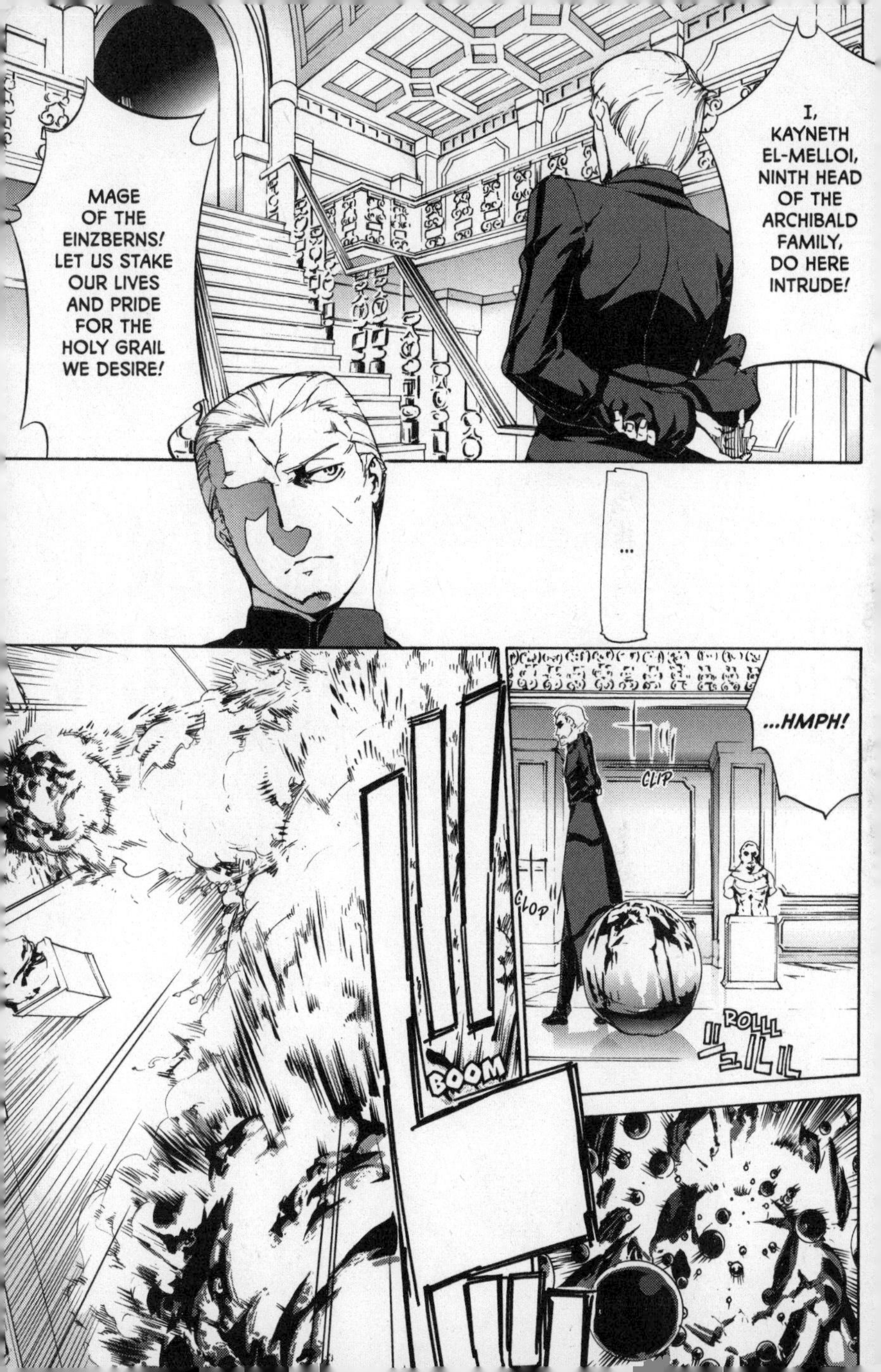
I, KAYNETH EL-MELLOI, NINTH HEAD OF THE ARCHIBALD FAMILY, DO HERE INTRUDE!
MAGE OF THE EINZBERNS! LET US STAKE OUR LIVES AND PRIDE FOR THE HOLY GRAIL WE DESIRE!
...
...HMPH!
CLIP
CLOP
ROLLL
BOOM

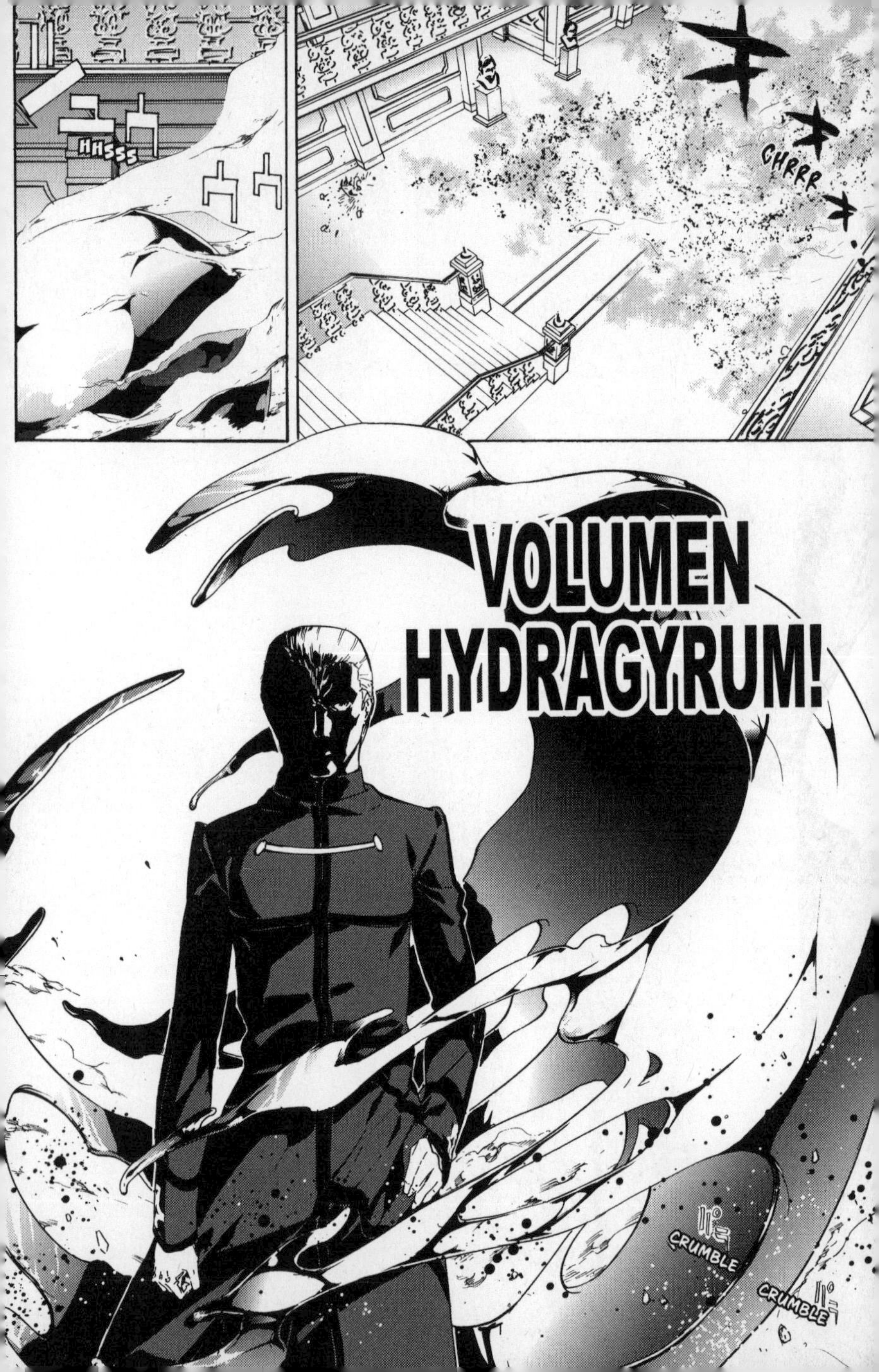
CHRRR
HHSSS
VOLUMEN HYDRAGYRUM!
CRUMBLE
CRUMBLE

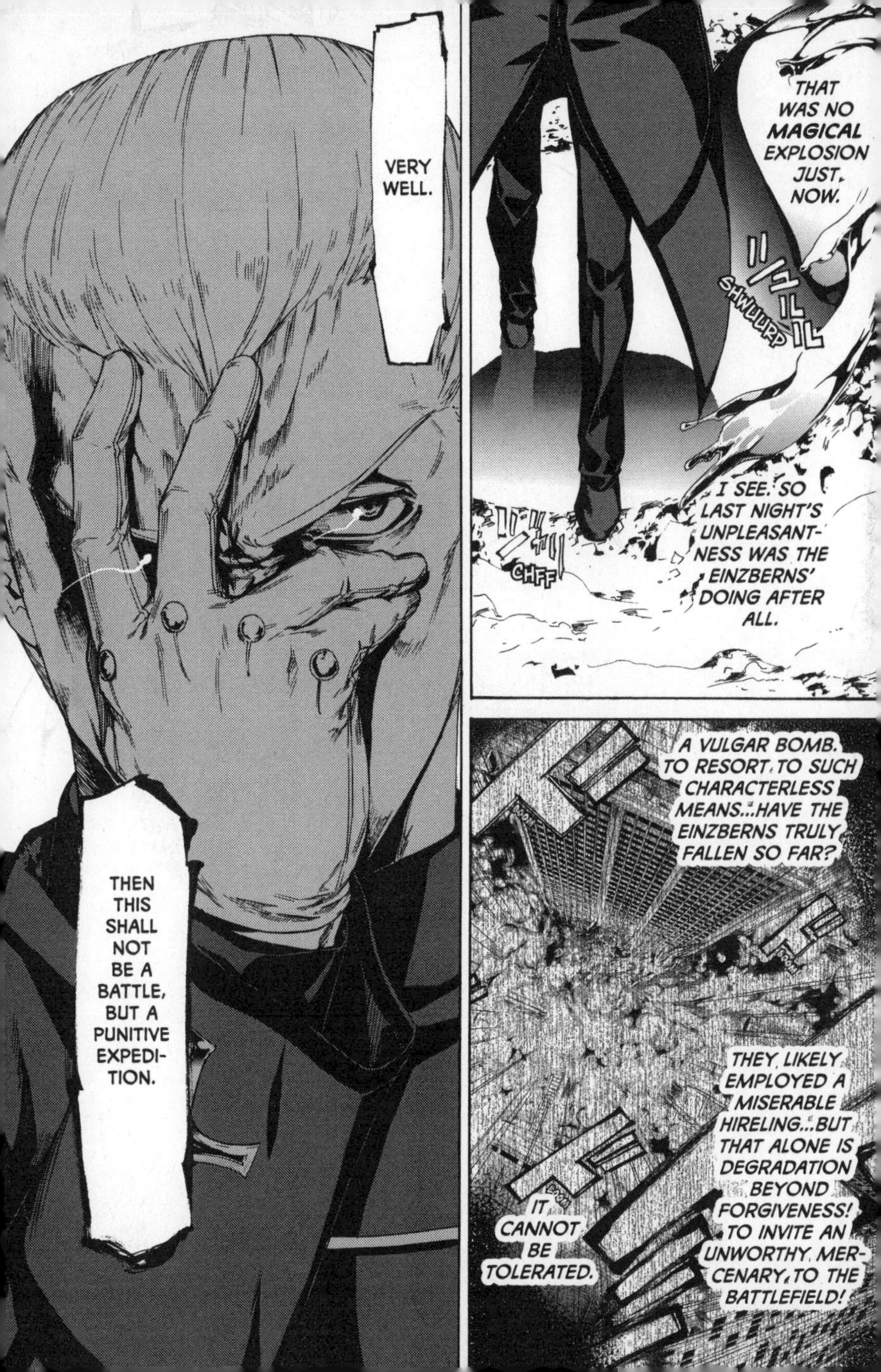
THAT WAS NO MAGICAL EXPLOSION JUST NOW.
SHWUURP
I SEE. SO LAST NIGHT'S UNPLEASANTNESS WAS THE EINZBERNS' DOING AFTER ALL.
CHFF
A VULGAR BOMB. TO RESORT TO SUCH CHARACTERLESS MEANS...HAVE THE EINZBERNS TRULY FALLEN SO FAR?
THEY LIKELY EMPLOYED A MISERABLE HIRELING...BUT THAT ALONE IS DEGRADATION BEYOND FORGIVENESS! TO INVITE AN UNWORTHY MERCENARY TO THE BATTLEFIELD!
IT CANNOT BE TOLERATED.
VERY WELL.
THEN THIS SHALL NOT BE A BATTLE, BUT A PUNITIVE EXPEDITION.

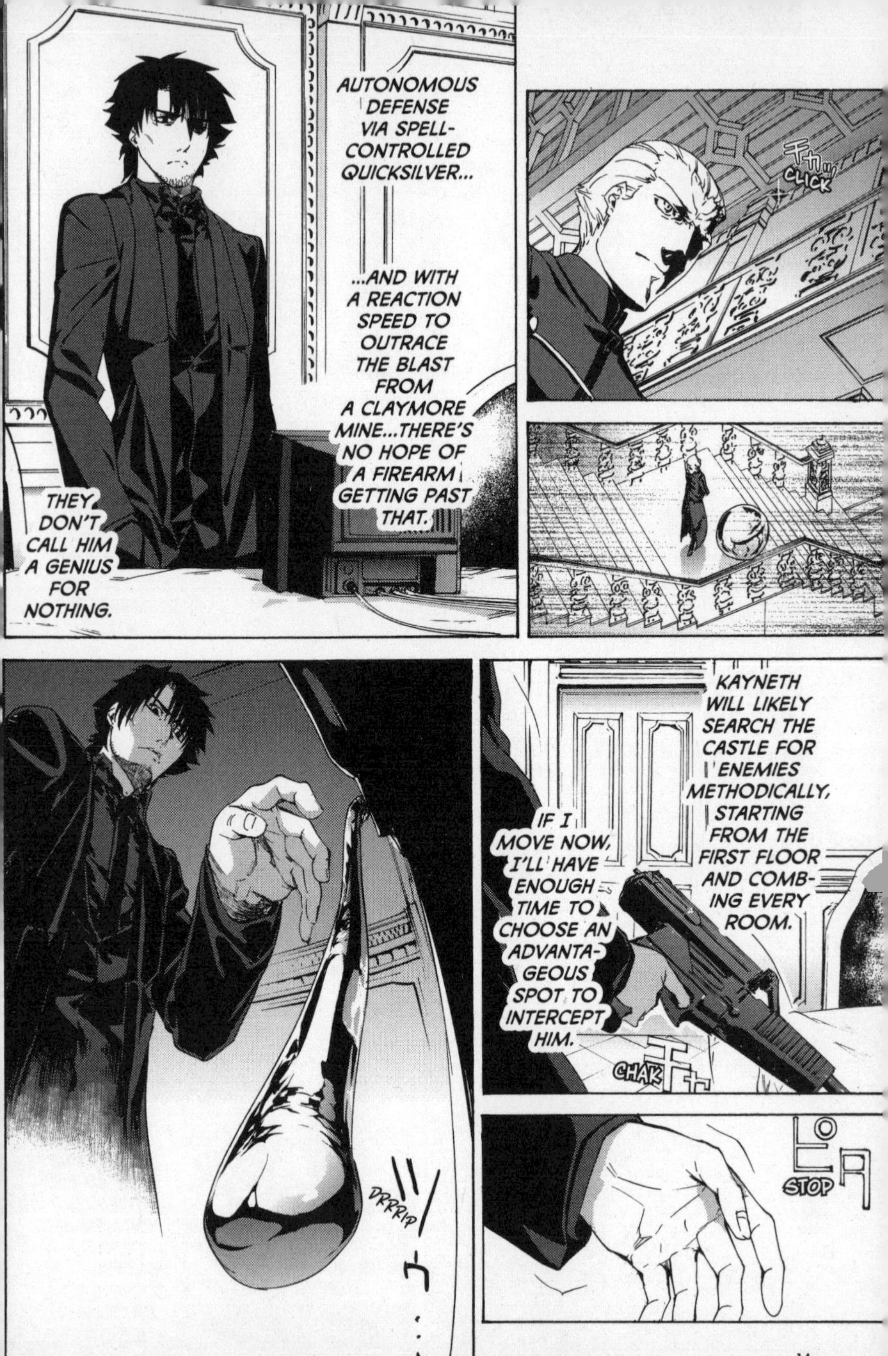
CLICK
AUTONOMOUS DEFENSE VIA SPELL-CONTROLLED QUICKSILVER...
...AND WITH A REACTION SPEED TO OUTRACE THE BLAST FROM A CLAYMORE MINE...THERE'S NO HOPE OF A FIREARM GETTING PAST THAT.
THEY DON'T CALL HIM A GENIUS FOR NOTHING.
KAYNETH WILL LIKELY SEARCH THE CASTLE FOR ENEMIES METHODICALLY, STARTING FROM THE FIRST FLOOR AND COMBING EVERY ROOM.
IF I MOVE NOW, I'LL HAVE ENOUGH TIME TO CHOOSE AN ADVANTAGEOUS SPOT TO INTERCEPT HIM.
CHAK
STOP
DRRRIP

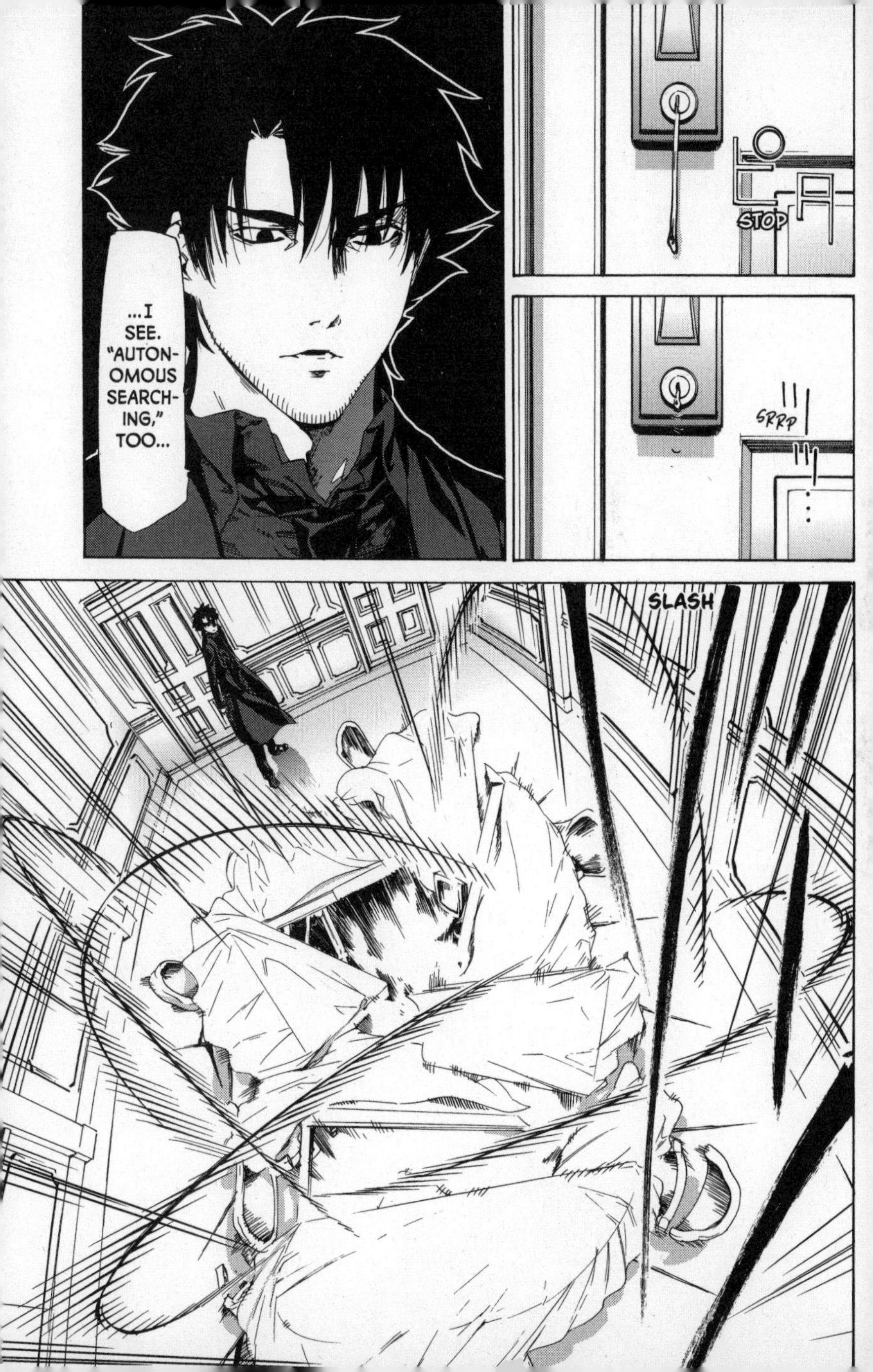
STOP
SRRP
...I SEE. "AUTONOMOUS SEARCHING," TOO...
SLASH

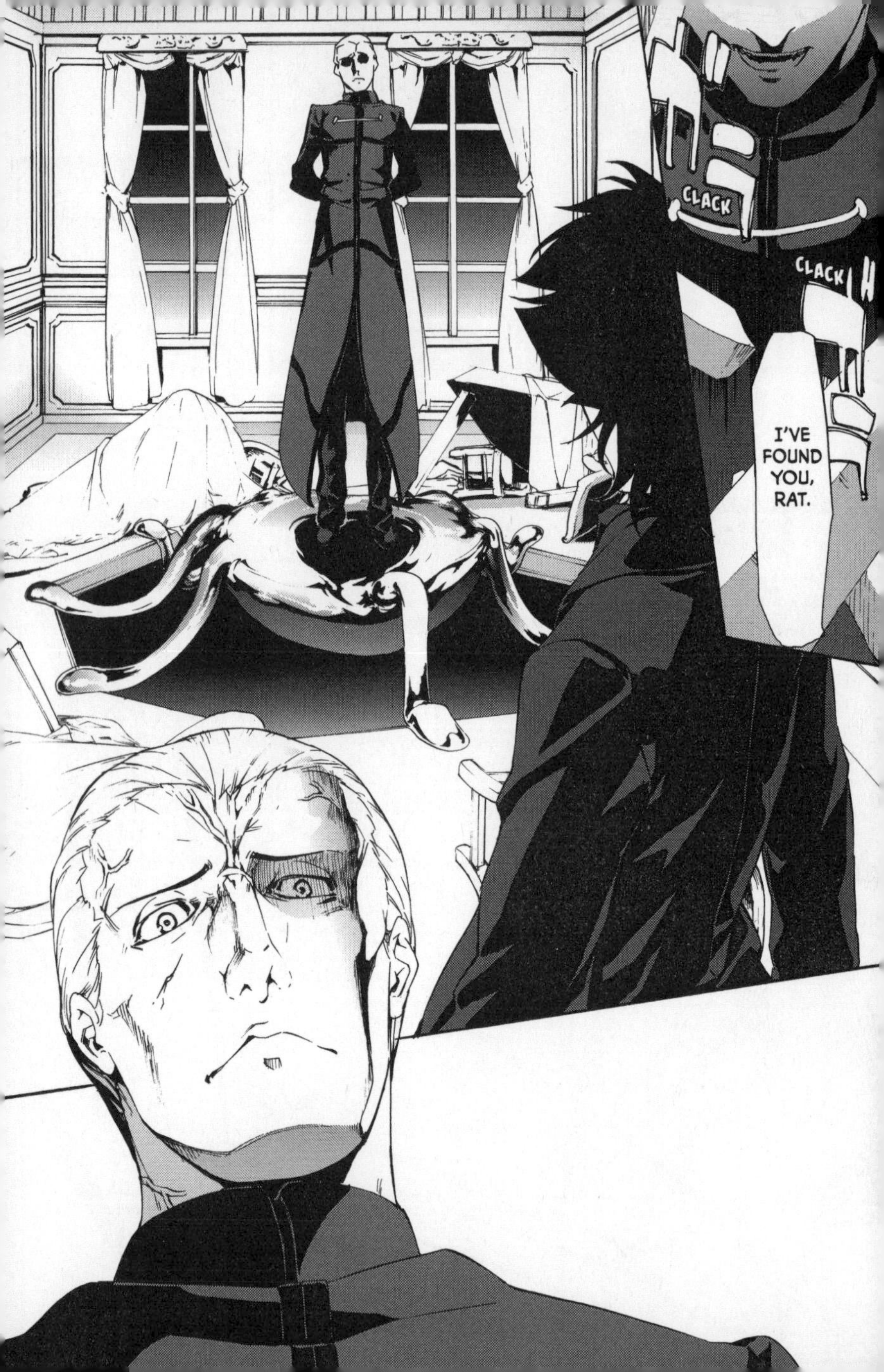
CLACK
CLACK
I'VE FOUND YOU, RAT.

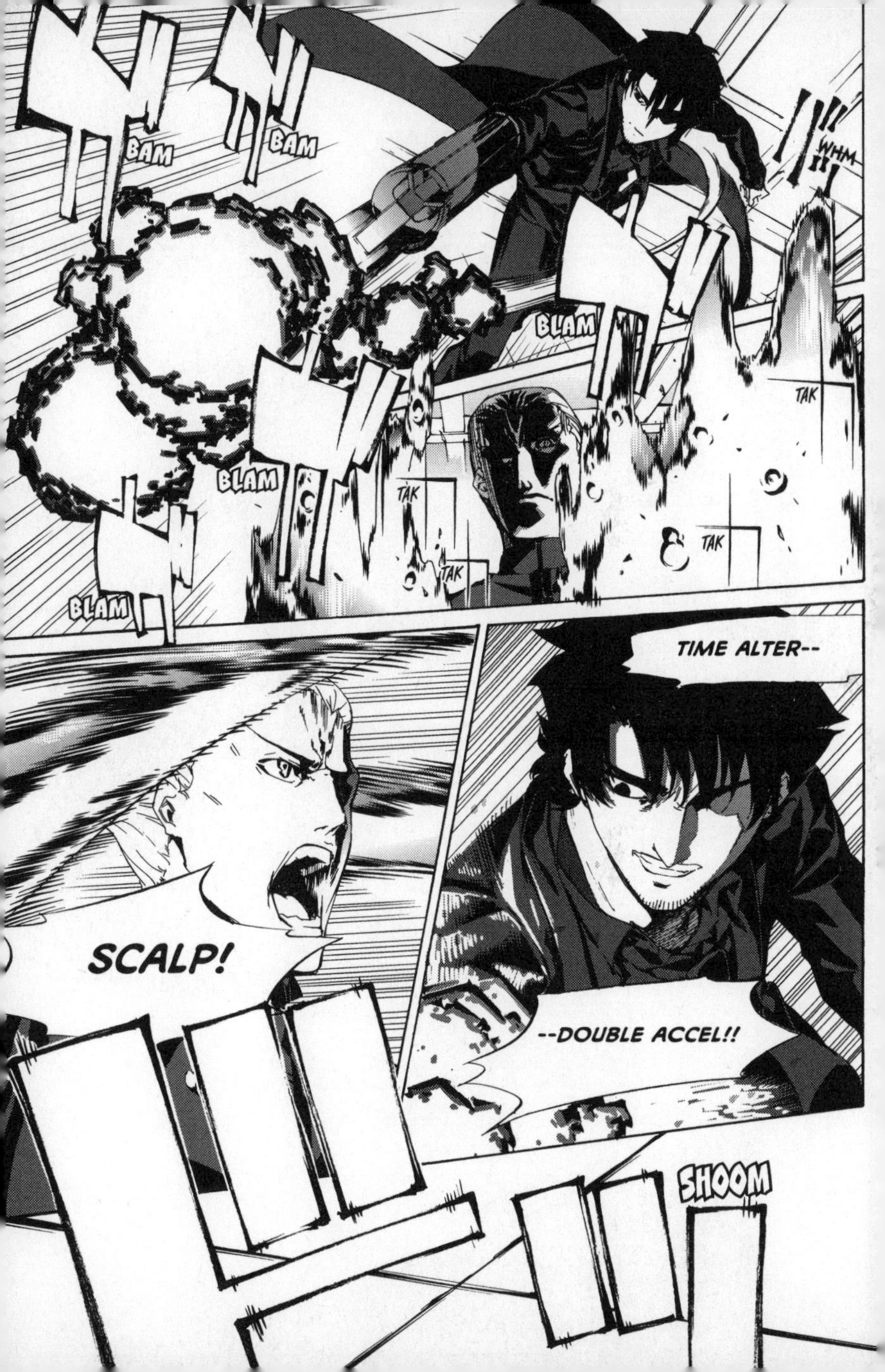
WHM
BAM
BAM
BLAM
TAK
TAK
BLAM
TAK
TAK
BLAM
TIME ALTER--
--DOUBLE ACCEL!!
SCALP!
SHOOM

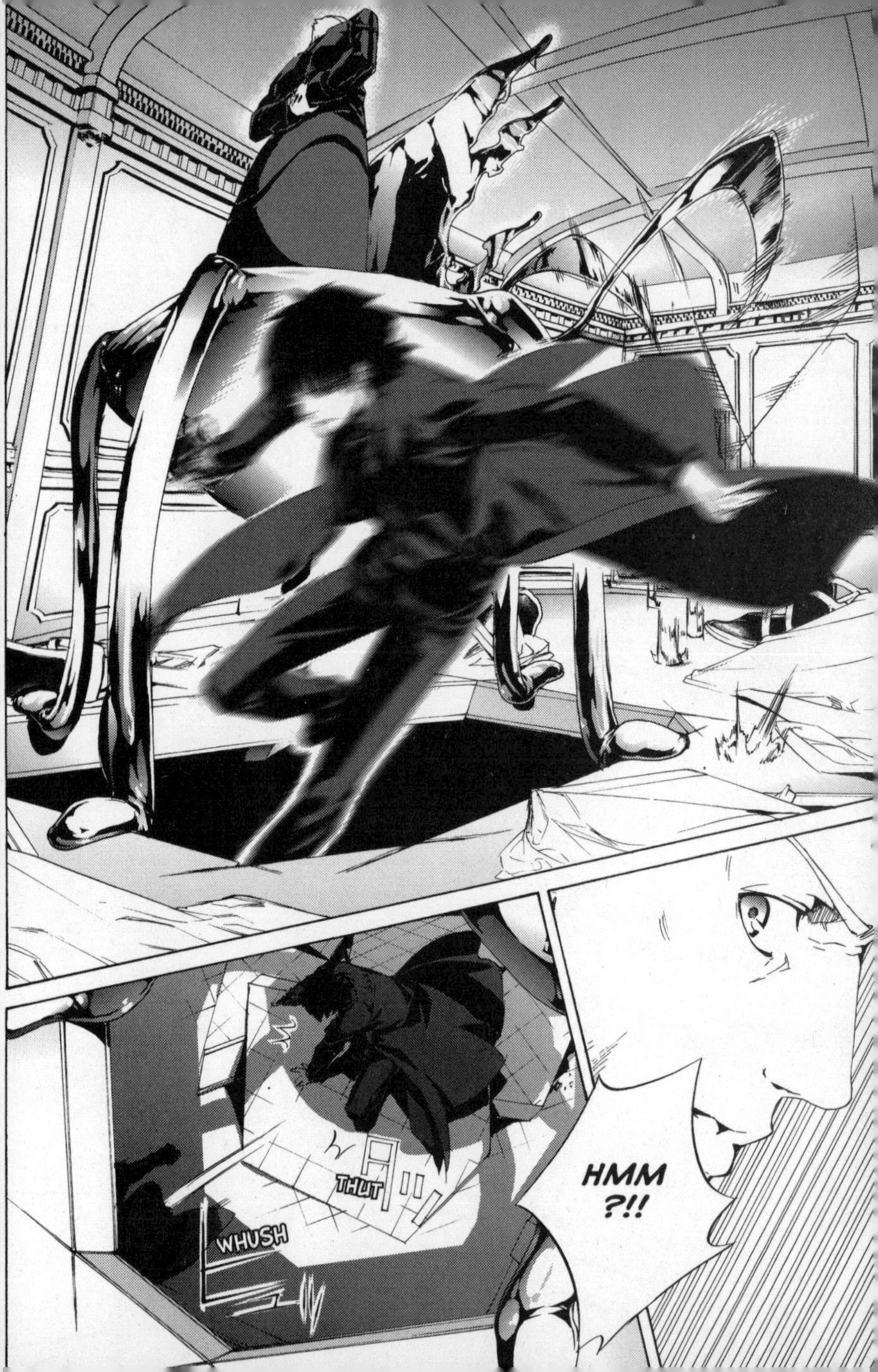
HMM ?!!
THUT
WHUSH

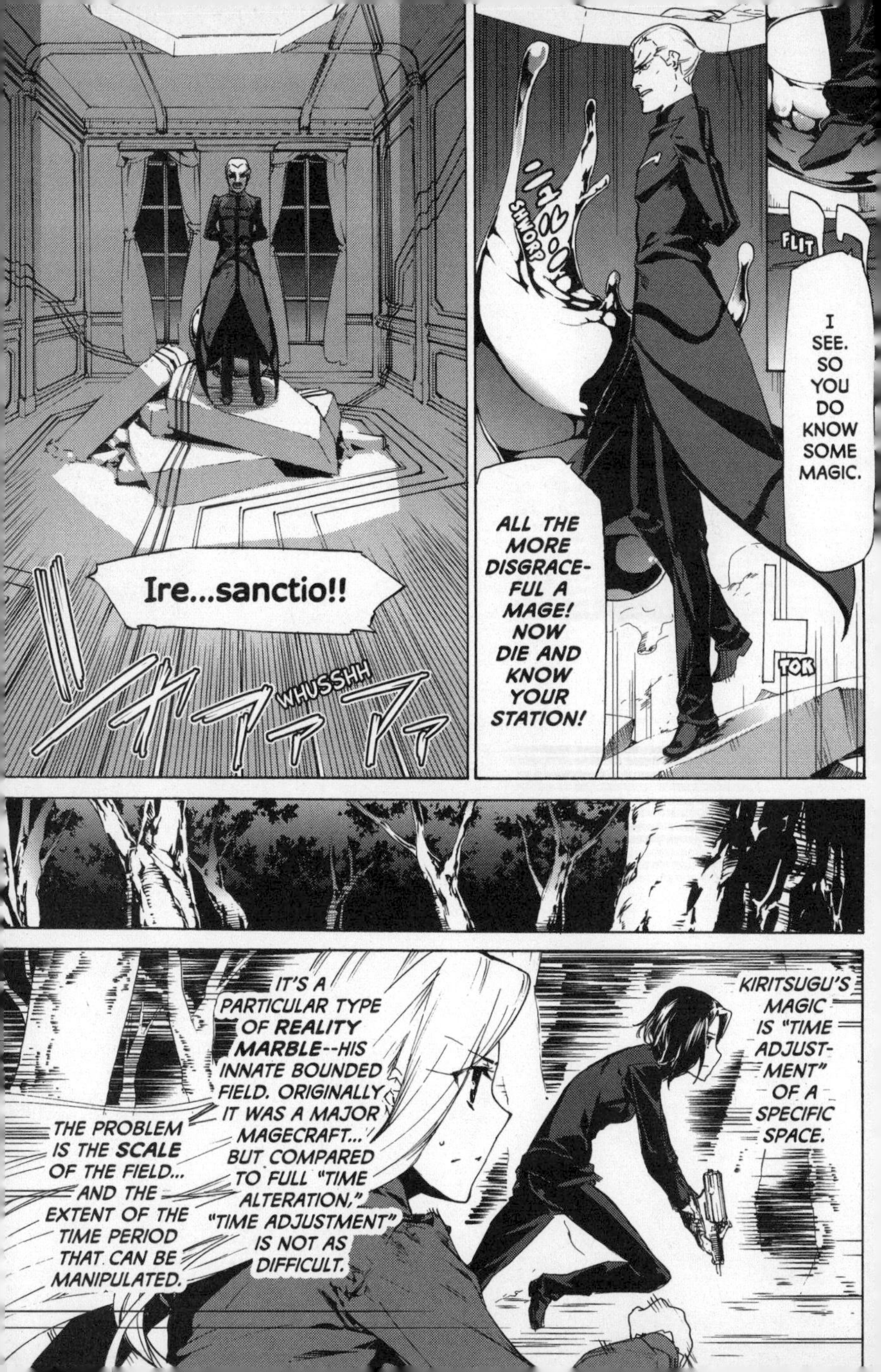
SHWORP
FLIT
I SEE. SO YOU DO KNOW SOME MAGIC.
ALL THE MORE DISGRACEFUL A MAGE! NOW DIE AND KNOW YOUR STATION!
TOK
Ire...sanctio!!
WHUSSHH
KIRITSUGU'S MAGIC IS "TIME ADJUSTMENT" OF A SPECIFIC SPACE.
IT'S A PARTICULAR TYPE OF REALITY MARBLE--HIS INNATE BOUNDED FIELD. ORIGINALLY IT WAS A MAJOR MAGECRAFT... BUT COMPARED TO FULL "TIME ALTERATION," "TIME ADJUSTMENT" IS NOT AS DIFFICULT.
THE PROBLEM IS THE SCALE OF THE FIELD... AND THE EXTENT OF THE TIME PERIOD THAT CAN BE MANIPULATED.

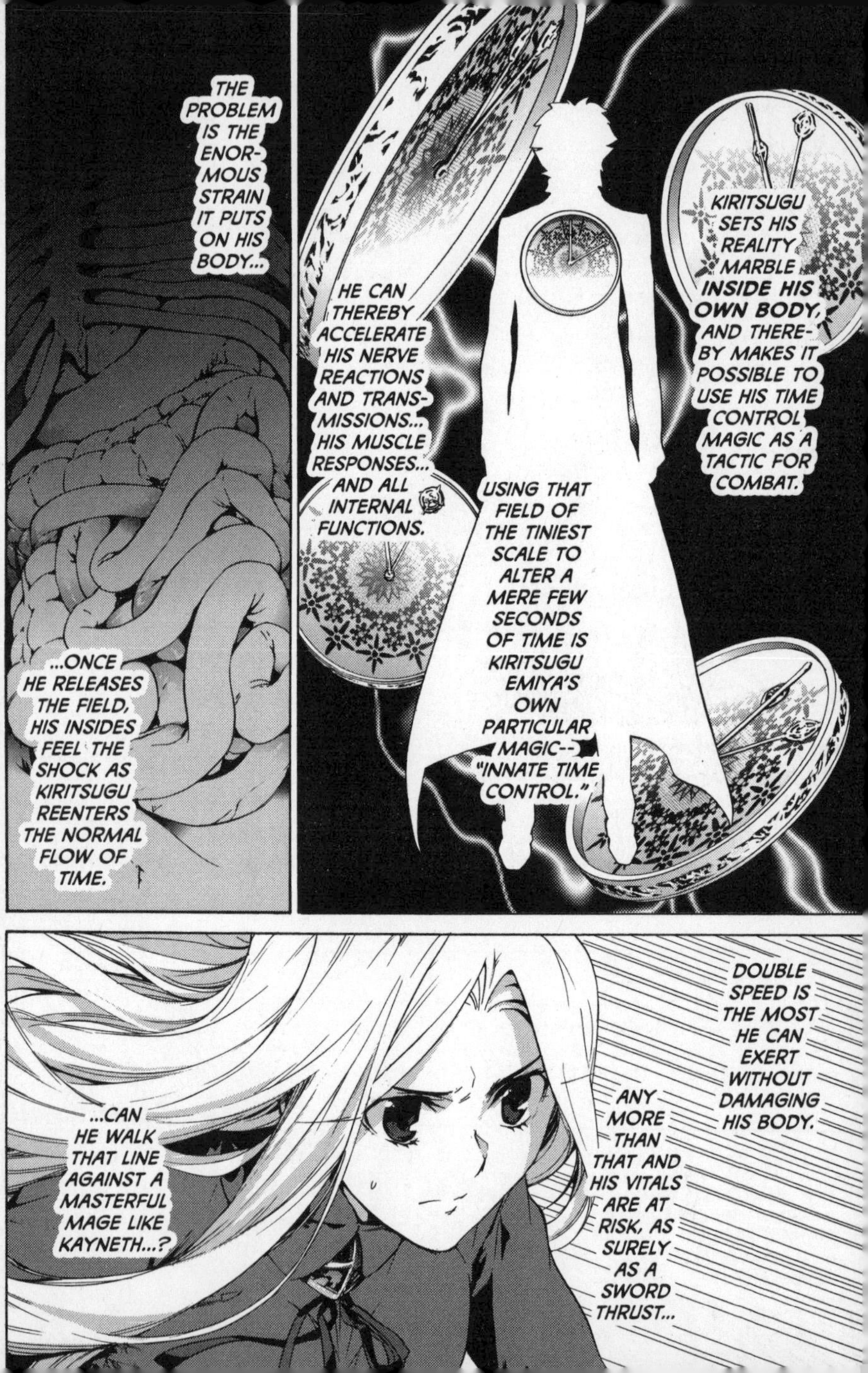
KIRITSUGU SETS HIS REALITY MARBLE **INSIDE HIS OWN BODY,** AND THEREBY MAKES IT POSSIBLE TO USE HIS TIME CONTROL MAGIC AS A TACTIC FOR COMBAT.
HE CAN THEREBY ACCELERATE HIS NERVE REACTIONS AND TRANSMISSIONS... HIS MUSCLE RESPONSES... AND ALL INTERNAL FUNCTIONS.
USING THAT FIELD OF THE TINIEST SCALE TO ALTER A MERE FEW SECONDS OF TIME IS KIRITSUGU EMIYA'S OWN PARTICULAR MAGIC-- "INNATE TIME CONTROL."
THE PROBLEM IS THE ENORMOUS STRAIN IT PUTS ON HIS BODY...
...ONCE HE RELEASES THE FIELD, HIS INSIDES FEEL THE SHOCK AS KIRITSUGU REENTERS THE NORMAL FLOW OF TIME.
DOUBLE SPEED IS THE MOST HE CAN EXERT WITHOUT DAMAGING HIS BODY.
ANY MORE THAN THAT AND HIS VITALS ARE AT RISK, AS SURELY AS A SWORD THRUST...
...CAN HE WALK THAT LINE AGAINST A MASTERFUL MAGE LIKE KAYNETH...?

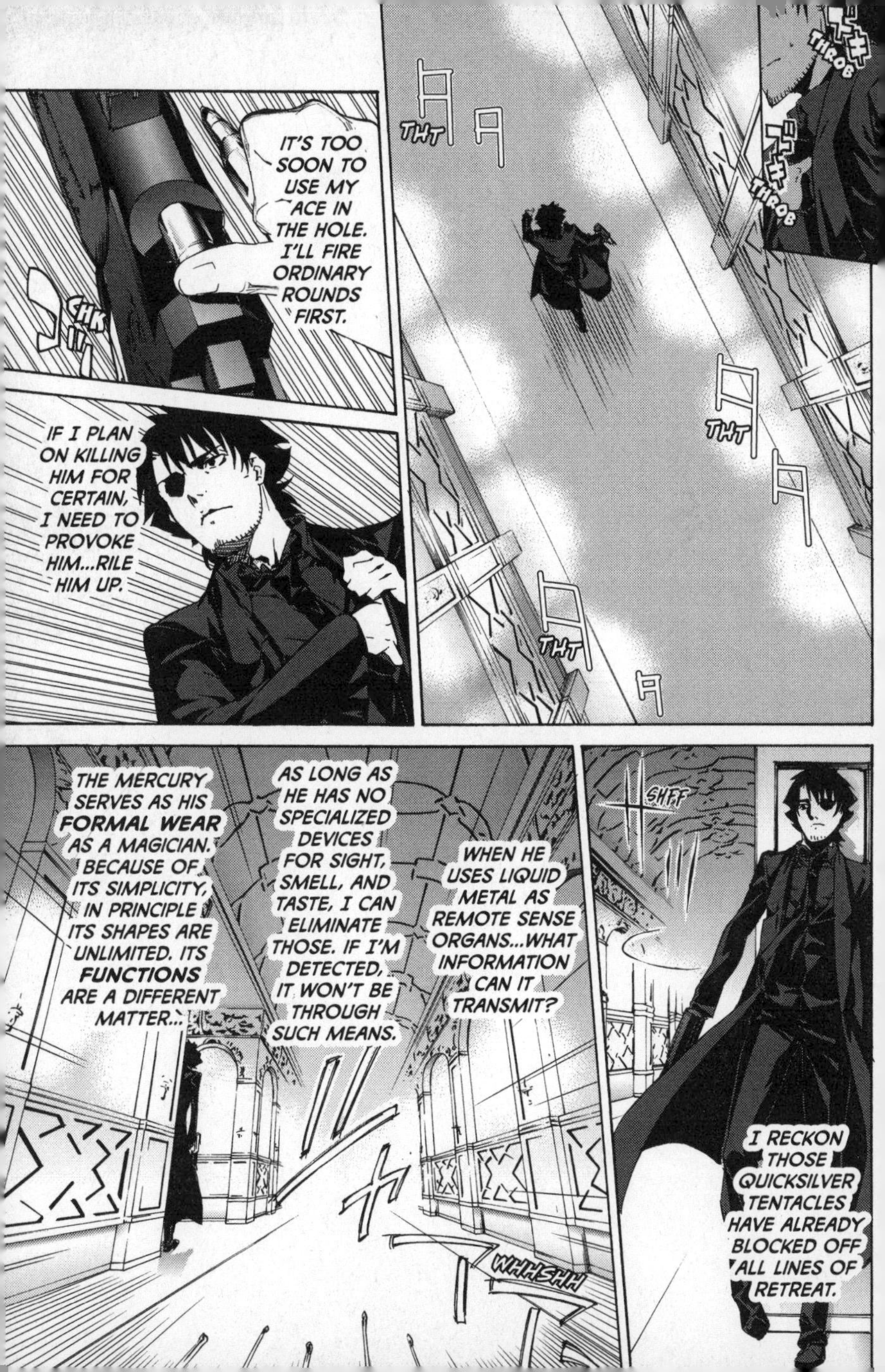
THROB
THROB
THT
THT
THT
IT'S TOO SOON TO USE MY ACE IN THE HOLE. I'LL FIRE ORDINARY ROUNDS FIRST.
CHK
IF I PLAN ON KILLING HIM FOR CERTAIN, I NEED TO PROVOKE HIM...RILE HIM UP.
SHFF
I RECKON THOSE QUICKSILVER TENTACLES HAVE ALREADY BLOCKED OFF ALL LINES OF RETREAT.
WHEN HE USES LIQUID METAL AS REMOTE SENSE ORGANS...WHAT INFORMATION CAN IT TRANSMIT?
AS LONG AS HE HAS NO SPECIALIZED DEVICES FOR SIGHT, SMELL, AND TASTE, I CAN ELIMINATE THOSE. IF I'M DETECTED, IT WON'T BE THROUGH SUCH MEANS.
THE MERCURY SERVES AS HIS FORMAL WEAR AS A MAGICIAN. BECAUSE OF ITS SIMPLICITY, IN PRINCIPLE ITS SHAPES ARE UNLIMITED. ITS FUNCTIONS ARE A DIFFERENT MATTER...
WHHSHH

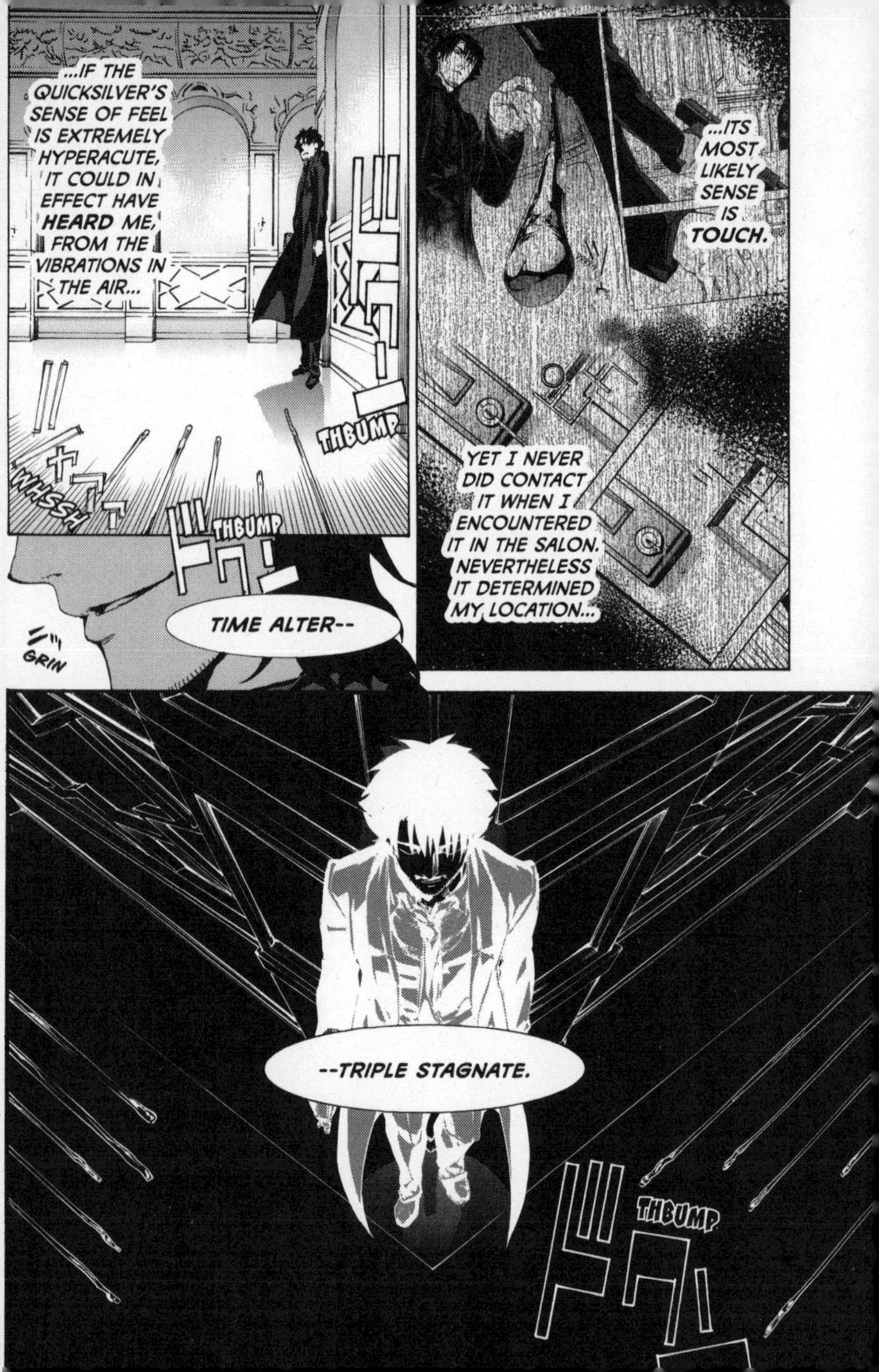
...ITS MOST LIKELY SENSE IS TOUCH.
YET I NEVER DID CONTACT IT WHEN I ENCOUNTERED IT IN THE SALON. NEVERTHELESS IT DETERMINED MY LOCATION...
...IF THE QUICKSILVER'S SENSE OF FEEL IS EXTREMELY HYPERACUTE, IT COULD IN EFFECT HAVE HEARD ME, FROM THE VIBRATIONS IN THE AIR...
THBUMP
WHSSH
THBUMP
TIME ALTER--
GRIN
--TRIPLE STAGNATE.
THBUMP

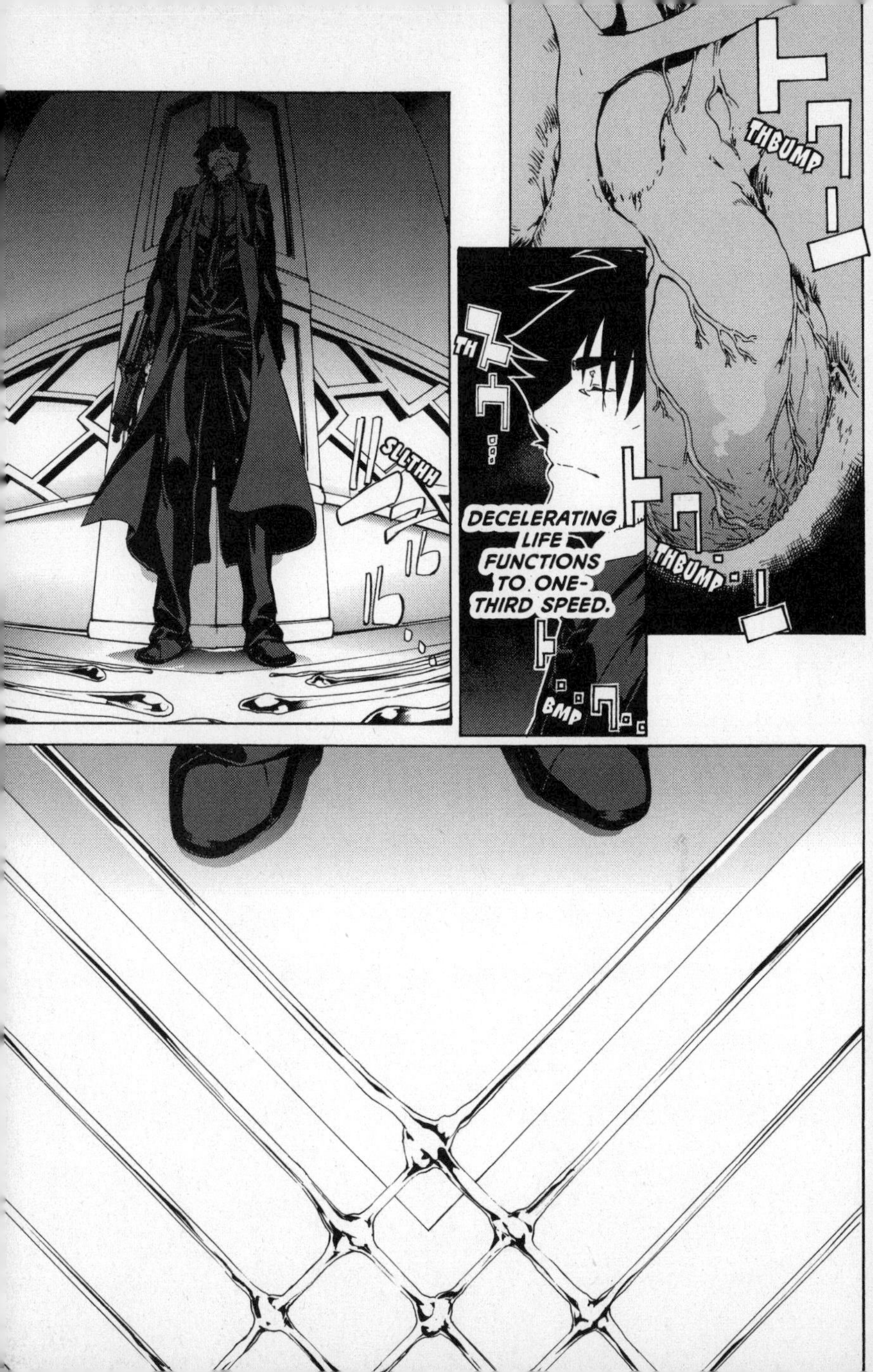
THBUMP
THBUMP
TH
DECELERATING LIFE FUNCTIONS TO ONE-THIRD SPEED.
BMP
SLLTHH

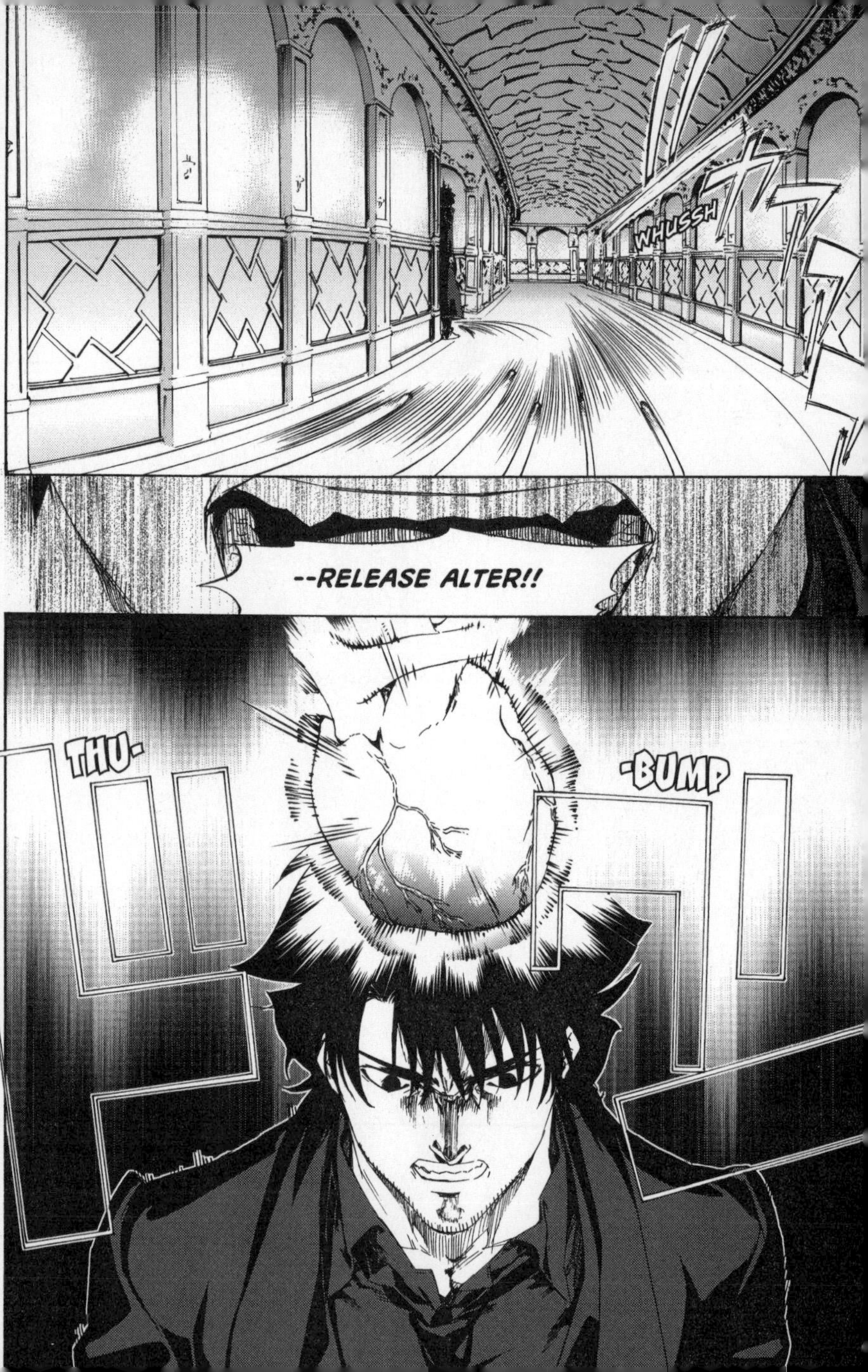
WHUSSH
--RELEASE ALTER!!
THU-
-BUMP

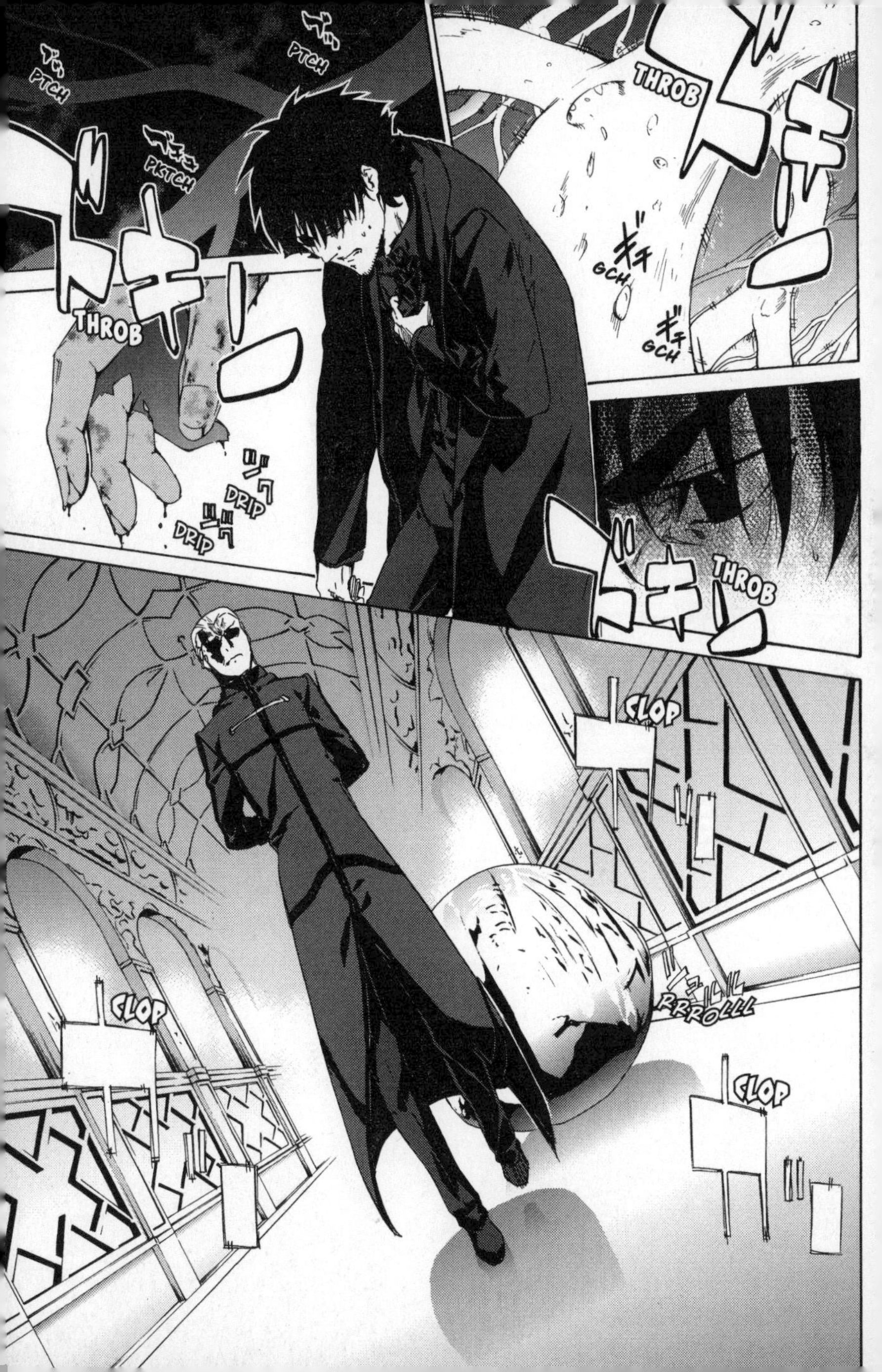
THROB
GCH
GCH
THROB
PTCH
PTCH
PKTCH
THROB
DRIP
DRIP
CLOP
RRROLLL
CLOP
CLOP

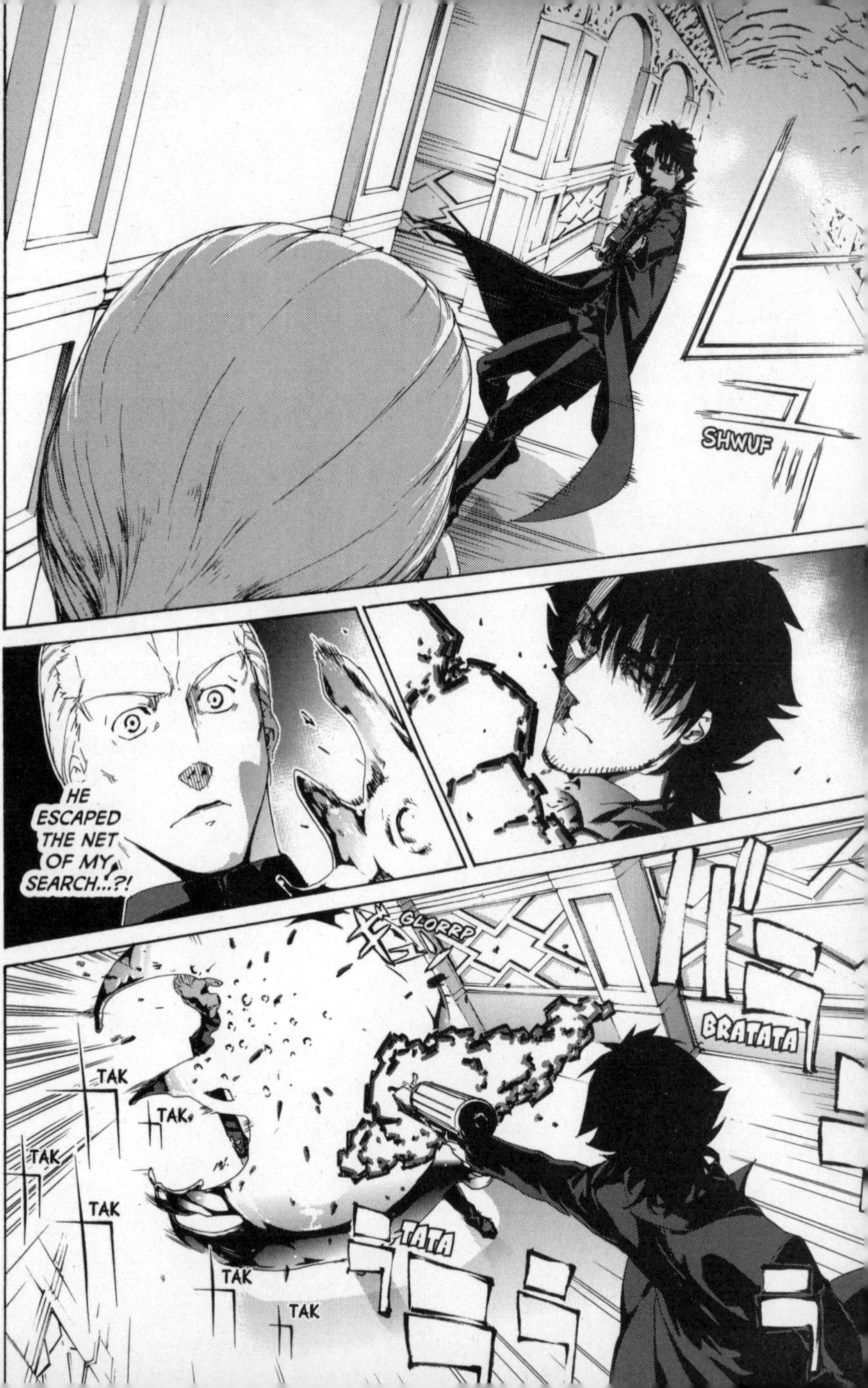
SHWUF
HE ESCAPED THE NET OF MY SEARCH...?!
GLORRP
BRATATA
TAK
TAK
TAK
TAK
TATA
TAK
TAK

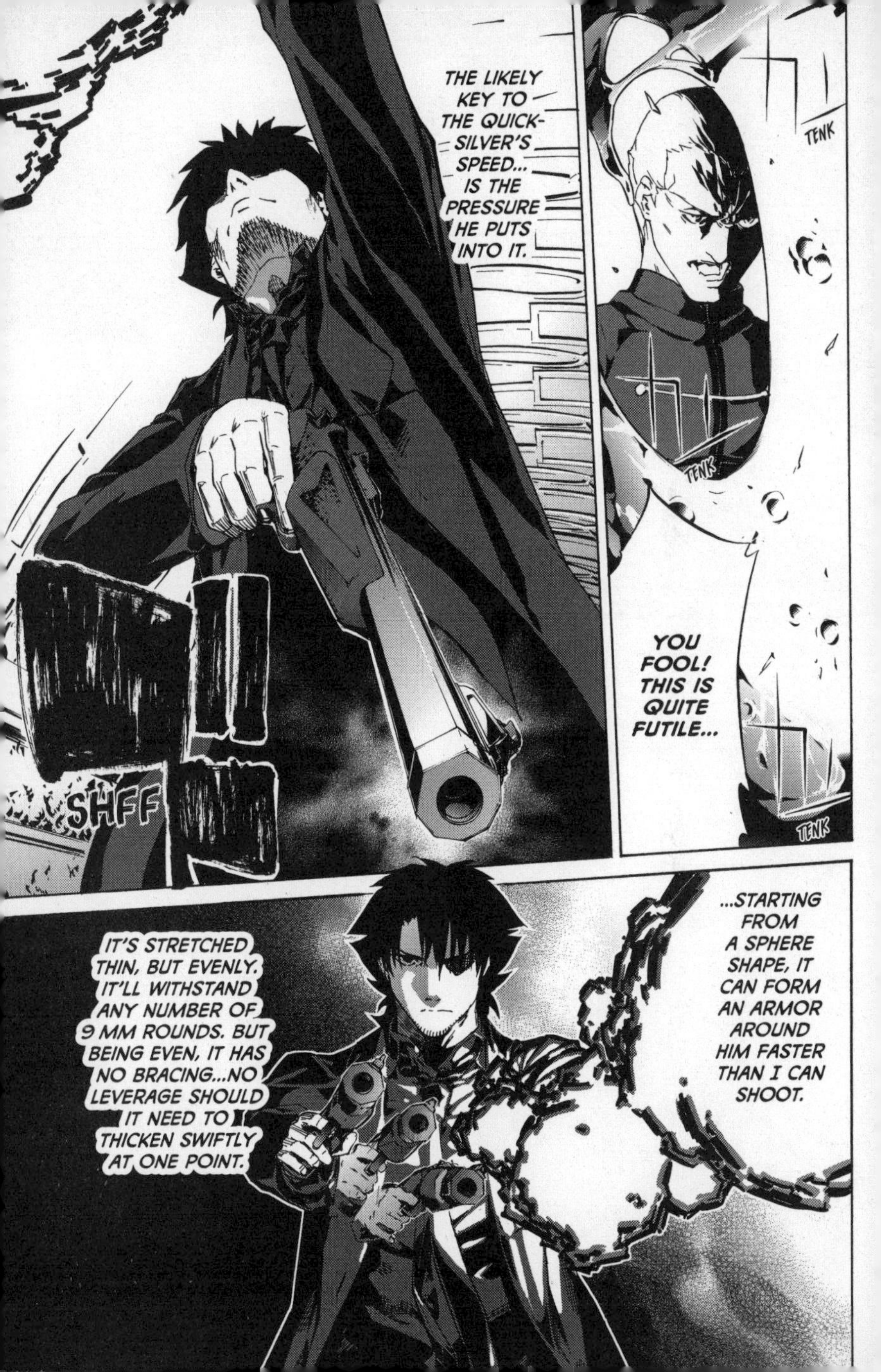

TENK
TENK
YOU FOOL! THIS IS QUITE FUTILE...
TENK
THE LIKELY KEY TO THE QUICK-SILVER'S SPEED... IS THE PRESSURE HE PUTS INTO IT.
SHFF
...STARTING FROM A SPHERE SHAPE, IT CAN FORM AN ARMOR AROUND HIM FASTER THAN I CAN SHOOT.
IT'S STRETCHED THIN, BUT EVENLY. IT'LL WITHSTAND ANY NUMBER OF 9 MM ROUNDS. BUT BEING EVEN, IT HAS NO BRACING...NO LEVERAGE SHOULD IT NEED TO THICKEN SWIFTLY AT ONE POINT.

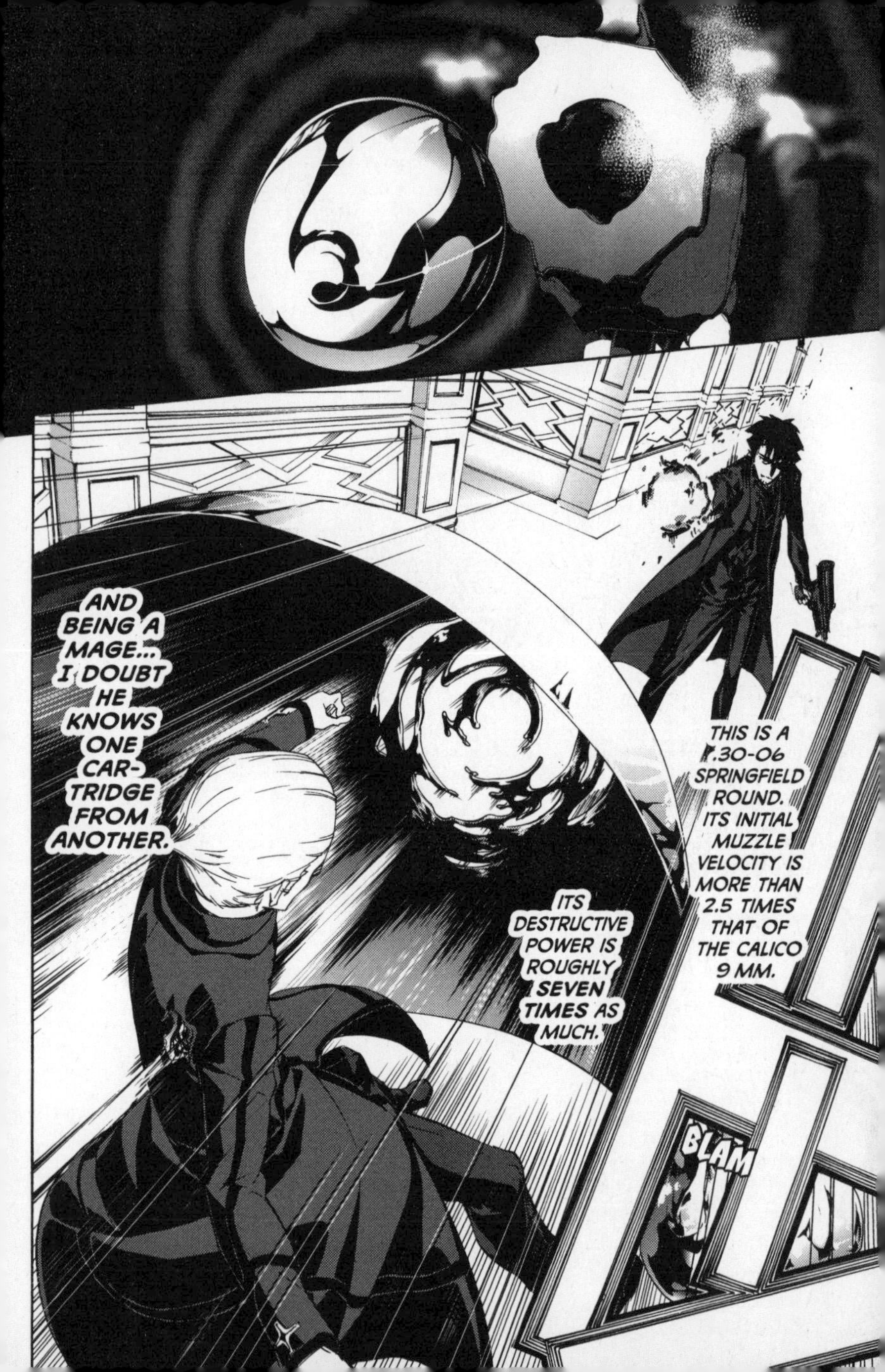
THIS IS A .30-06 SPRINGFIELD ROUND. ITS INITIAL MUZZLE VELOCITY IS MORE THAN 2.5 TIMES THAT OF THE CALICO 9 MM.
ITS DESTRUCTIVE POWER IS ROUGHLY SEVEN TIMES AS MUCH.
AND BEING A MAGE... I DOUBT HE KNOWS ONE CAR-TRIDGE FROM ANOTHER.
BLAM

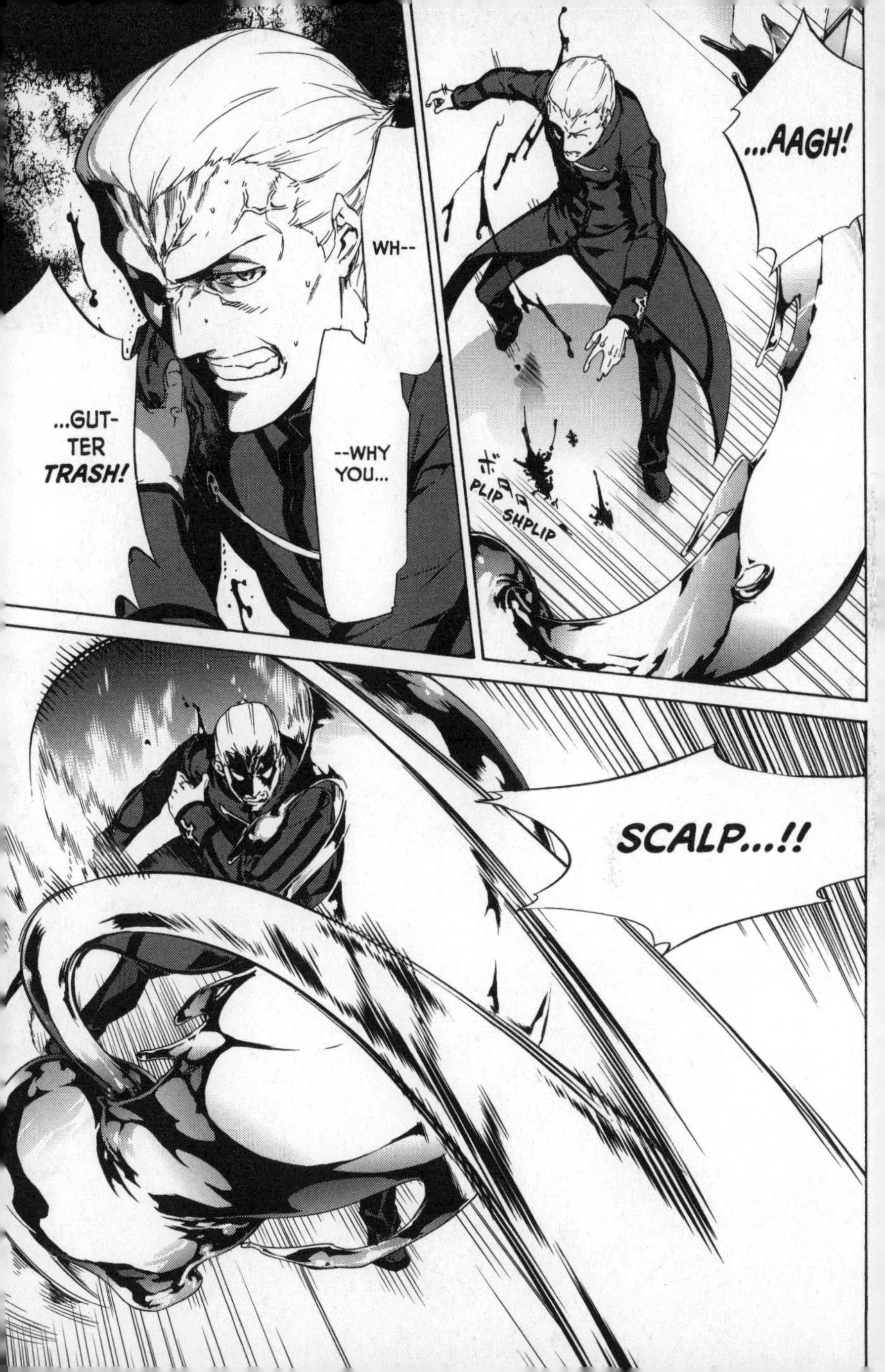
...AAGH!
PLIP
SHPLIP
WH--
--WHY YOU...
...GUT-
TER
TRASH!
SCALP...!!

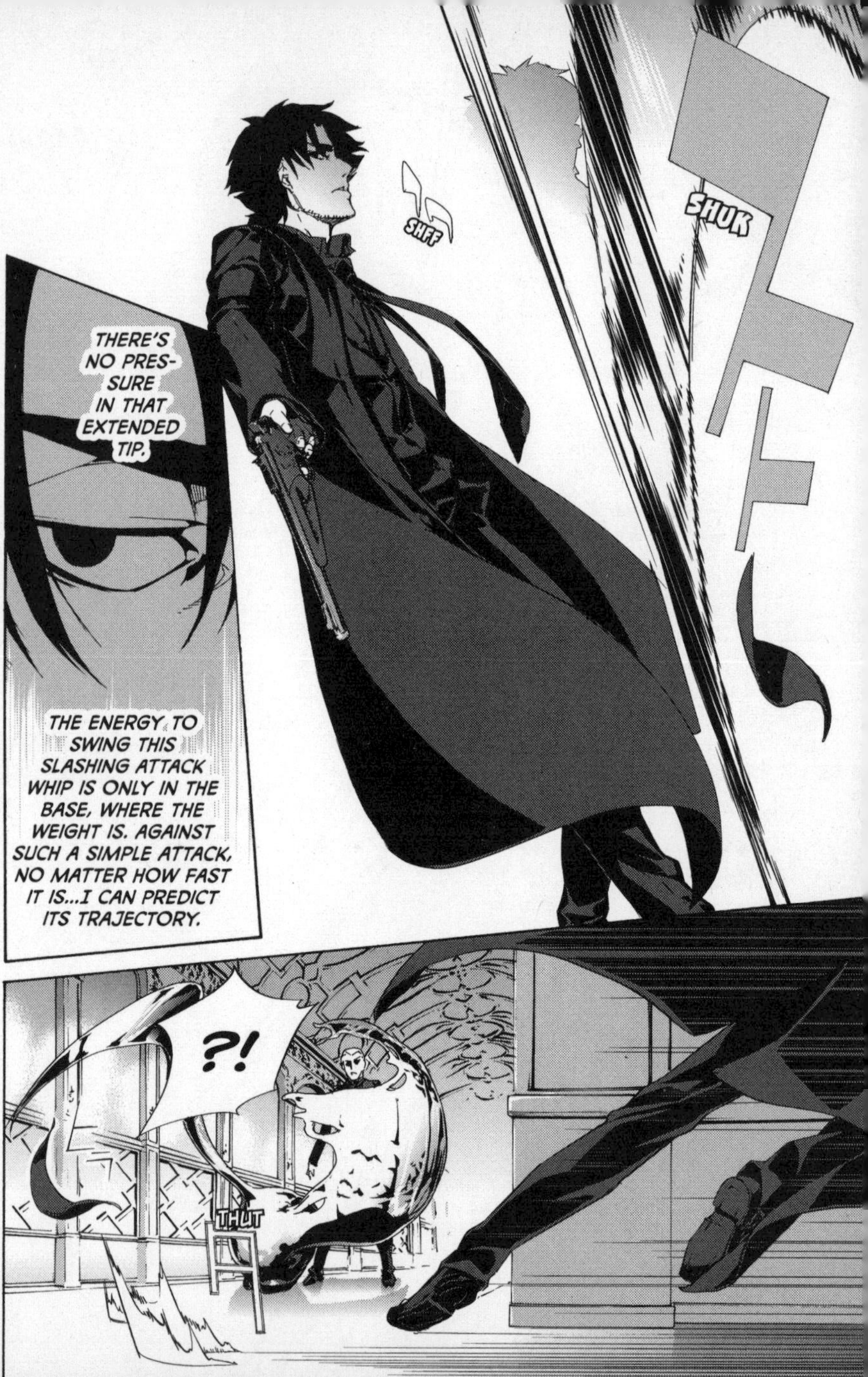
SHUK
SHFF
THERE'S NO PRES-SURE IN THAT EXTENDED TIP.
THE ENERGY TO SWING THIS SLASHING ATTACK WHIP IS ONLY IN THE BASE, WHERE THE WEIGHT IS. AGAINST SUCH A SIMPLE ATTACK, NO MATTER HOW FAST IT IS...I CAN PREDICT ITS TRAJECTORY.
?!
THUT

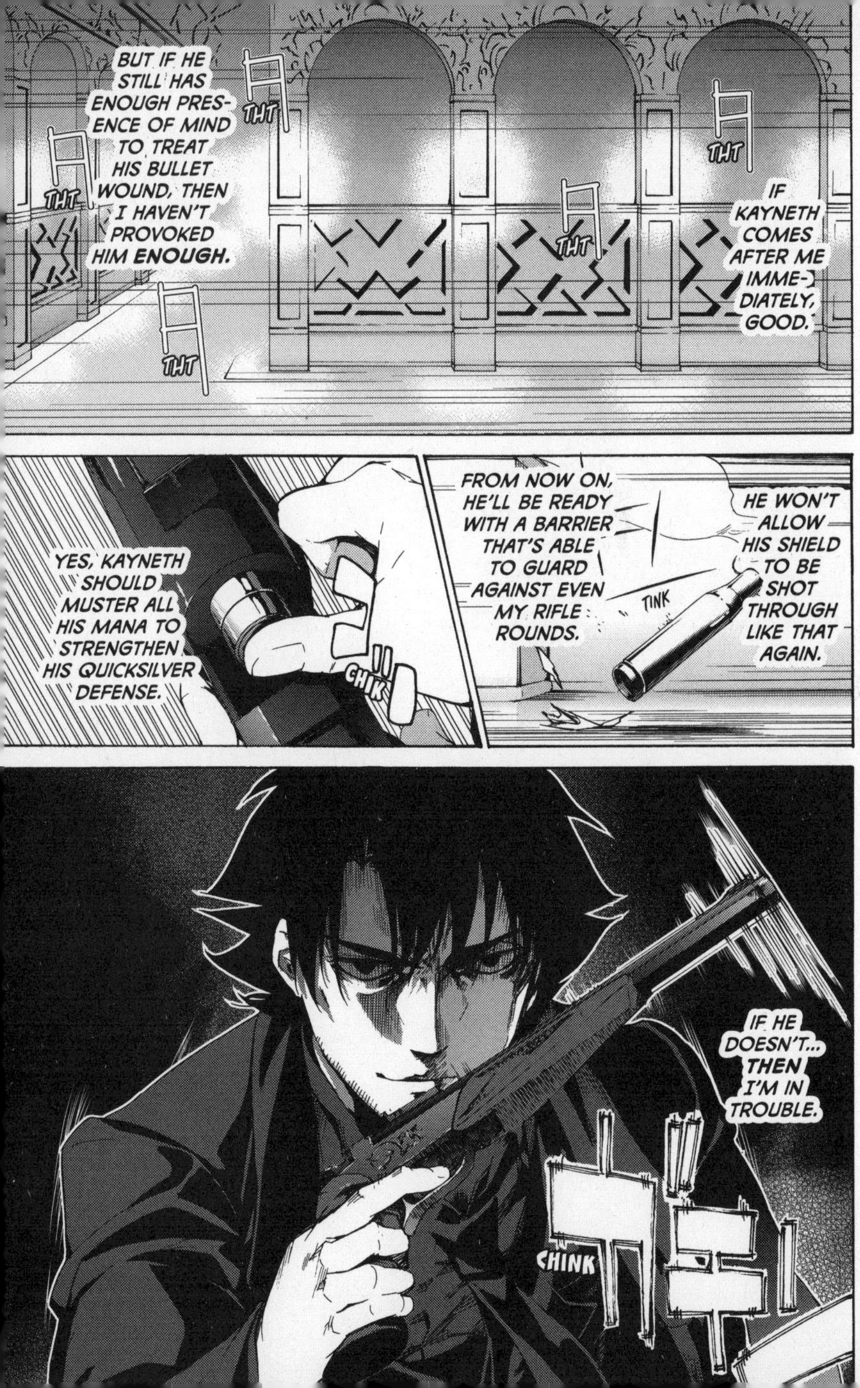
IF KAYNETH COMES AFTER ME IMMEDIATELY, GOOD.
THT
THT
BUT IF HE STILL HAS ENOUGH PRESENCE OF MIND TO TREAT HIS BULLET WOUND, THEN I HAVEN'T PROVOKED HIM **ENOUGH.**
THT
THT
THT
HE WON'T ALLOW HIS SHIELD TO BE SHOT THROUGH LIKE THAT AGAIN.
FROM NOW ON, HE'LL BE READY WITH A BARRIER THAT'S ABLE TO GUARD AGAINST EVEN MY RIFLE ROUNDS.
TINK
YES, KAYNETH SHOULD MUSTER ALL HIS MANA TO STRENGTHEN HIS QUICKSILVER DEFENSE.
CHIK
IF HE DOESN'T... **THEN** I'M IN TROUBLE.
CHINK

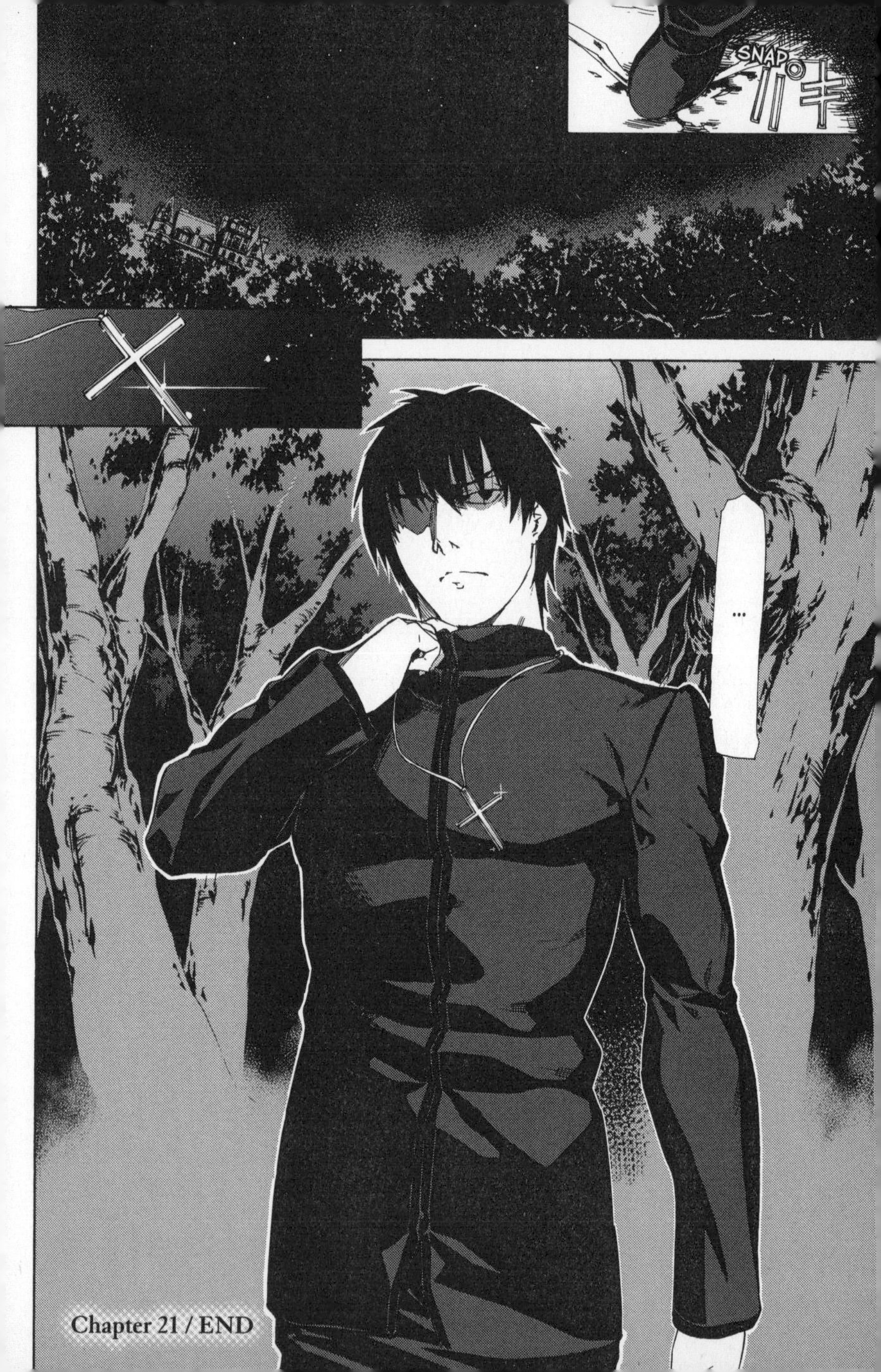
SNAP
...

Chapter 21 / END

CHAPTER 22

—130 : 44 : 57

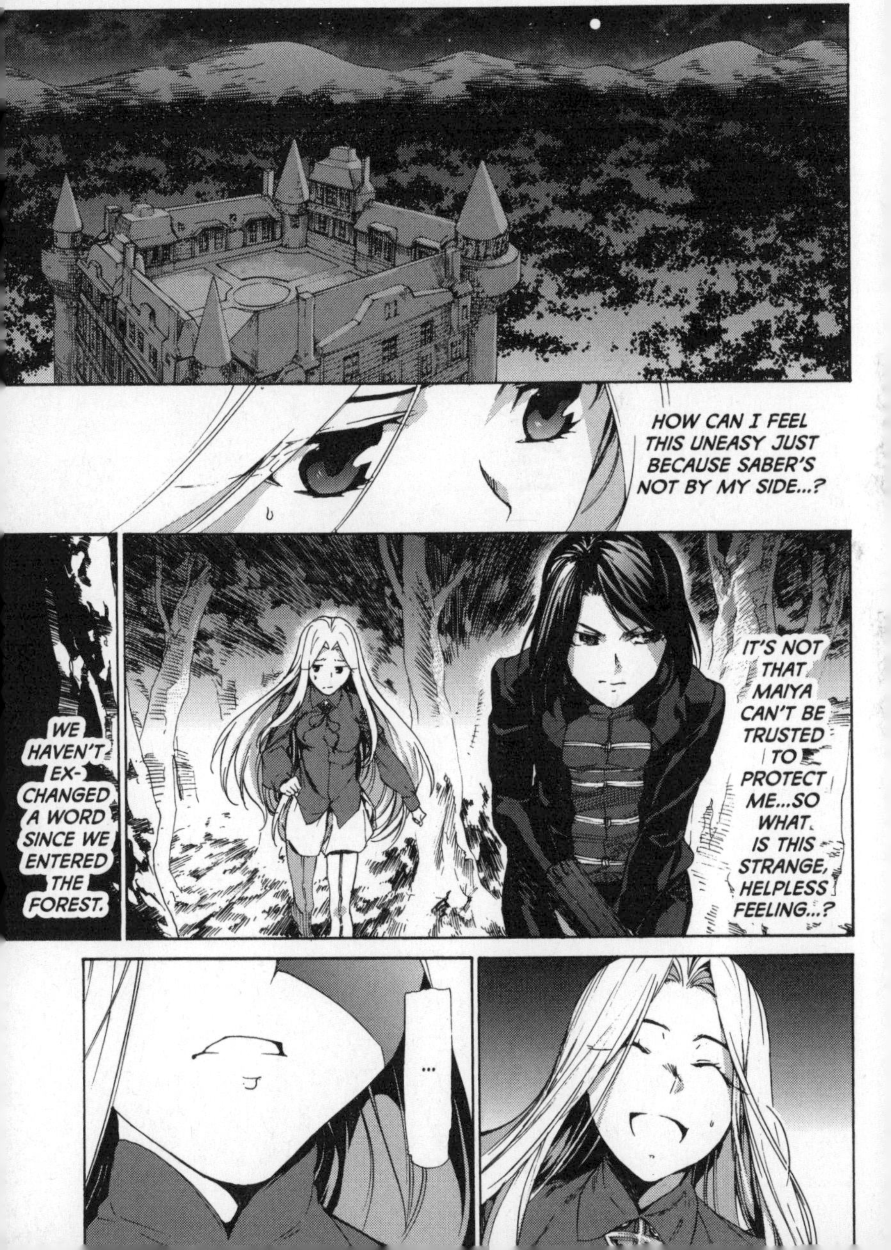
HOW CAN I FEEL THIS UNEASY JUST BECAUSE SABER'S NOT BY MY SIDE...?
IT'S NOT THAT MAIYA CAN'T BE TRUSTED TO PROTECT ME...SO WHAT IS THIS STRANGE, HELPLESS FEELING...?
WE HAVEN'T EX-CHANGED A WORD SINCE WE ENTERED THE FOREST.
...

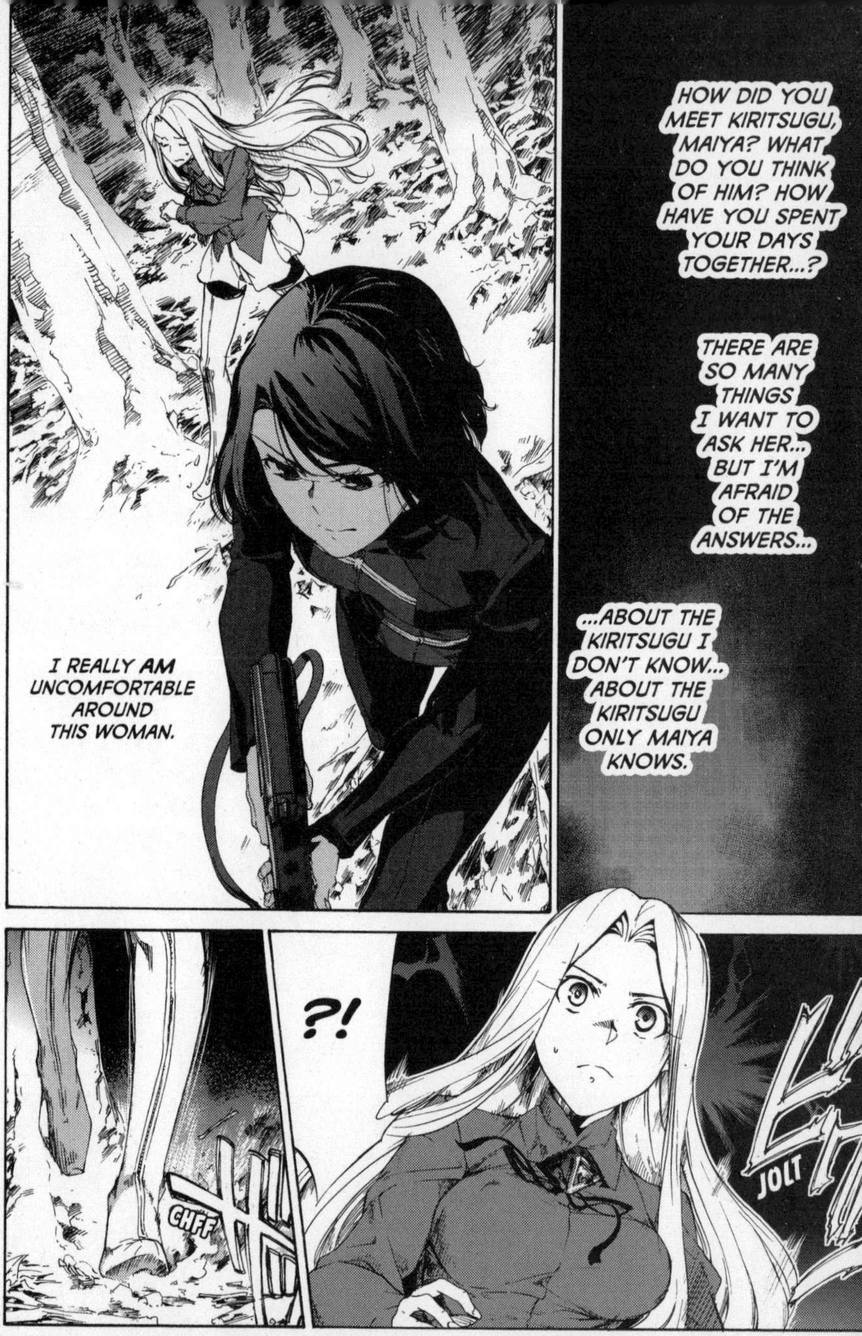
HOW DID YOU MEET KIRITSUGU, MAIYA? WHAT DO YOU THINK OF HIM? HOW HAVE YOU SPENT YOUR DAYS TOGETHER...?
THERE ARE SO MANY THINGS I WANT TO ASK HER... BUT I'M AFRAID OF THE ANSWERS...
...ABOUT THE KIRITSUGU I DON'T KNOW... ABOUT THE KIRITSUGU ONLY MAIYA KNOWS.
I REALLY AM UNCOMFORTABLE AROUND THIS WOMAN.
?!
JOLT
CHFF

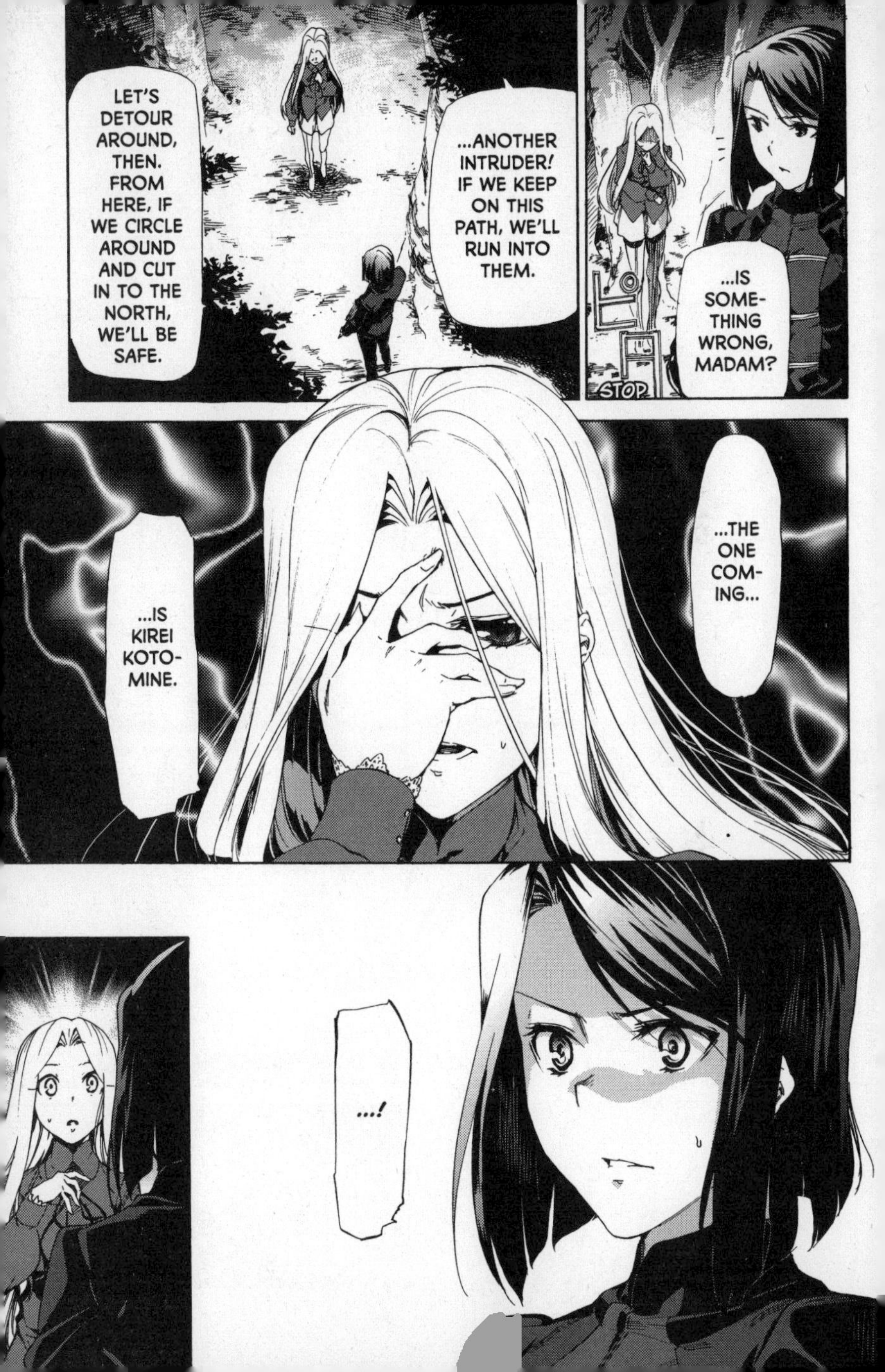
STOP
...IS SOMETHING WRONG, MADAM?
...ANOTHER INTRUDER! IF WE KEEP ON THIS PATH, WE'LL RUN INTO THEM.
LET'S DETOUR AROUND, THEN. FROM HERE, IF WE CIRCLE AROUND AND CUT IN TO THE NORTH, WE'LL BE SAFE.
...THE ONE COMING...
...IS KIREI KOTOMINE.
...!

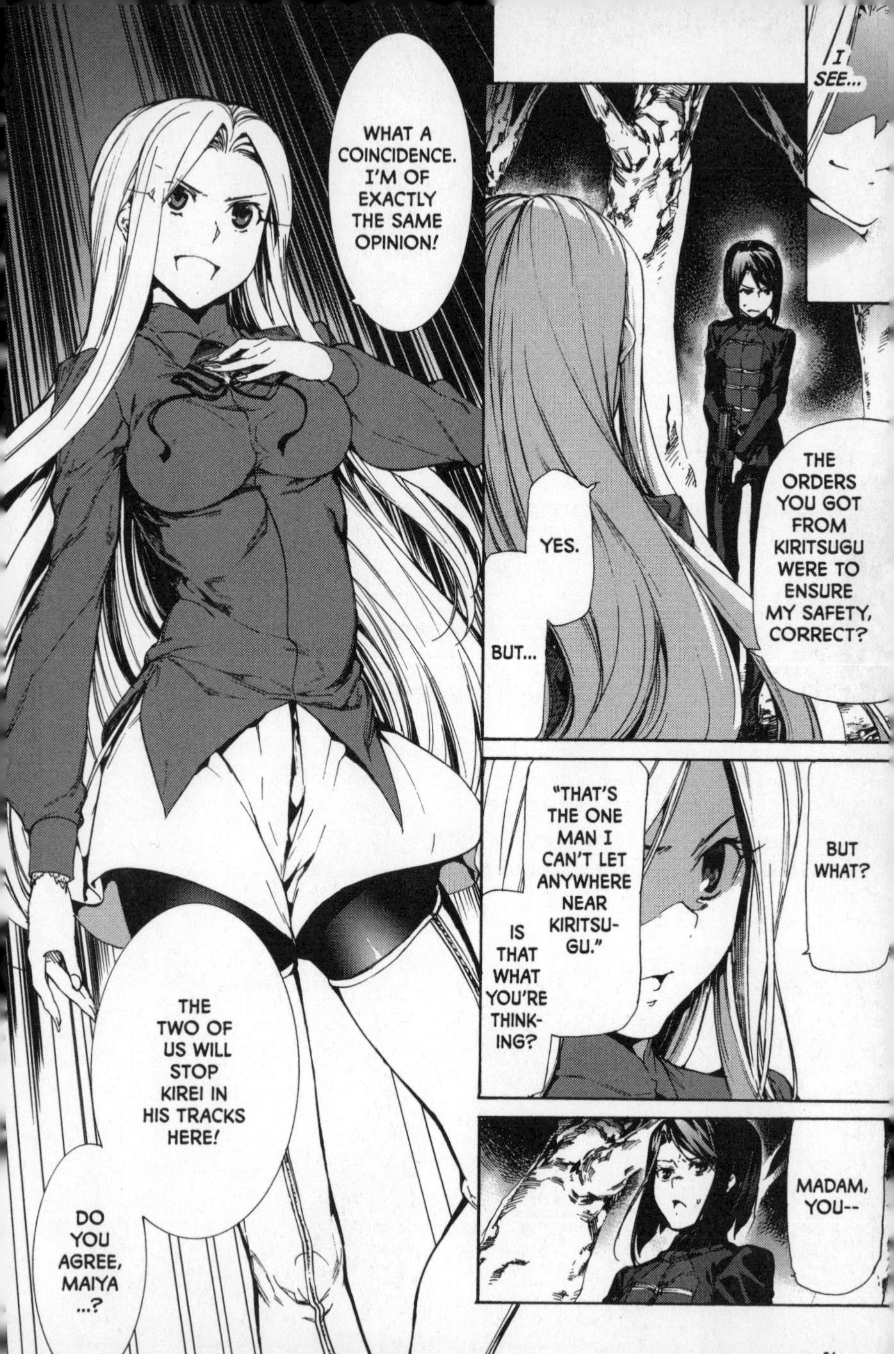
I SEE...
THE ORDERS YOU GOT FROM KIRITSUGU WERE TO ENSURE MY SAFETY, CORRECT?
YES.
BUT...
BUT WHAT?
"THAT'S THE ONE MAN I CAN'T LET ANYWHERE NEAR KIRITSU-GU."
IS THAT WHAT YOU'RE THINK-ING?
MADAM, YOU--
WHAT A COINCIDENCE. I'M OF EXACTLY THE SAME OPINION!
THE TWO OF US WILL STOP KIREI IN HIS TRACKS HERE!
DO YOU AGREE, MAIYA ...?

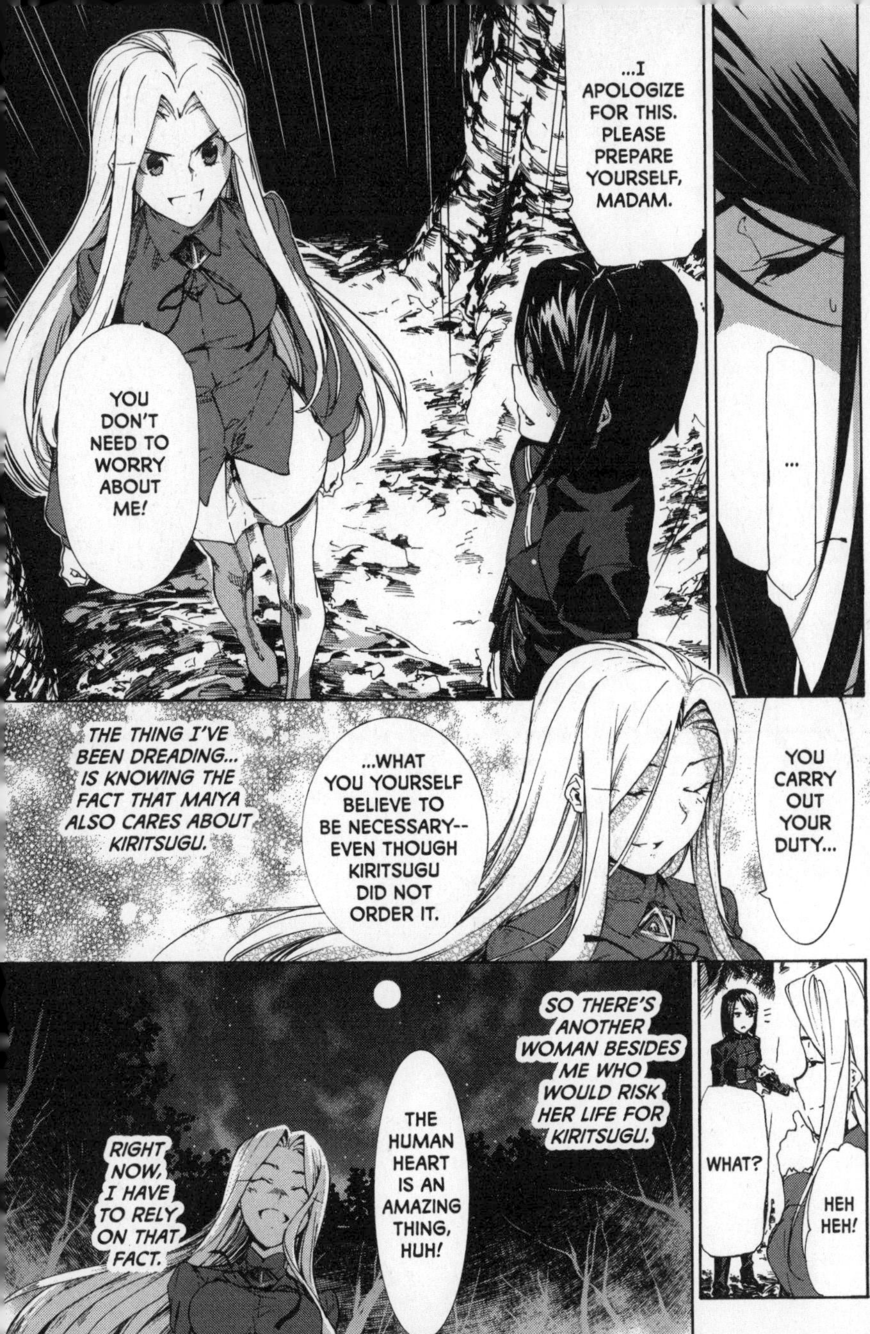
...
...I APOLOGIZE FOR THIS. PLEASE PREPARE YOURSELF, MADAM.
YOU DON'T NEED TO WORRY ABOUT ME!
YOU CARRY OUT YOUR DUTY...
...WHAT YOU YOURSELF BELIEVE TO BE NECESSARY-- EVEN THOUGH KIRITSUGU DID NOT ORDER IT.
THE THING I'VE BEEN DREADING... IS KNOWING THE FACT THAT MAIYA ALSO CARES ABOUT KIRITSUGU.
HEH HEH!
WHAT?
SO THERE'S ANOTHER WOMAN BESIDES ME WHO WOULD RISK HER LIFE FOR KIRITSUGU.
THE HUMAN HEART IS AN AMAZING THING, HUH!
RIGHT NOW, I HAVE TO RELY ON THAT FACT.

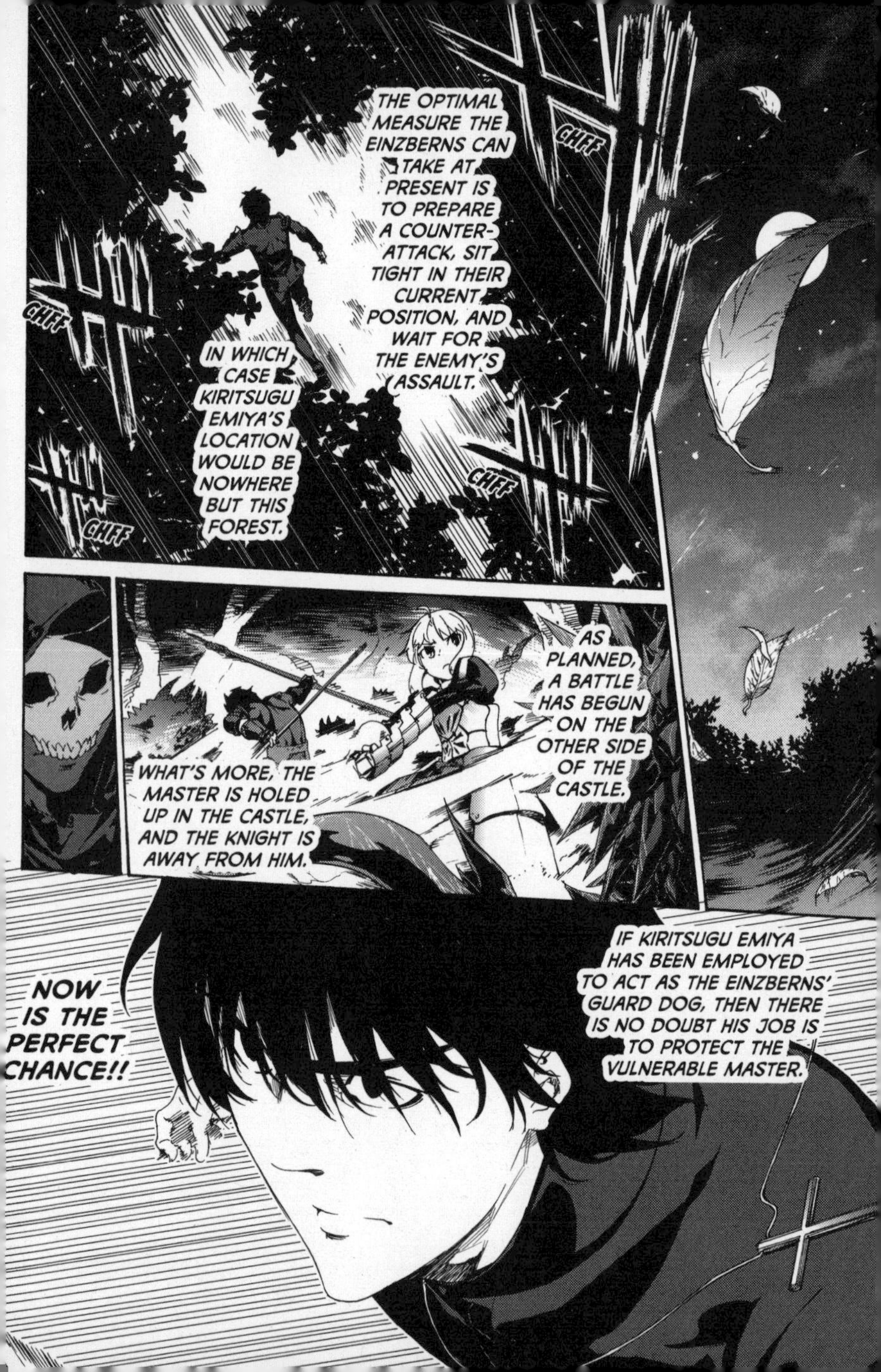
THE OPTIMAL MEASURE THE EINZBERNS CAN TAKE AT PRESENT IS TO PREPARE A COUNTER-ATTACK, SIT TIGHT IN THEIR CURRENT POSITION, AND WAIT FOR THE ENEMY'S ASSAULT.
CHFF
CHFF
IN WHICH CASE KIRITSUGU EMIYA'S LOCATION WOULD BE NOWHERE BUT THIS FOREST.
CHFF
CHFF
AS PLANNED, A BATTLE HAS BEGUN ON THE OTHER SIDE OF THE CASTLE.
WHAT'S MORE, THE MASTER IS HOLED UP IN THE CASTLE, AND THE KNIGHT IS AWAY FROM HIM.
IF KIRITSUGU EMIYA HAS BEEN EMPLOYED TO ACT AS THE EINZBERNS' GUARD DOG, THEN THERE IS NO DOUBT HIS JOB IS TO PROTECT THE VULNERABLE MASTER.
NOW IS THE PERFECT CHANCE!!

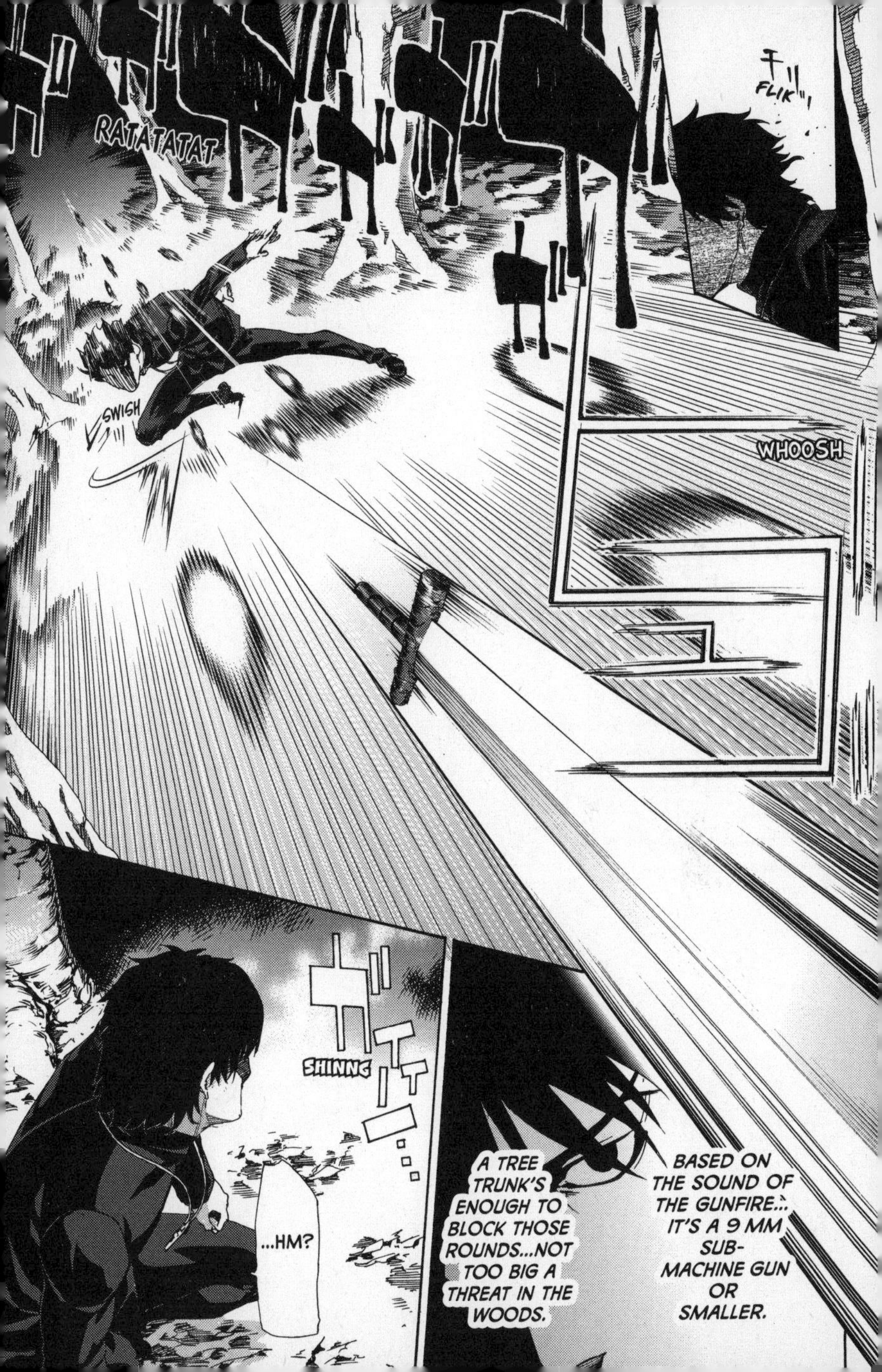

FLIK
RATATATAT
WHOOSH
SWISH
BASED ON THE SOUND OF THE GUNFIRE... IT'S A 9 MM SUB-MACHINE GUN OR SMALLER.
A TREE TRUNK'S ENOUGH TO BLOCK THOSE ROUNDS...NOT TOO BIG A THREAT IN THE WOODS.
SHINNG
...HM?

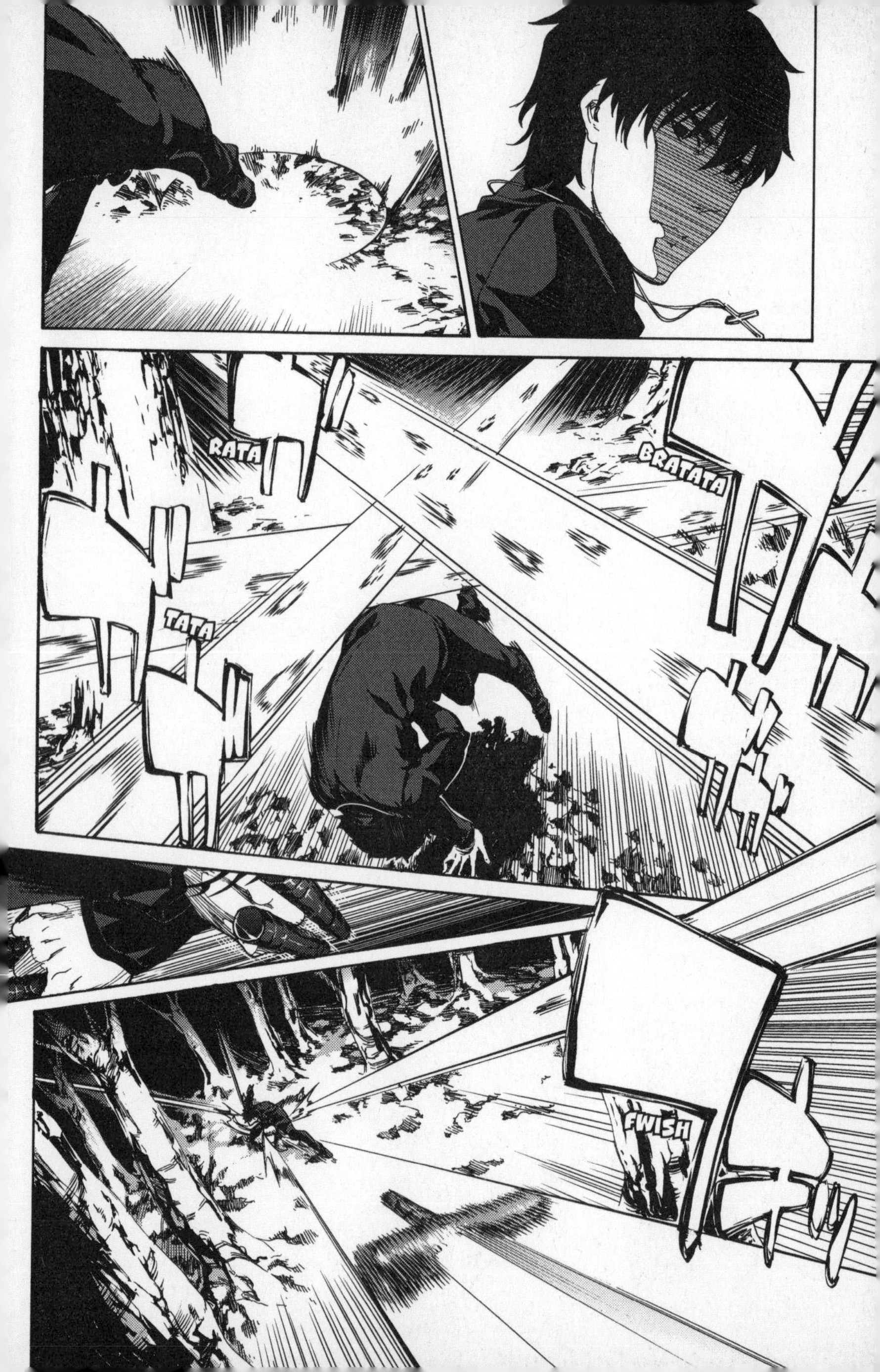
BRATATA
RATA
TATA
FWISH

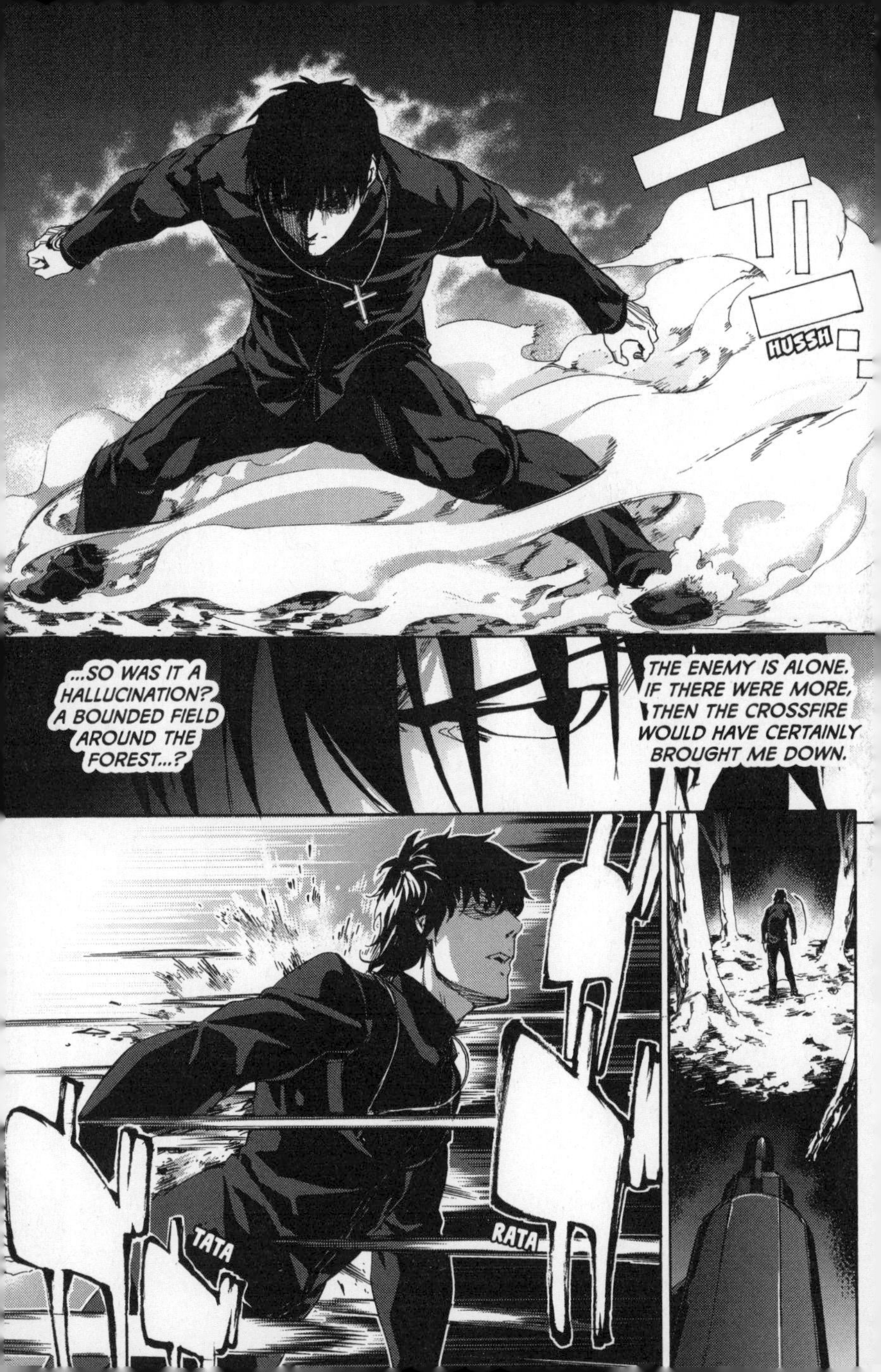
HUSSH
THE ENEMY IS ALONE. IF THERE WERE MORE, THEN THE CROSSFIRE WOULD HAVE CERTAINLY BROUGHT ME DOWN.
...SO WAS IT A HALLUCINATION? A BOUNDED FIELD AROUND THE FOREST...?
RATA
TATA

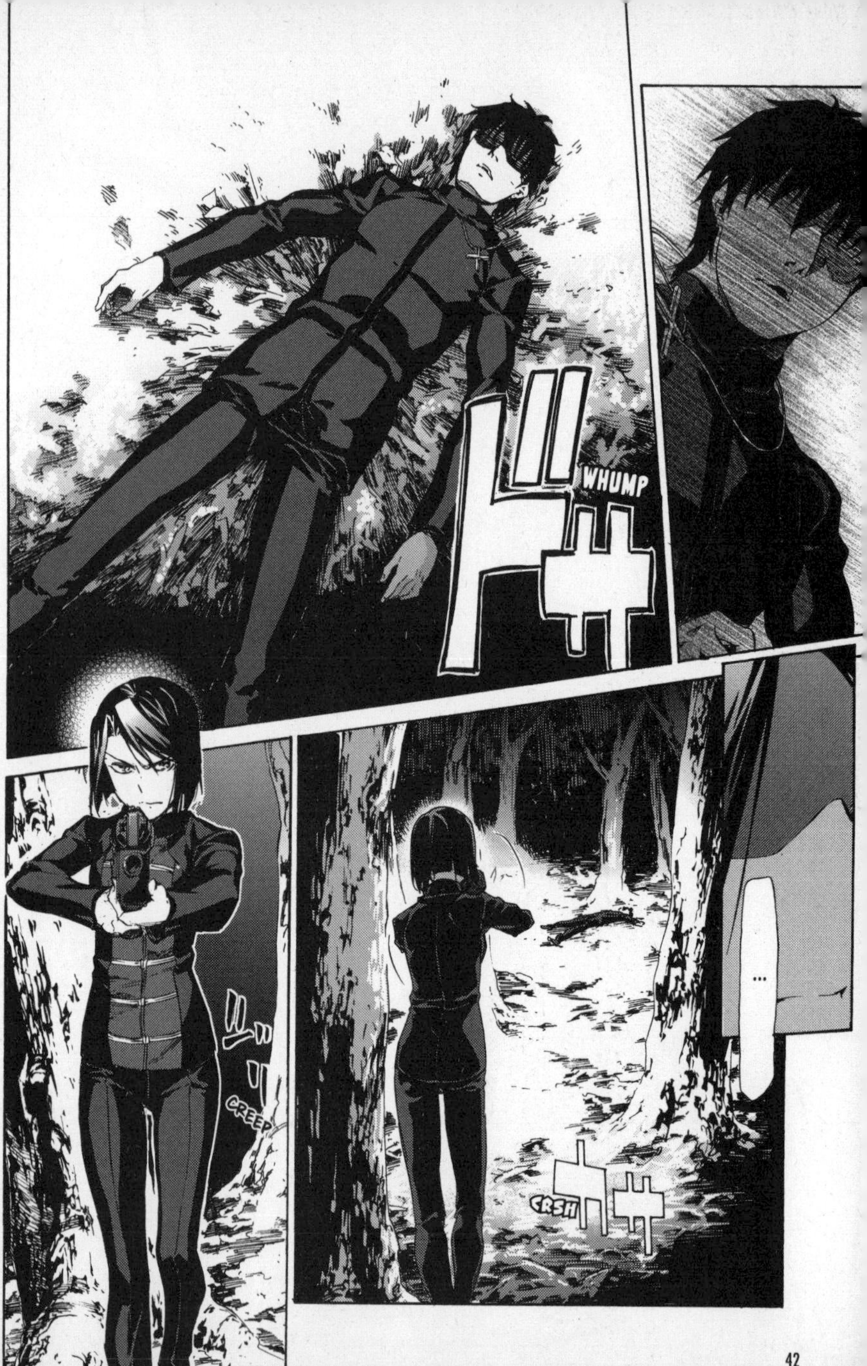
WHUMP
...
CRSH
CREEP

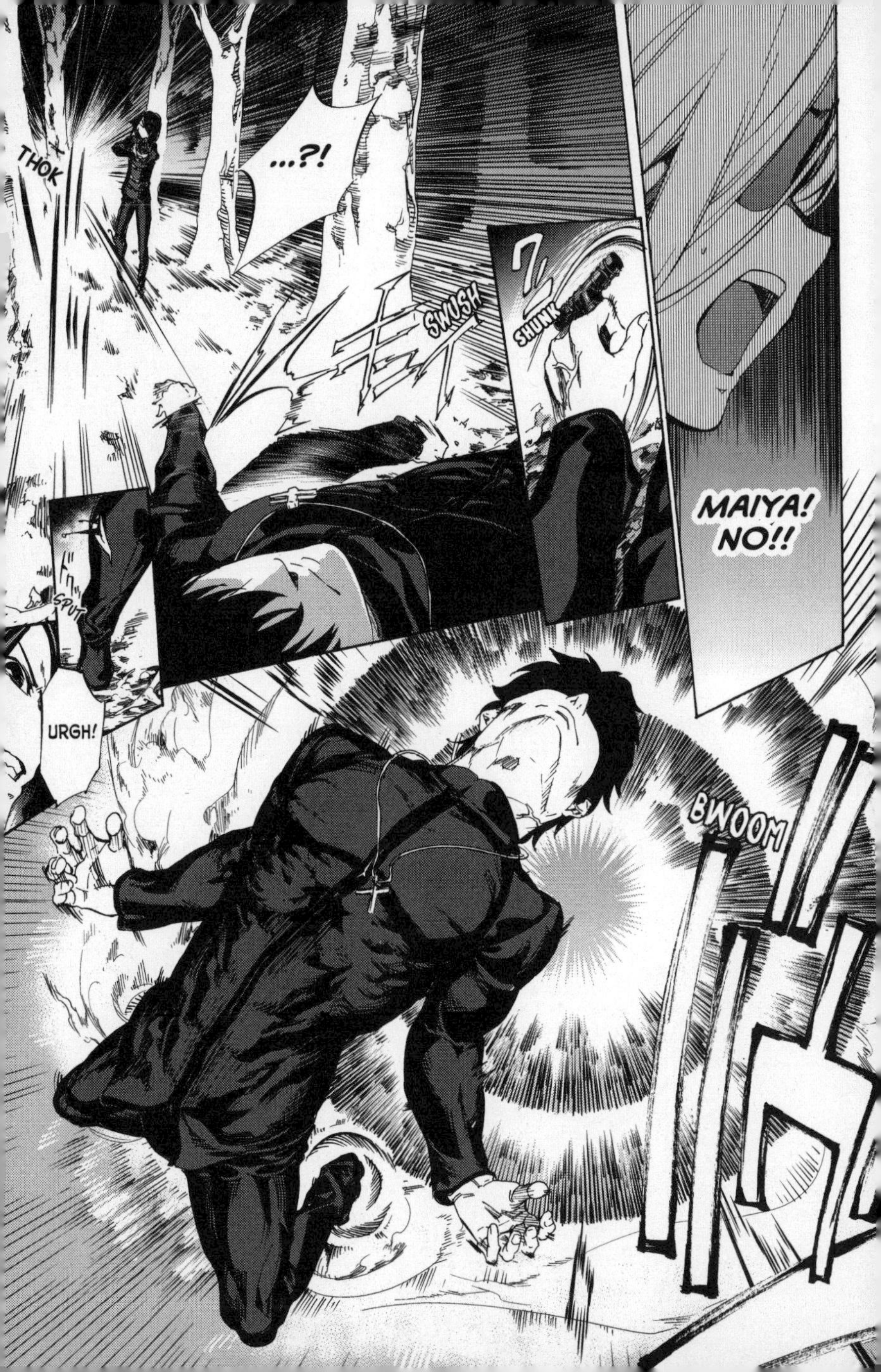
MAIYA! NO!!
...?!
THOK
SHUNK
SWUSH
SPUT
URGH!
BWOOM

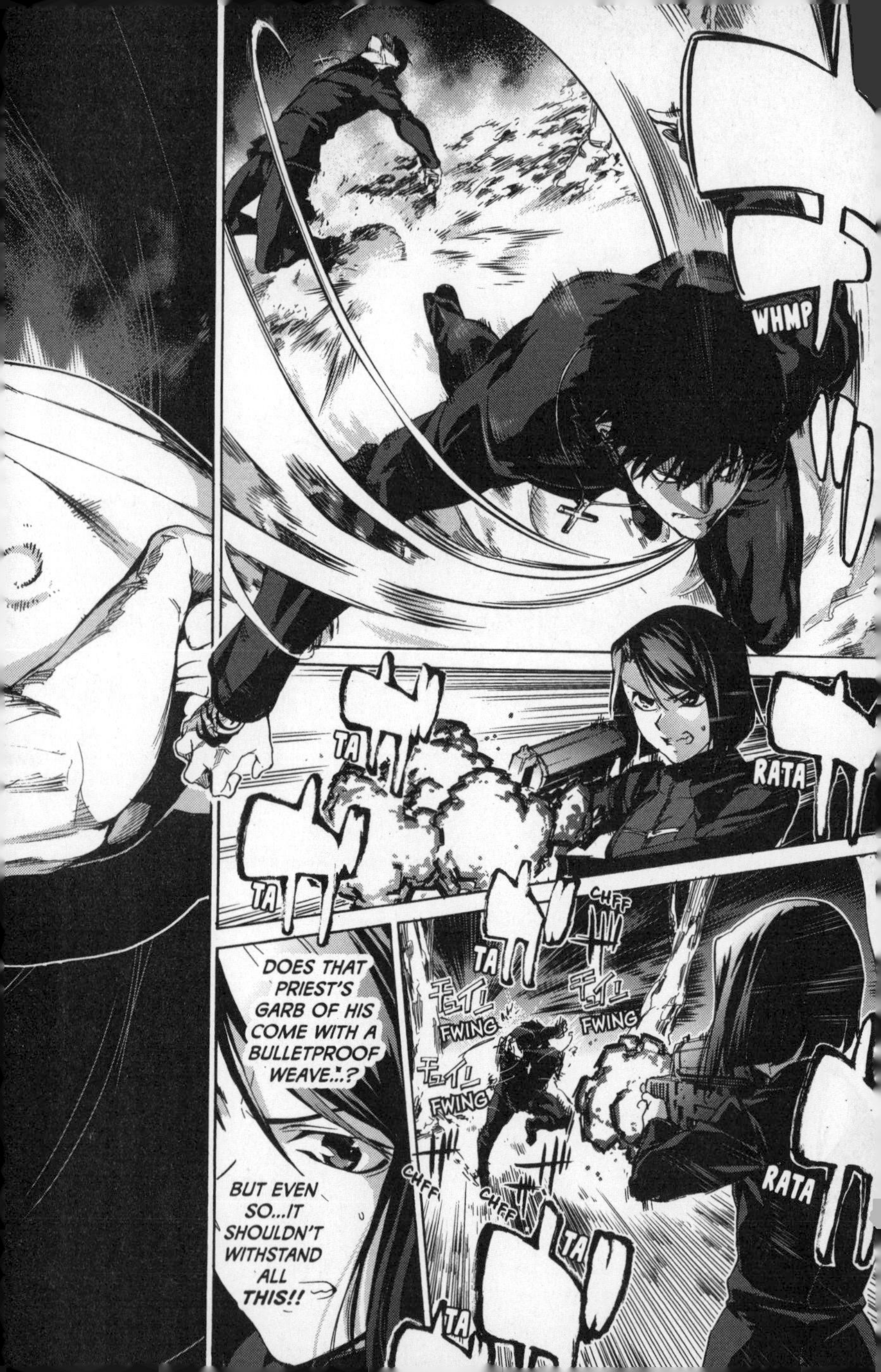
WHMP
RATA
TA
TA
CHFF
TA
FWING
FWING
FWING
RATA
CHFF
CHFF
TA
TA
DOES THAT PRIEST'S GARB OF HIS COME WITH A BULLETPROOF WEAVE...?
BUT EVEN SO...IT SHOULDN'T WITHSTAND ALL THIS!!

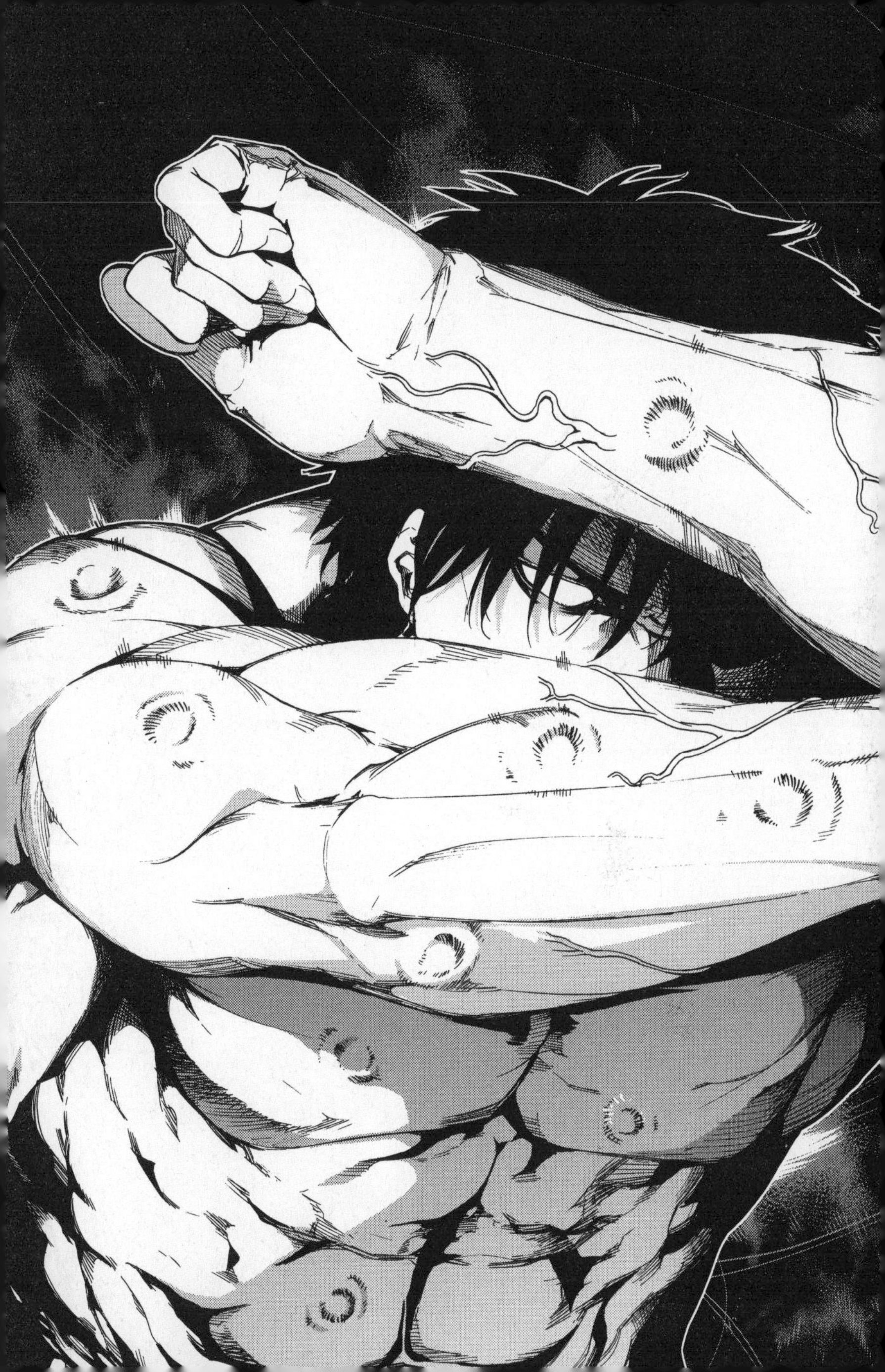

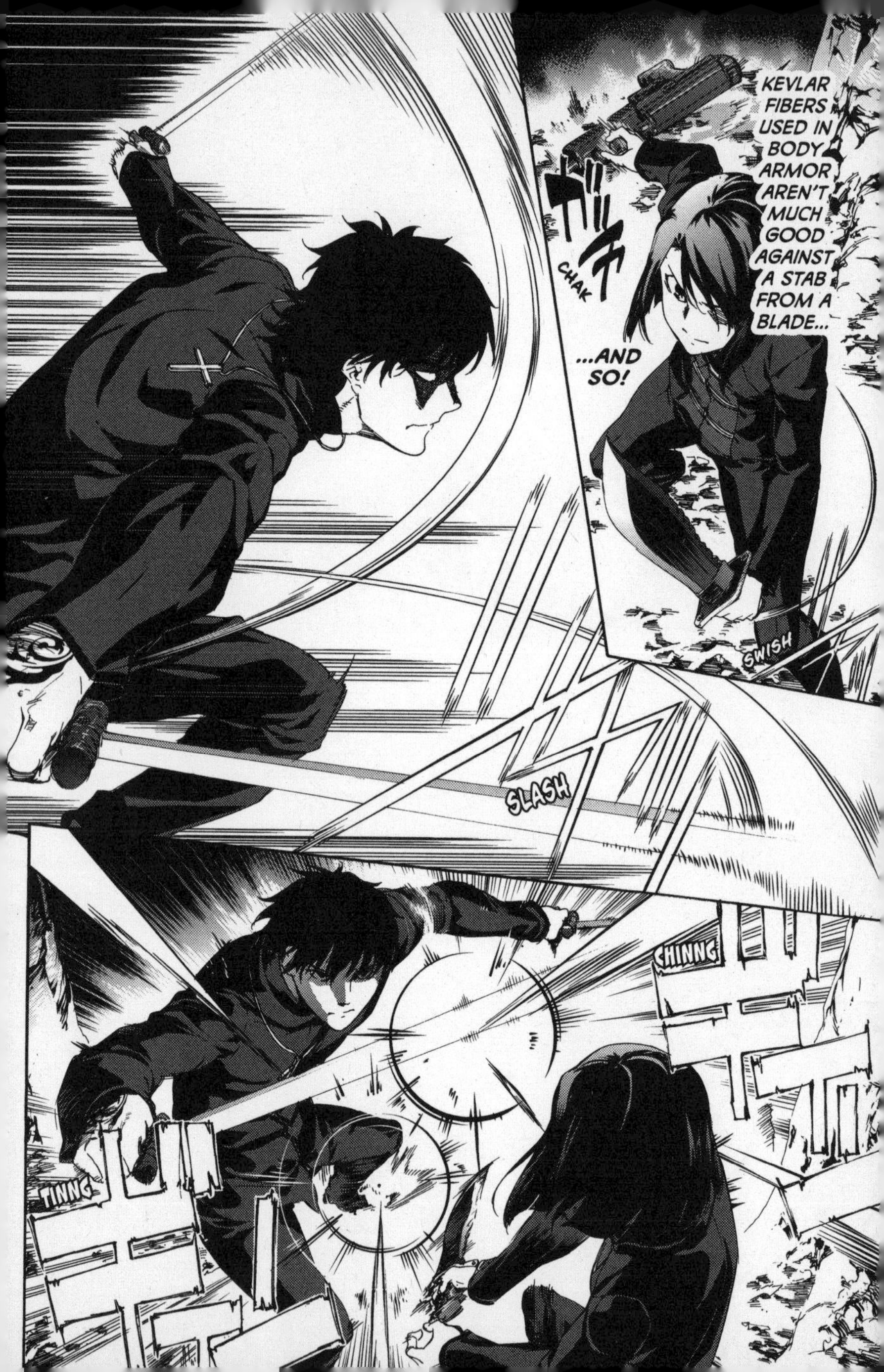

KEVLAR FIBERS USED IN BODY ARMOR AREN'T MUCH GOOD AGAINST A STAB FROM A BLADE...
CHAK
...AND SO!
SWISH
SLASH
CHINNG
TINNG

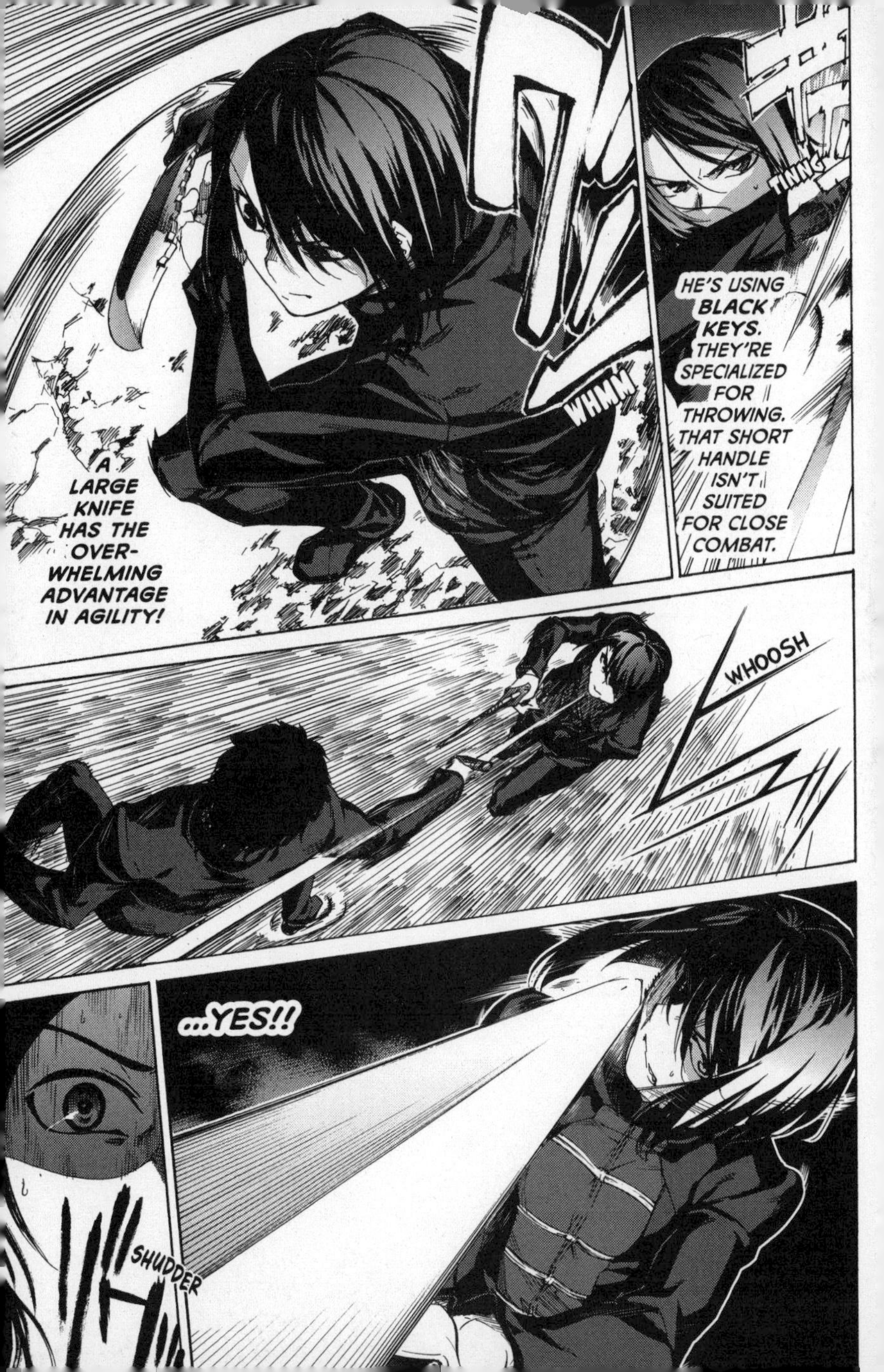
TINNG
HE'S USING BLACK KEYS. THEY'RE SPECIALIZED FOR THROWING. THAT SHORT HANDLE ISN'T SUITED FOR CLOSE COMBAT.
WHMM
A LARGE KNIFE HAS THE OVER-WHELMING ADVANTAGE IN AGILITY!
WHOOSH
...YES!!
SHUDDER

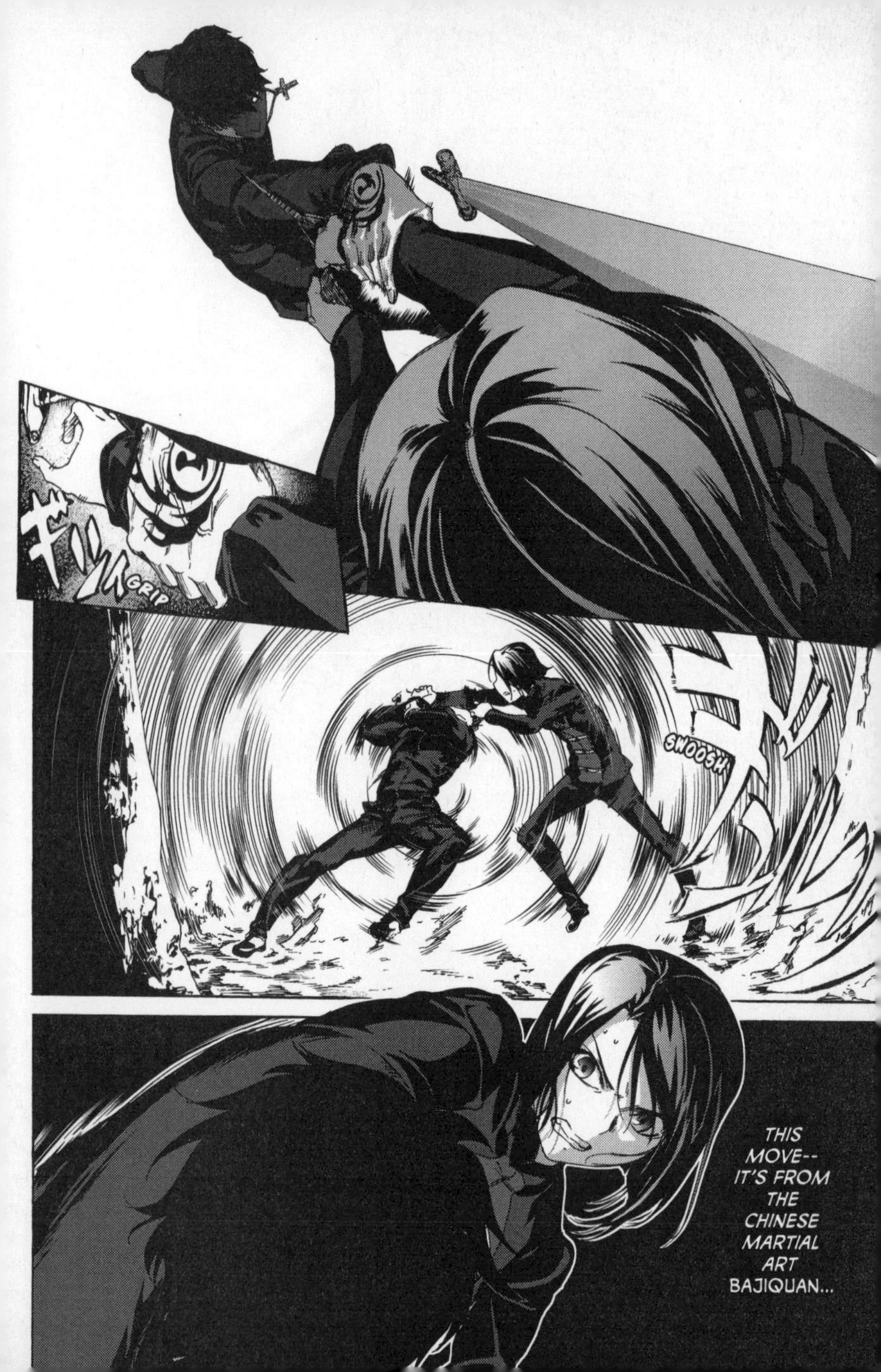
GRIP
SWOOSH
THIS MOVE-- IT'S FROM THE CHINESE MARTIAL ART BAJIQUAN...

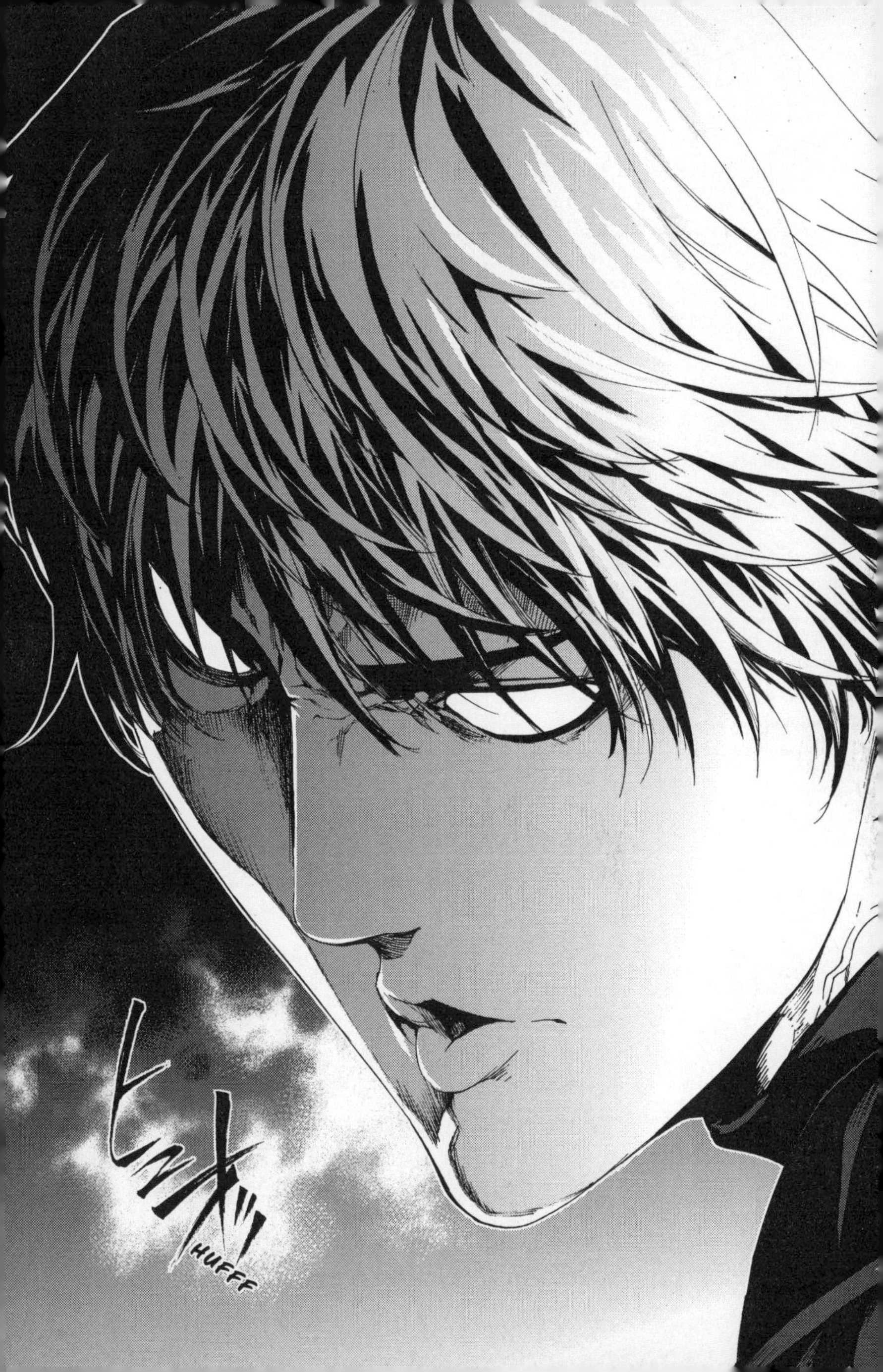
ヒハッ
HUFFF

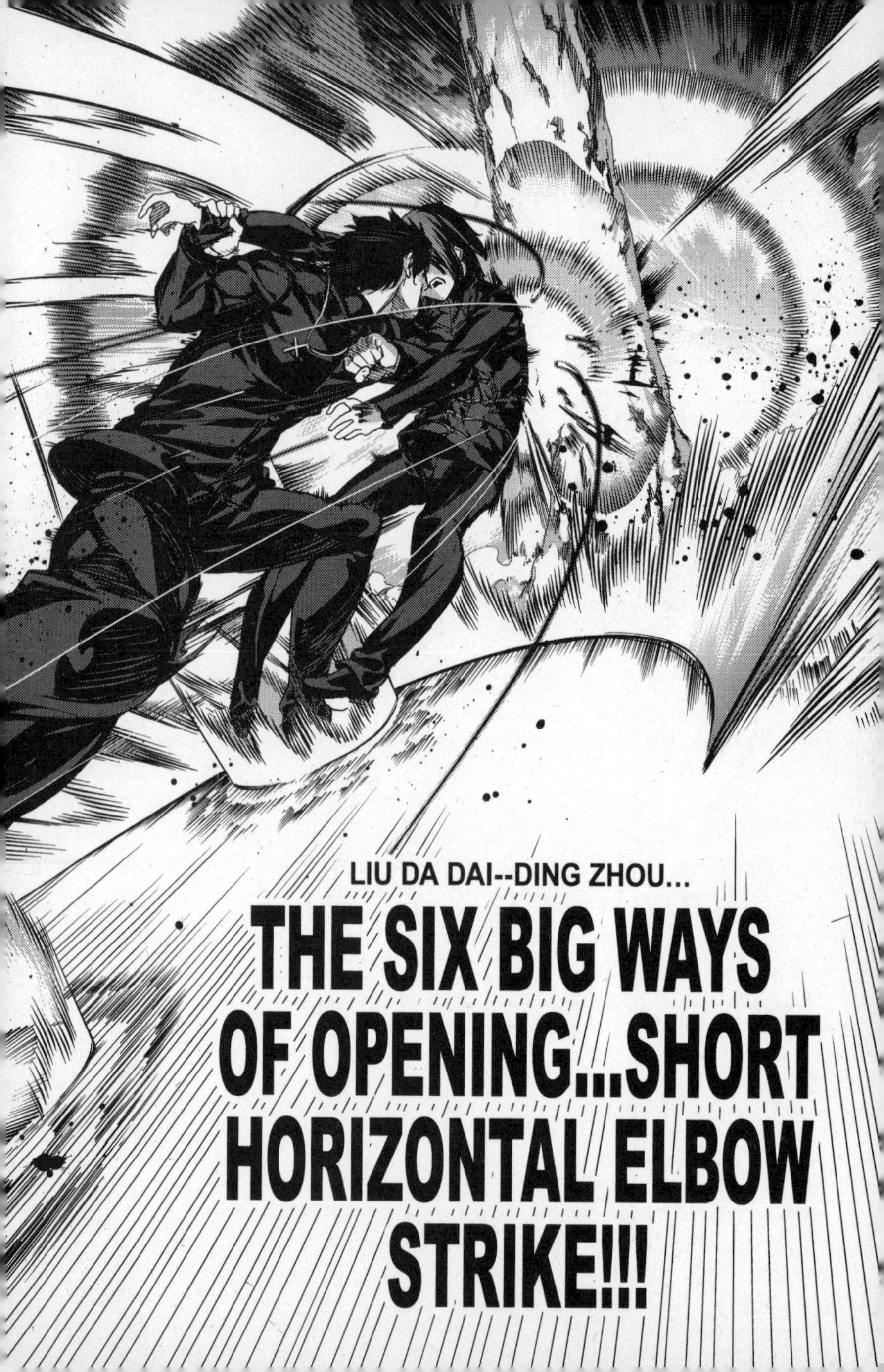
LIU DA DAI--DING ZHOU...
THE SIX BIG WAYS OF OPENING...SHORT HORIZONTAL ELBOW STRIKE!!!

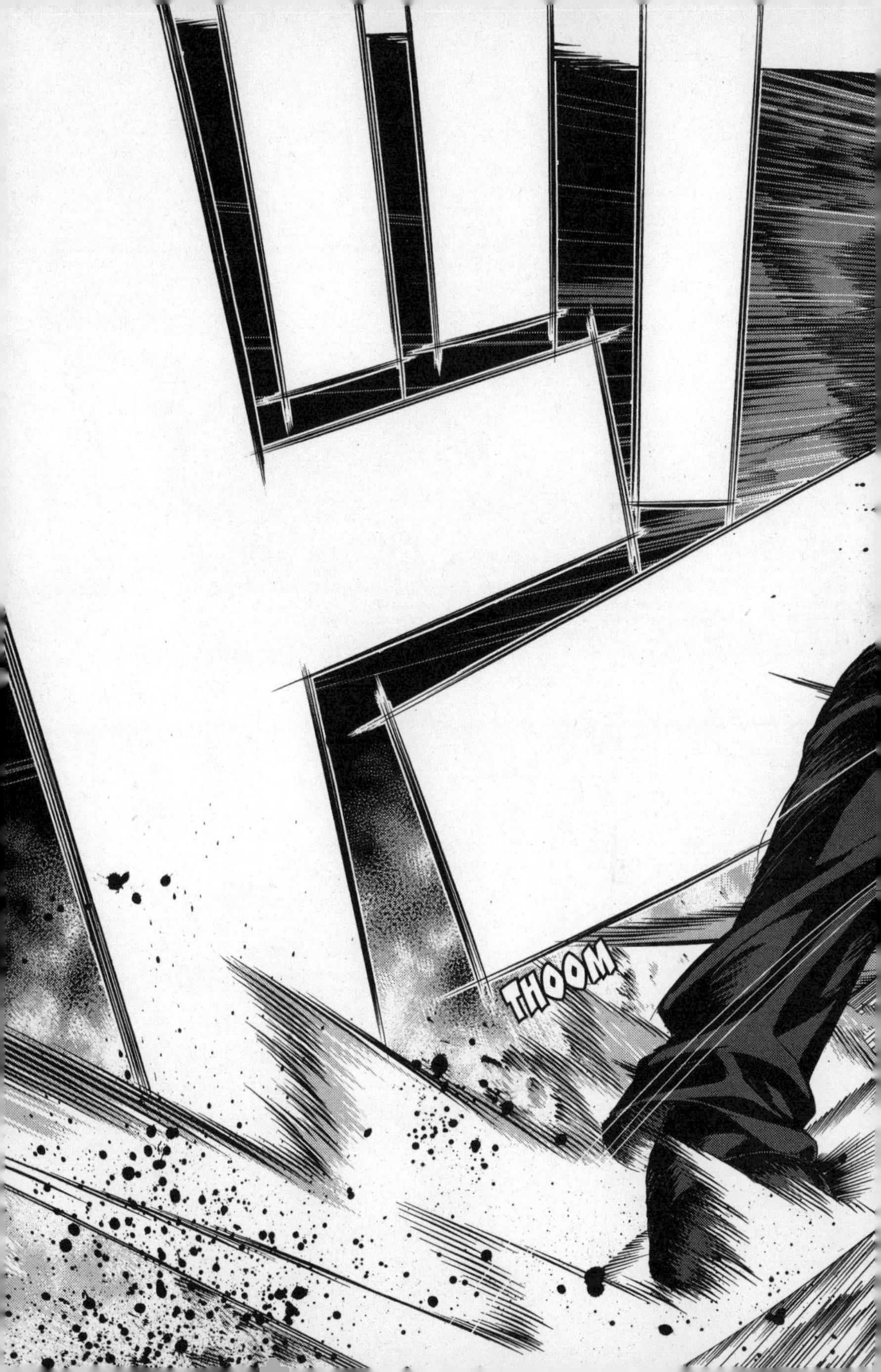
THOOM

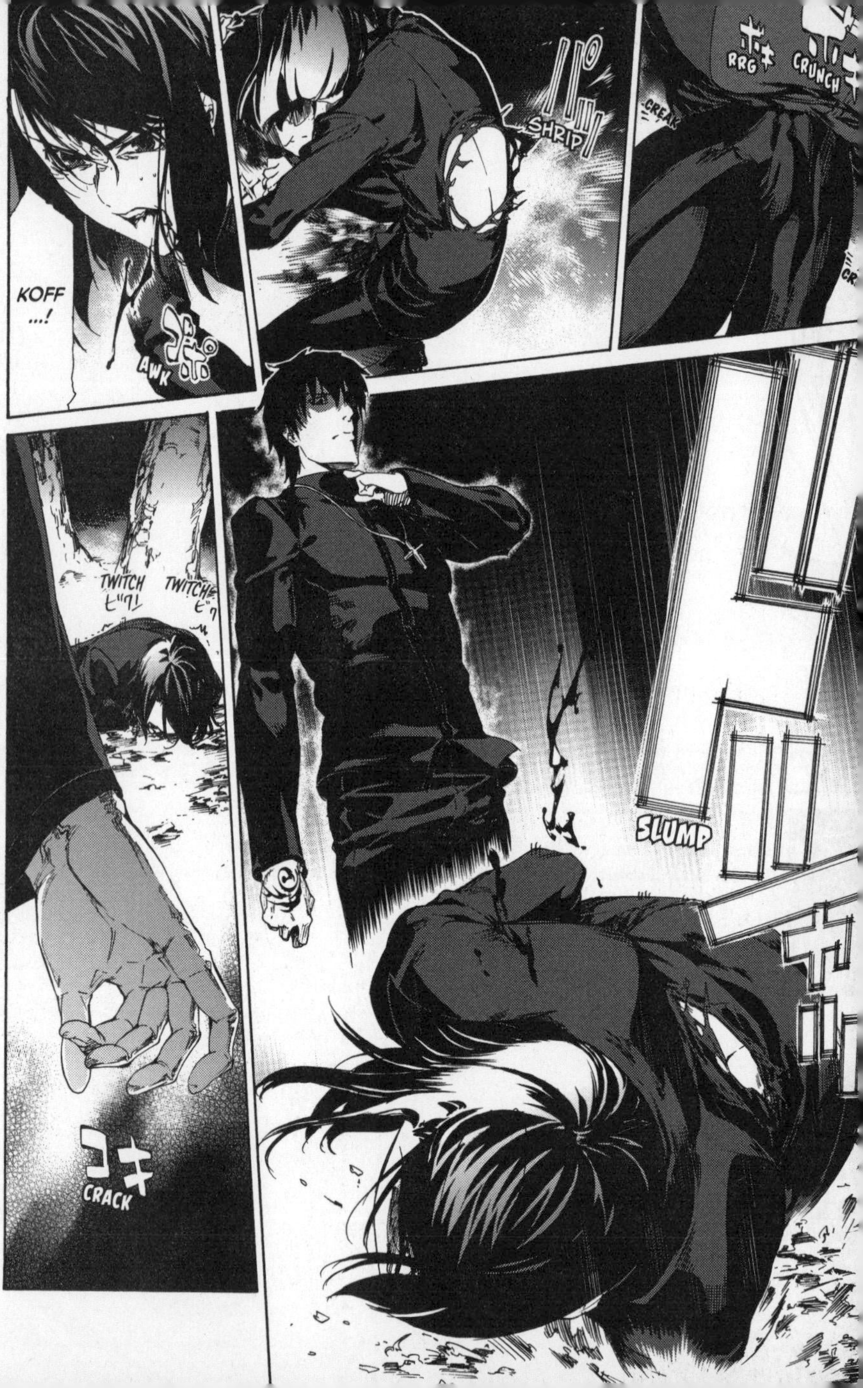

RRG
CRUNCH
CREAK
SHRIP
KOFF
...!
AWK
SLUMP
TWITCH
TWITCH
CRACK

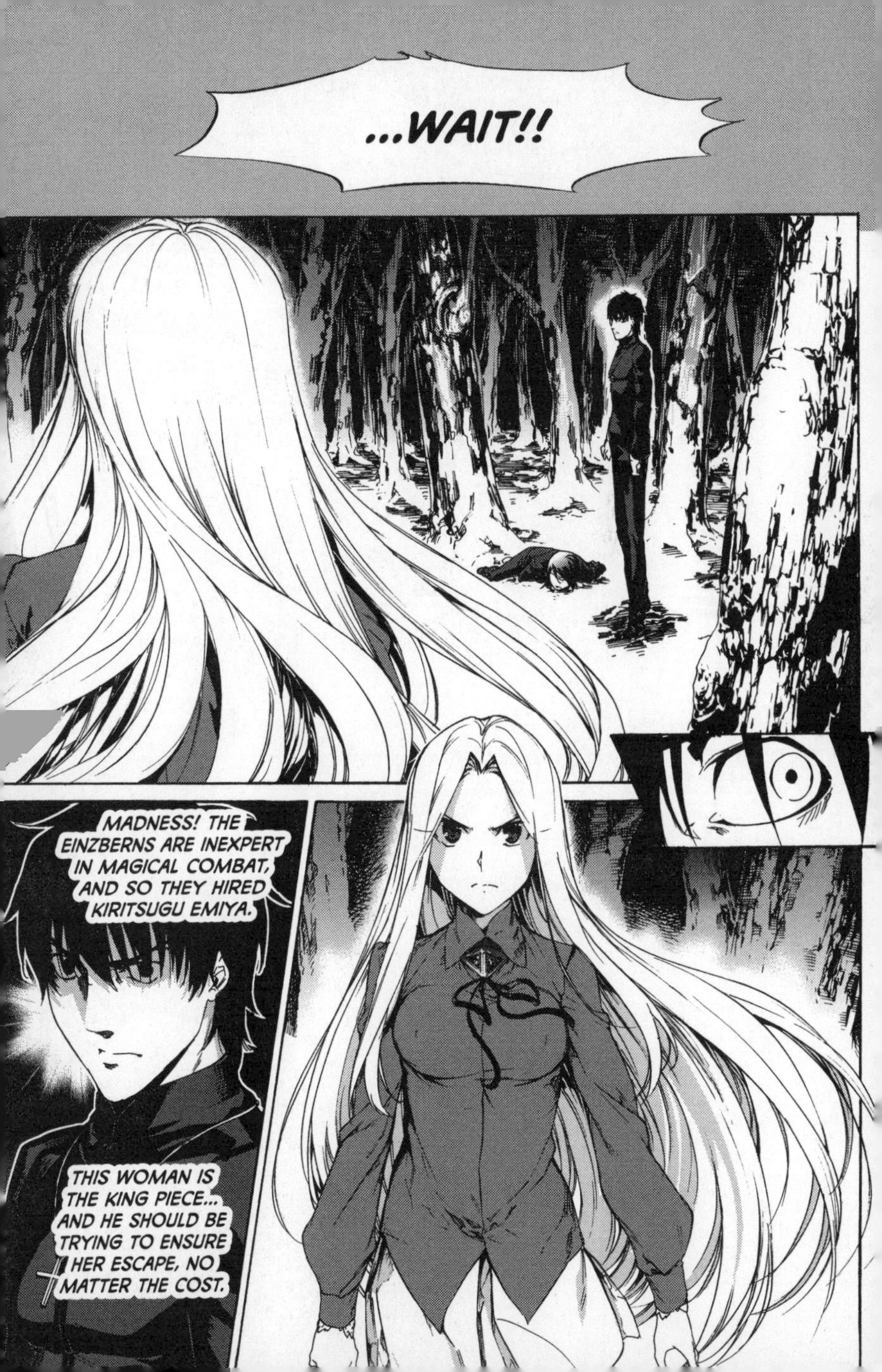
...WAIT!!
MADNESS! THE EINZBERNS ARE INEXPERT IN MAGICAL COMBAT, AND SO THEY HIRED KIRITSUGU EMIYA.
THIS WOMAN IS THE KING PIECE... AND HE SHOULD BE TRYING TO ENSURE HER ESCAPE, NO MATTER THE COST.

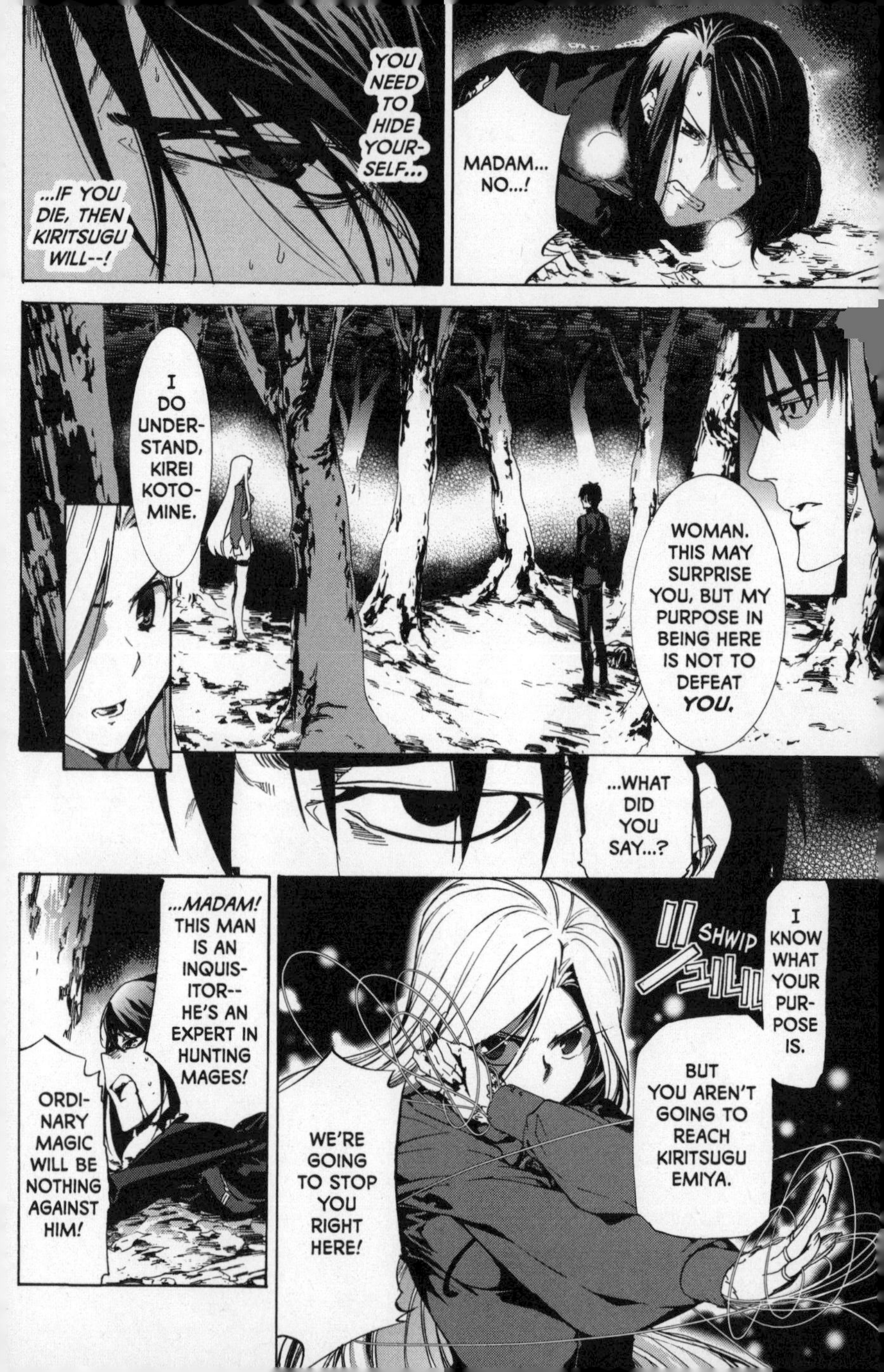
MADAM... NO...!
YOU NEED TO HIDE YOURSELF...
...IF YOU DIE, THEN KIRITSUGU WILL--!
WOMAN. THIS MAY SURPRISE YOU, BUT MY PURPOSE IN BEING HERE IS NOT TO DEFEAT *YOU.*
I DO UNDERSTAND, KIREI KOTOMINE.
...WHAT DID YOU SAY...?
I KNOW WHAT YOUR PURPOSE IS.
SHWIP
BUT YOU AREN'T GOING TO REACH KIRITSUGU EMIYA.
WE'RE GOING TO STOP YOU RIGHT HERE!
...MADAM! THIS MAN IS AN INQUISITOR-- HE'S AN EXPERT IN HUNTING MAGES!
ORDINARY MAGIC WILL BE NOTHING AGAINST HIM!

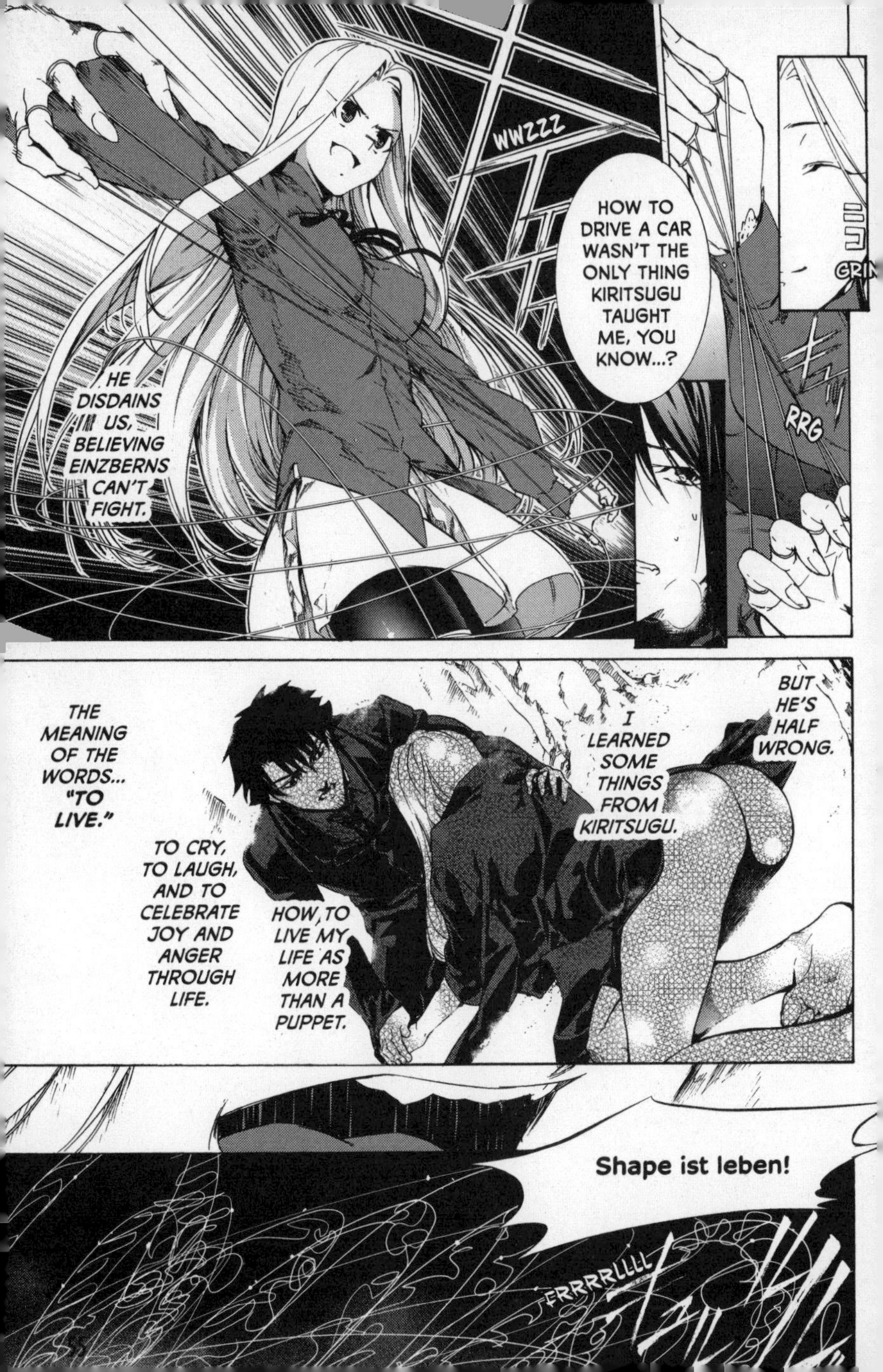

WWZZZ
HOW TO DRIVE A CAR WASN'T THE ONLY THING KIRITSUGU TAUGHT ME, YOU KNOW...?
GRIN
HE DISDAINS US, BELIEVING EINZBERNS CAN'T FIGHT.
RRG
BUT HE'S HALF WRONG.
I LEARNED SOME THINGS FROM KIRITSUGU.
THE MEANING OF THE WORDS... "TO LIVE."
HOW TO LIVE MY LIFE AS MORE THAN A PUPPET.
TO CRY, TO LAUGH, AND TO CELEBRATE JOY AND ANGER THROUGH LIFE.
Shape ist leben!
FRRRRLLLL

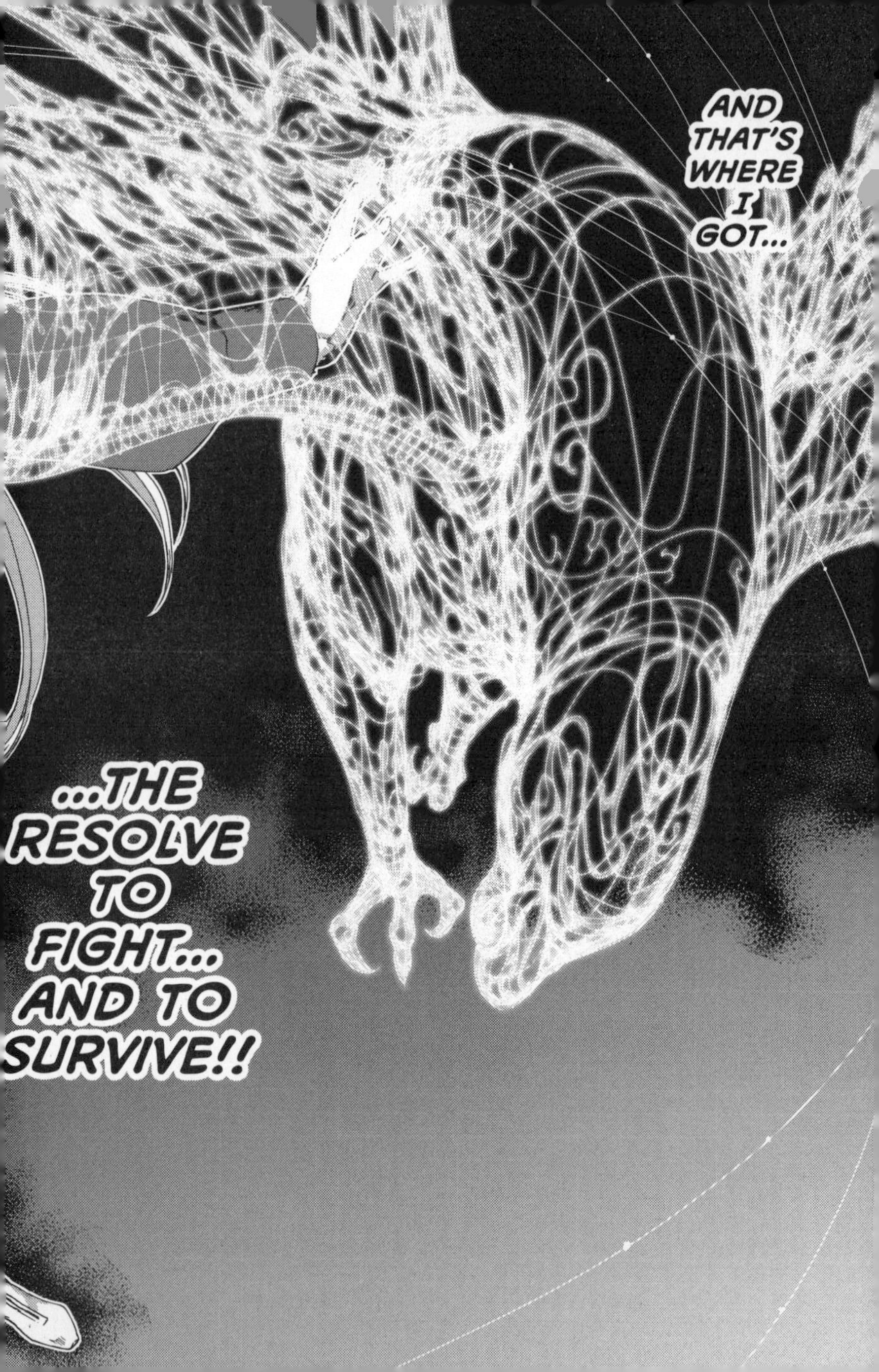
AND THAT'S WHERE I GOT...
...THE RESOLVE TO FIGHT... AND TO SURVIVE!!

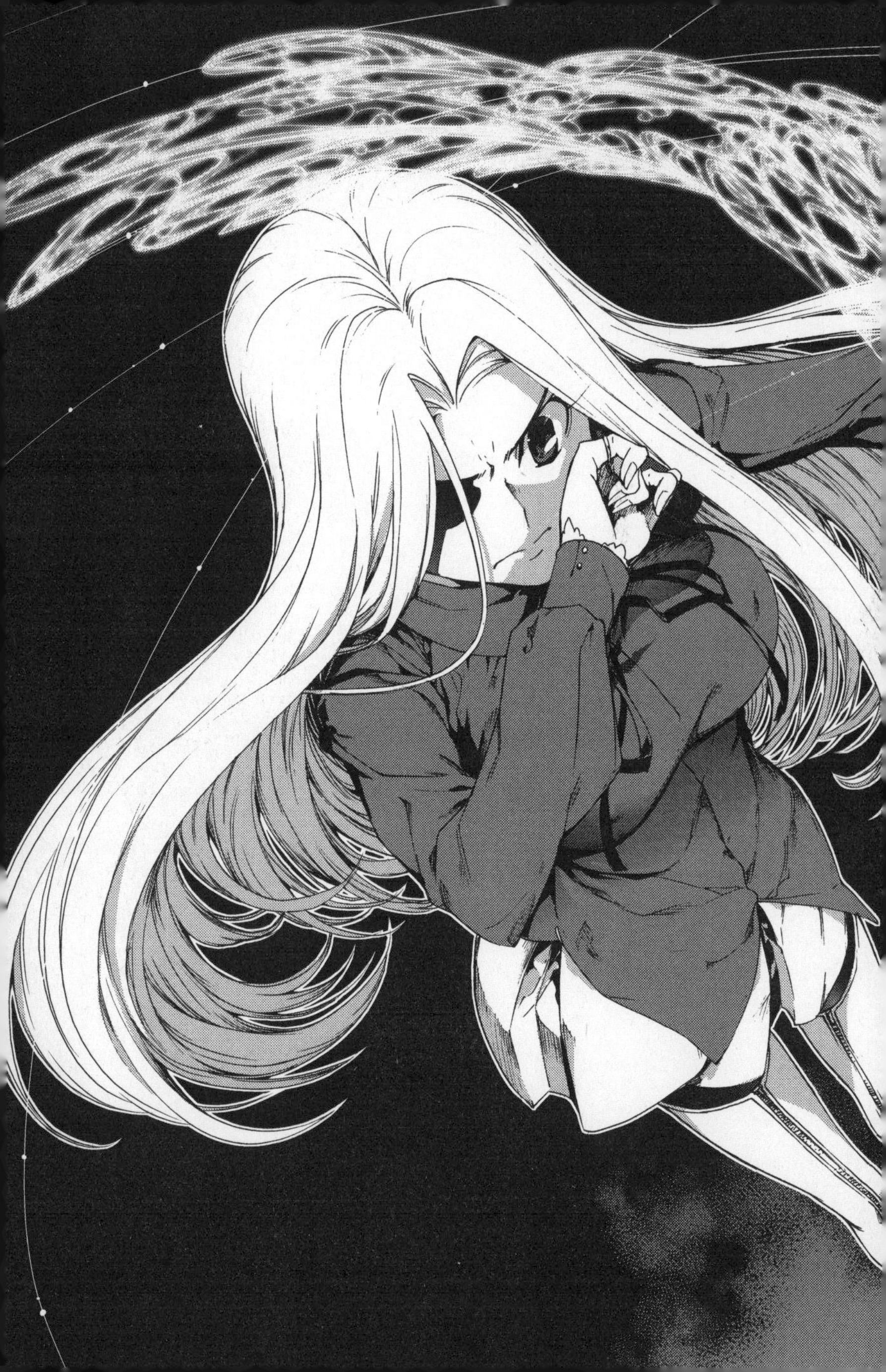

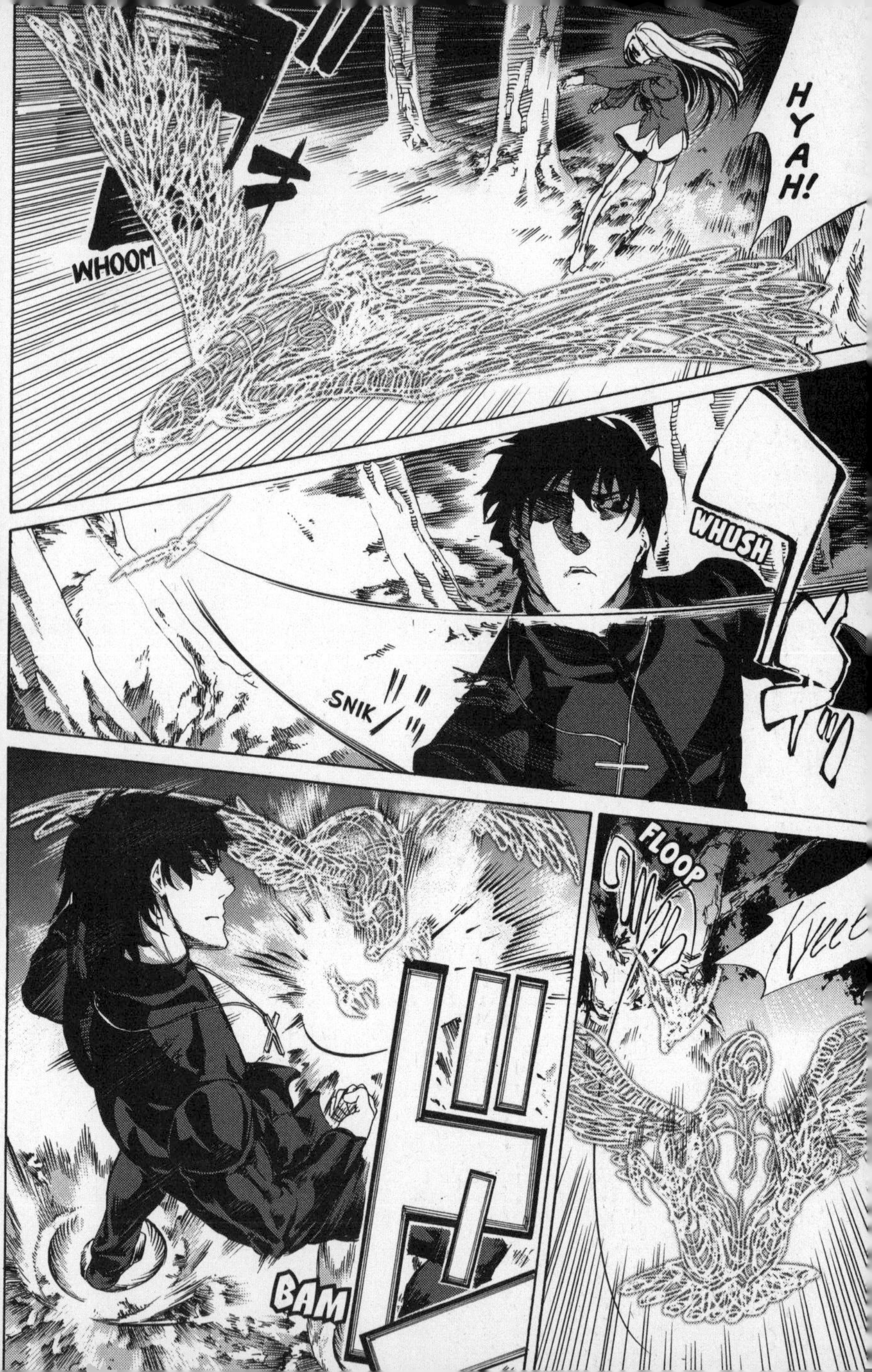
HYAH!
WHOOM
WHUSH
SNIK
FLOOP
Kyee
BAM

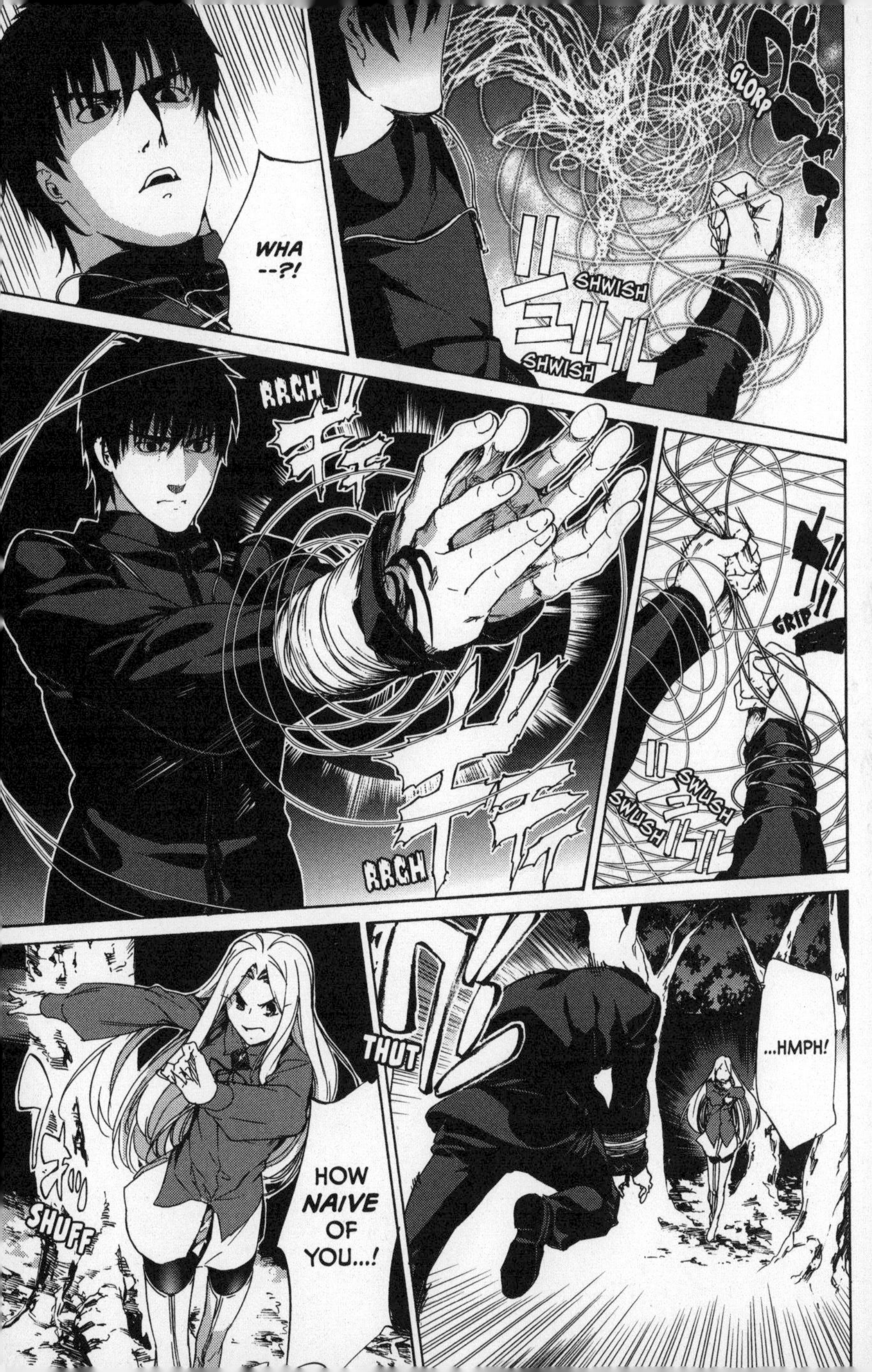
GLORP
SHWISH
SHWISH
WHA --?!
GRIP!!
SWUSH
SWUSH
RRCH
RRCH
...HMPH!
THUT
HOW *NAIVE* OF YOU...!
SHUFF

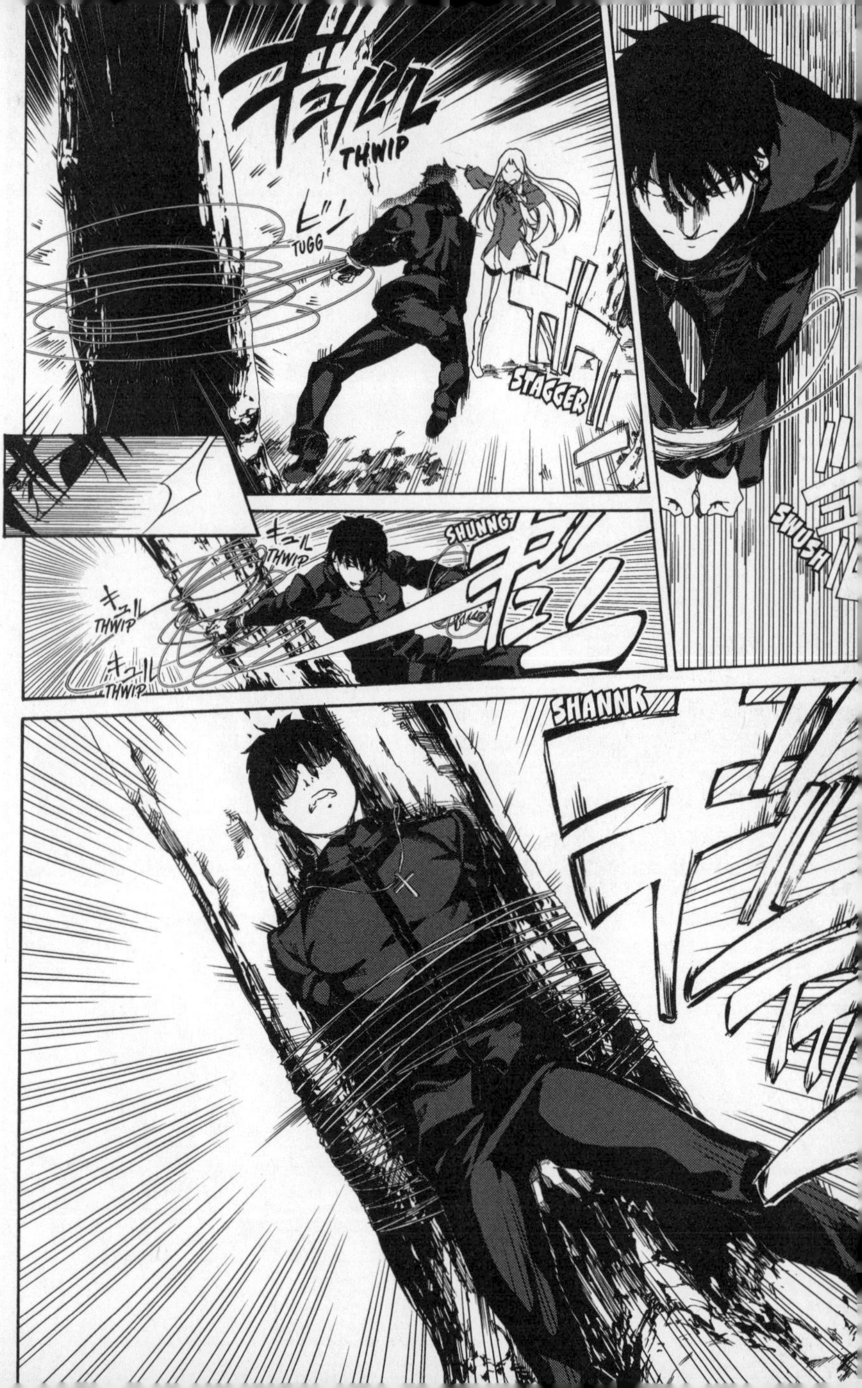
SWUSH
THWIP
TUGG
STAGGER
SHUNNG
THWIP
THWIP
THWIP
SHANNK

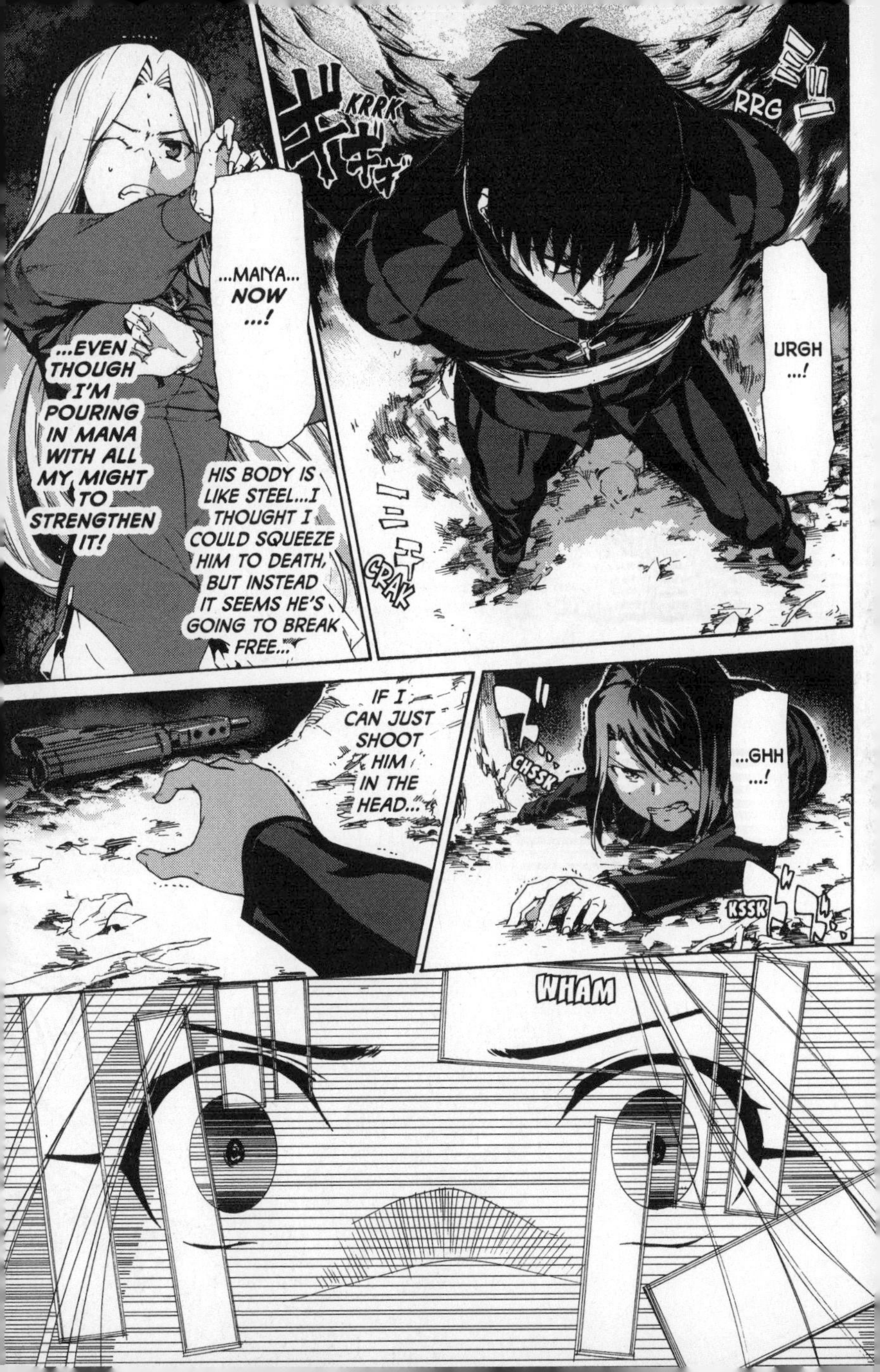
RRG
KRRK
URGH ...!
CRAK
...MAIYA... NOW ...!
...EVEN THOUGH I'M POURING IN MANA WITH ALL MY MIGHT TO STRENGTHEN IT!
HIS BODY IS LIKE STEEL...I THOUGHT I COULD SQUEEZE HIM TO DEATH, BUT INSTEAD IT SEEMS HE'S GOING TO BREAK FREE...
CHSSK
...GHH ...!
KSSK
IF I CAN JUST SHOOT HIM IN THE HEAD...
WHAM

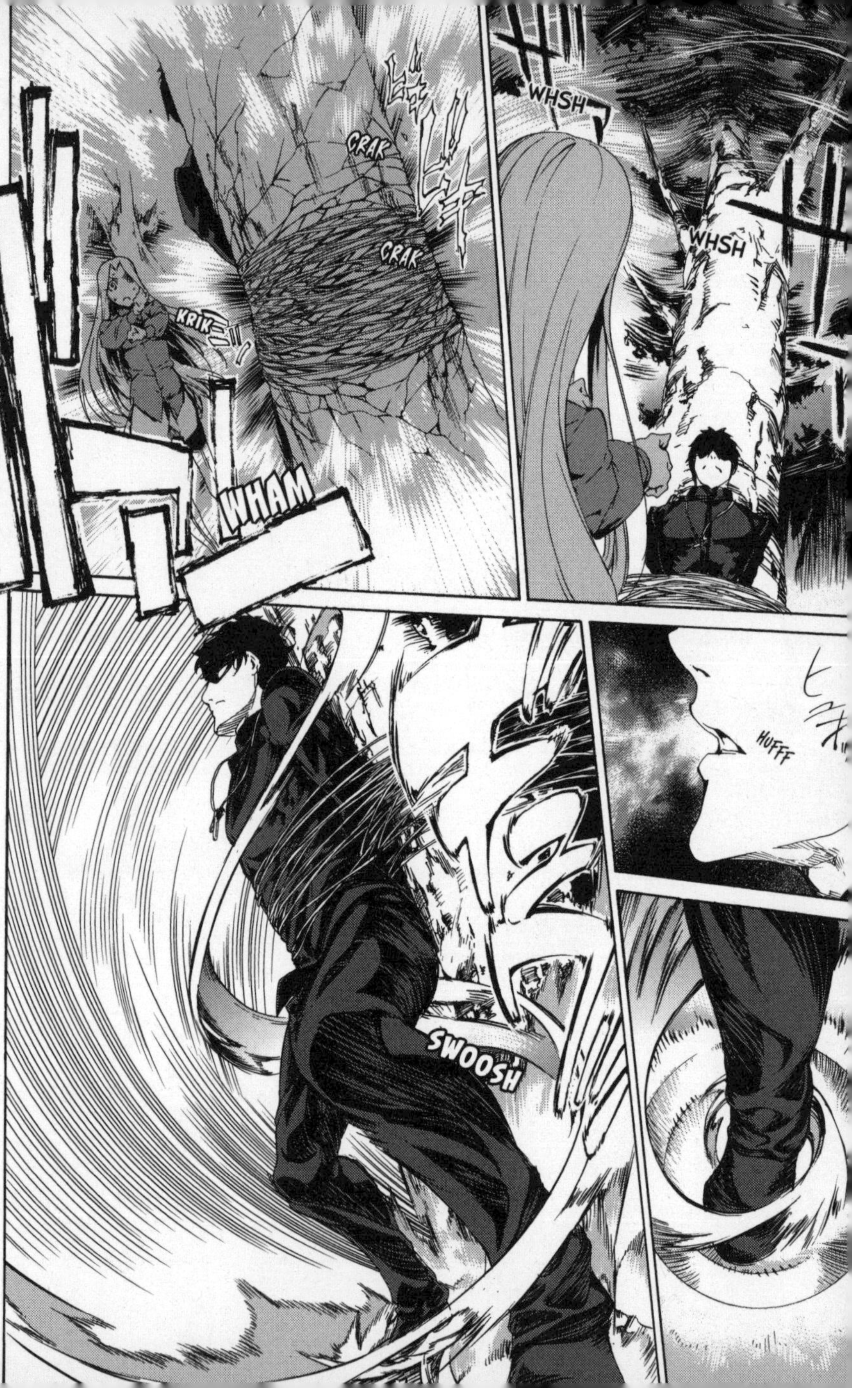
WHSH
WHSH
CRAK
CRAK
KRIK
WHAM
HUFFF
SWOOSH

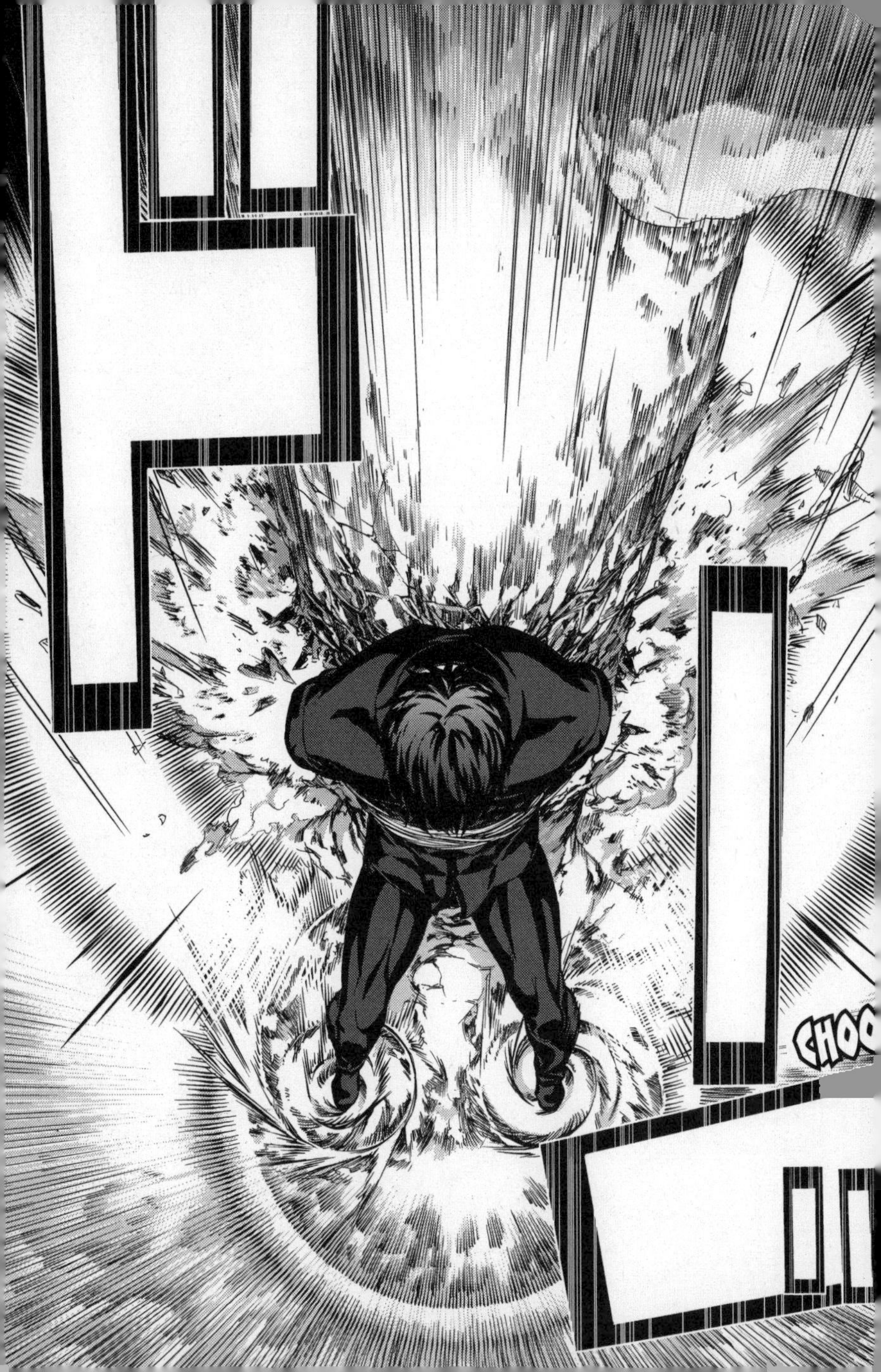
CHOO

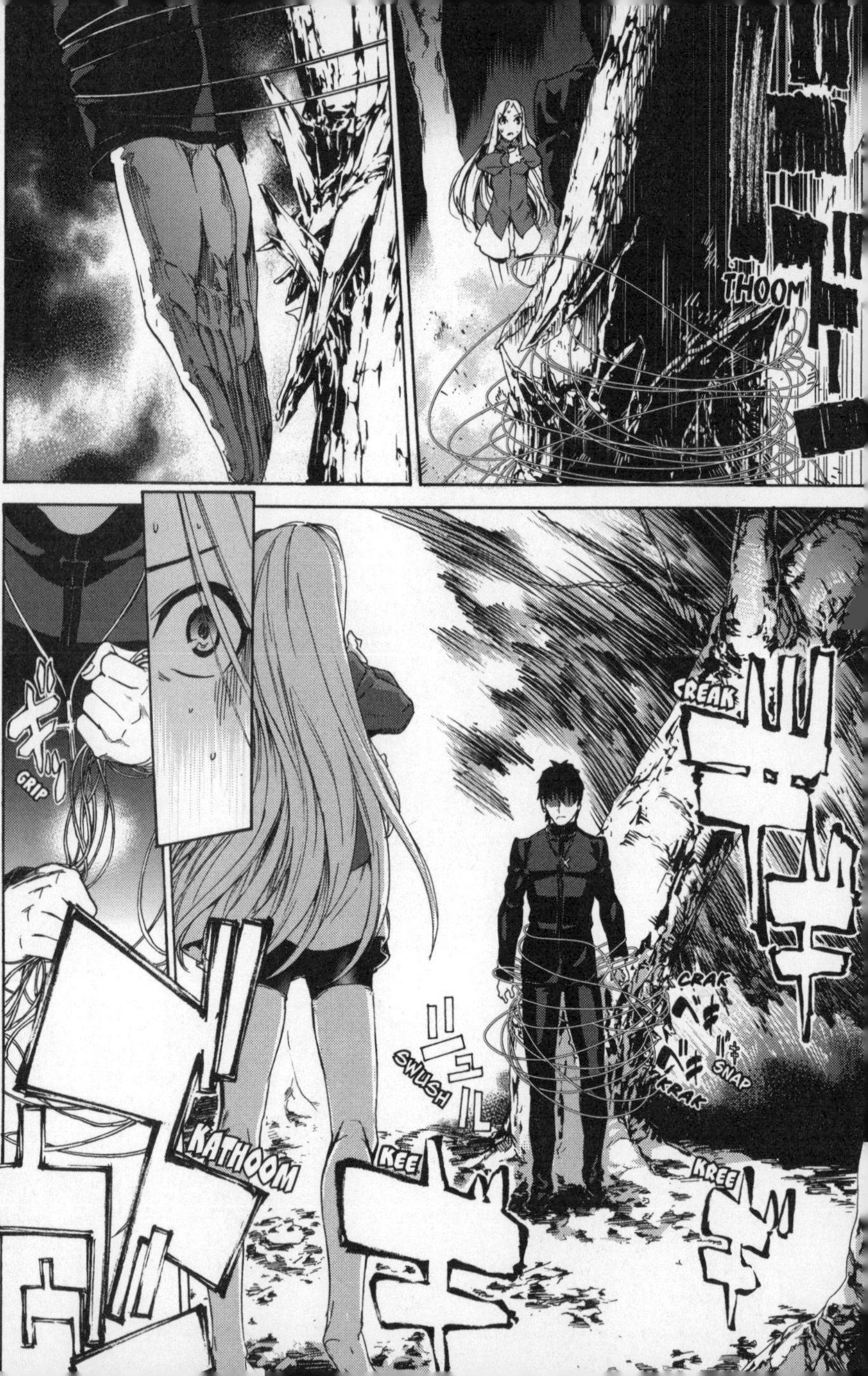
THOOM
CREAK
CRAK
SNAP
KRAK
KREE
SWUSH
KEE
KATHOOM
GRIP

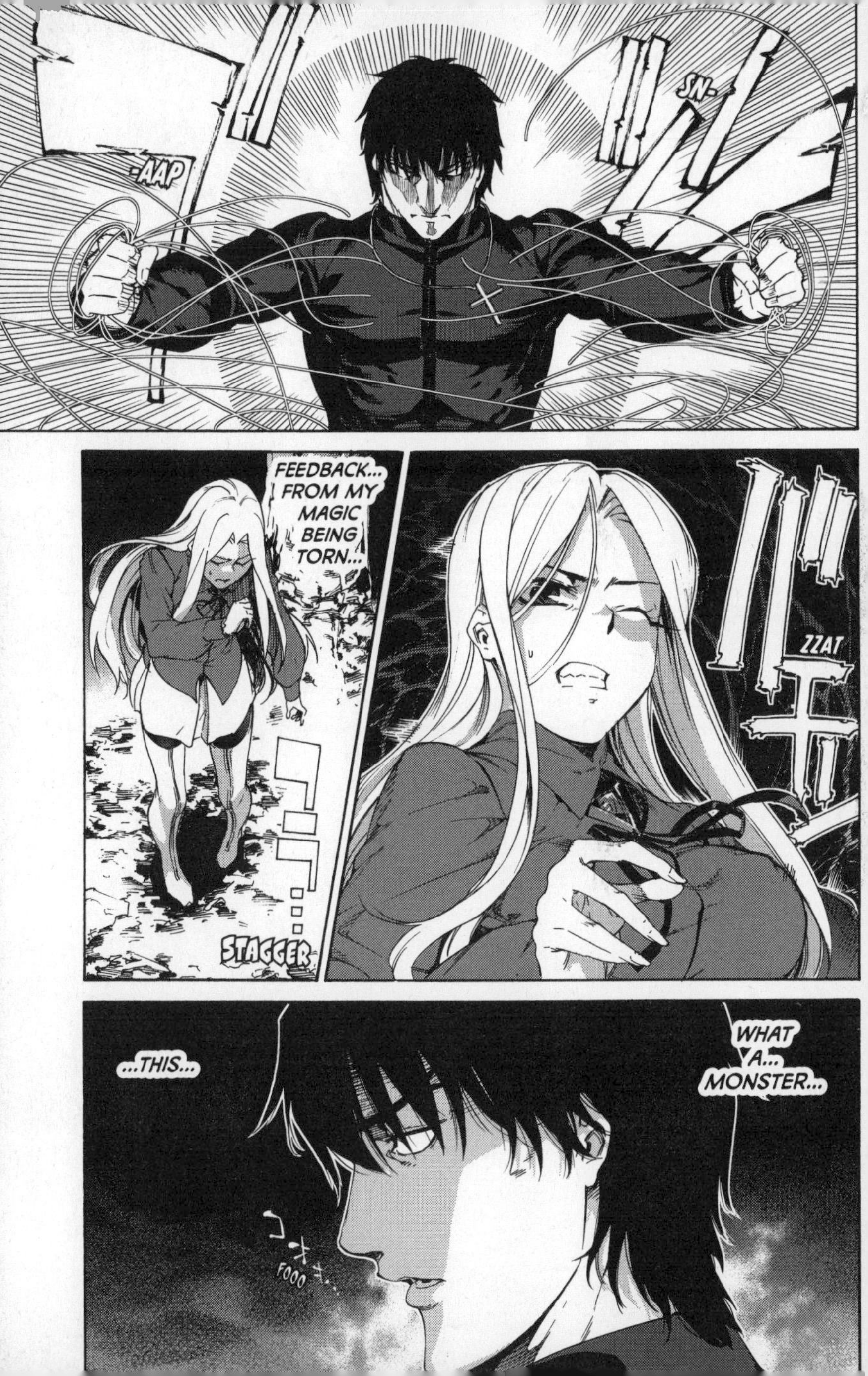
SN-
-AAP
ZZAT
FEEDBACK... FROM MY MAGIC BEING TORN...
STAGGER
WHAT A... MONSTER...
...THIS...
FOOO

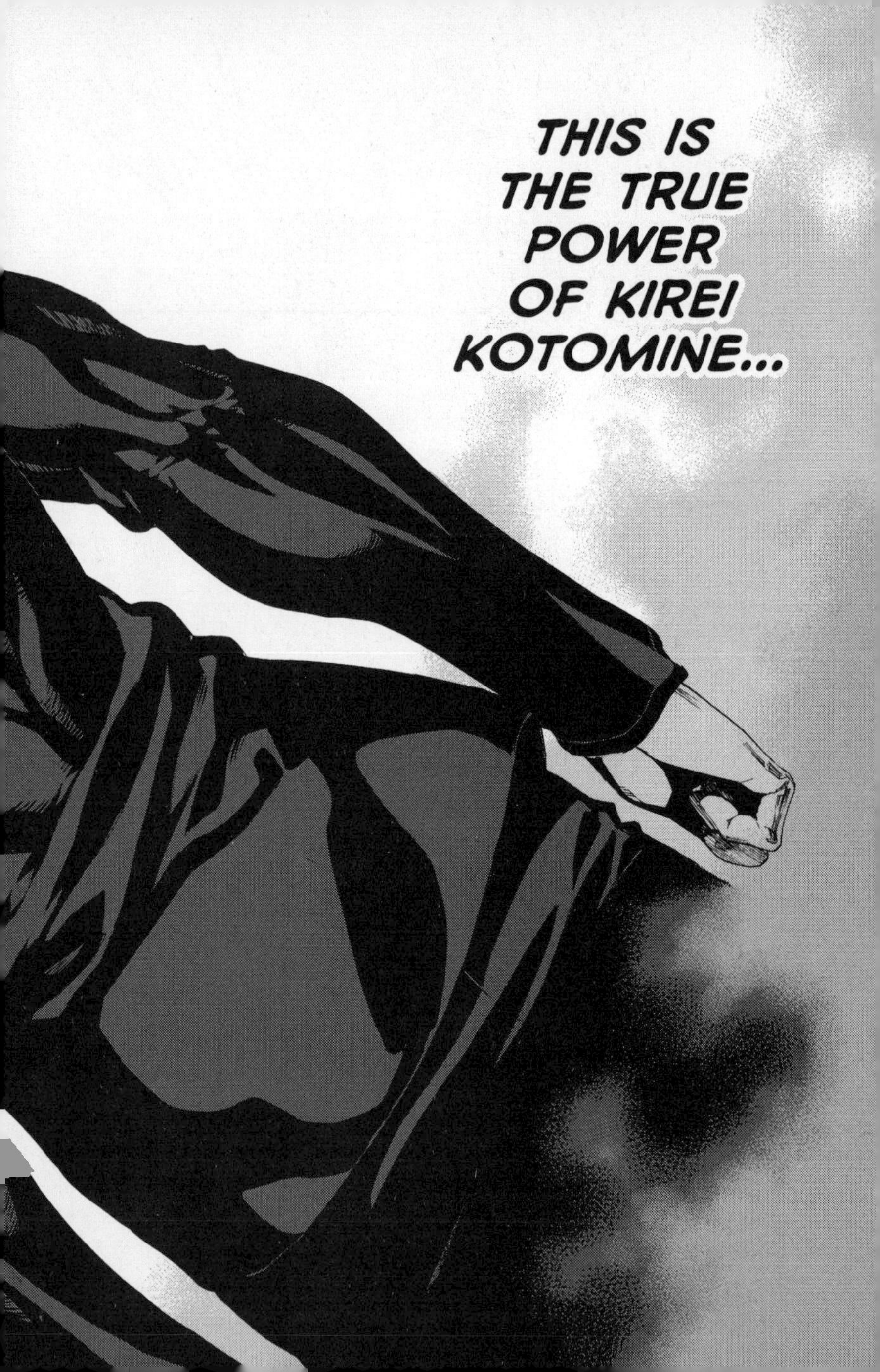
THIS IS THE TRUE POWER OF KIREI KOTOMINE...

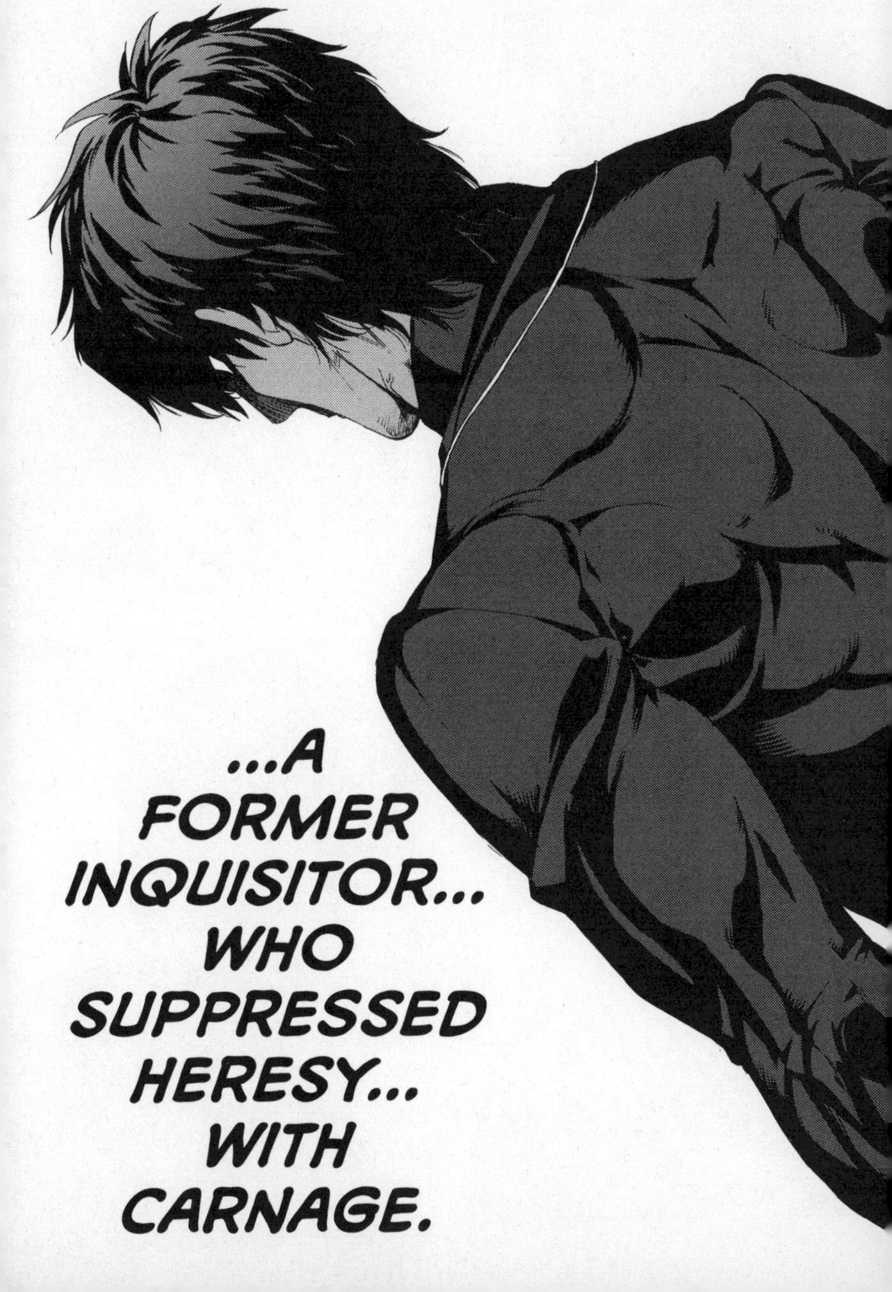
...A FORMER INQUISITOR... WHO SUPPRESSED HERESY... WITH CARNAGE.

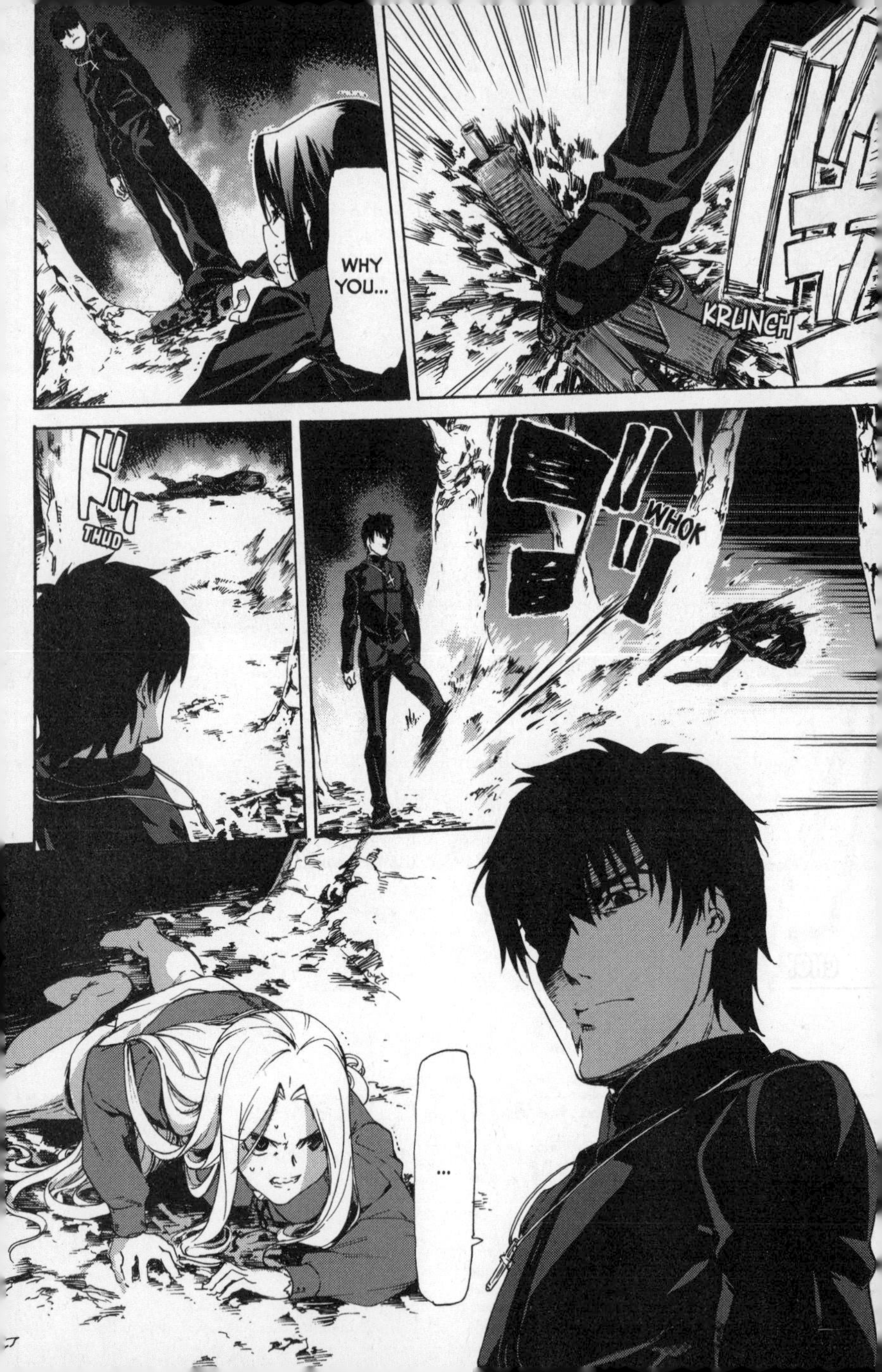
KRUNCH
WHY YOU...
WHOK
THUD
...

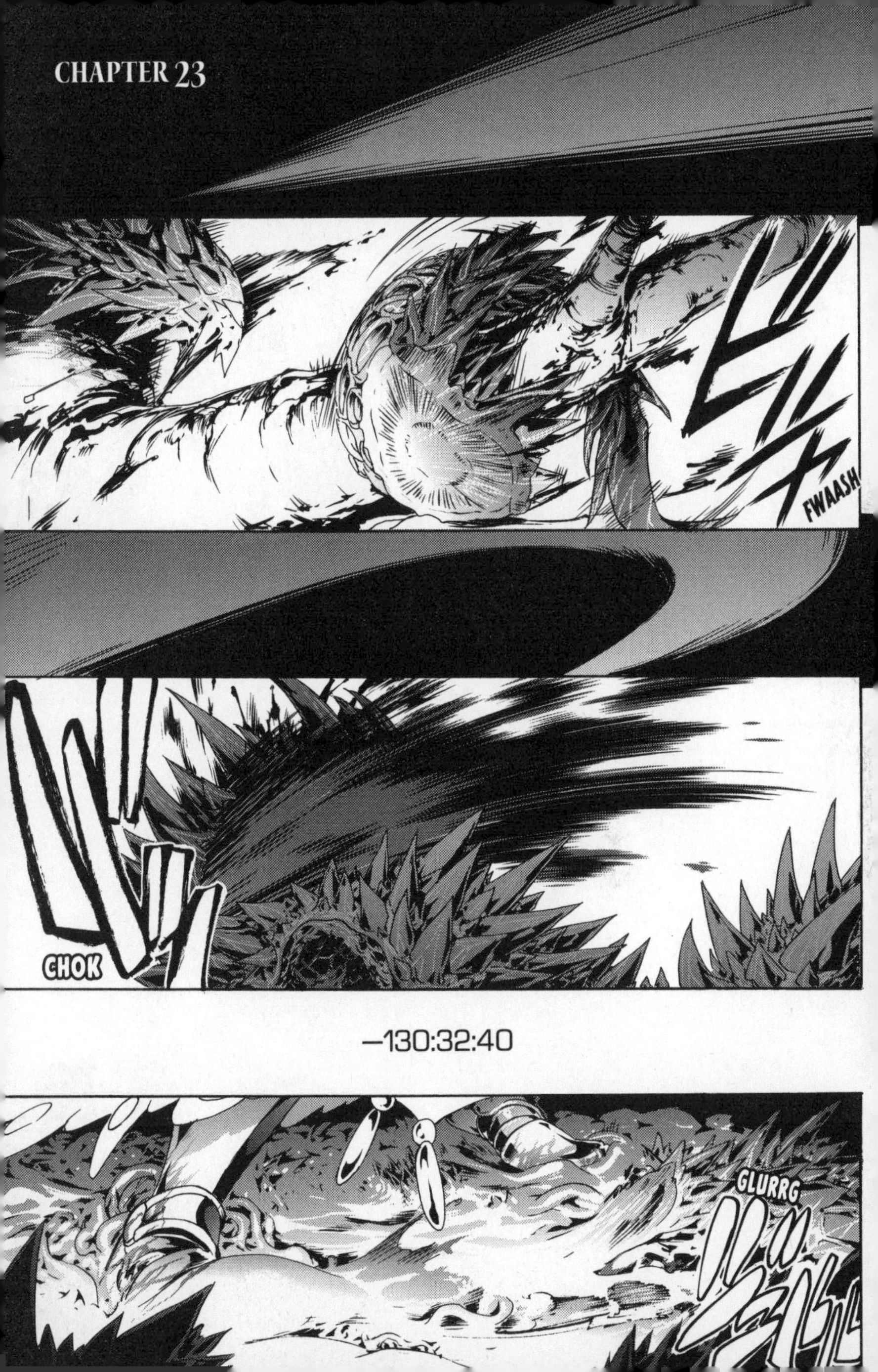
CHAPTER 23
FWAASH
CHOK
–130:32:40
GLURRG

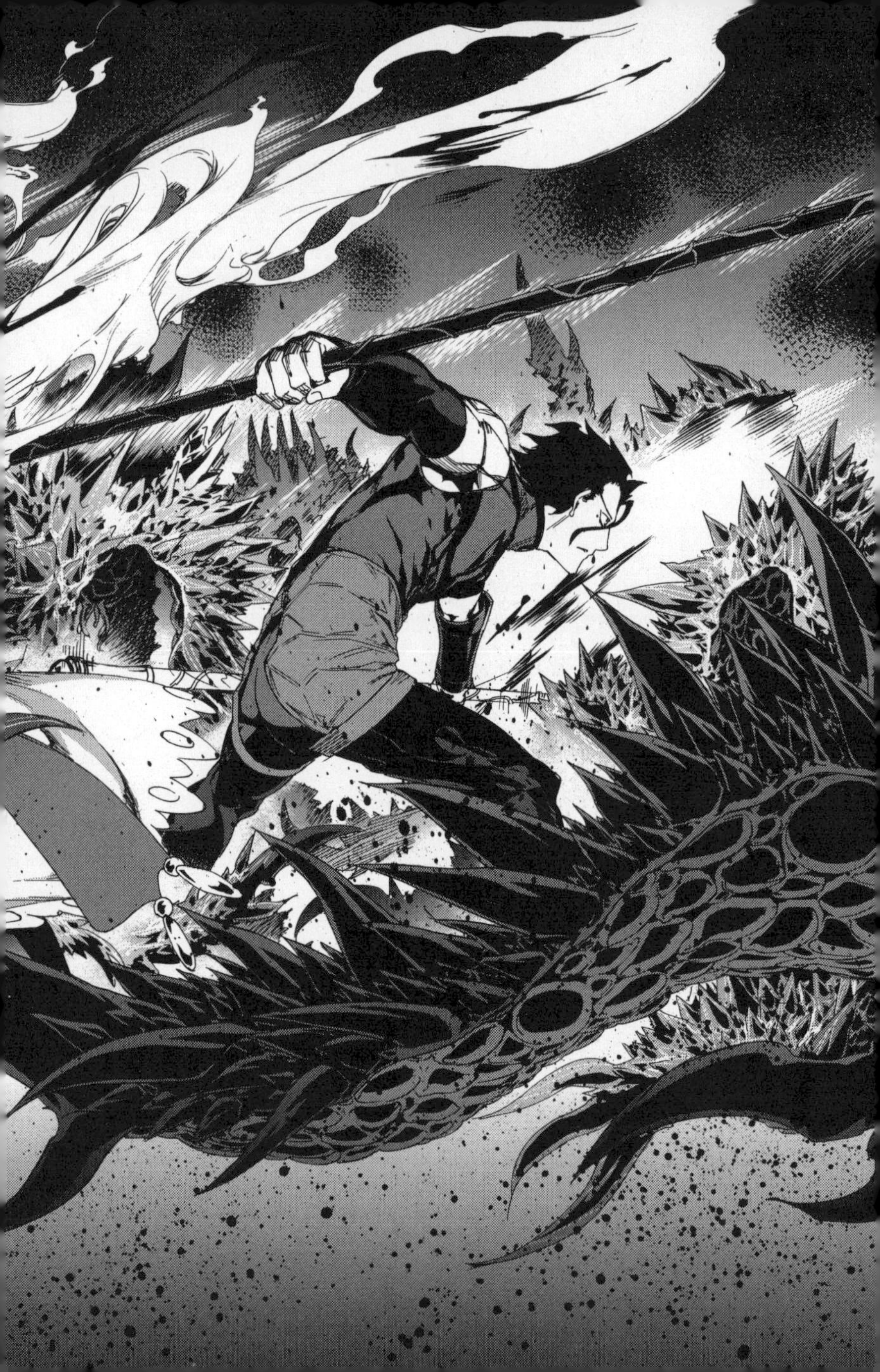

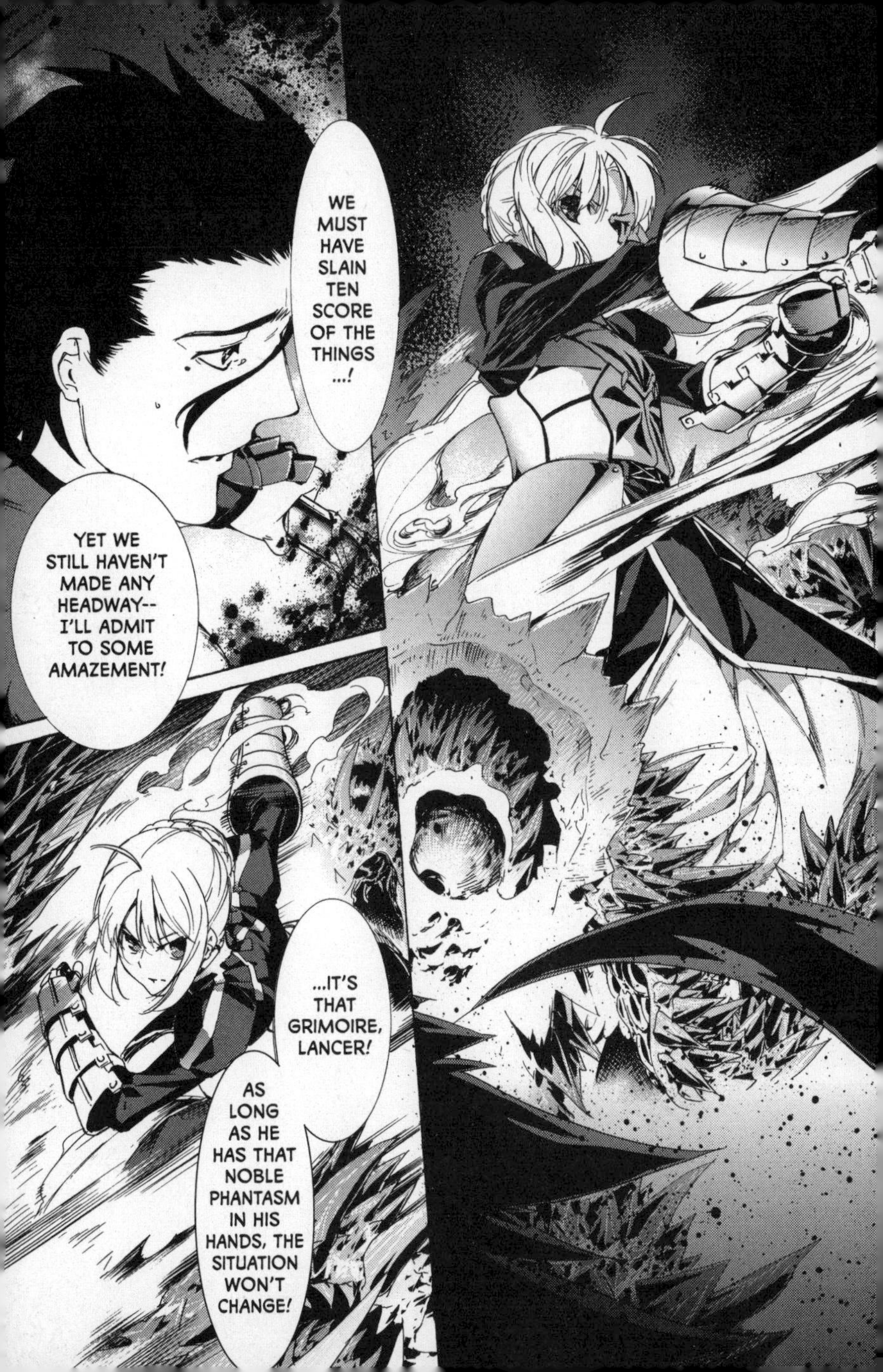
WE MUST HAVE SLAIN TEN SCORE OF THE THINGS ...!
YET WE STILL HAVEN'T MADE ANY HEADWAY-- I'LL ADMIT TO SOME AMAZEMENT!
...IT'S THAT GRIMOIRE, LANCER!
AS LONG AS HE HAS THAT NOBLE PHANTASM IN HIS HANDS, THE SITUATION WON'T CHANGE!

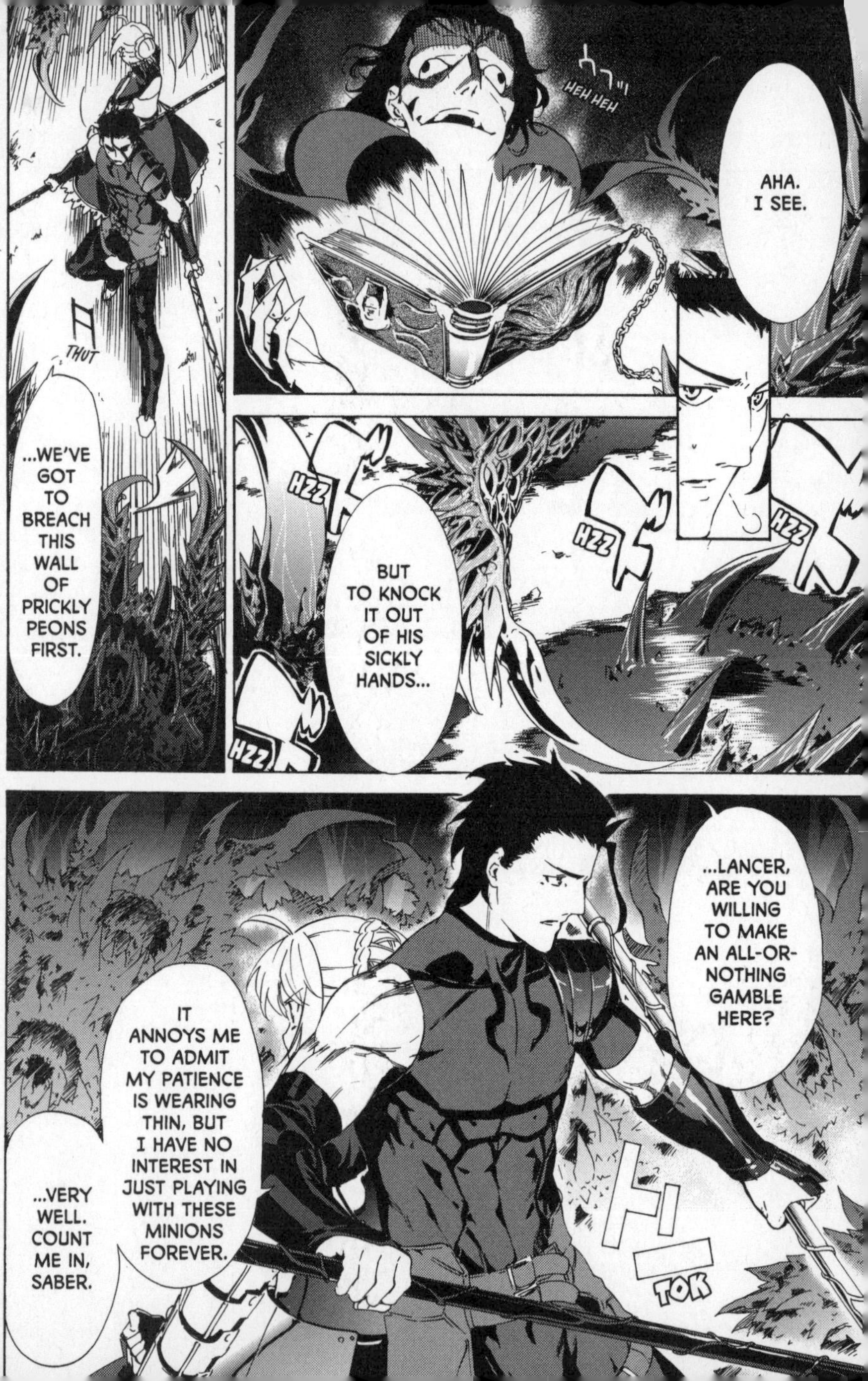

AHA. I SEE.
HEH HEH
HZZ
HZZ
BUT TO KNOCK IT OUT OF HIS SICKLY HANDS...
HZZ
THUT
...WE'VE GOT TO BREACH THIS WALL OF PRICKLY PEONS FIRST.
...LANCER, ARE YOU WILLING TO MAKE AN ALL-OR-NOTHING GAMBLE HERE?
TOK
IT ANNOYS ME TO ADMIT MY PATIENCE IS WEARING THIN, BUT I HAVE NO INTEREST IN JUST PLAYING WITH THESE MINIONS FOREVER.
...VERY WELL. COUNT ME IN, SABER.

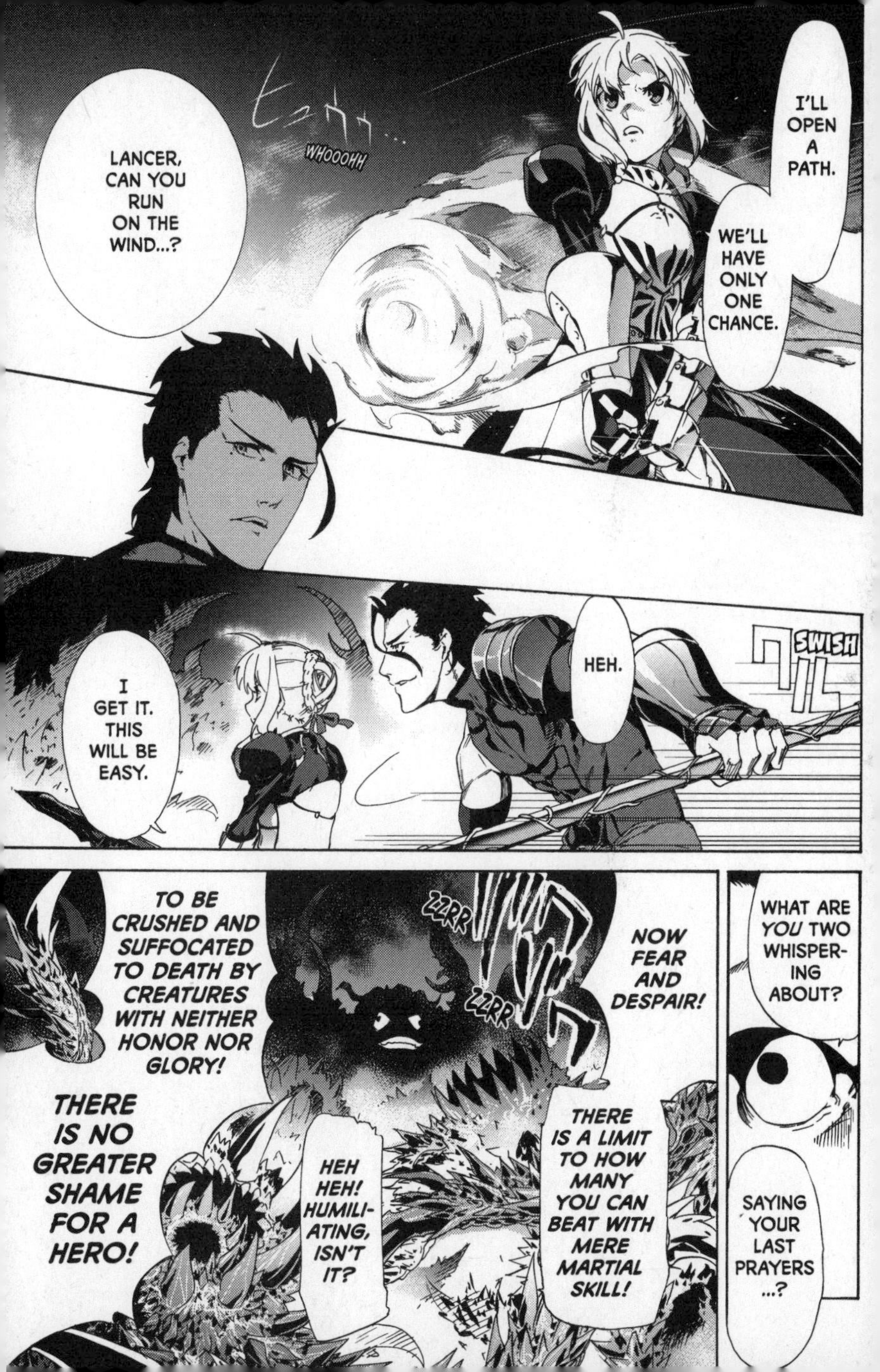
I'LL OPEN A PATH.
WE'LL HAVE ONLY ONE CHANCE.
WHOOOHH
LANCER, CAN YOU RUN ON THE WIND...?
SWISH
HEH.
I GET IT. THIS WILL BE EASY.
WHAT ARE *YOU* TWO WHISPER-ING ABOUT?
SAYING YOUR LAST PRAYERS ...?
ZZRR
ZZRR
NOW FEAR AND DESPAIR!
TO BE CRUSHED AND SUFFOCATED TO DEATH BY CREATURES WITH NEITHER HONOR NOR GLORY!
THERE IS A LIMIT TO HOW MANY YOU CAN BEAT WITH MERE MARTIAL SKILL!
HEH HEH! HUMILI-ATING, ISN'T IT?
THERE IS NO GREATER SHAME FOR A HERO!

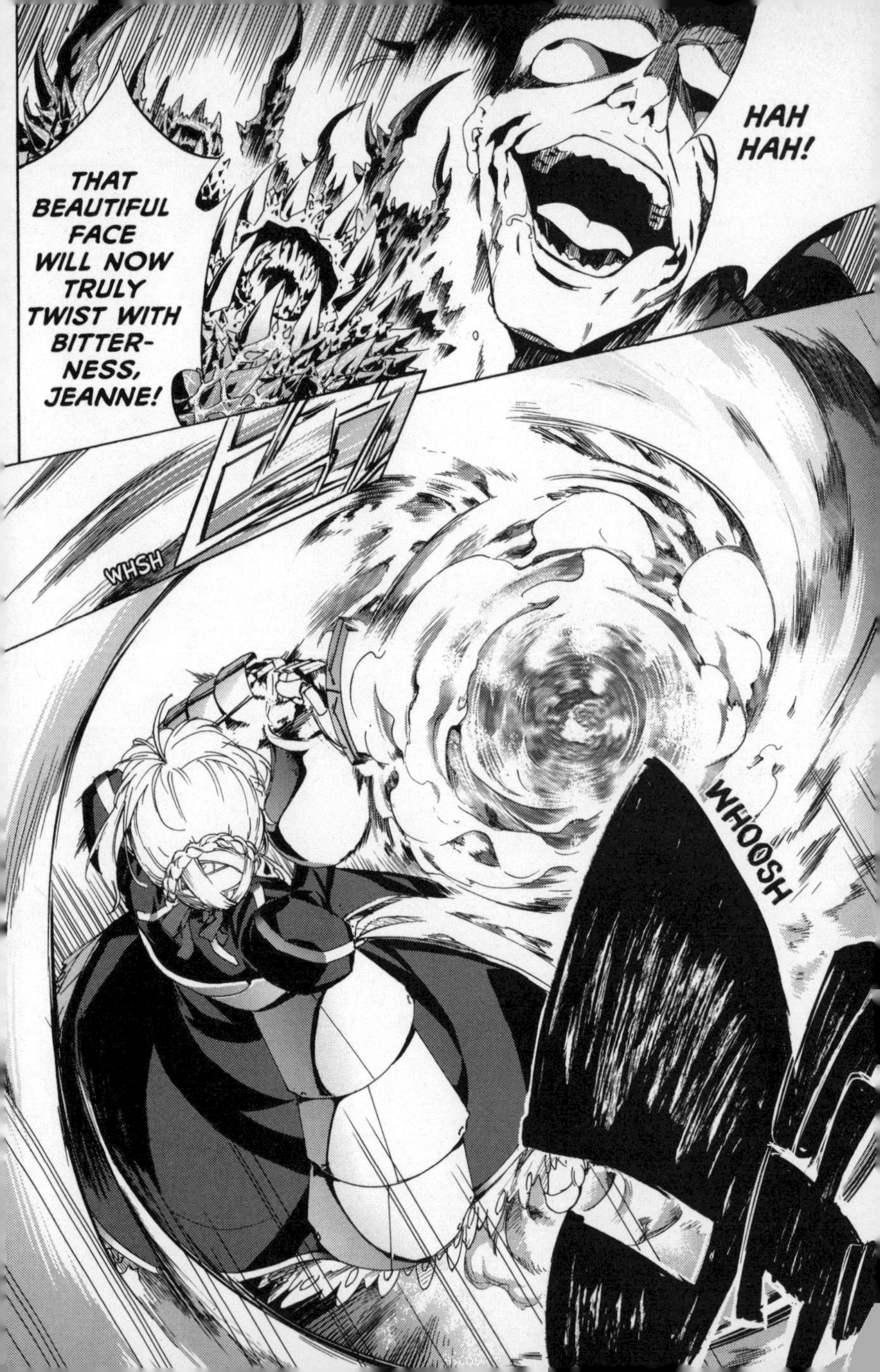
HAH HAH!
THAT BEAUTIFUL FACE WILL NOW TRULY TWIST WITH BITTER-NESS, JEANNE!
WHSH
WHOOSH

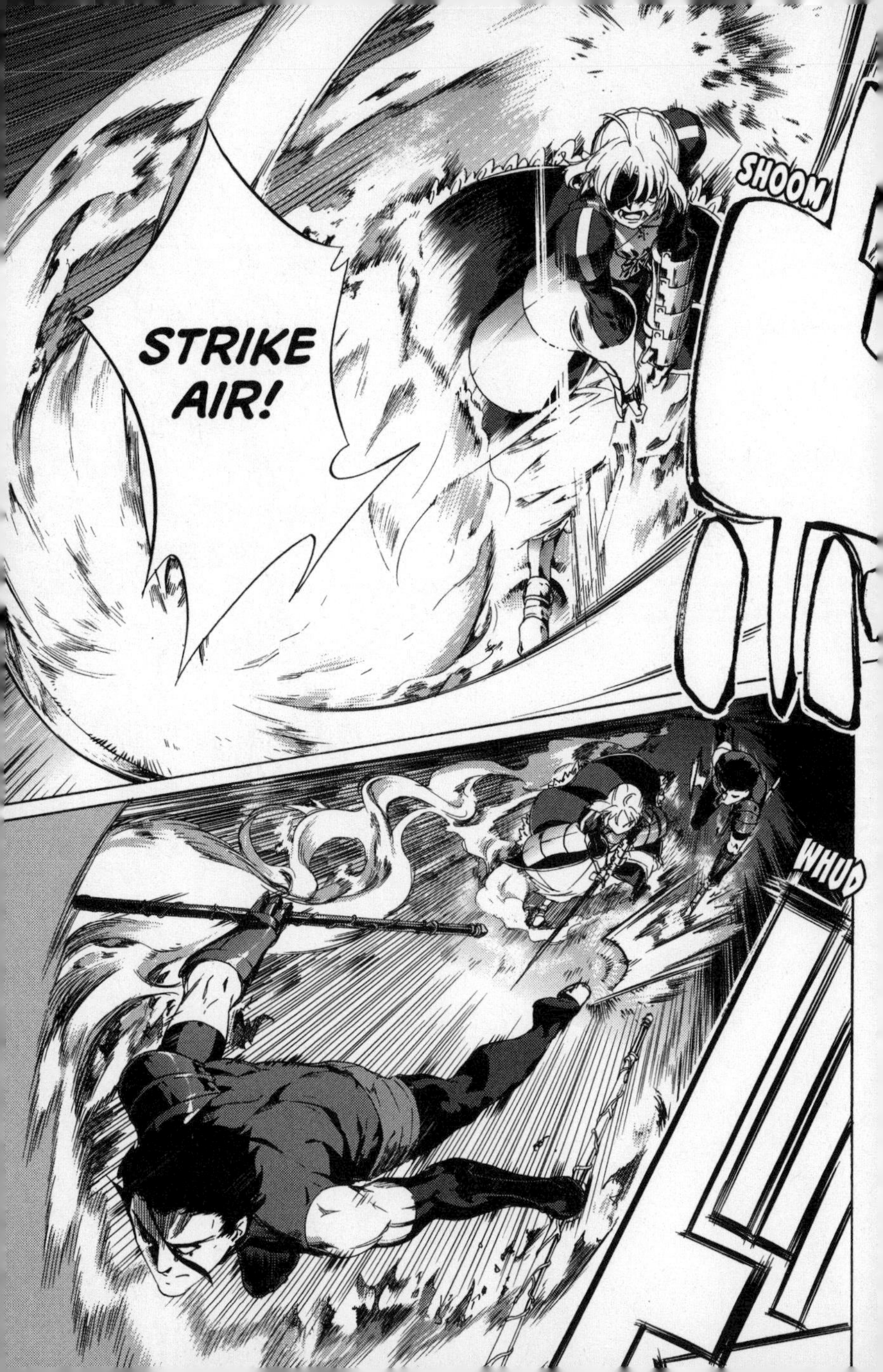
SHOOM
STRIKE AIR!
WHUD

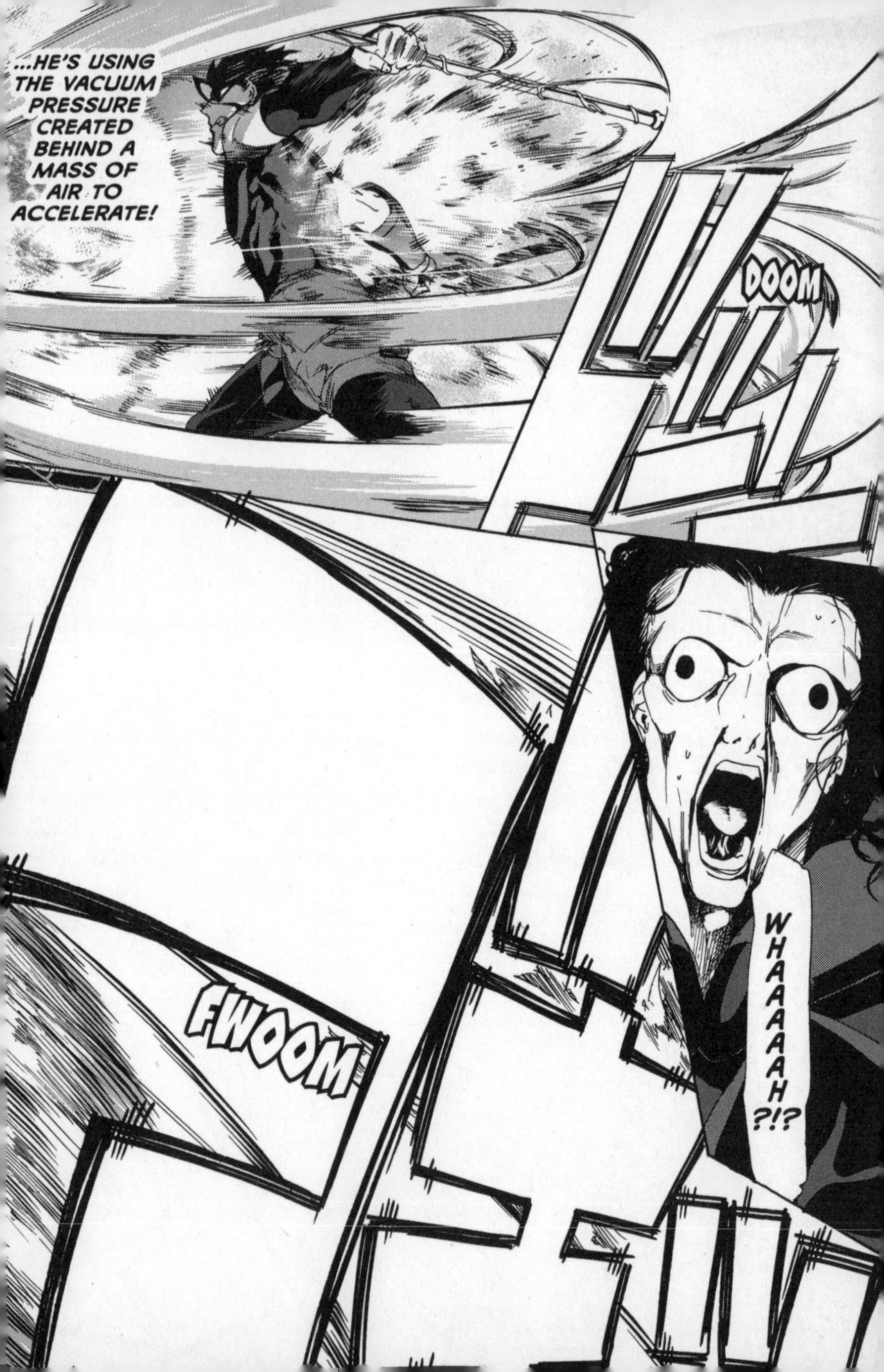
...HE'S USING THE VACUUM PRESSURE CREATED BEHIND A MASS OF AIR TO ACCELERATE!
DOOM
WHAAAAAAH?!?
FWOOM

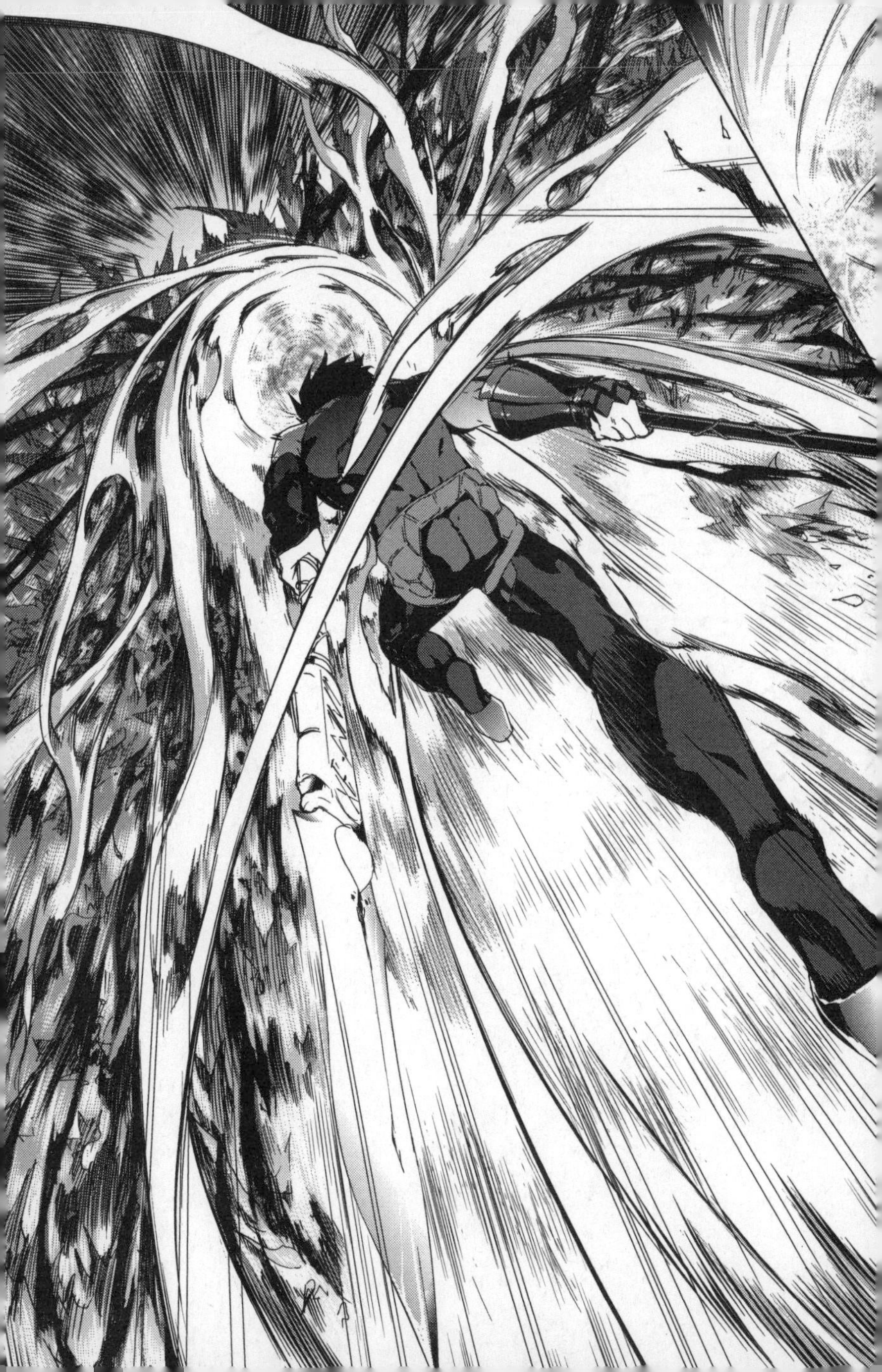

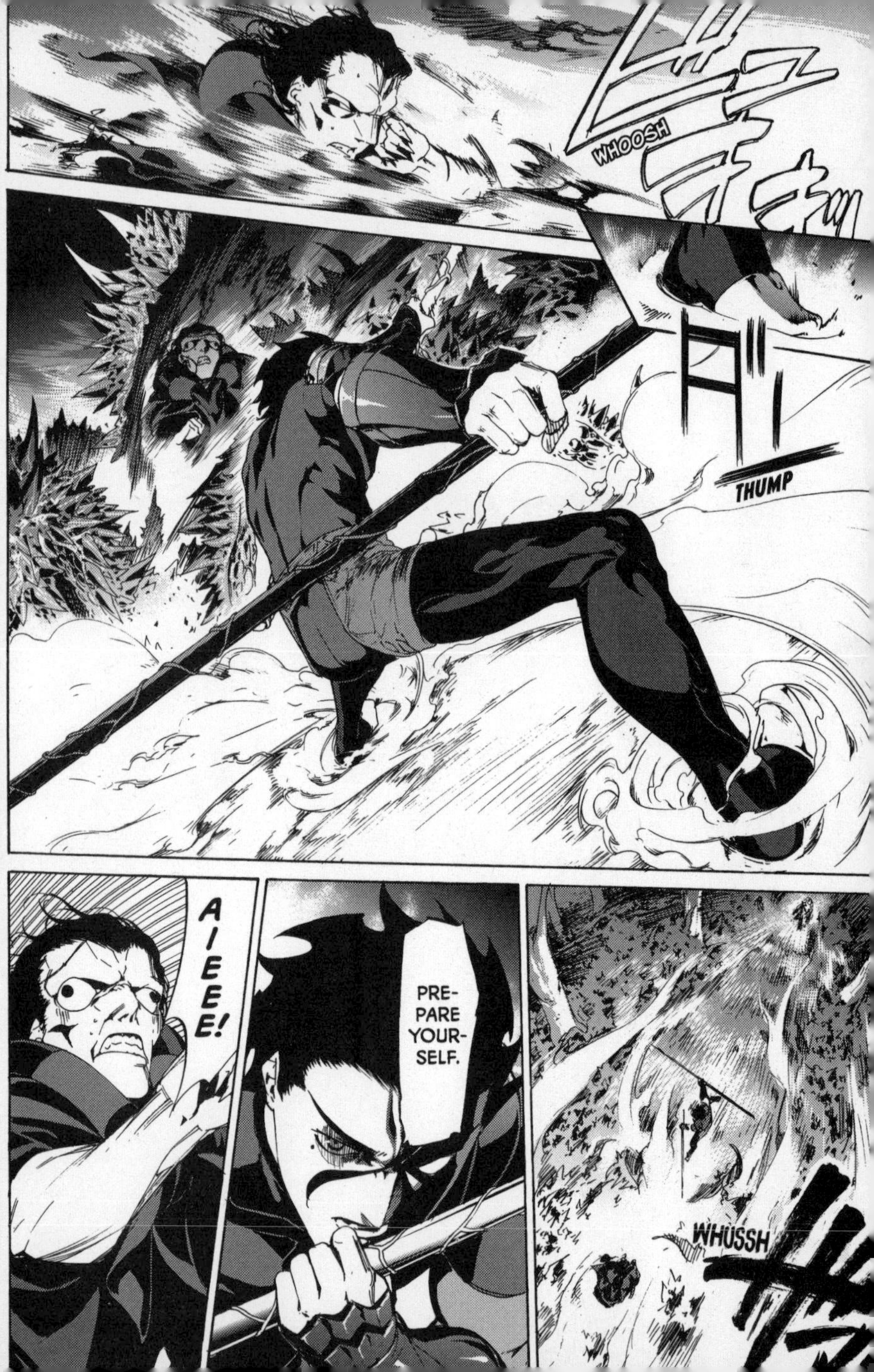

WHOOSH
THUMP
AIEEEE!
PRE-
PARE
YOUR-
SELF.
WHUSSH

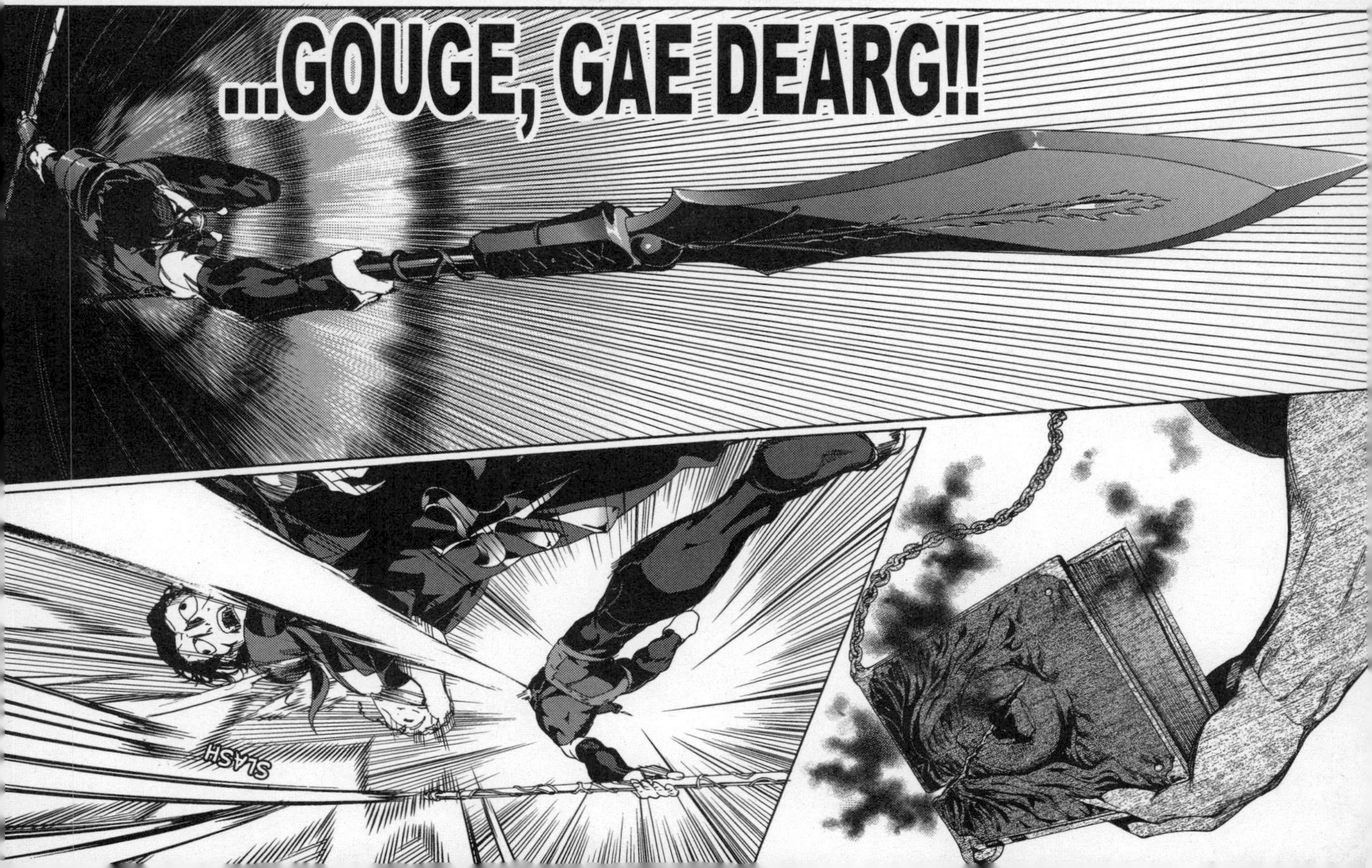
...GOUGE, GAE DEARG!!
SLASH

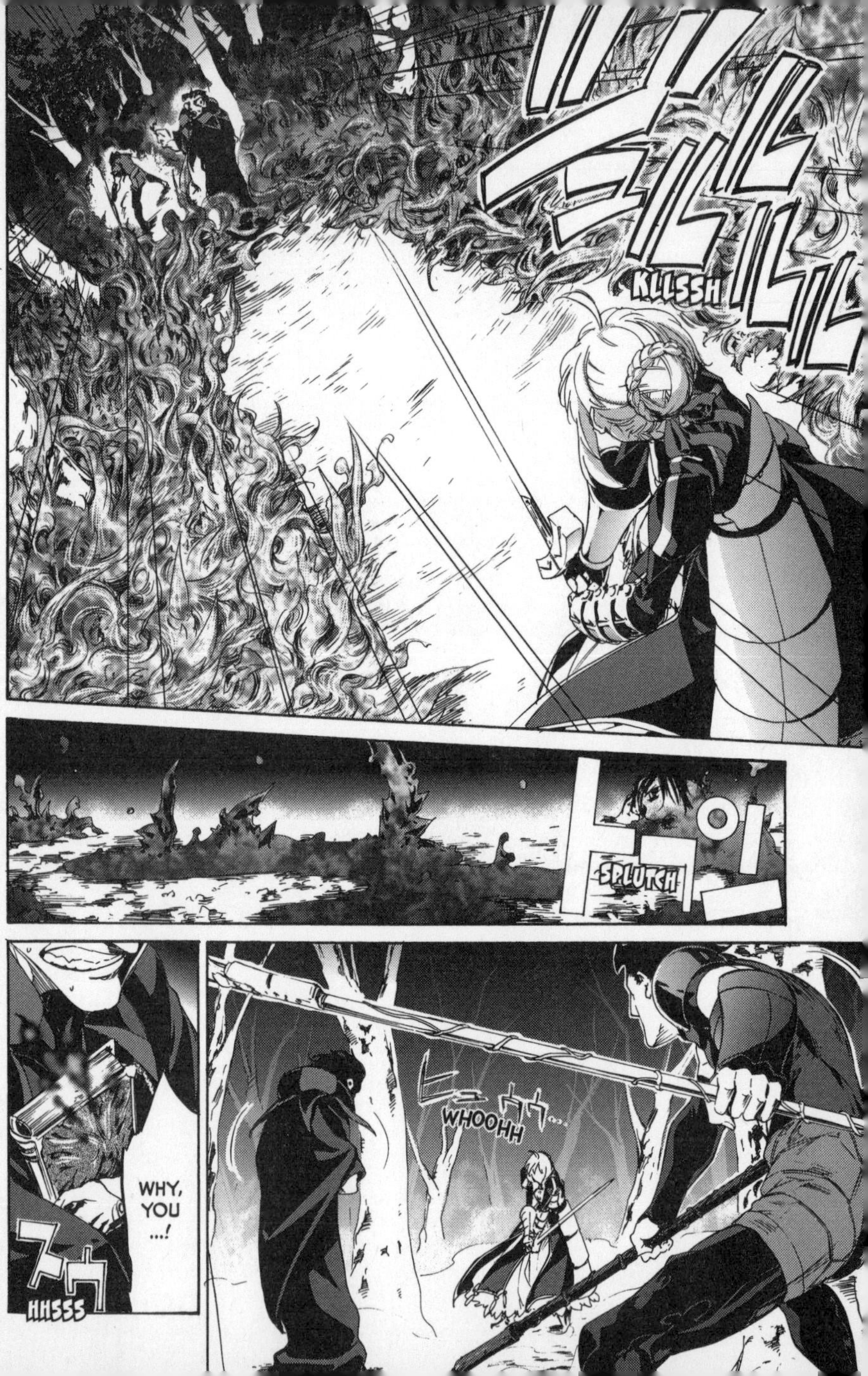
KLLSSH
SPLUTCH
WHOOHH
WHY, YOU ...!
HHSSS

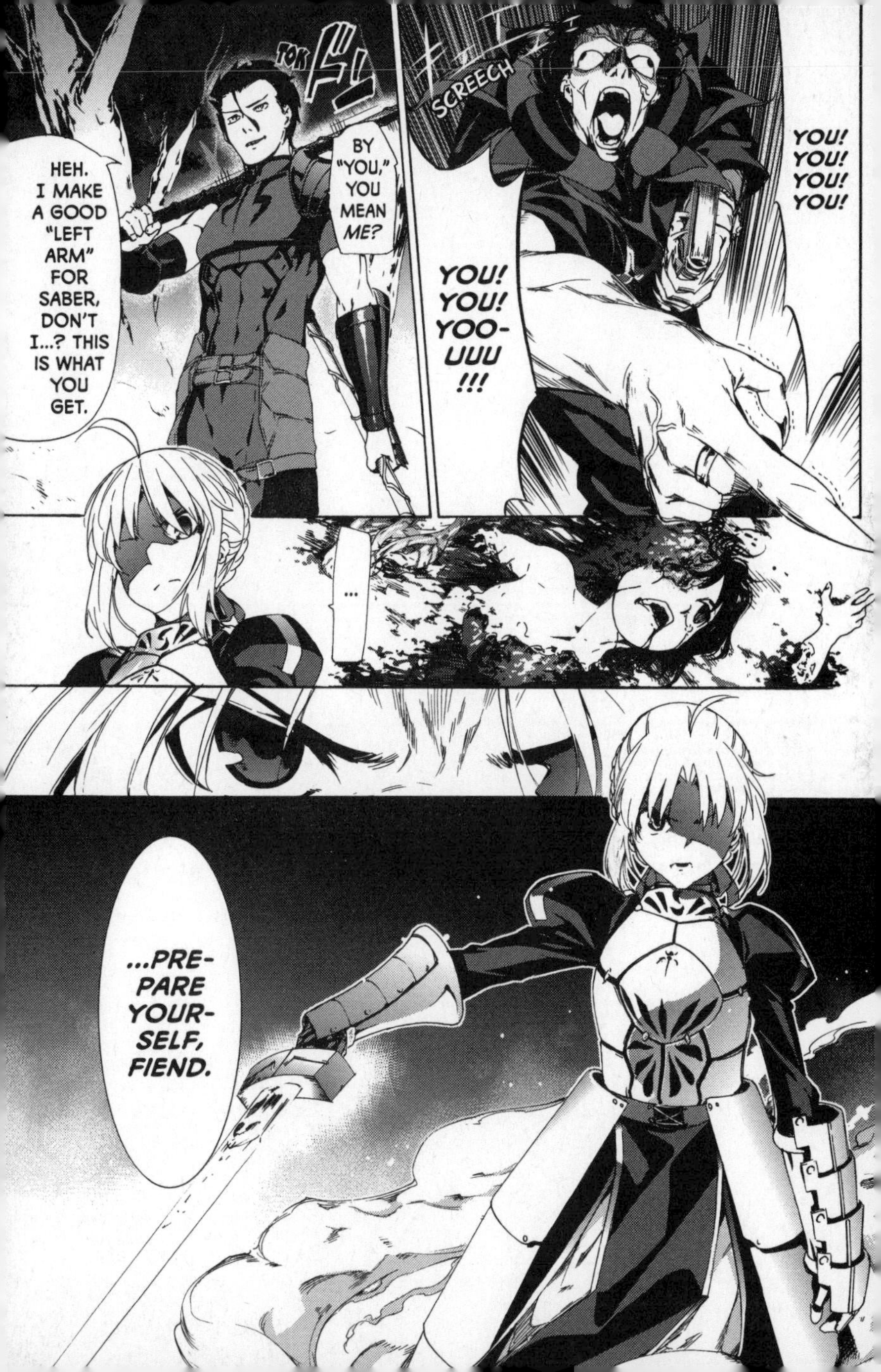
SCREECH
YOU! YOU! YOU! YOU!
YOU! YOU! YOO-UUU!!!
TOK
BY "YOU," YOU MEAN *ME?*
HEH. I MAKE A GOOD "LEFT ARM" FOR SABER, DON'T I...? THIS IS WHAT YOU GET.
...
...PRE-PARE YOUR-SELF, FIEND.

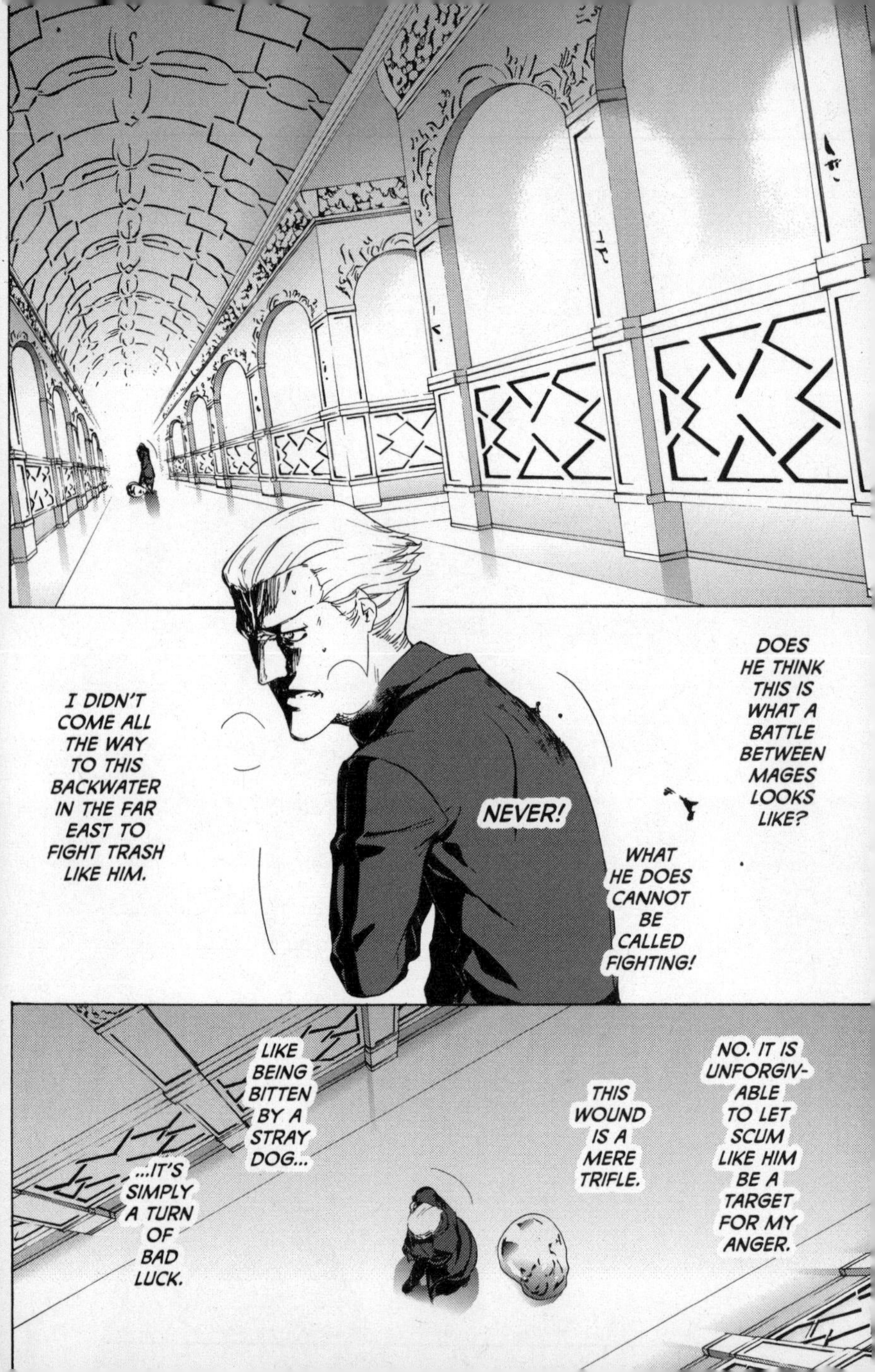
DOES HE THINK THIS IS WHAT A BATTLE BETWEEN MAGES LOOKS LIKE?
WHAT HE DOES CANNOT BE CALLED FIGHTING!
NEVER!
I DIDN'T COME ALL THE WAY TO THIS BACKWATER IN THE FAR EAST TO FIGHT TRASH LIKE HIM.
NO. IT IS UNFORGIV-ABLE TO LET SCUM LIKE HIM BE A TARGET FOR MY ANGER.
THIS WOUND IS A MERE TRIFLE.
LIKE BEING BITTEN BY A STRAY DOG...
...IT'S SIMPLY A TURN OF BAD LUCK.

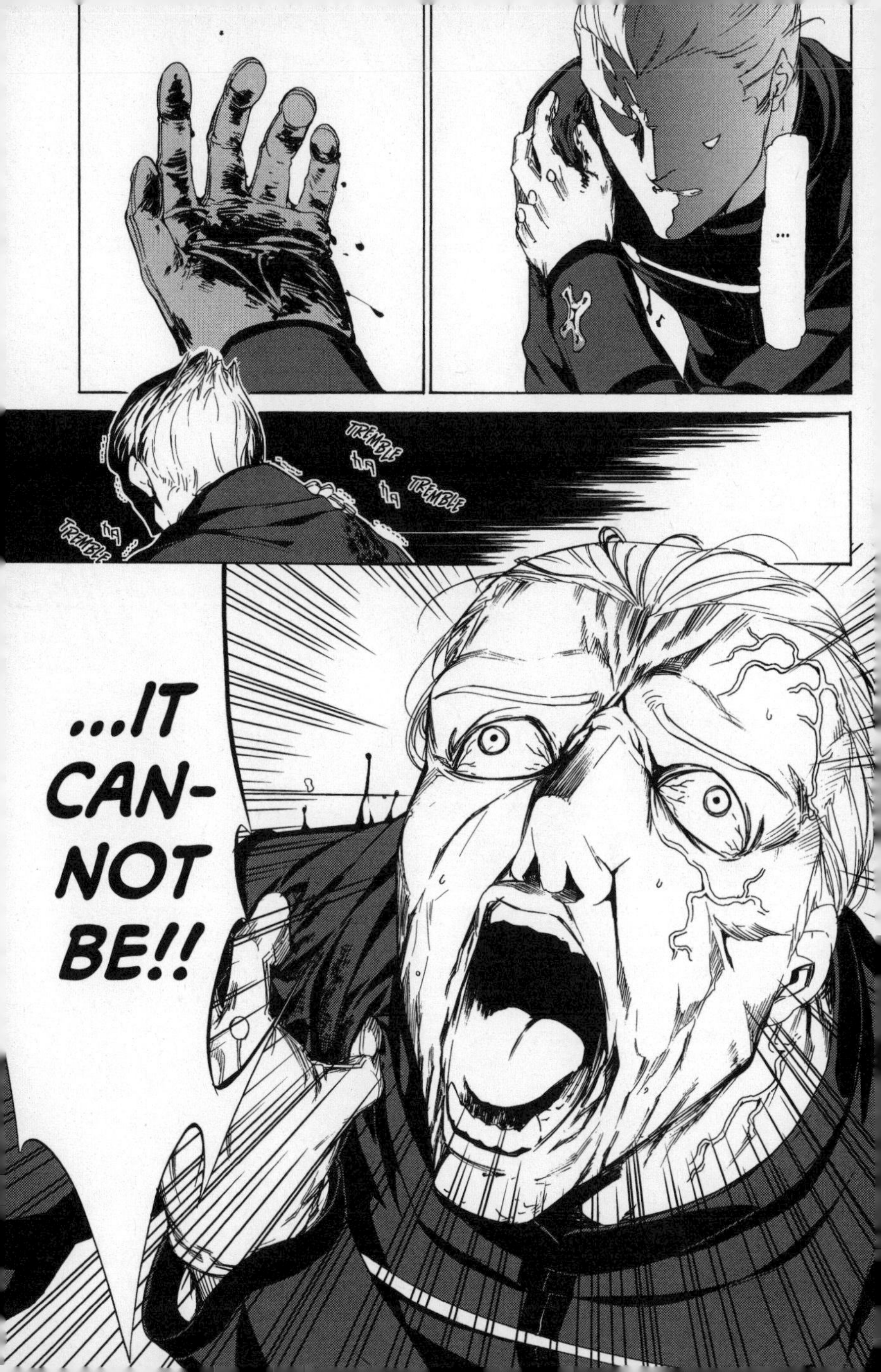
...
TREMBLE
TREMBLE
TREMBLE
...IT CAN-NOT BE!!

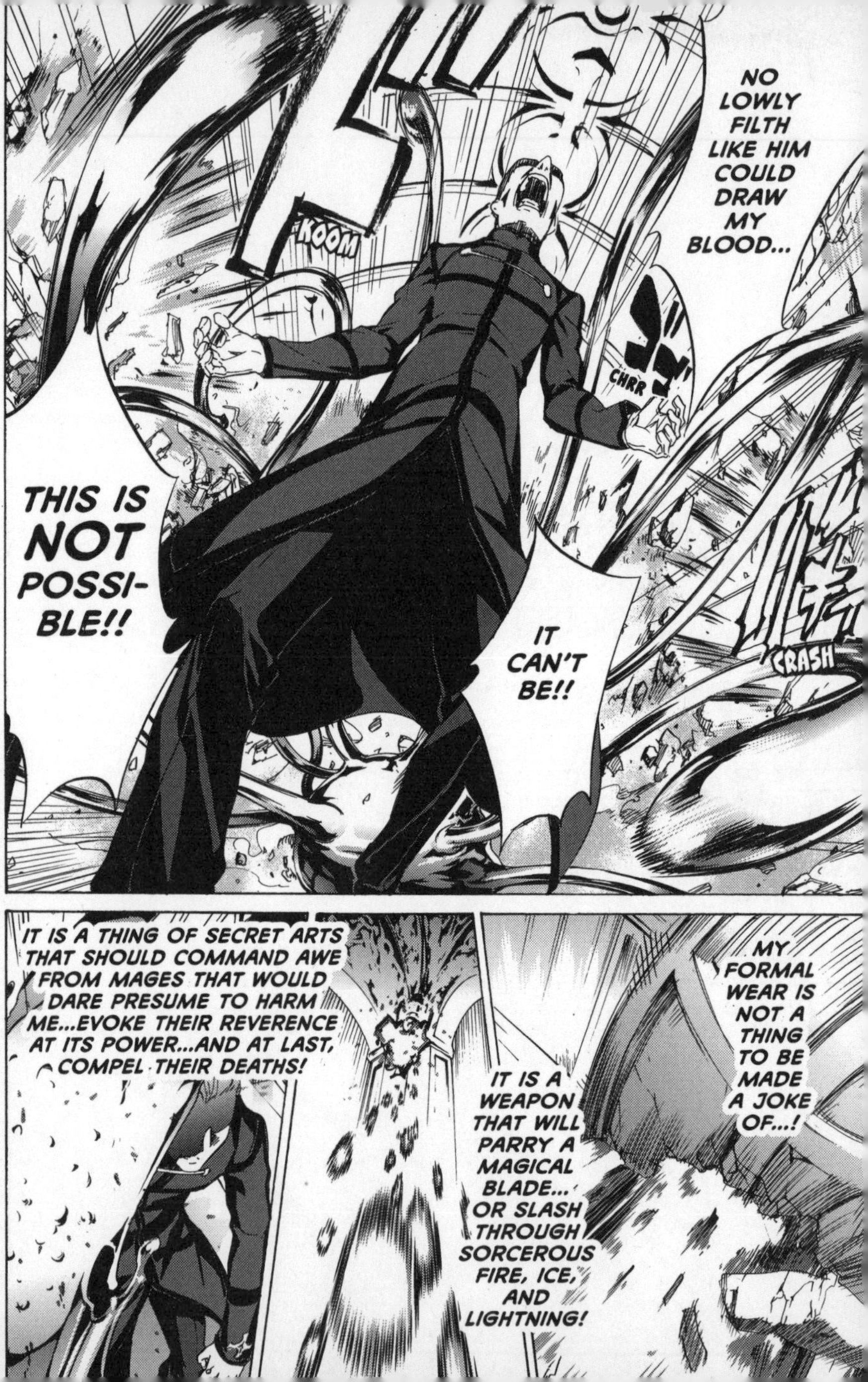
NO LOWLY FILTH LIKE HIM COULD DRAW MY BLOOD...
KOOM
CHRR
IT CAN'T BE!!
THIS IS NOT POSSI-BLE!!
CRASH
MY FORMAL WEAR IS NOT A THING TO BE MADE A JOKE OF...!
IT IS A WEAPON THAT WILL PARRY A MAGICAL BLADE... OR SLASH THROUGH SORCEROUS FIRE, ICE, AND LIGHTNING!
IT IS A THING OF SECRET ARTS THAT SHOULD COMMAND AWE FROM MAGES THAT WOULD DARE PRESUME TO HARM ME...EVOKE THEIR REVERENCE AT ITS POWER...AND AT LAST, COMPEL THEIR DEATHS!

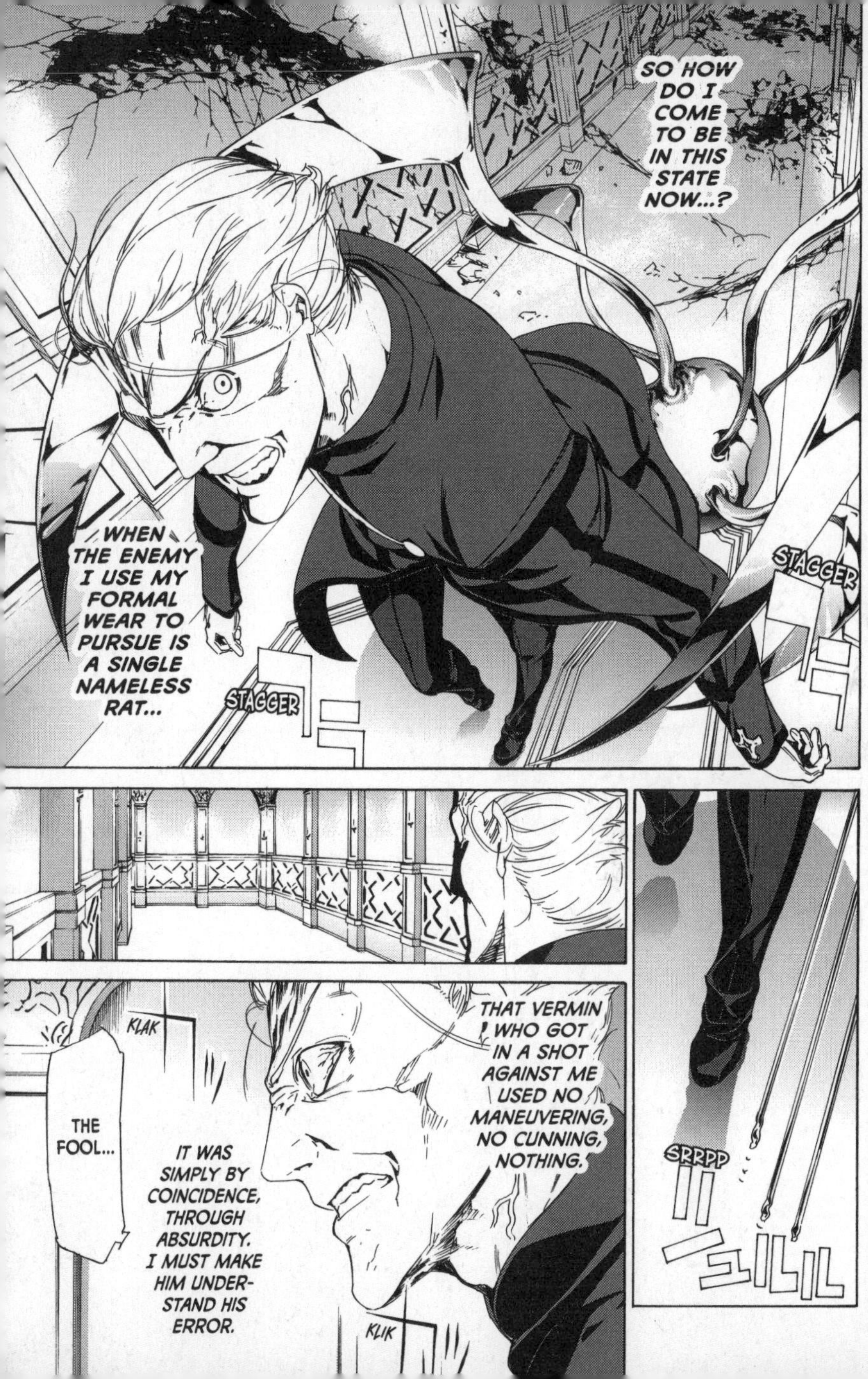
SO HOW DO I COME TO BE IN THIS STATE NOW...?
STAGGER
WHEN THE ENEMY I USE MY FORMAL WEAR TO PURSUE IS A SINGLE NAMELESS RAT...
STAGGER
SRRPP
THAT VERMIN WHO GOT IN A SHOT AGAINST ME USED NO MANEUVERING, NO CUNNING, NOTHING.
KLAK
THE FOOL...
IT WAS SIMPLY BY COINCIDENCE, THROUGH ABSURDITY. I MUST MAKE HIM UNDER-STAND HIS ERROR.
KLIK

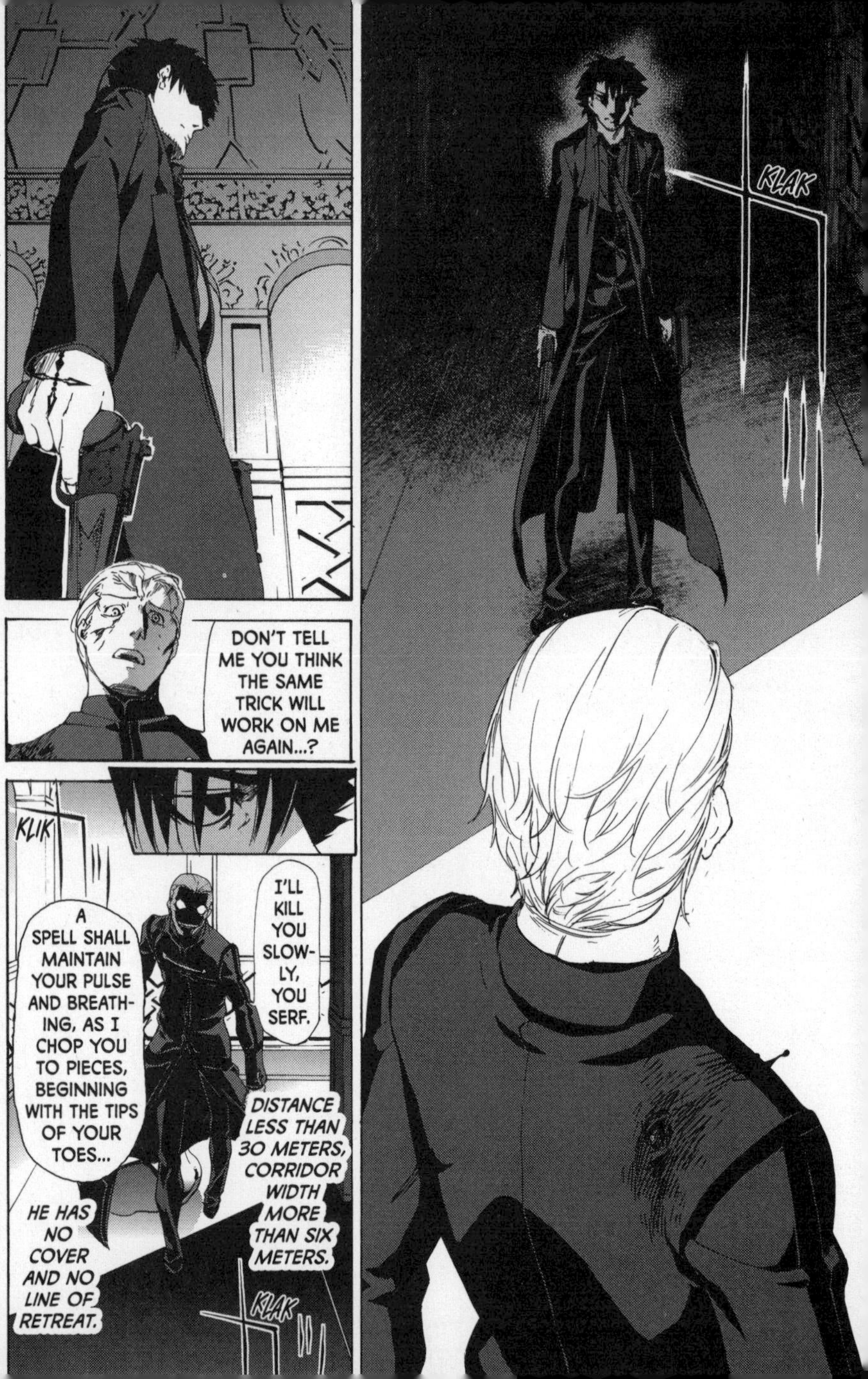
KLAK
DON'T TELL ME YOU THINK THE SAME TRICK WILL WORK ON ME AGAIN...?
KLIK
I'LL KILL YOU SLOW-LY, YOU SERF.
A SPELL SHALL MAINTAIN YOUR PULSE AND BREATH-ING, AS I CHOP YOU TO PIECES, BEGINNING WITH THE TIPS OF YOUR TOES...
DISTANCE LESS THAN 30 METERS, CORRIDOR WIDTH MORE THAN SIX METERS.
HE HAS NO COVER AND NO LINE OF RETREAT.
KLAK

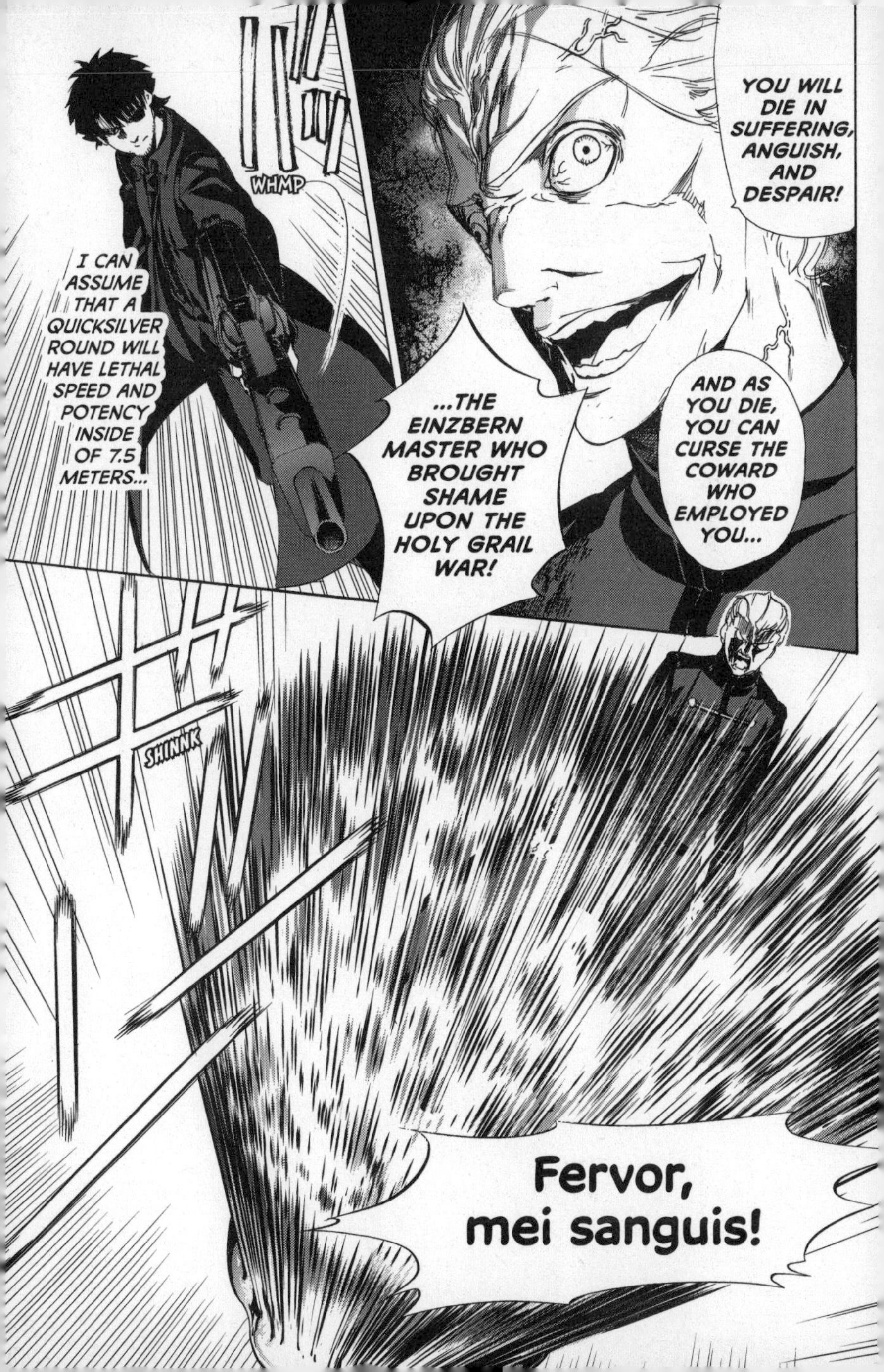
YOU WILL DIE IN SUFFERING, ANGUISH, AND DESPAIR!
AND AS YOU DIE, YOU CAN CURSE THE COWARD WHO EMPLOYED YOU...
...THE EINZBERN MASTER WHO BROUGHT SHAME UPON THE HOLY GRAIL WAR!
WHMP
I CAN ASSUME THAT A QUICKSILVER ROUND WILL HAVE LETHAL SPEED AND POTENCY INSIDE OF 7.5 METERS...
SHINNK
Fervor, mei sanguis!

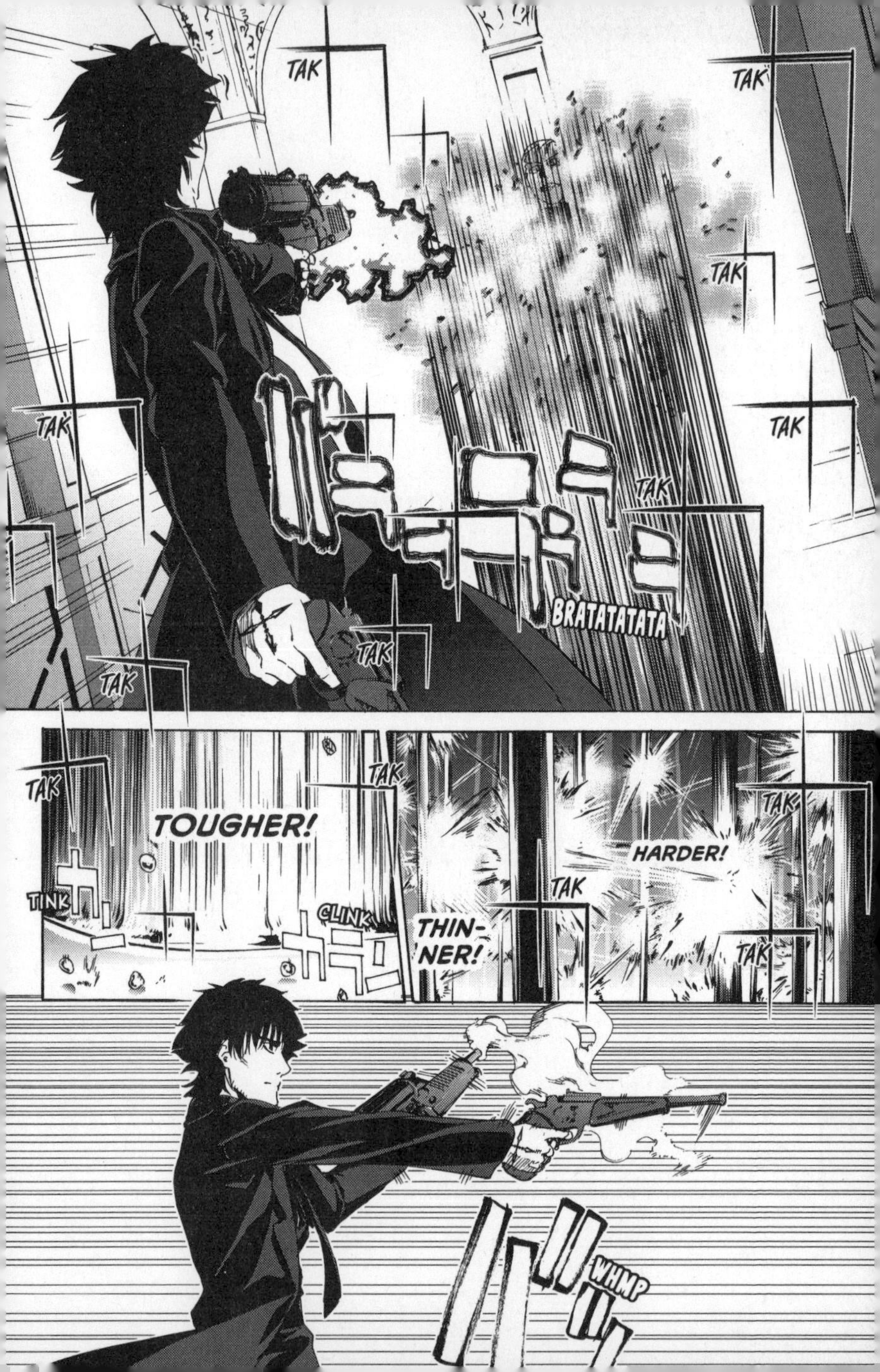
TAK
TAK
TAK
TAK
TAK
TAK
BRATATATATA
TAK
TAK
TAK
HARDER!
TAK
TAK
TAK
THIN-
NER!
TOUGHER!
CLINK
TINK
TAK
WHMP

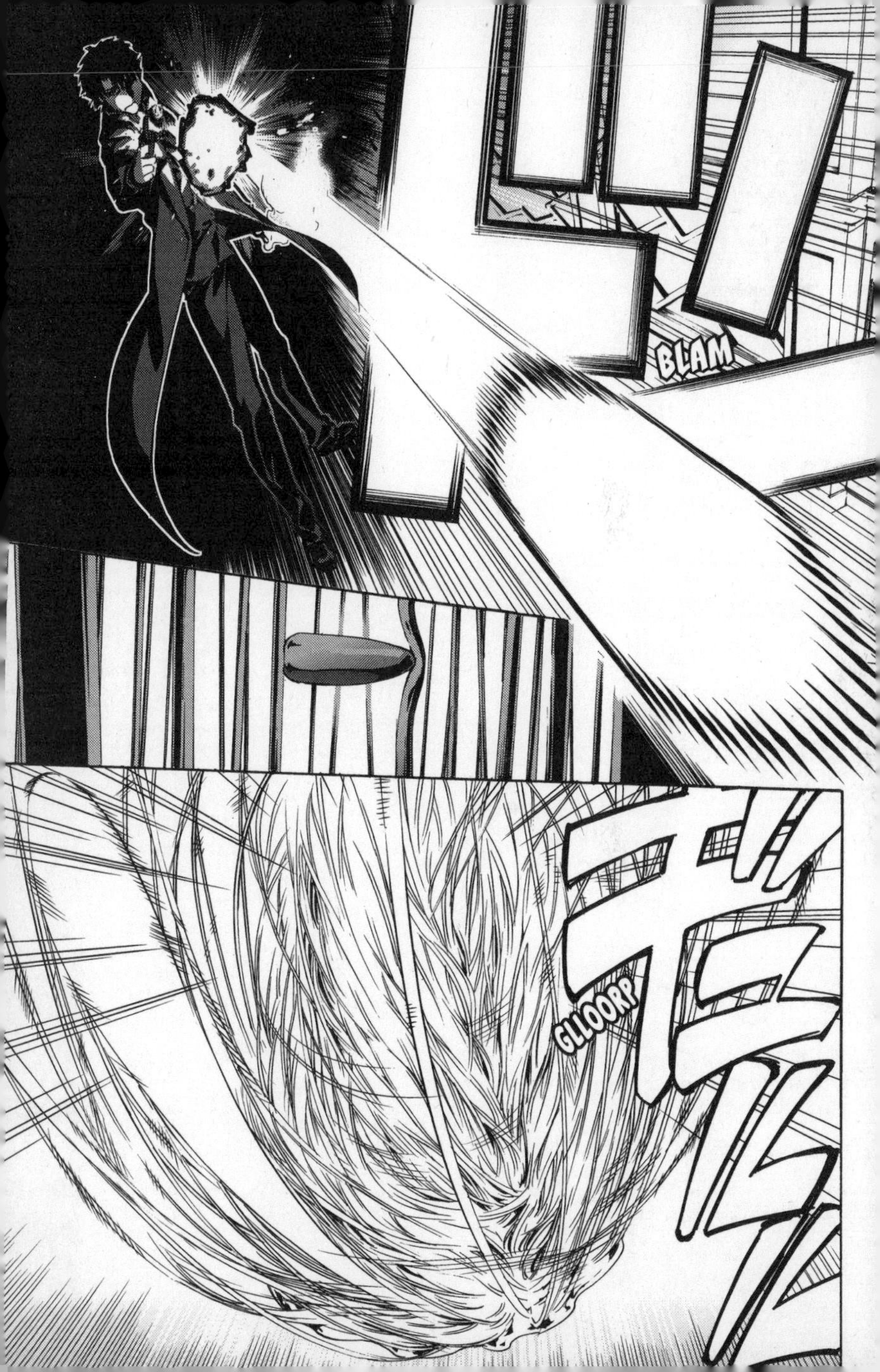
BLAM
GLLOORP

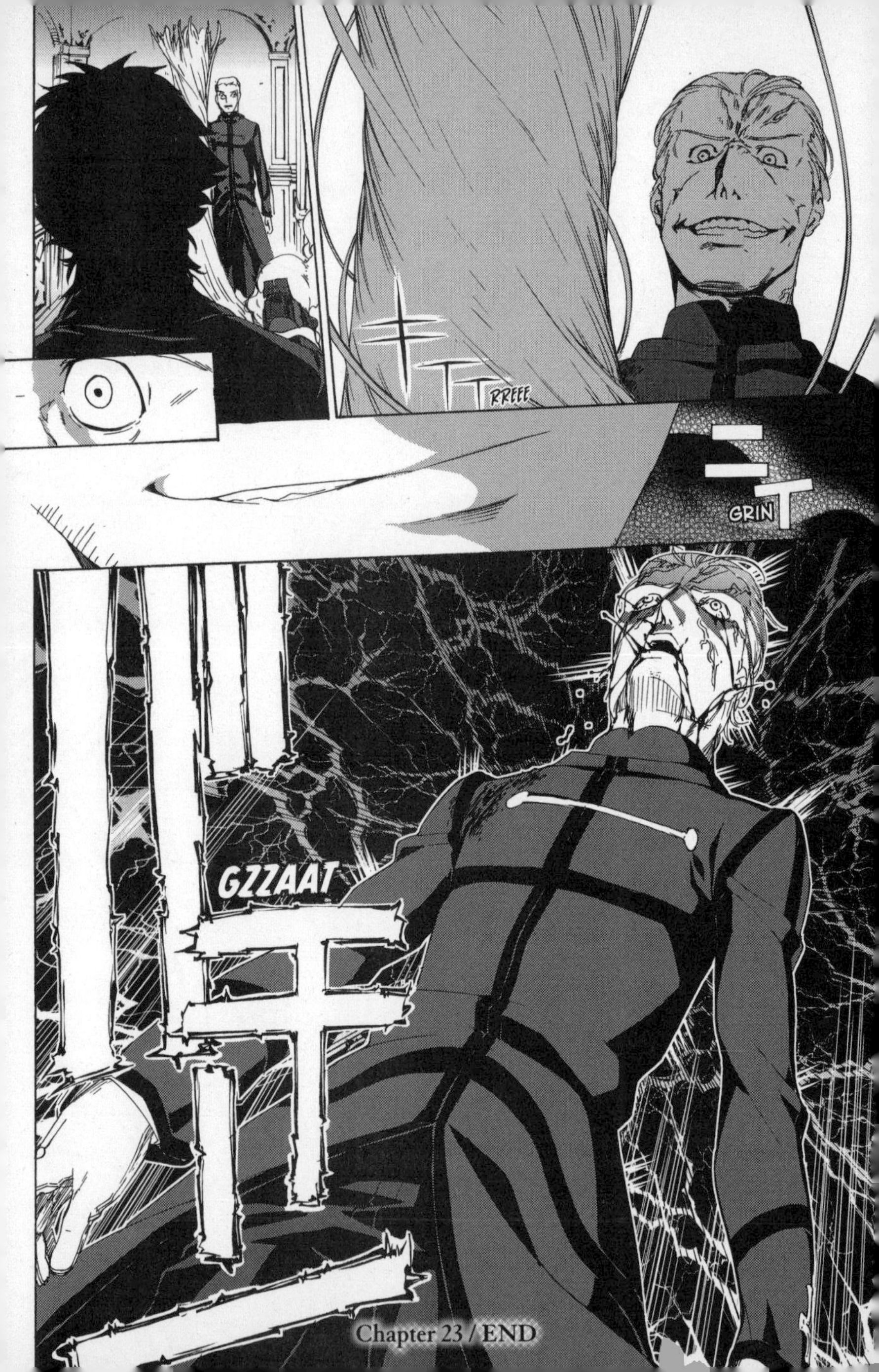
RREEE
GRIN
GZZAAT
Chapter 23 / END

CHAPTER 24

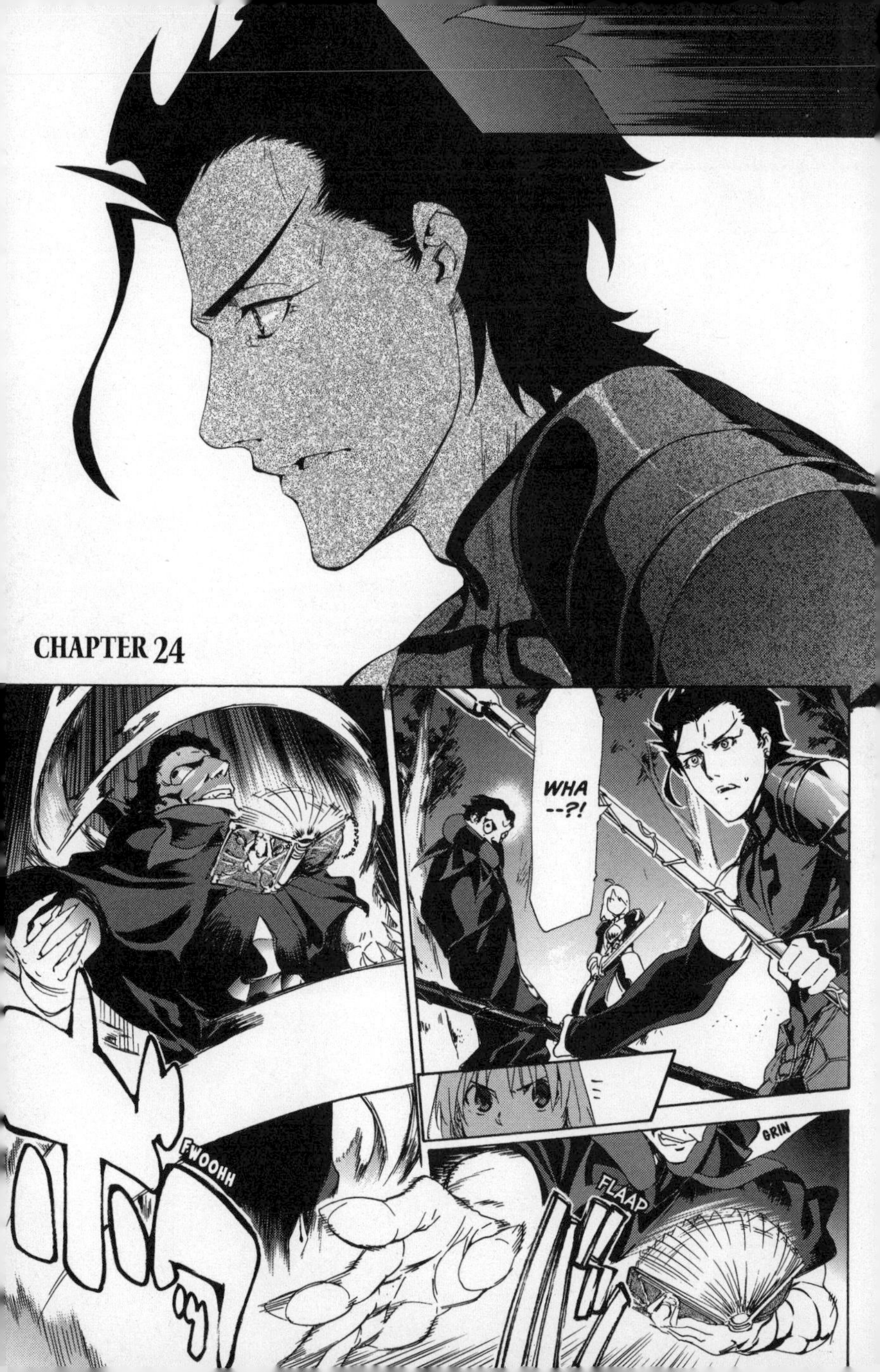
WHA --?!
GRIN
FLAAP
FWOOHH

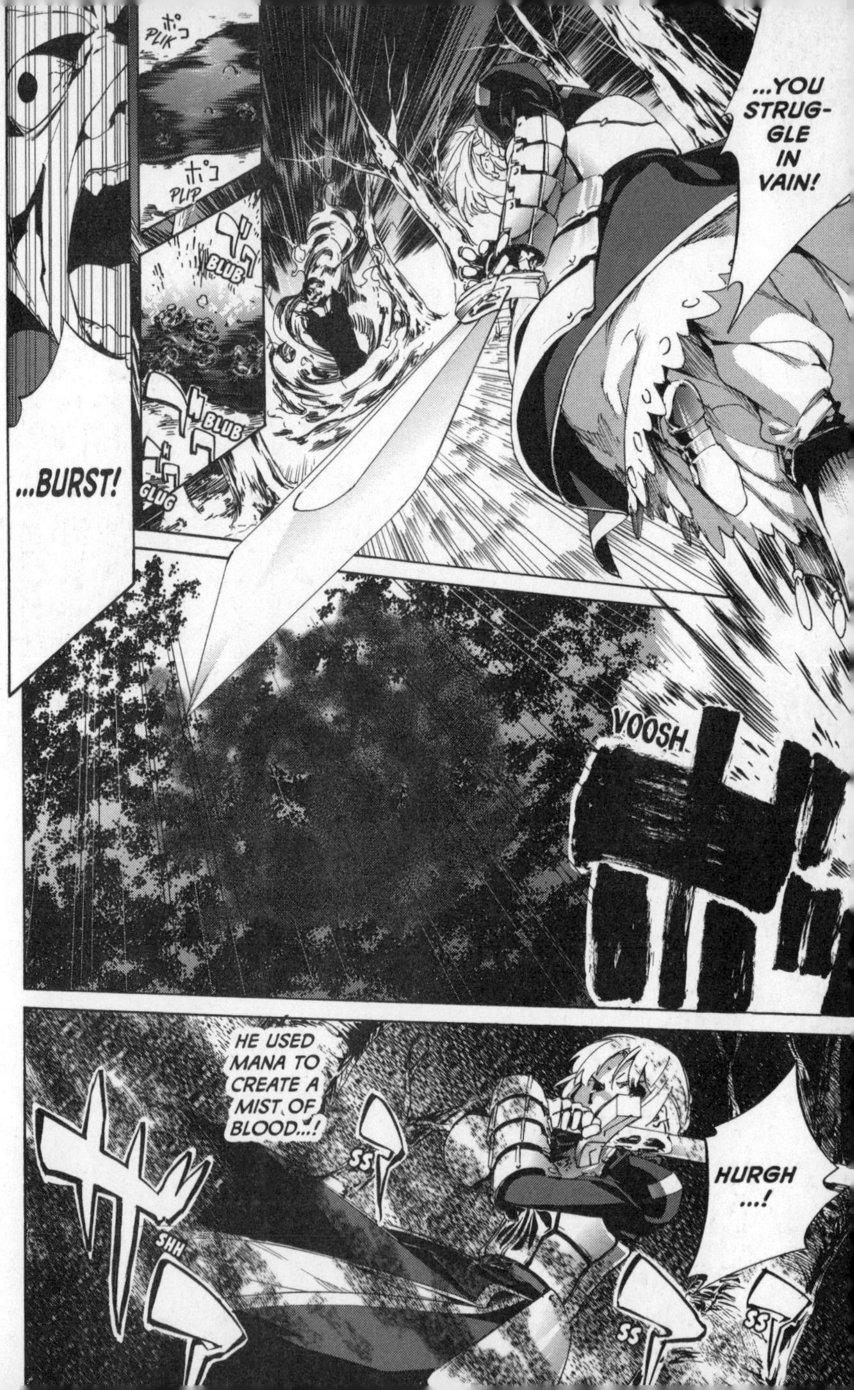
...YOU STRUG-GLE IN VAIN!
ポコ PLIK
ポコ PLIP
BLUB
BLUB
GLUG
...BURST!
VOOSH
HURGH ...!
HE USED MANA TO CREATE A MIST OF BLOOD...!
SS
SHH
SS
SS

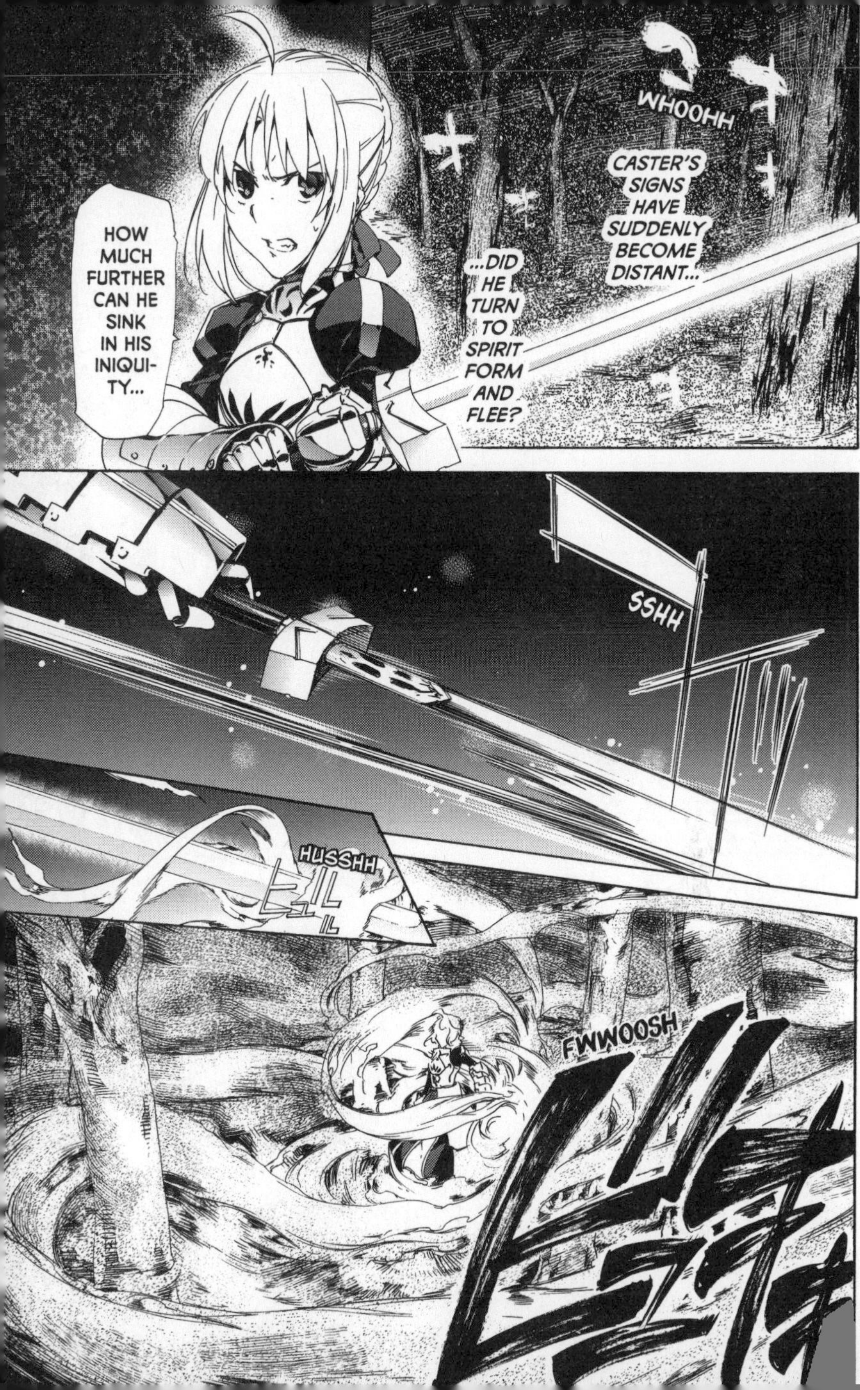
WHOOHH
CASTER'S SIGNS HAVE SUDDENLY BECOME DISTANT...
...DID HE TURN TO SPIRIT FORM AND FLEE?
HOW MUCH FURTHER CAN HE SINK IN HIS INIQUI-TY...
SSHH
HUSSHH
FWWOOSH

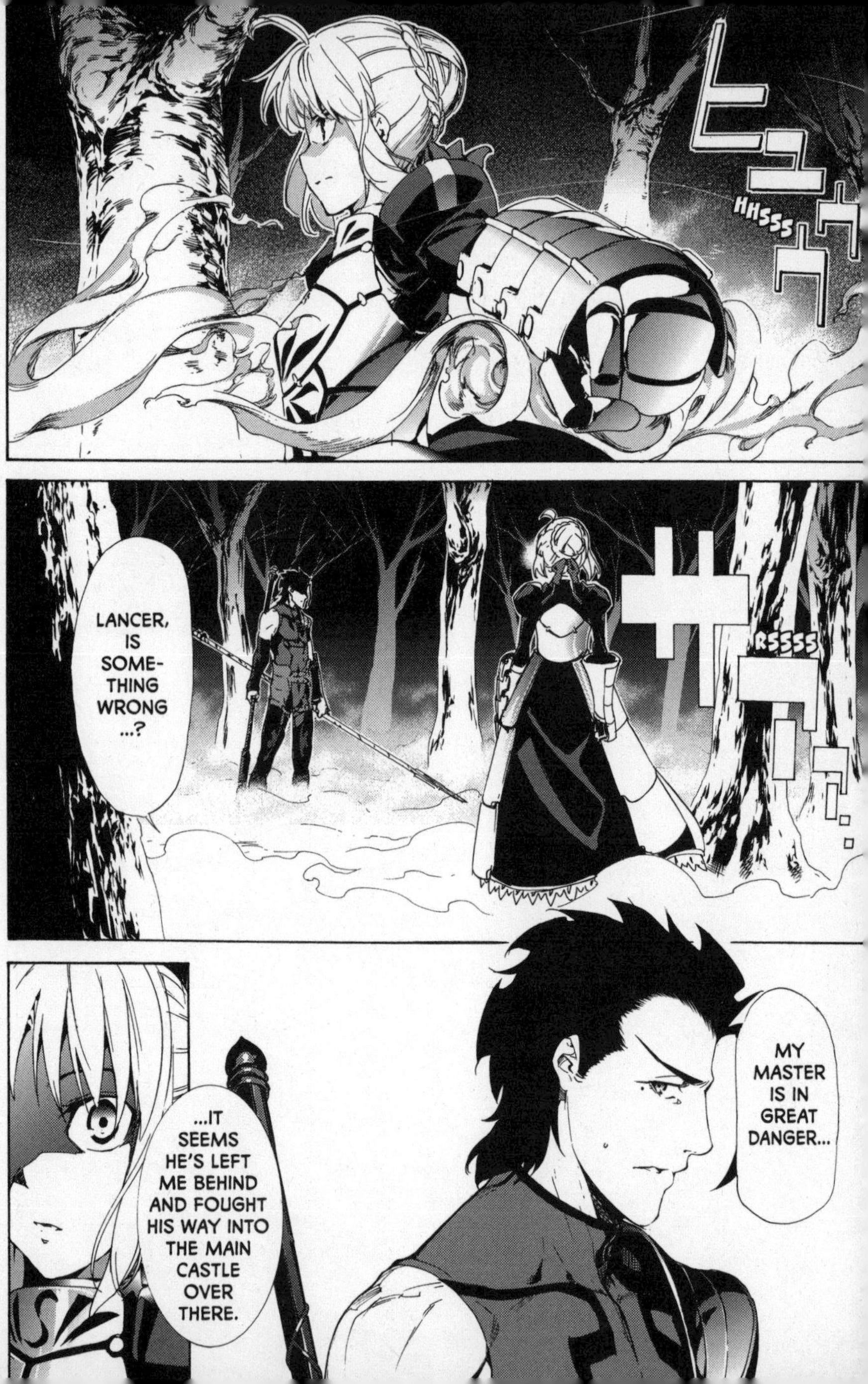
HHSSS
RSSSS
LANCER, IS SOME-THING WRONG ...?
MY MASTER IS IN GREAT DANGER...
...IT SEEMS HE'S LEFT ME BEHIND AND FOUGHT HIS WAY INTO THE MAIN CASTLE OVER THERE.

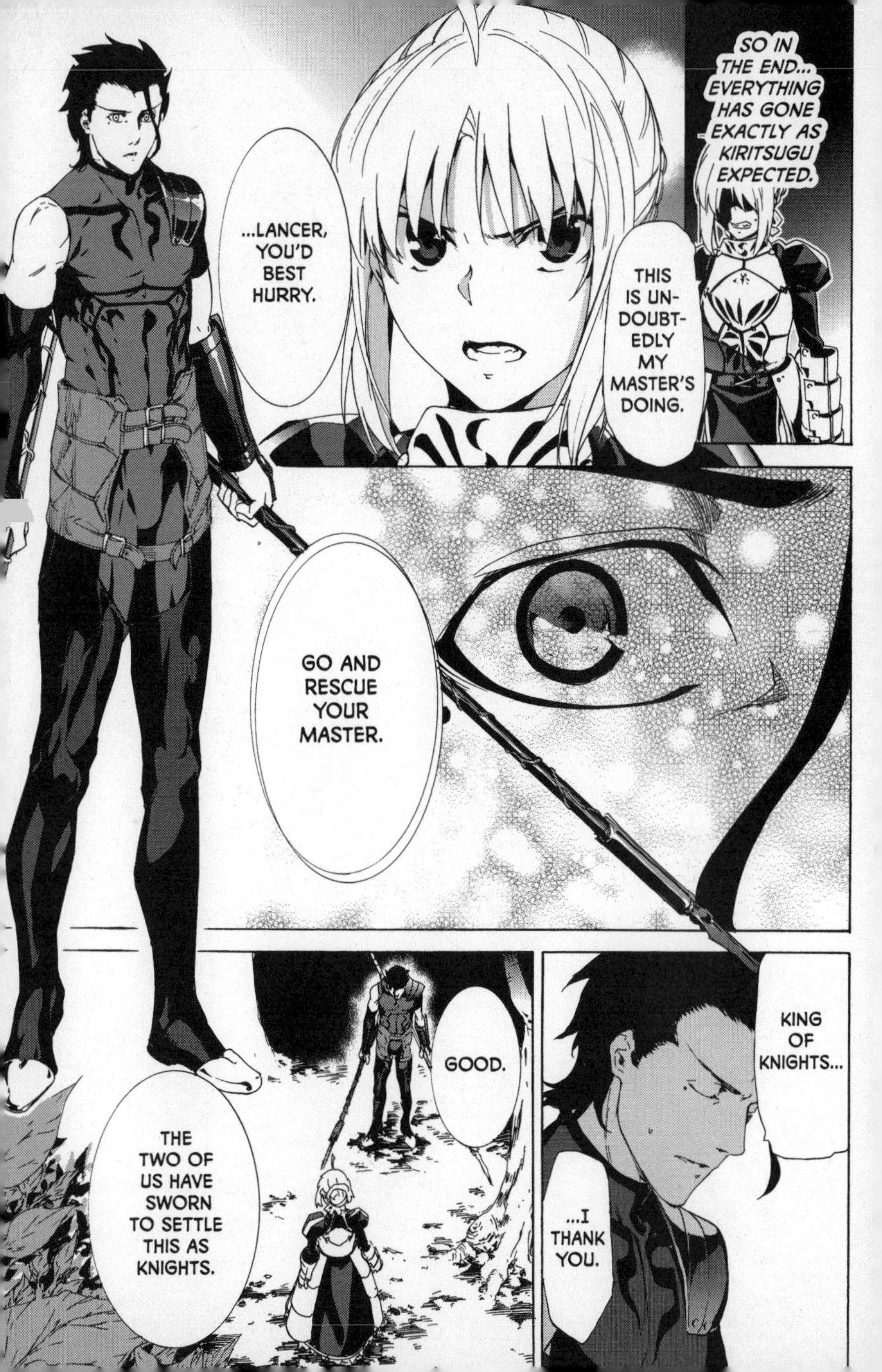
SO IN THE END... EVERYTHING HAS GONE EXACTLY AS KIRITSUGU EXPECTED.
THIS IS UNDOUBTEDLY MY MASTER'S DOING.
...LANCER, YOU'D BEST HURRY.
GO AND RESCUE YOUR MASTER.
KING OF KNIGHTS...
...I THANK YOU.
GOOD.
THE TWO OF US HAVE SWORN TO SETTLE THIS AS KNIGHTS.

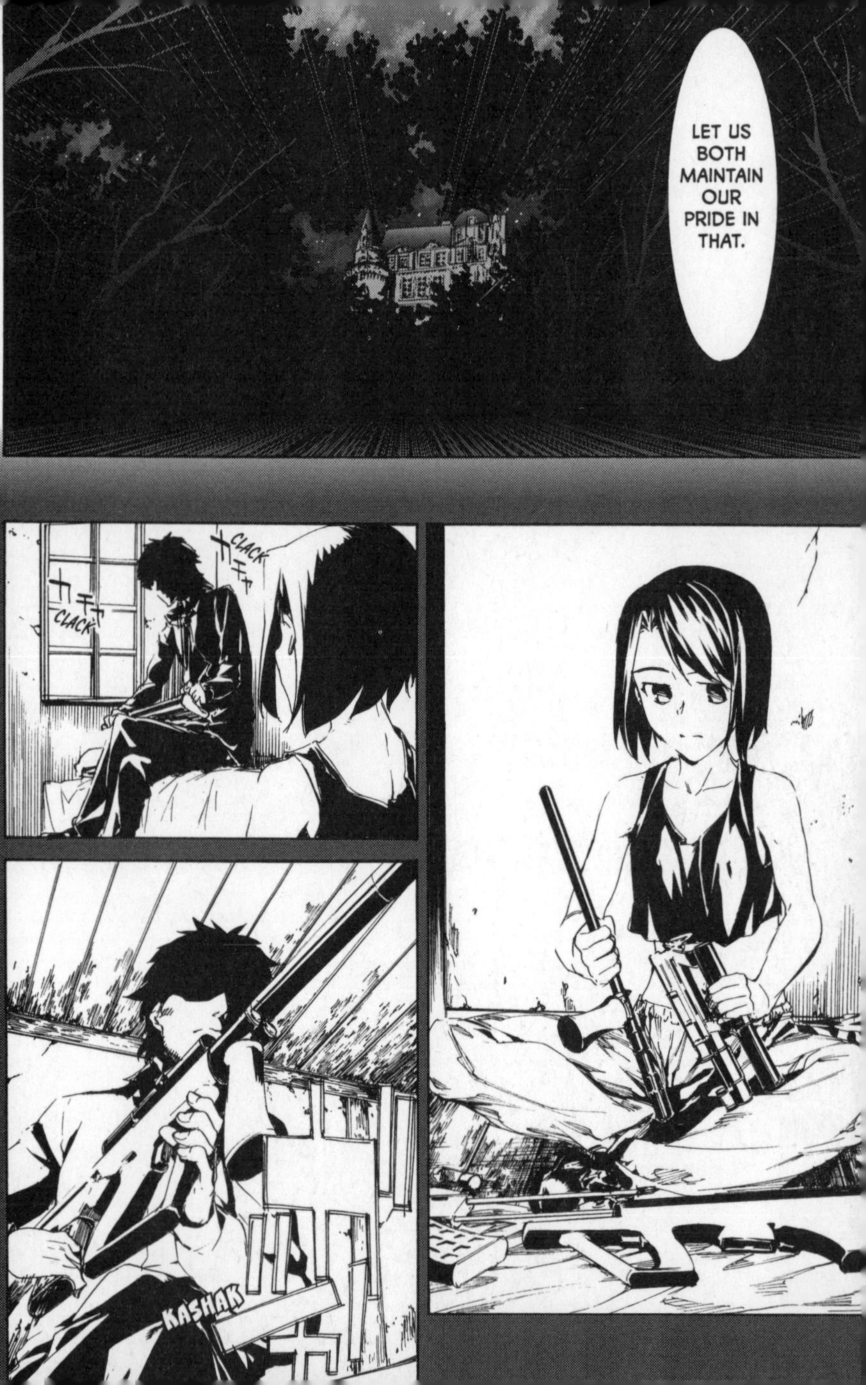
LET US BOTH MAINTAIN OUR PRIDE IN THAT.
CLACK
CLACK
KASHAK

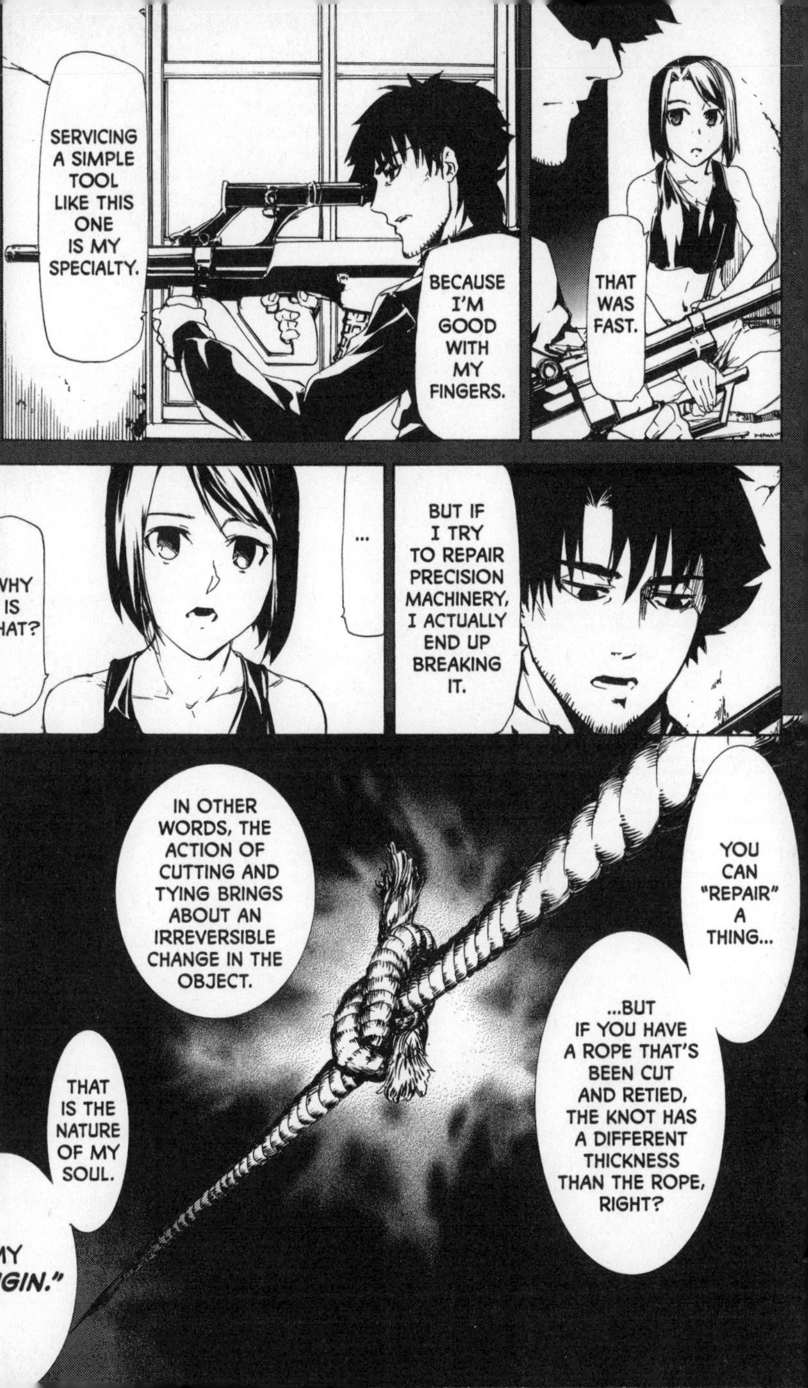
THAT WAS FAST.
SERVICING A SIMPLE TOOL LIKE THIS ONE IS MY SPECIALTY.
BECAUSE I'M GOOD WITH MY FINGERS.
BUT IF I TRY TO REPAIR PRECISION MACHINERY, I ACTUALLY END UP BREAKING IT.
...
WHY IS THAT?
YOU CAN "REPAIR" A THING...
...BUT IF YOU HAVE A ROPE THAT'S BEEN CUT AND RETIED, THE KNOT HAS A DIFFERENT THICKNESS THAN THE ROPE, RIGHT?
IN OTHER WORDS, THE ACTION OF CUTTING AND TYING BRINGS ABOUT AN IRREVERSIBLE CHANGE IN THE OBJECT.
THAT IS THE NATURE OF MY SOUL.
MY "*ORIGIN*."

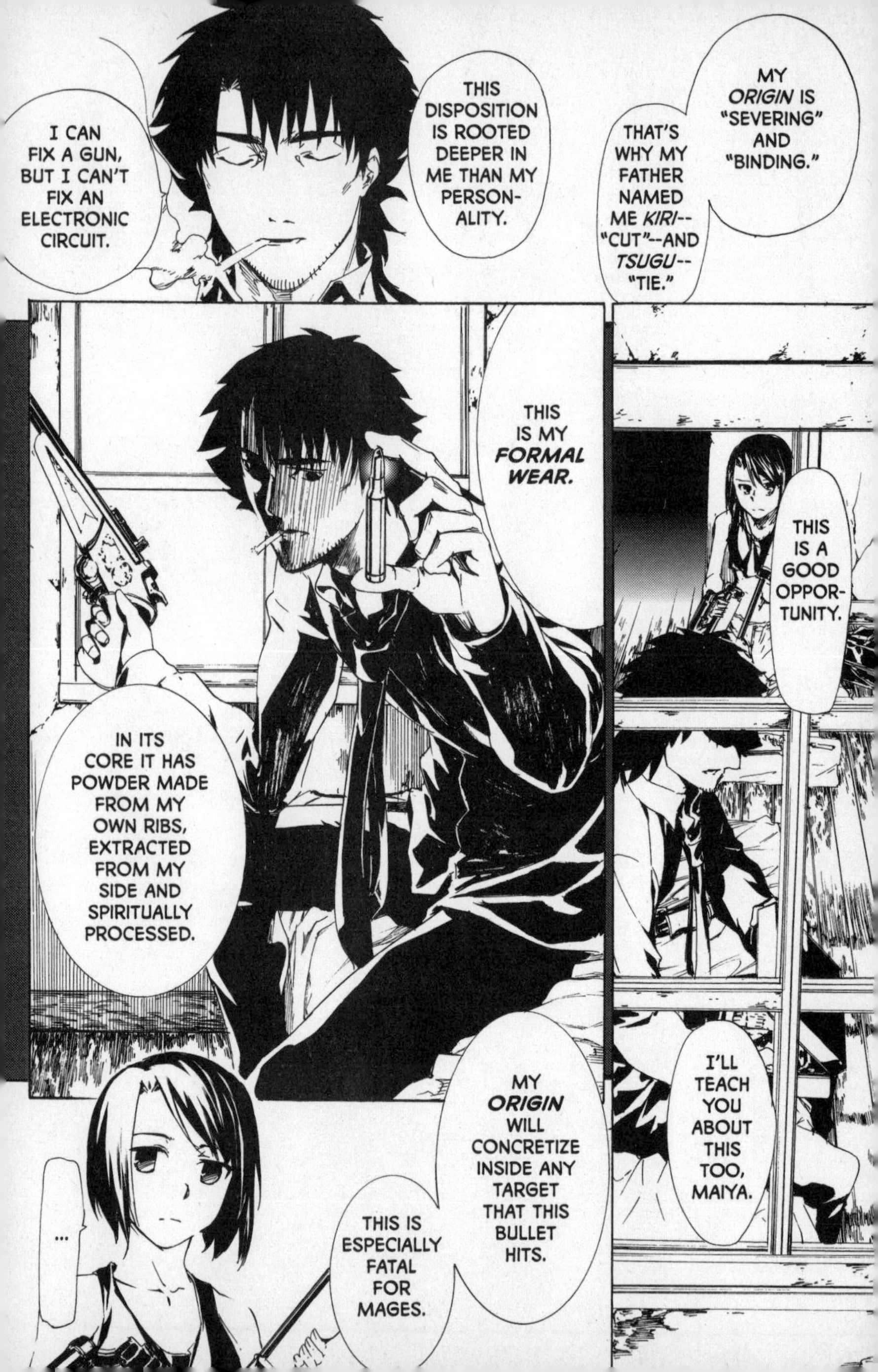
MY *ORIGIN* IS "SEVERING" AND "BINDING."
THAT'S WHY MY FATHER NAMED ME *KIRI*--"CUT"--AND *TSUGU*--"TIE."
THIS DISPOSITION IS ROOTED DEEPER IN ME THAN MY PERSON-ALITY.
I CAN FIX A GUN, BUT I CAN'T FIX AN ELECTRONIC CIRCUIT.
THIS IS A GOOD OPPOR-TUNITY.
I'LL TEACH YOU ABOUT THIS TOO, MAIYA.
THIS IS MY ***FORMAL WEAR.***
IN ITS CORE IT HAS POWDER MADE FROM MY OWN RIBS, EXTRACTED FROM MY SIDE AND SPIRITUALLY PROCESSED.
MY ***ORIGIN*** WILL CONCRETIZE INSIDE ANY TARGET THAT THIS BULLET HITS.
THIS IS ESPECIALLY FATAL FOR MAGES.
...

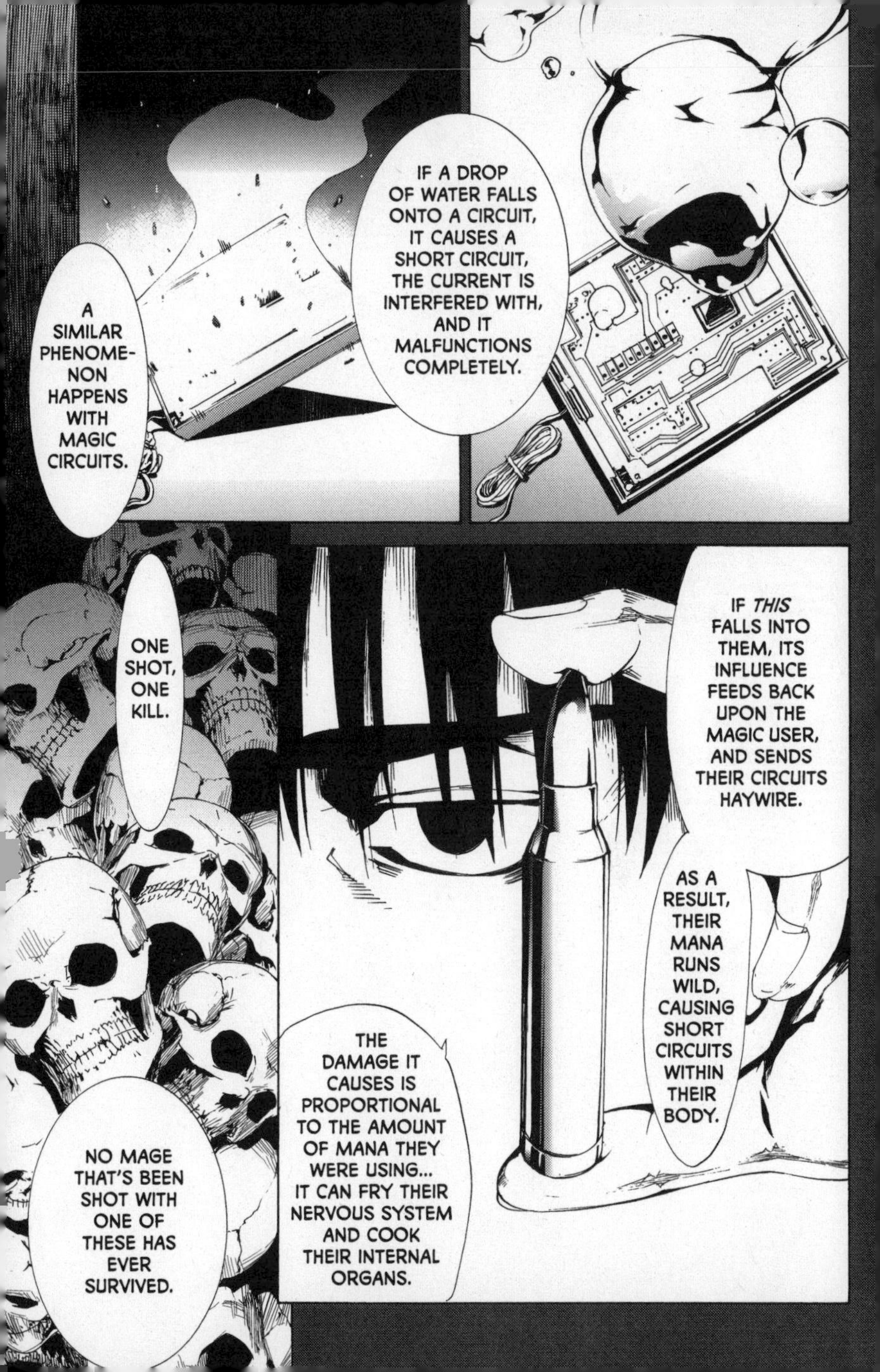
IF A DROP OF WATER FALLS ONTO A CIRCUIT, IT CAUSES A SHORT CIRCUIT, THE CURRENT IS INTERFERED WITH, AND IT MALFUNCTIONS COMPLETELY.
A SIMILAR PHENOMENON HAPPENS WITH MAGIC CIRCUITS.
IF *THIS* FALLS INTO THEM, ITS INFLUENCE FEEDS BACK UPON THE MAGIC USER, AND SENDS THEIR CIRCUITS HAYWIRE.
AS A RESULT, THEIR MANA RUNS WILD, CAUSING SHORT CIRCUITS WITHIN THEIR BODY.
THE DAMAGE IT CAUSES IS PROPORTIONAL TO THE AMOUNT OF MANA THEY WERE USING... IT CAN FRY THEIR NERVOUS SYSTEM AND COOK THEIR INTERNAL ORGANS.
ONE SHOT, ONE KILL.
NO MAGE THAT'S BEEN SHOT WITH ONE OF THESE HAS EVER SURVIVED.

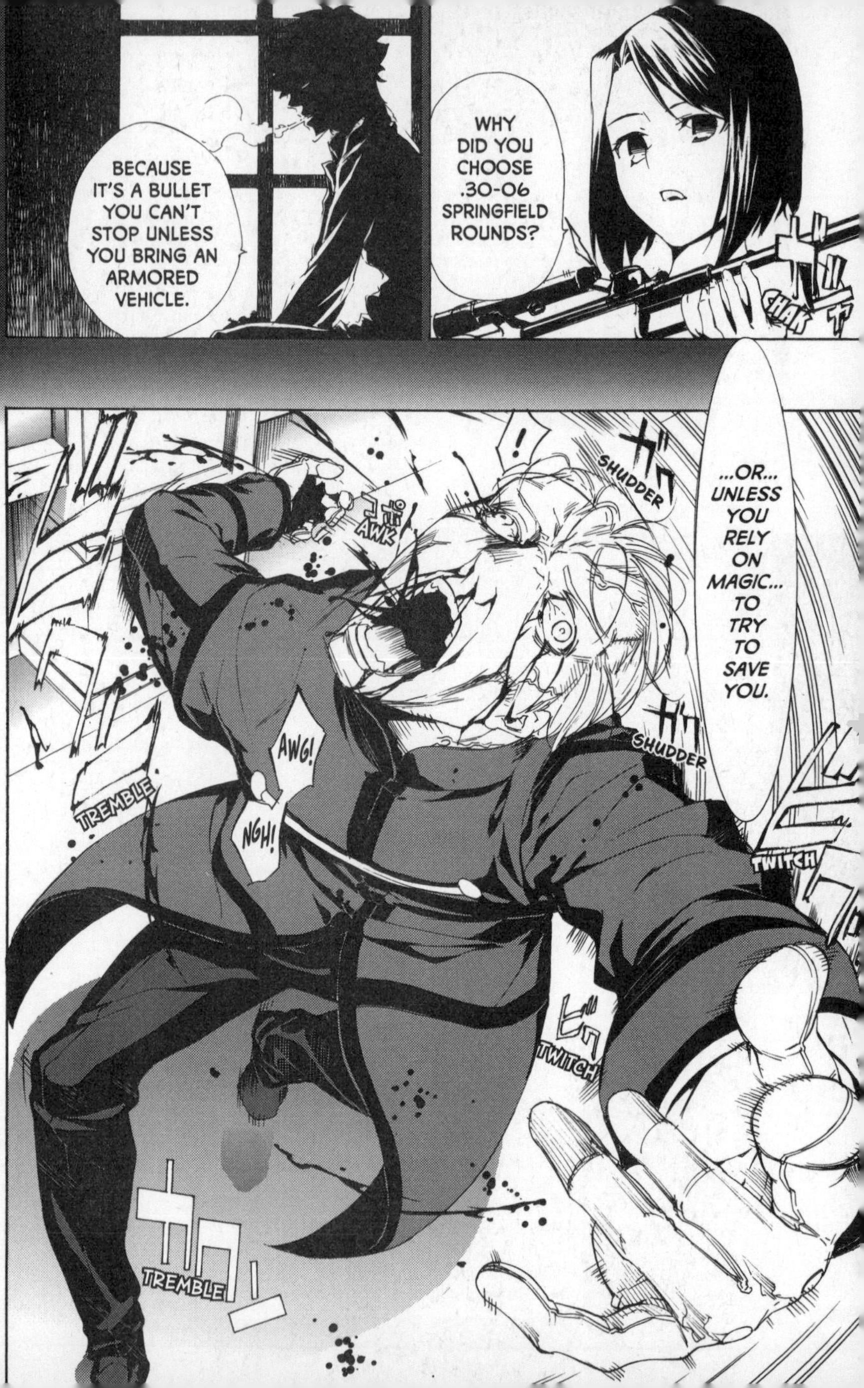
WHY DID YOU CHOOSE .30-06 SPRINGFIELD ROUNDS?
CHAK
BECAUSE IT'S A BULLET YOU CAN'T STOP UNLESS YOU BRING AN ARMORED VEHICLE.
...OR... UNLESS YOU RELY ON MAGIC... TO TRY TO SAVE YOU.
SHUDDER
!
AWK
SHUDDER
TWITCH
AWG!
NGH!
TREMBLE
TWITCH
TREMBLE

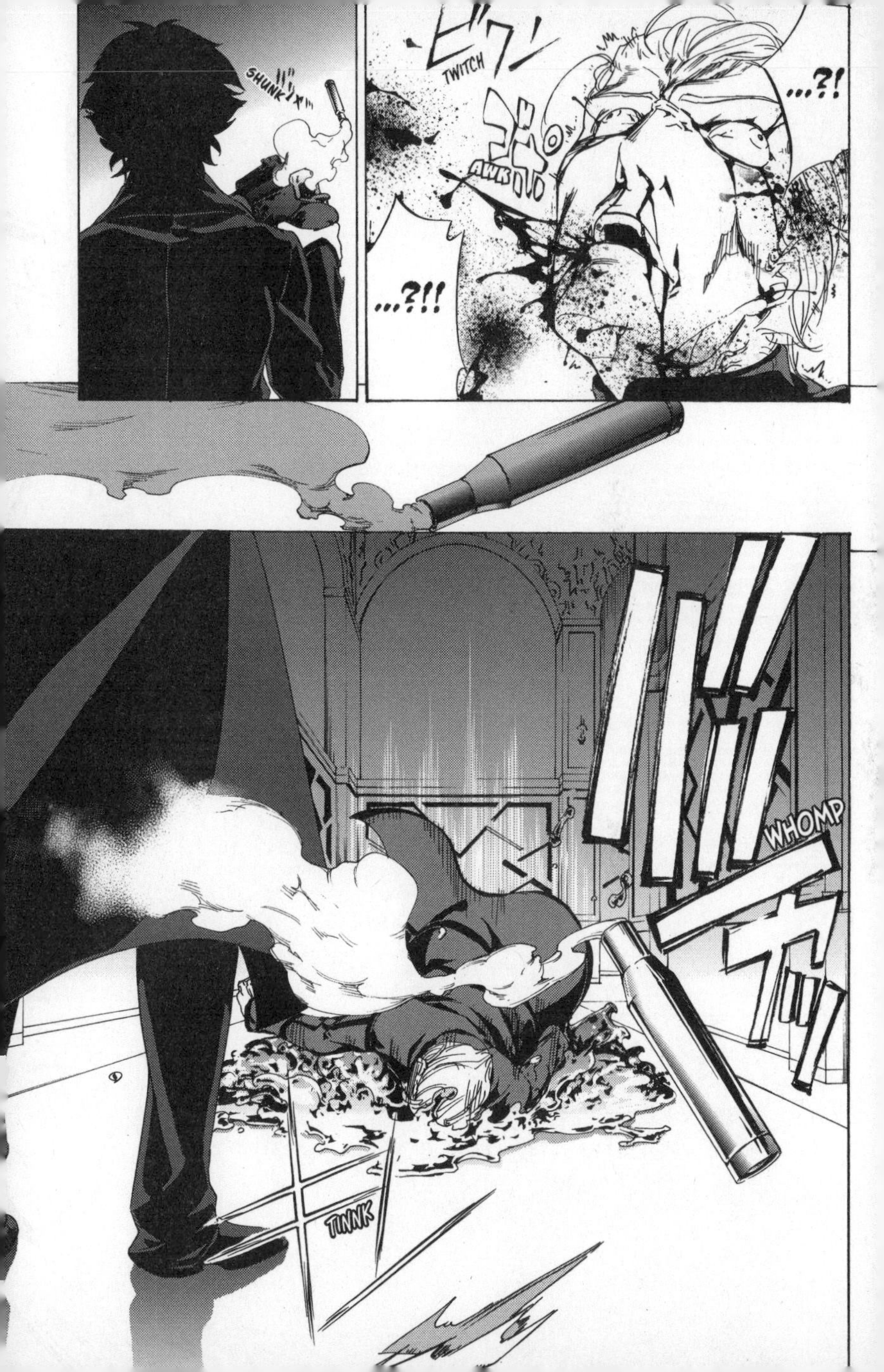
TWITCH
...?!
AWK
...?!!
SHUNK!
WHOMP
TINNK

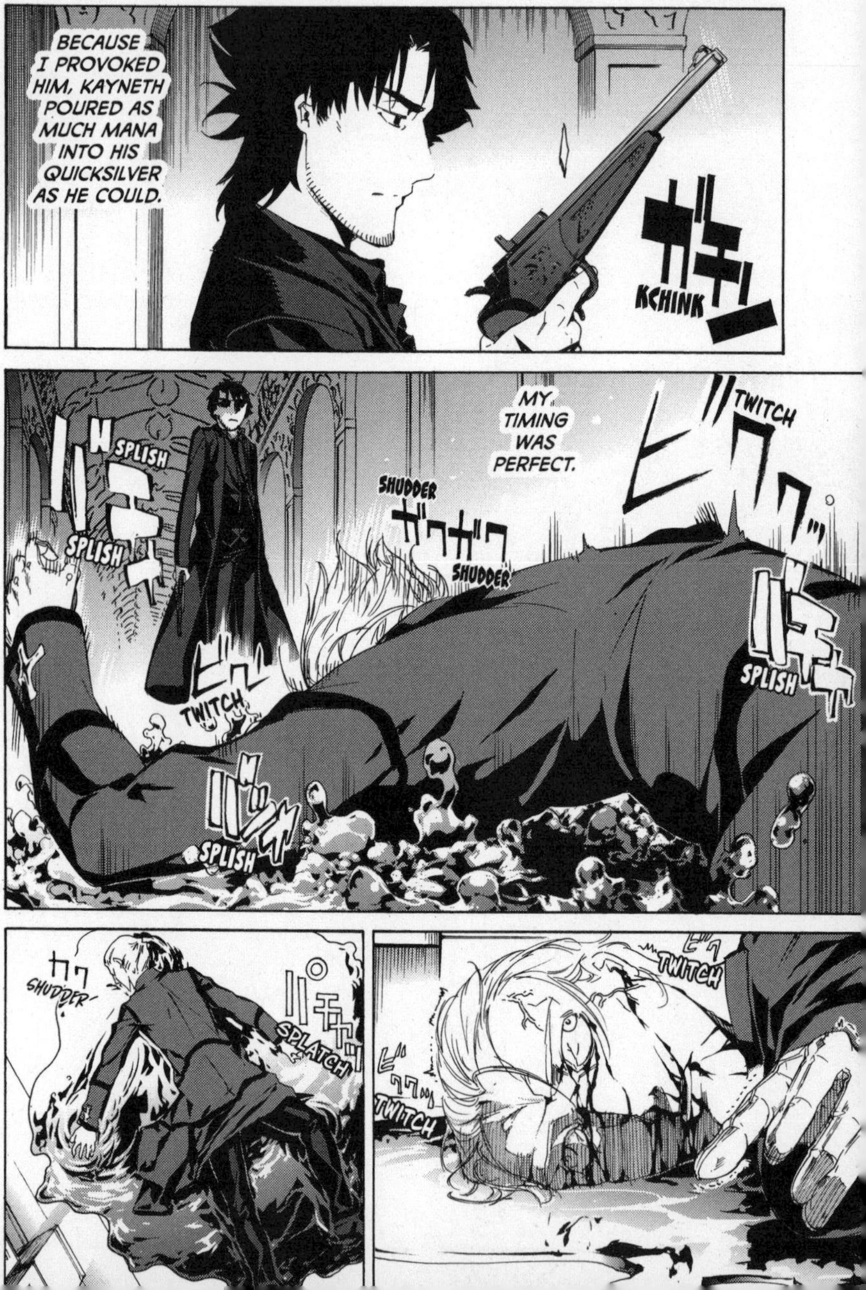
BECAUSE I PROVOKED HIM, KAYNETH POURED AS MUCH MANA INTO HIS QUICKSILVER AS HE COULD.
KCHINK
MY TIMING WAS PERFECT.
TWITCH
SHUDDER
SHUDDER
SPLISH
SPLISH
SPLISH
TWITCH
SPLISH
TWITCH
TWITCH
SPLATCH
SHUDDER

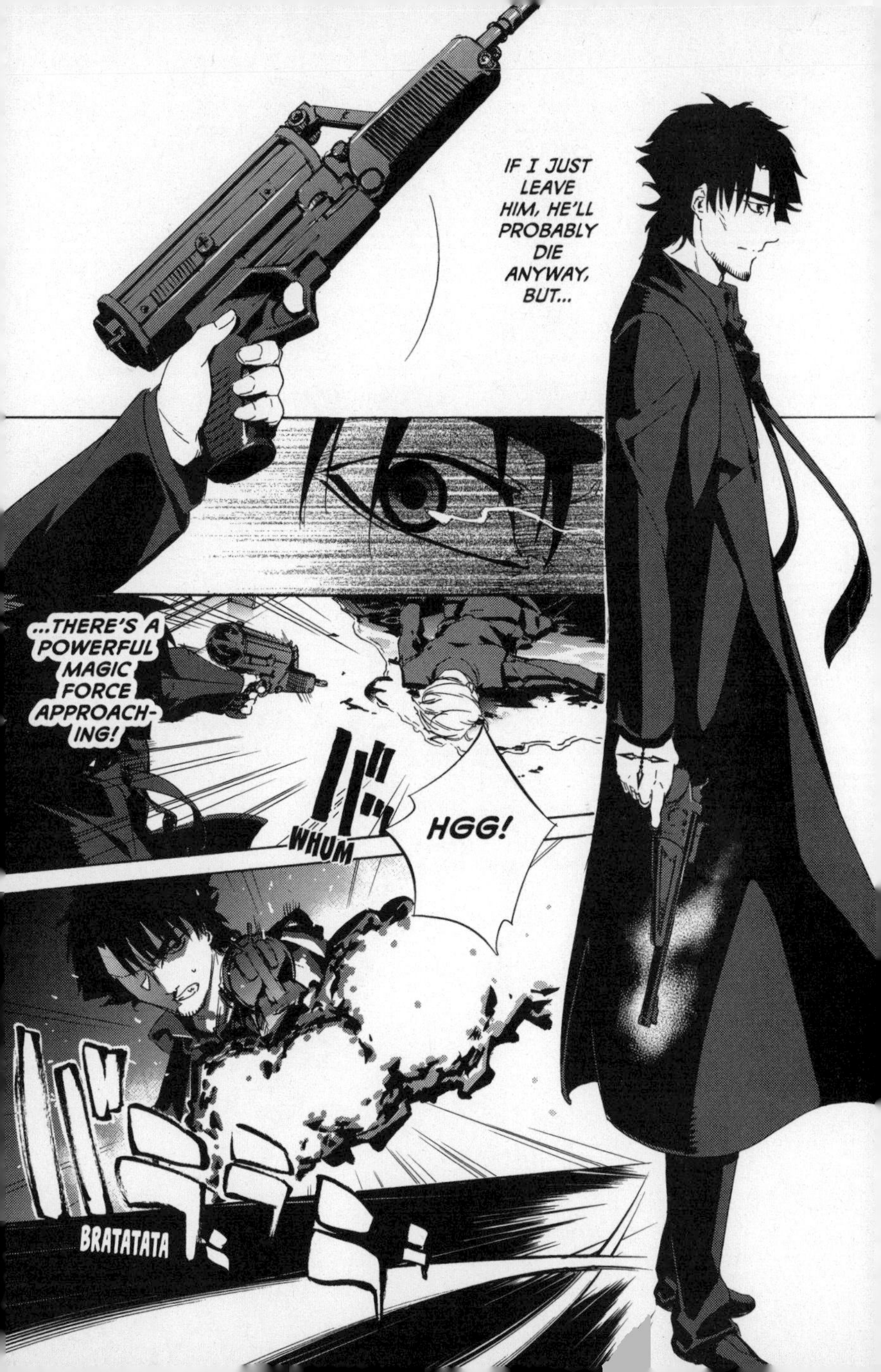
IF I JUST LEAVE HIM, HE'LL PROBABLY DIE ANYWAY, BUT...
...THERE'S A POWERFUL MAGIC FORCE APPROACH-ING!
HGG!
WHUM
BRATATATA

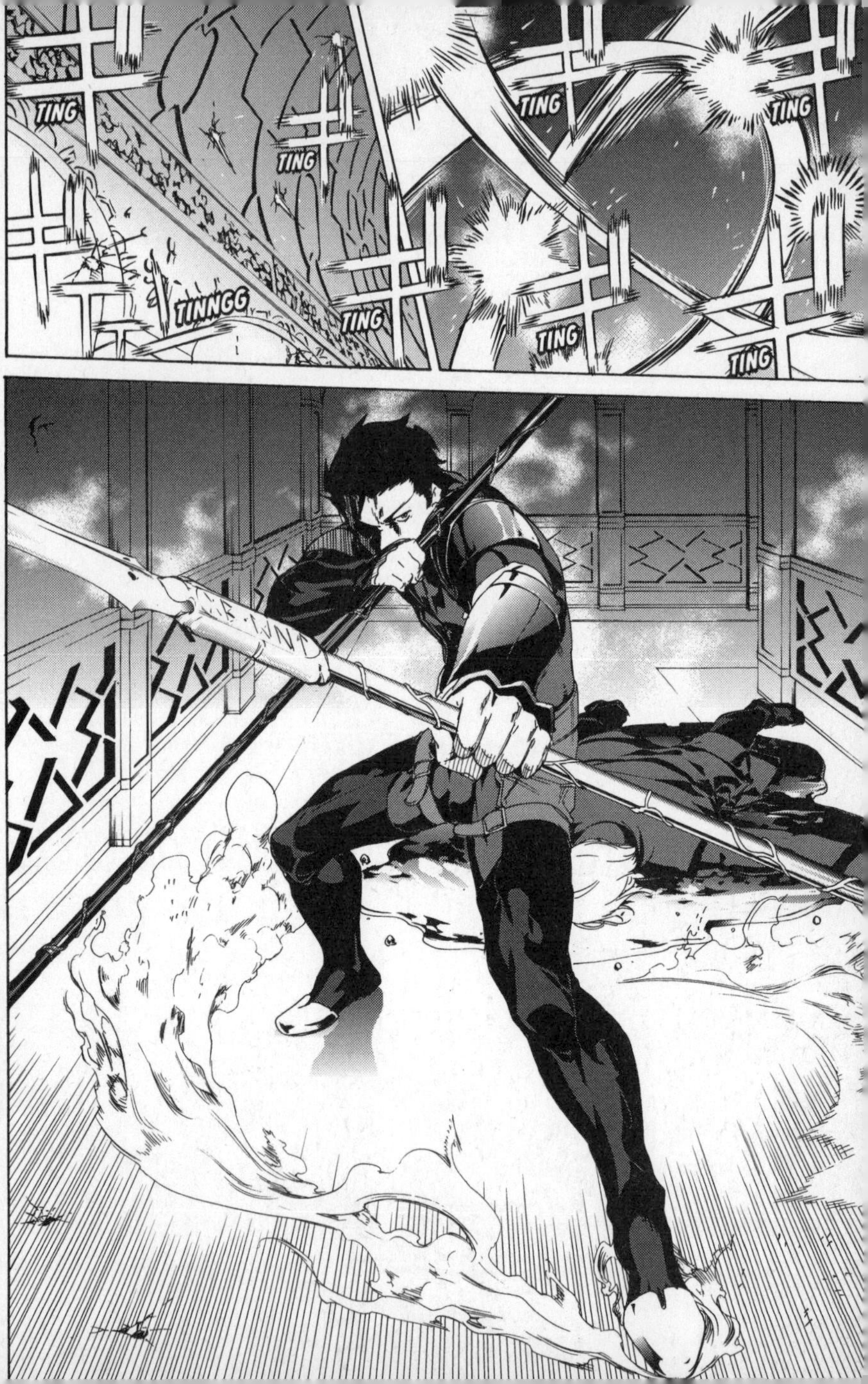
TING
TING
TING
TING
TING
TING
TINNGG
TING
TING

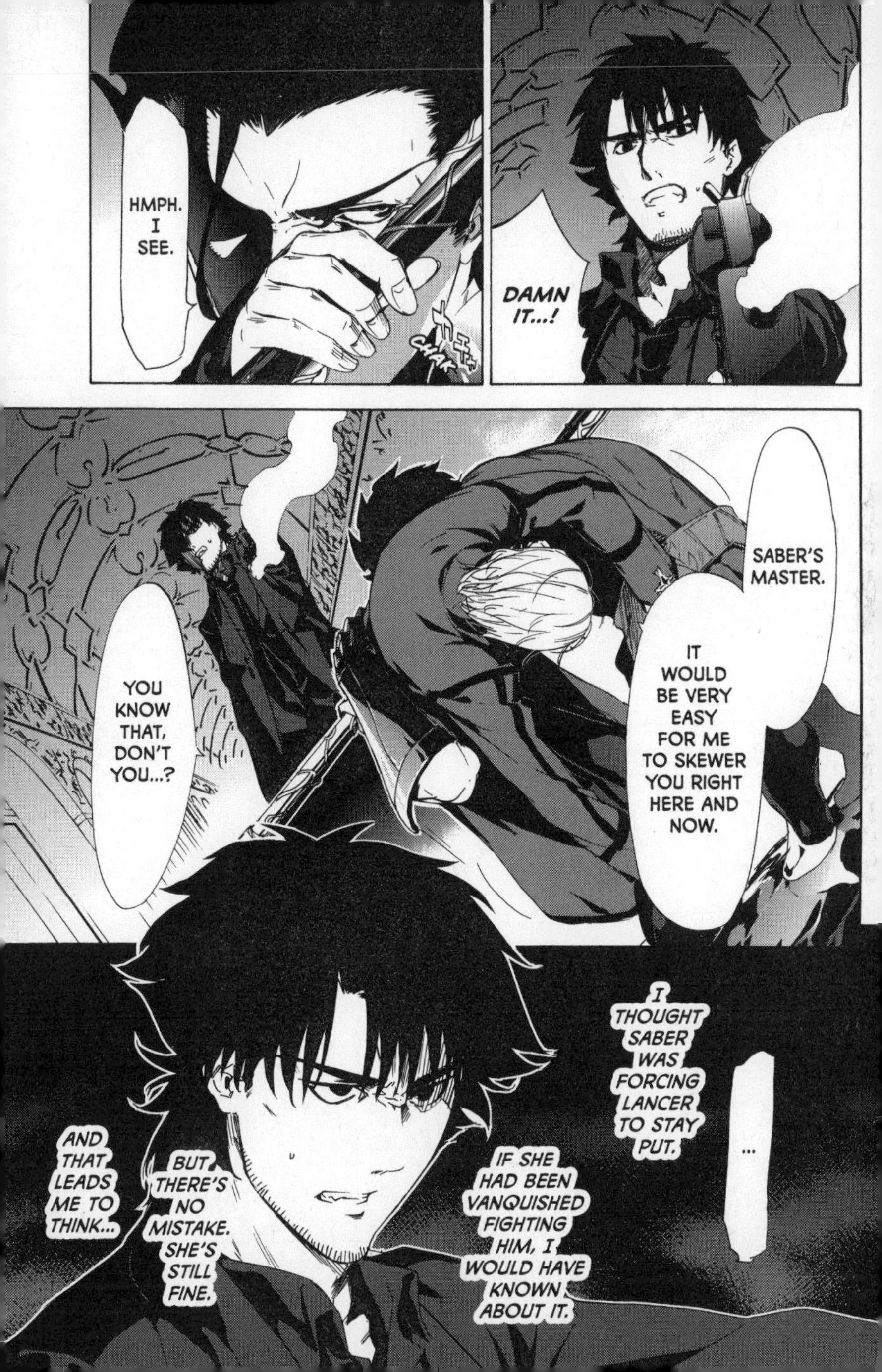
DAMN IT...!
HMPH. I SEE.
CHAK
SABER'S MASTER.
IT WOULD BE VERY EASY FOR ME TO SKEWER YOU RIGHT HERE AND NOW.
YOU KNOW THAT, DON'T YOU...?
...
I THOUGHT SABER WAS FORCING LANCER TO STAY PUT.
IF SHE HAD BEEN VANQUISHED FIGHTING HIM, I WOULD HAVE KNOWN ABOUT IT.
BUT THERE'S NO MISTAKE. SHE'S STILL FINE.
AND THAT LEADS ME TO THINK...

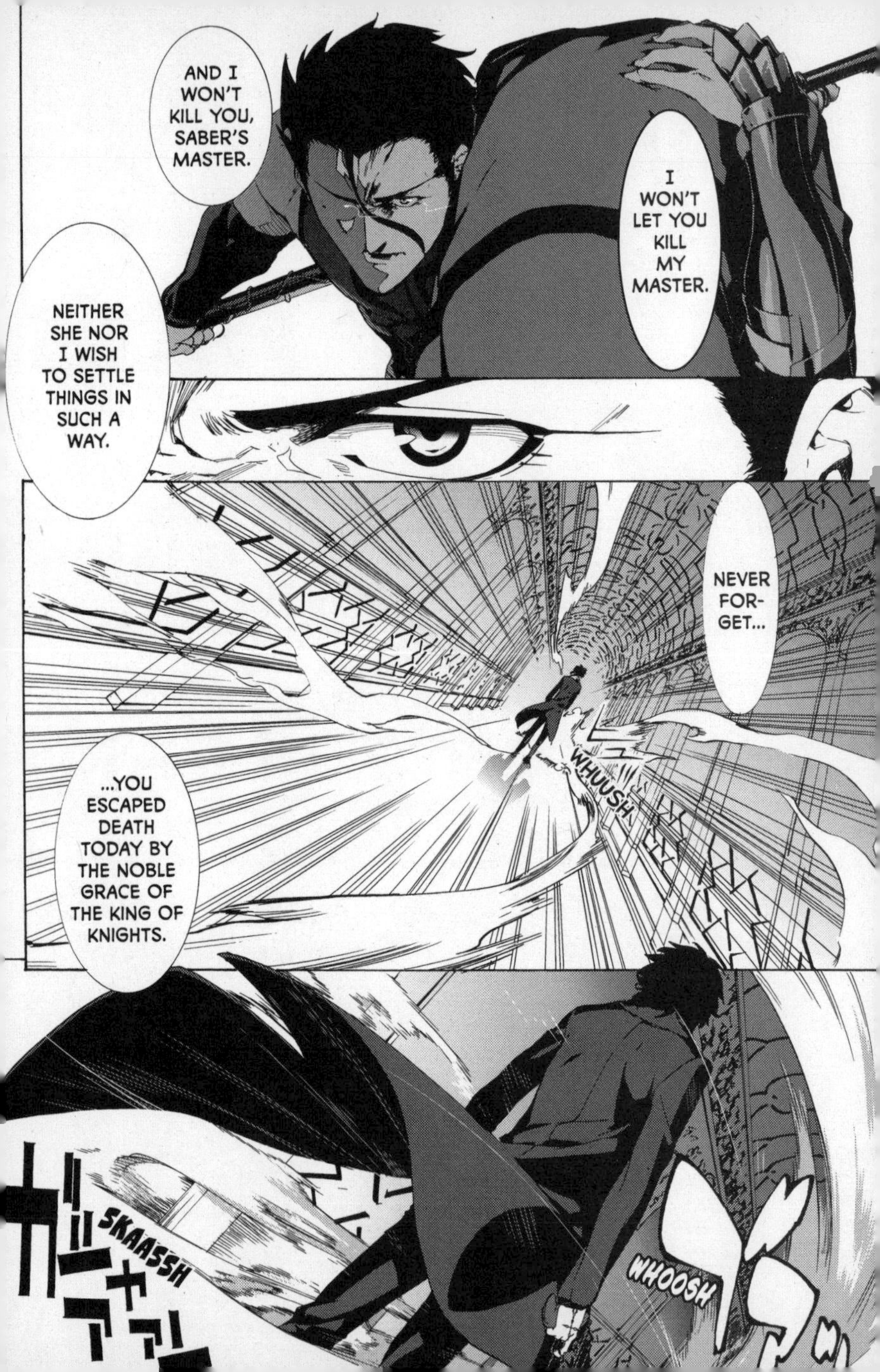
I WON'T LET YOU KILL MY MASTER.
AND I WON'T KILL YOU, SABER'S MASTER.
NEITHER SHE NOR I WISH TO SETTLE THINGS IN SUCH A WAY.
NEVER FOR-GET...
WHUUSH
...YOU ESCAPED DEATH TODAY BY THE NOBLE GRACE OF THE KING OF KNIGHTS.
WHOOSH
SKAASSH

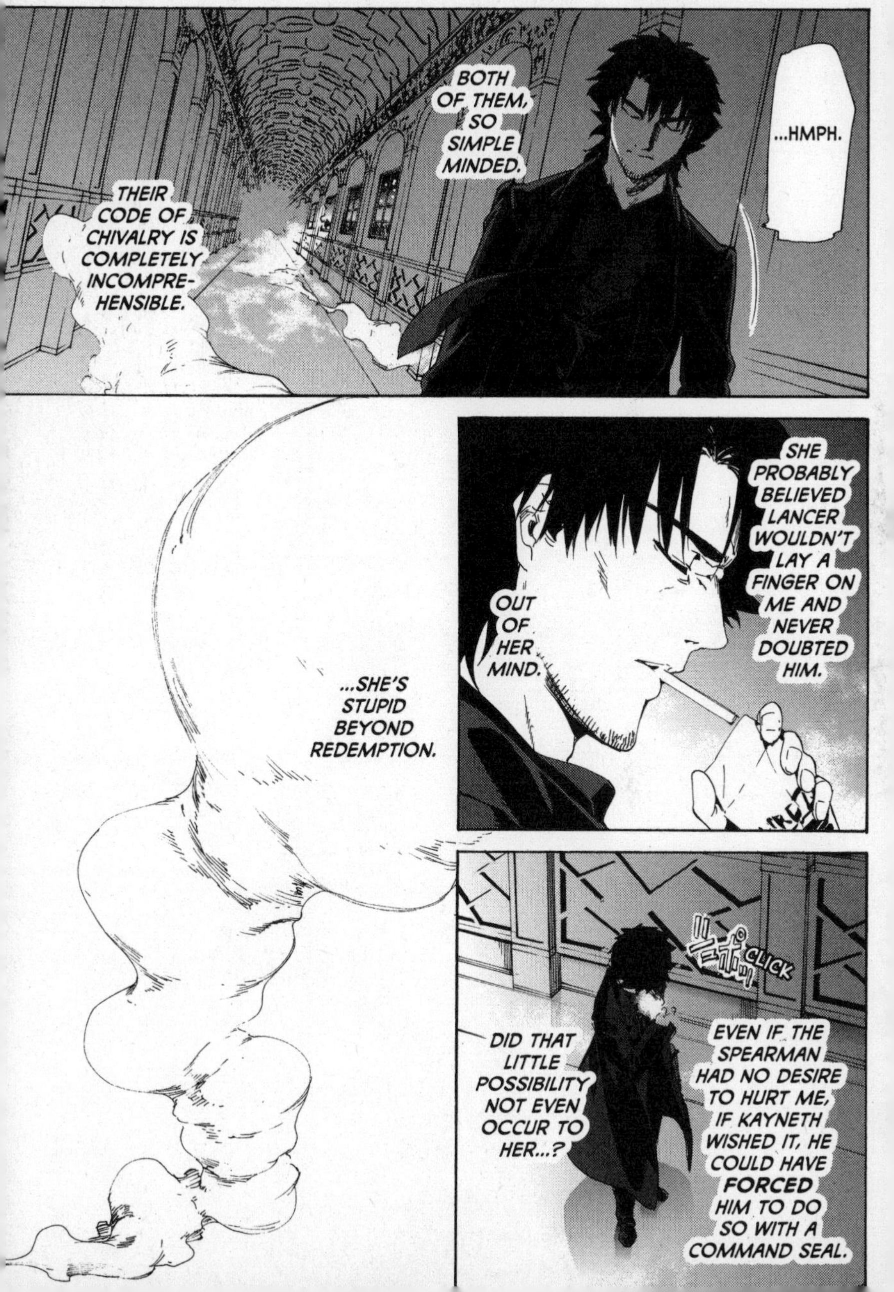
...HMPH.
BOTH OF THEM, SO SIMPLE MINDED.
THEIR CODE OF CHIVALRY IS COMPLETELY INCOMPRE-HENSIBLE.
SHE PROBABLY BELIEVED LANCER WOULDN'T LAY A FINGER ON ME AND NEVER DOUBTED HIM.
OUT OF HER MIND.
...SHE'S STUPID BEYOND REDEMPTION.
CLICK
EVEN IF THE SPEARMAN HAD NO DESIRE TO HURT ME, IF KAYNETH WISHED IT, HE COULD HAVE **FORCED** HIM TO DO SO WITH A COMMAND SEAL.
DID THAT LITTLE POSSIBILITY NOT EVEN OCCUR TO HER...?

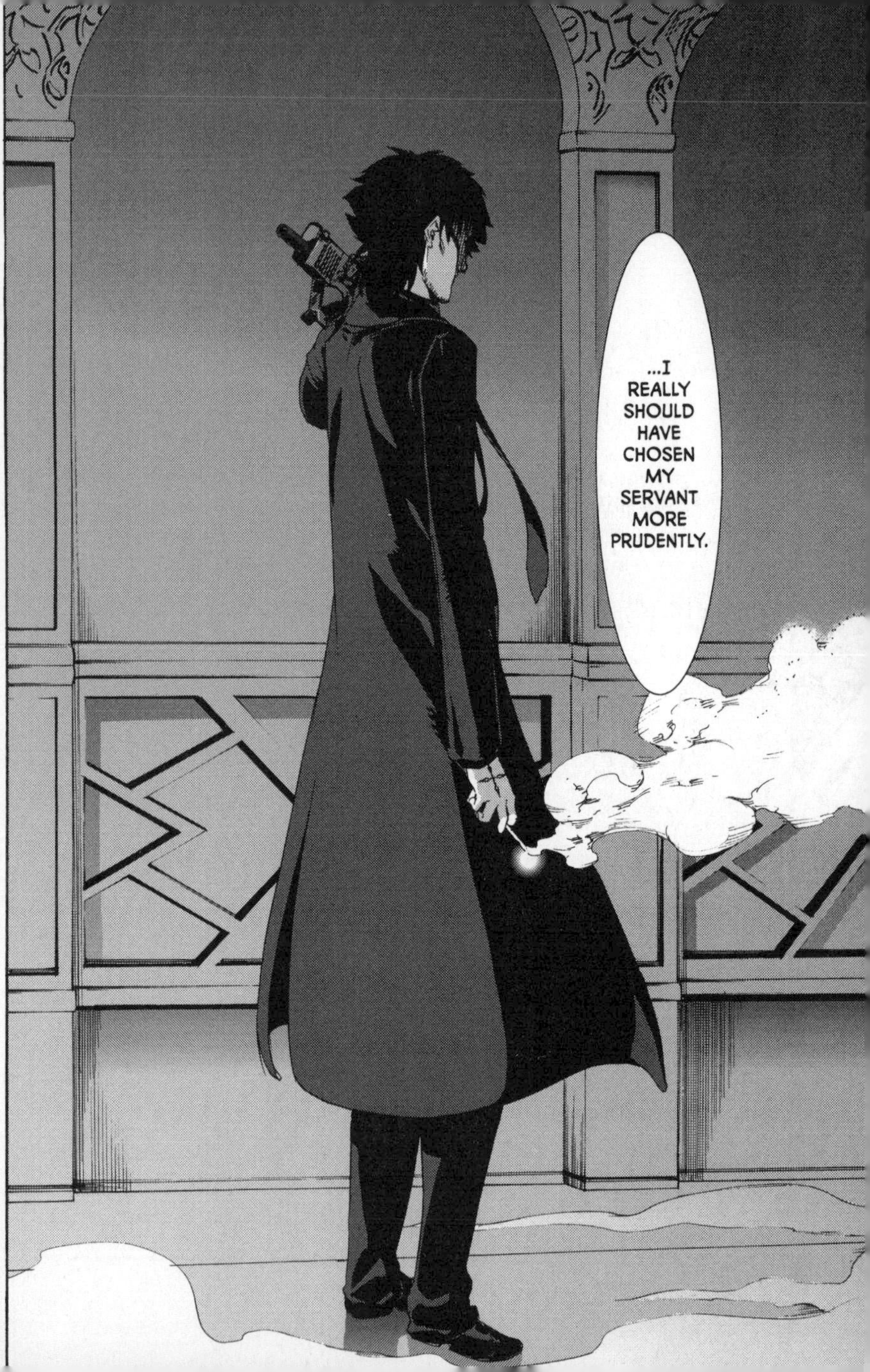
...I REALLY SHOULD HAVE CHOSEN MY SERVANT MORE PRUDENTLY.

— 130 : 32 : 15

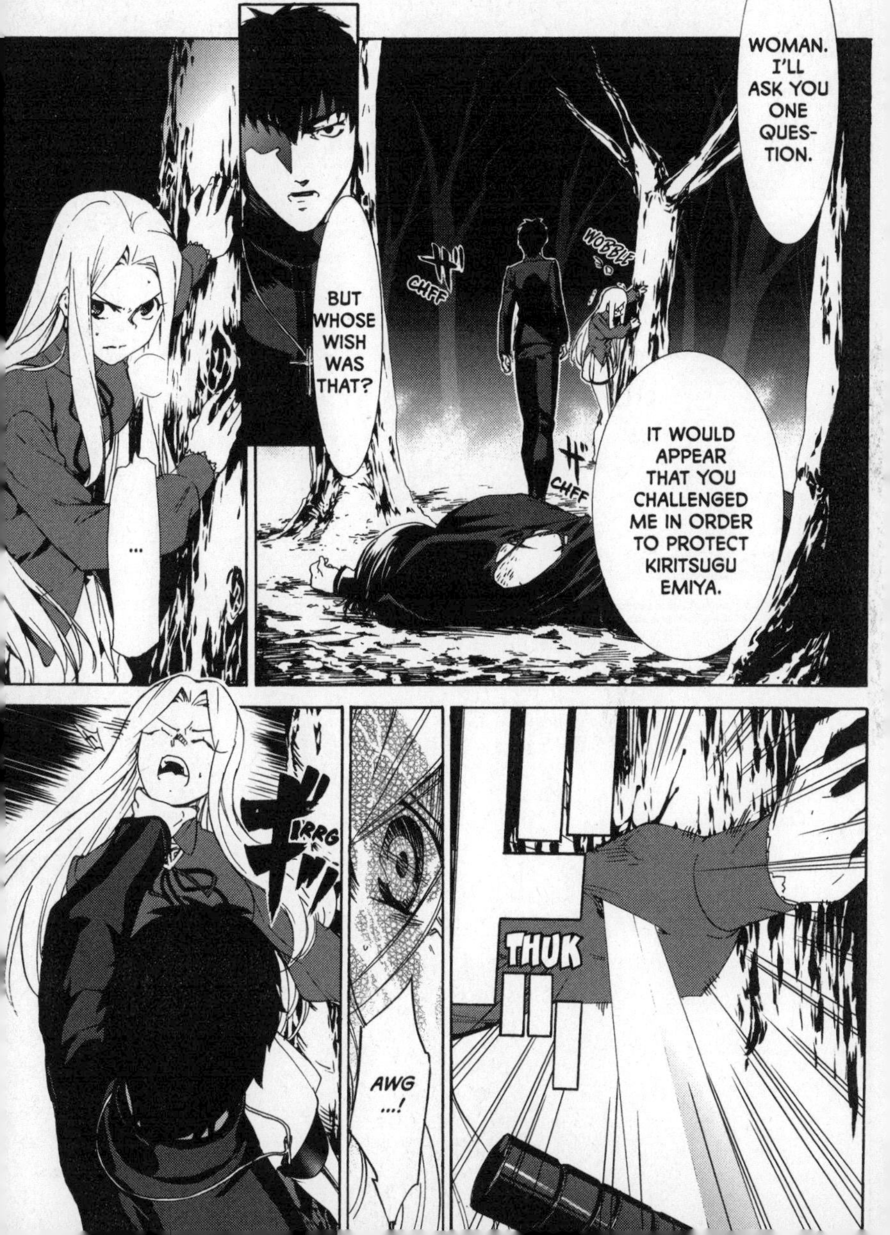
WOMAN. I'LL ASK YOU ONE QUES-TION.
WOBBLE
CHFF
IT WOULD APPEAR THAT YOU CHALLENGED ME IN ORDER TO PROTECT KIRITSUGU EMIYA.
CHFF
BUT WHOSE WISH WAS THAT?
...
THUK
AWG ...!
IRRG

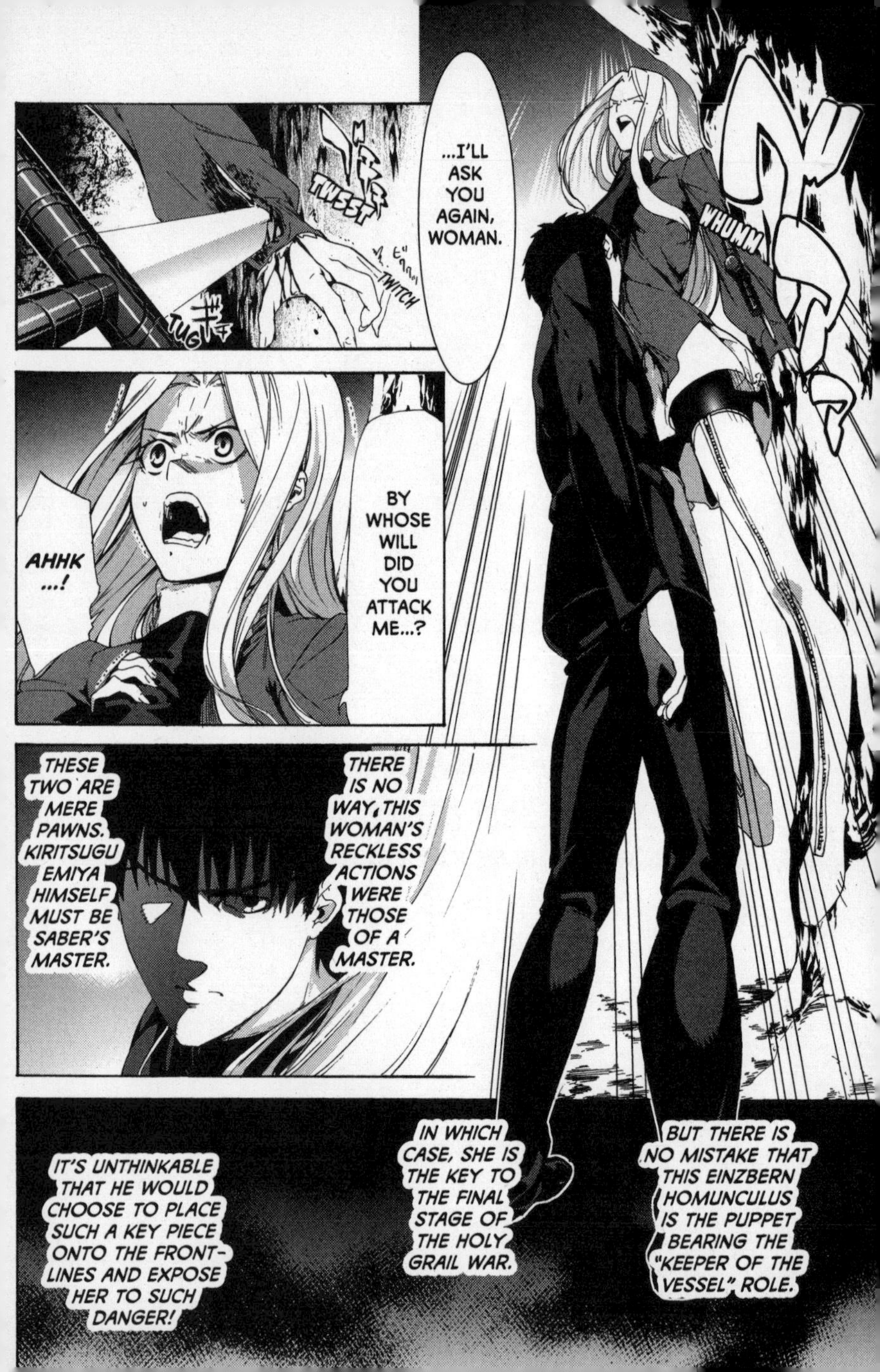

...I'LL ASK YOU AGAIN, WOMAN.
WHUMM
TWSST
TWITCH
TUG
BY WHOSE WILL DID YOU ATTACK ME...?
AHHK ...!
THERE IS NO WAY THIS WOMAN'S RECKLESS ACTIONS WERE THOSE OF A MASTER.
THESE TWO ARE MERE PAWNS. KIRITSUGU EMIYA HIMSELF MUST BE SABER'S MASTER.
BUT THERE IS NO MISTAKE THAT THIS EINZBERN HOMUNCULUS IS THE PUPPET BEARING THE "KEEPER OF THE VESSEL" ROLE.
IN WHICH CASE, SHE IS THE KEY TO THE FINAL STAGE OF THE HOLY GRAIL WAR.
IT'S UNTHINKABLE THAT HE WOULD CHOOSE TO PLACE SUCH A KEY PIECE ONTO THE FRONT-LINES AND EXPOSE HER TO SUCH DANGER!

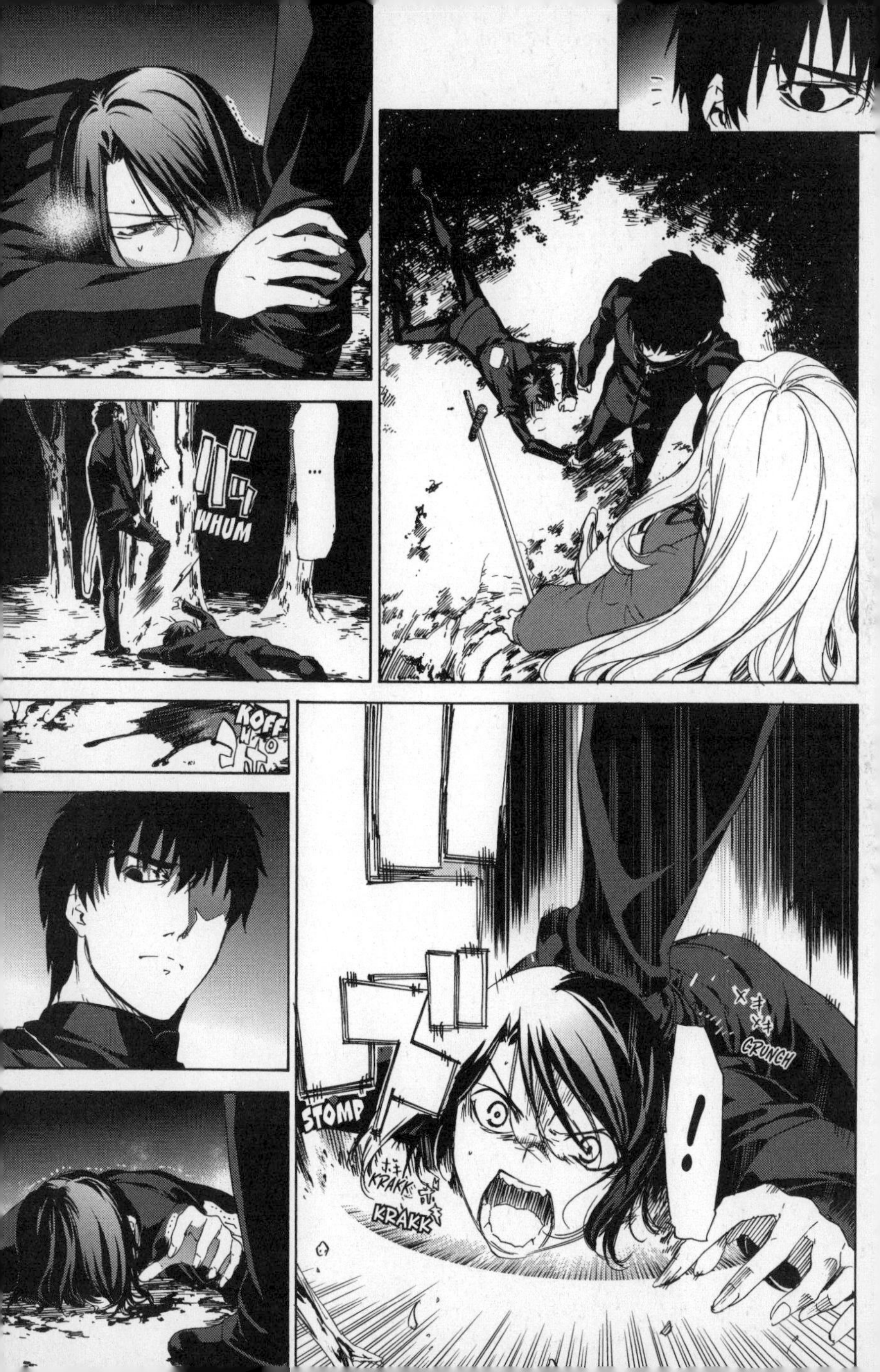
...
WHUM
CRUNCH
!
STOMP
KRAKK
KRAKK
KOFF

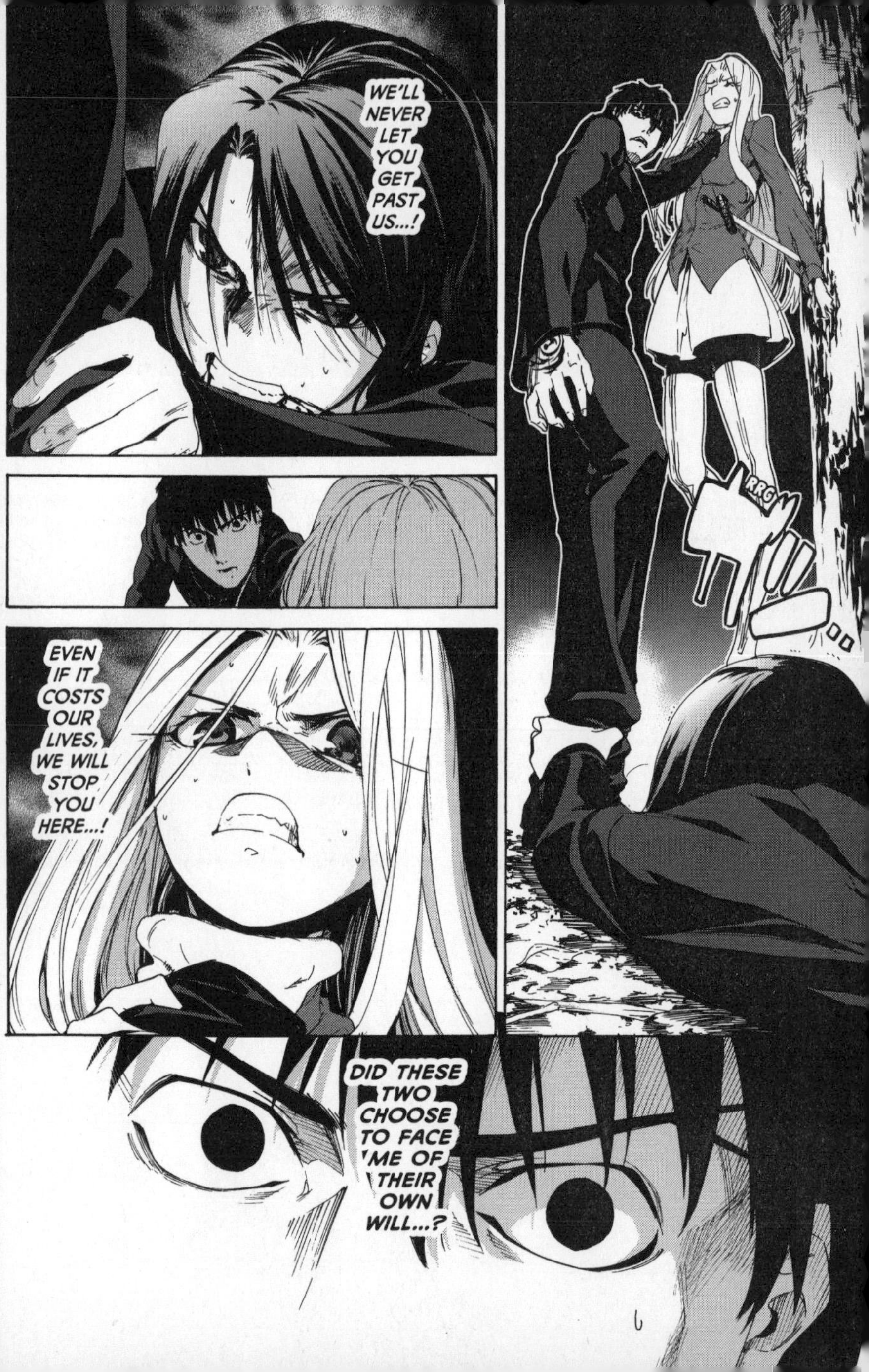
RRG
WE'LL NEVER LET YOU GET PAST US...!
EVEN IF IT COSTS OUR LIVES, WE WILL STOP YOU HERE...!
DID THESE TWO CHOOSE TO FACE ME OF THEIR OWN WILL...?

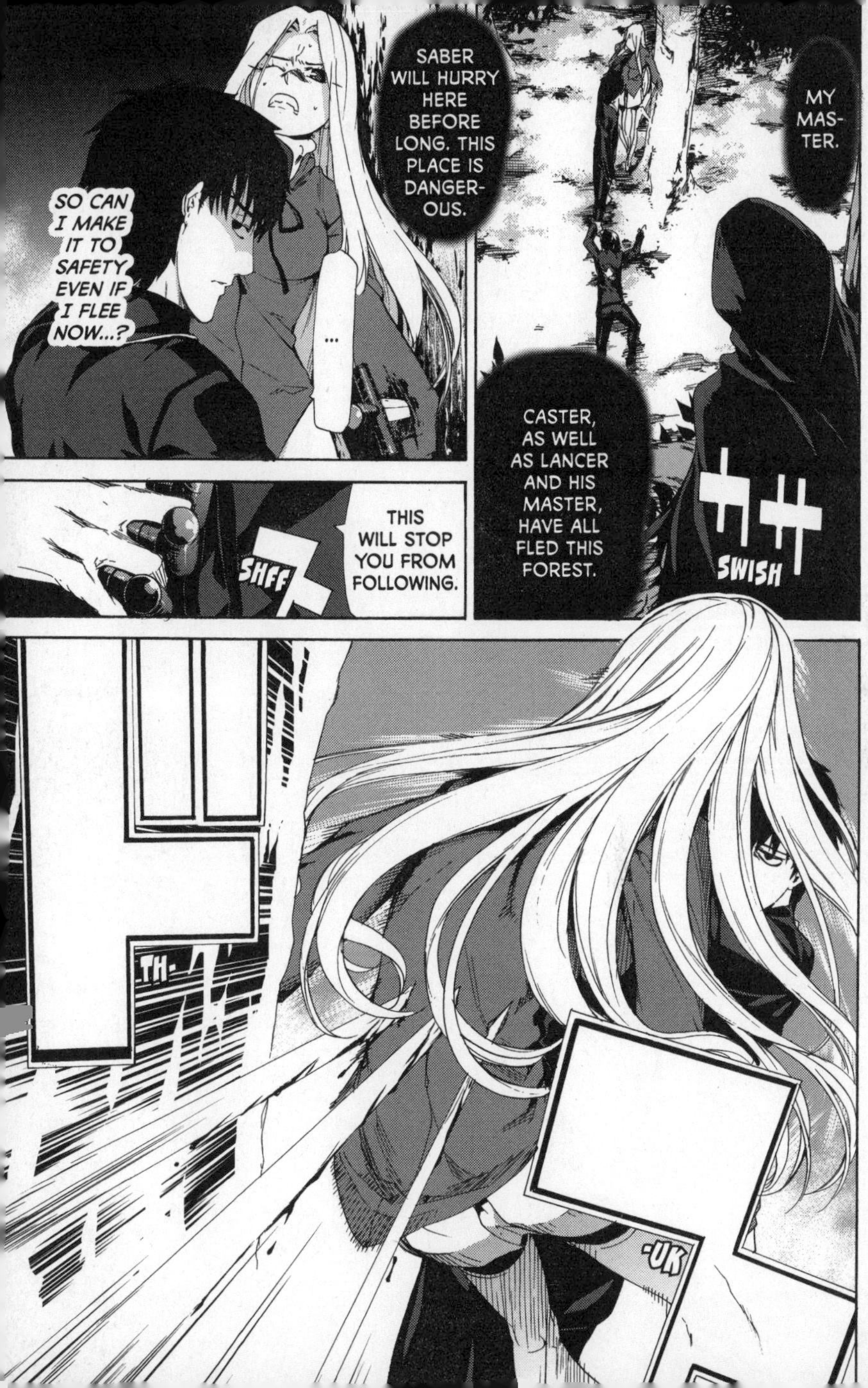

MY MASTER.
CASTER, AS WELL AS LANCER AND HIS MASTER, HAVE ALL FLED THIS FOREST.
SWISH
SABER WILL HURRY HERE BEFORE LONG. THIS PLACE IS DANGEROUS.
SO CAN I MAKE IT TO SAFETY EVEN IF I FLEE NOW...?
...
THIS WILL STOP YOU FROM FOLLOWING.
SHFF
TH-
-UK

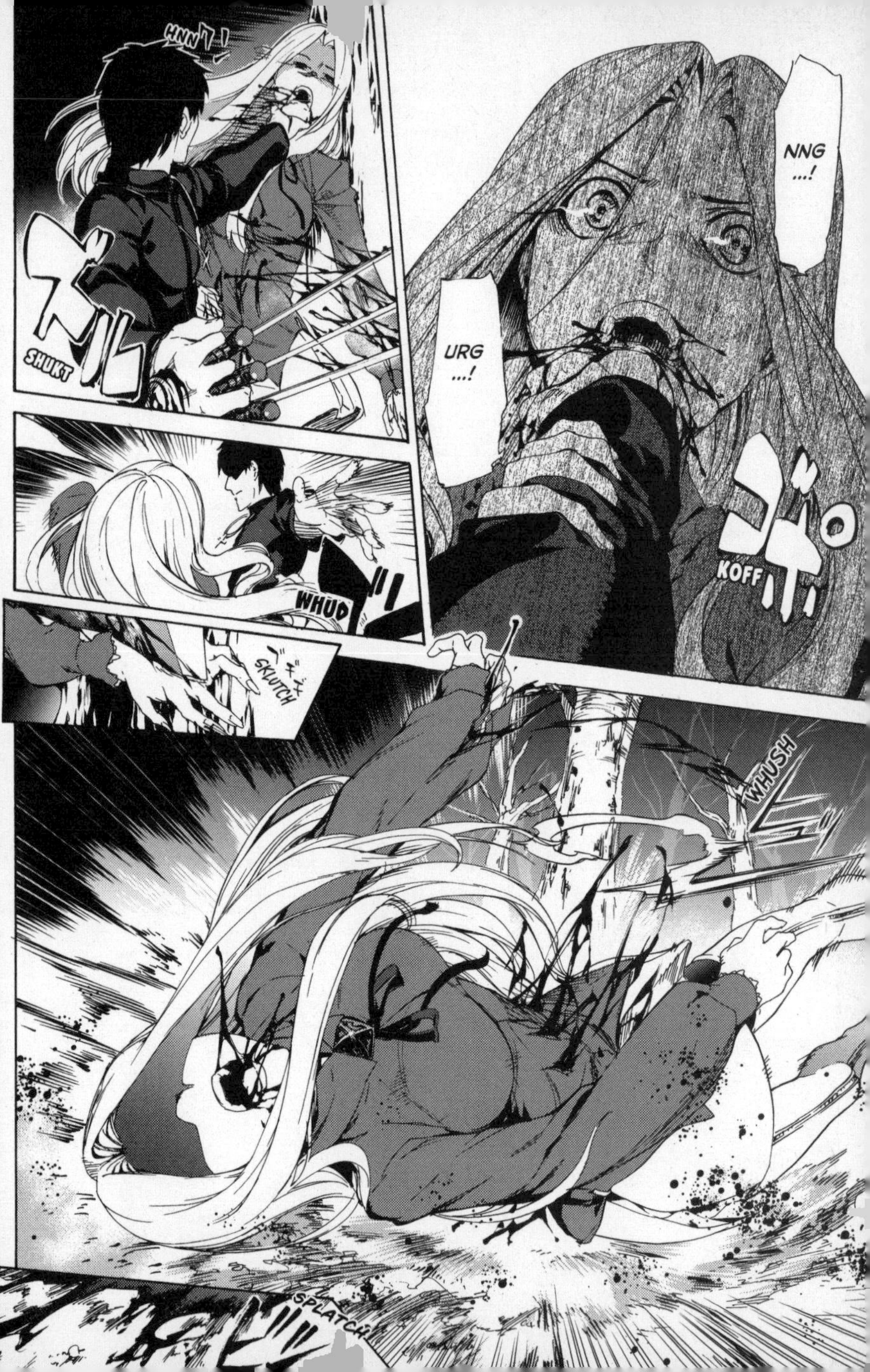
NNG
...!
URG
...!
KOFF
HNN !
SHUKT
WHUD
SKLUTCH
WHUSH
SPLATCH

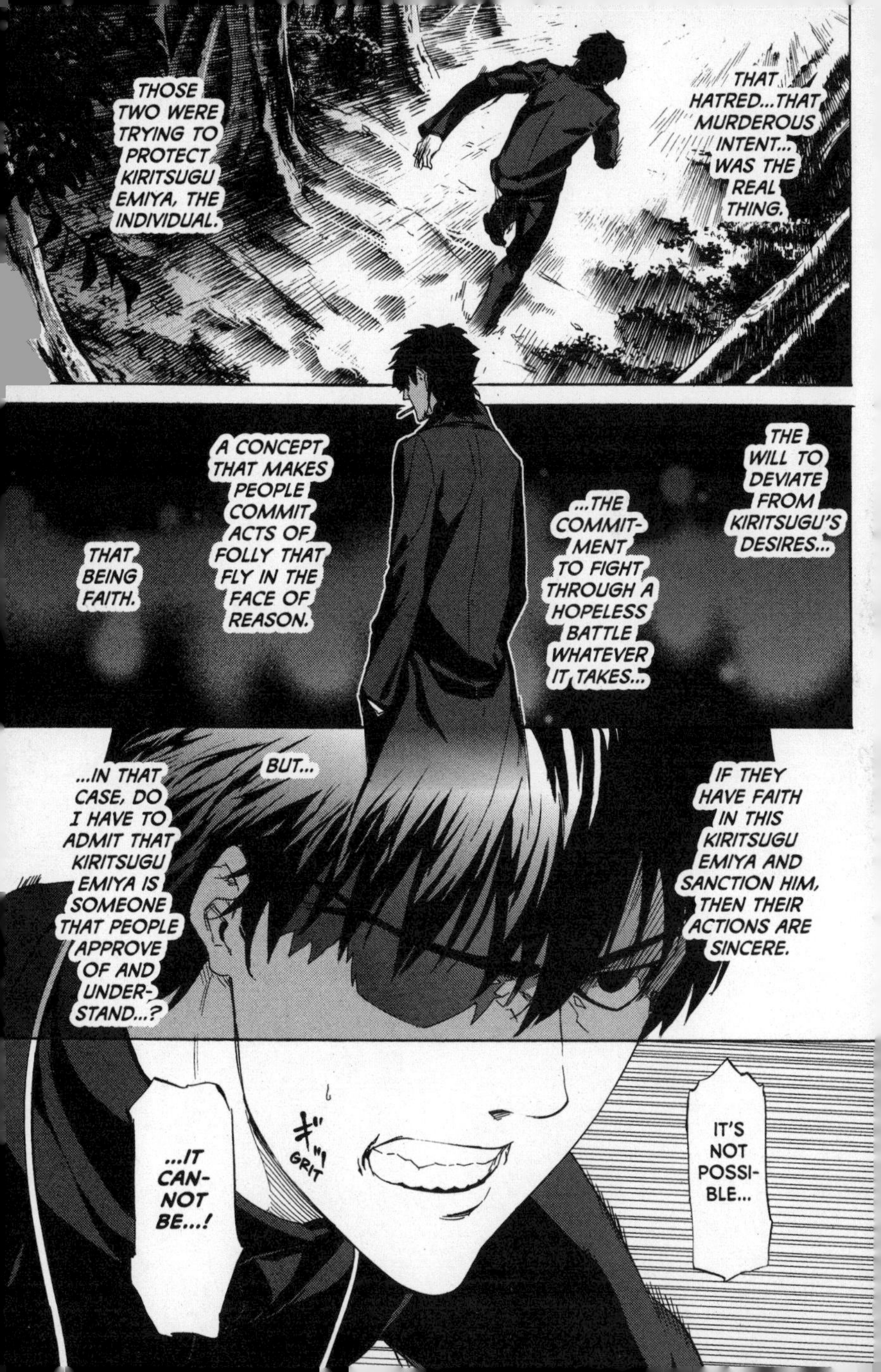
THAT HATRED...THAT MURDEROUS INTENT... WAS THE REAL THING.
THOSE TWO WERE TRYING TO PROTECT KIRITSUGU EMIYA, THE INDIVIDUAL.
THE WILL TO DEVIATE FROM KIRITSUGU'S DESIRES...
...THE COMMIT-MENT TO FIGHT THROUGH A HOPELESS BATTLE WHATEVER IT TAKES...
A CONCEPT THAT MAKES PEOPLE COMMIT ACTS OF FOLLY THAT FLY IN THE FACE OF REASON.
THAT BEING FAITH.
IF THEY HAVE FAITH IN THIS KIRITSUGU EMIYA AND SANCTION HIM, THEN THEIR ACTIONS ARE SINCERE.
BUT...
...IN THAT CASE, DO I HAVE TO ADMIT THAT KIRITSUGU EMIYA IS SOMEONE THAT PEOPLE APPROVE OF AND UNDER-STAND...?
IT'S NOT POSSI-BLE...
ギリ
GRIT
...IT CAN-NOT BE...!

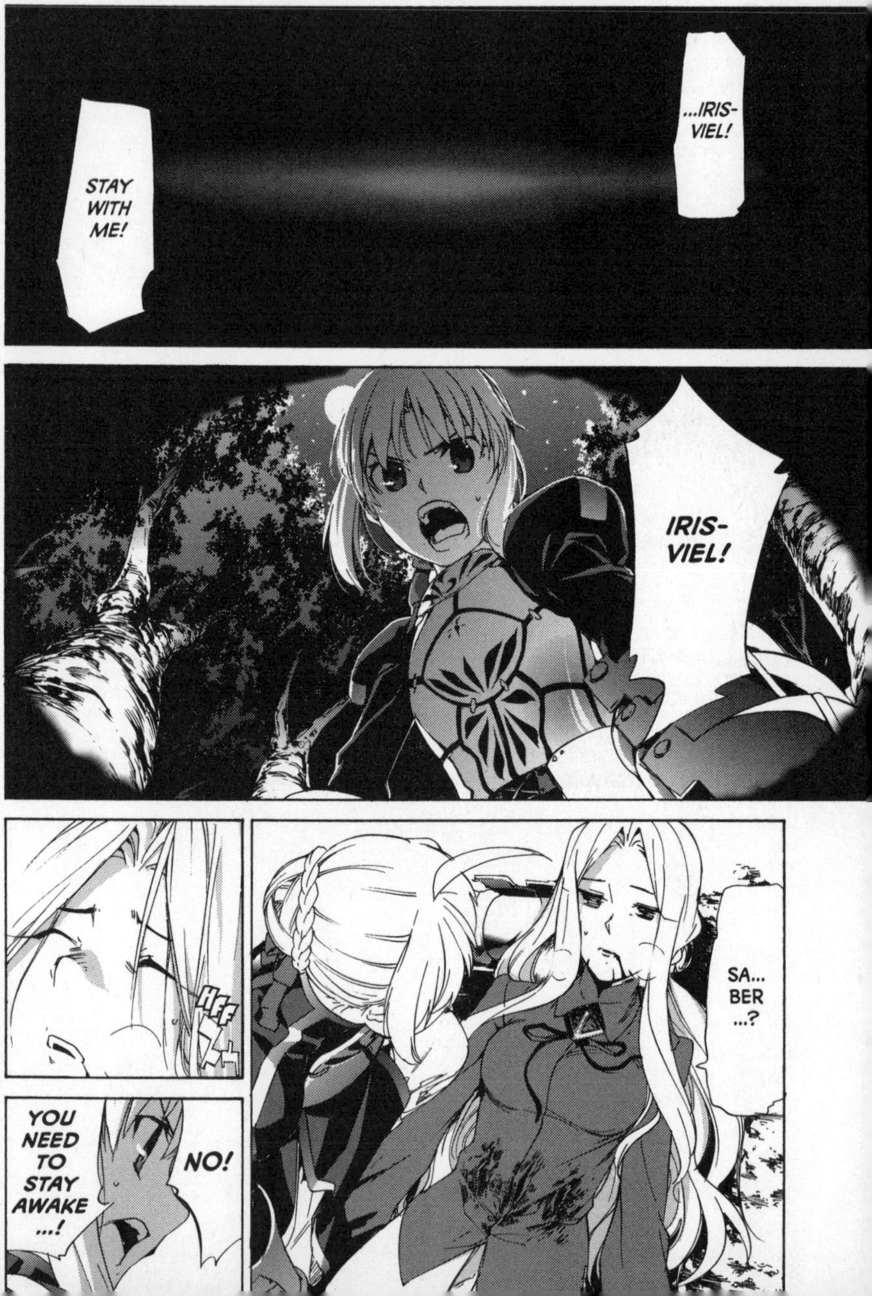
...IRIS-VIEL!
STAY WITH ME!
IRIS-VIEL!
SA... BER ...?
HFF
NO!
YOU NEED TO STAY AWAKE ...!

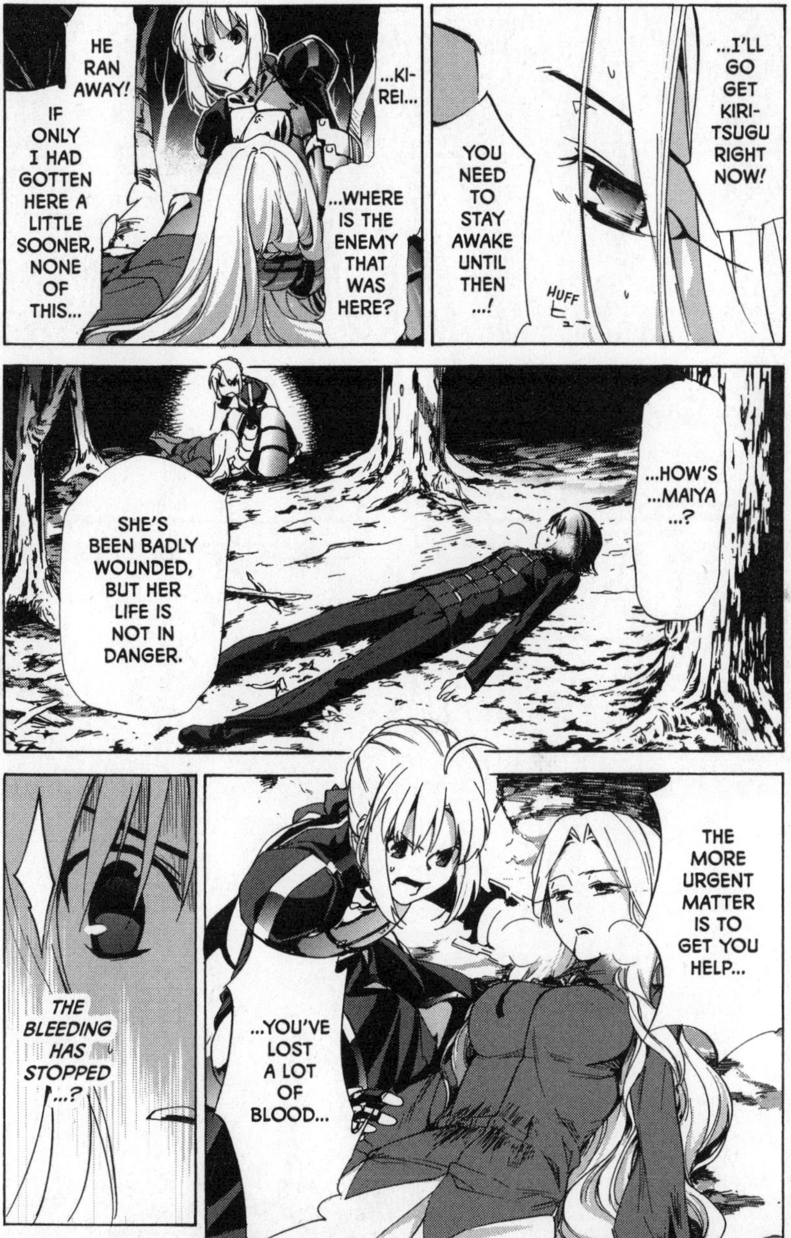
...I'LL GO GET KIRI-TSUGU RIGHT NOW!
YOU NEED TO STAY AWAKE UNTIL THEN ...!
HUFF
...KI-REI...
...WHERE IS THE ENEMY THAT WAS HERE?
HE RAN AWAY!
IF ONLY I HAD GOTTEN HERE A LITTLE SOONER, NONE OF THIS...
...HOW'S ...MAIYA ...?
SHE'S BEEN BADLY WOUNDED, BUT HER LIFE IS NOT IN DANGER.
THE MORE URGENT MATTER IS TO GET YOU HELP...
...YOU'VE LOST A LOT OF BLOOD...
THE BLEEDING HAS STOPPED ...?

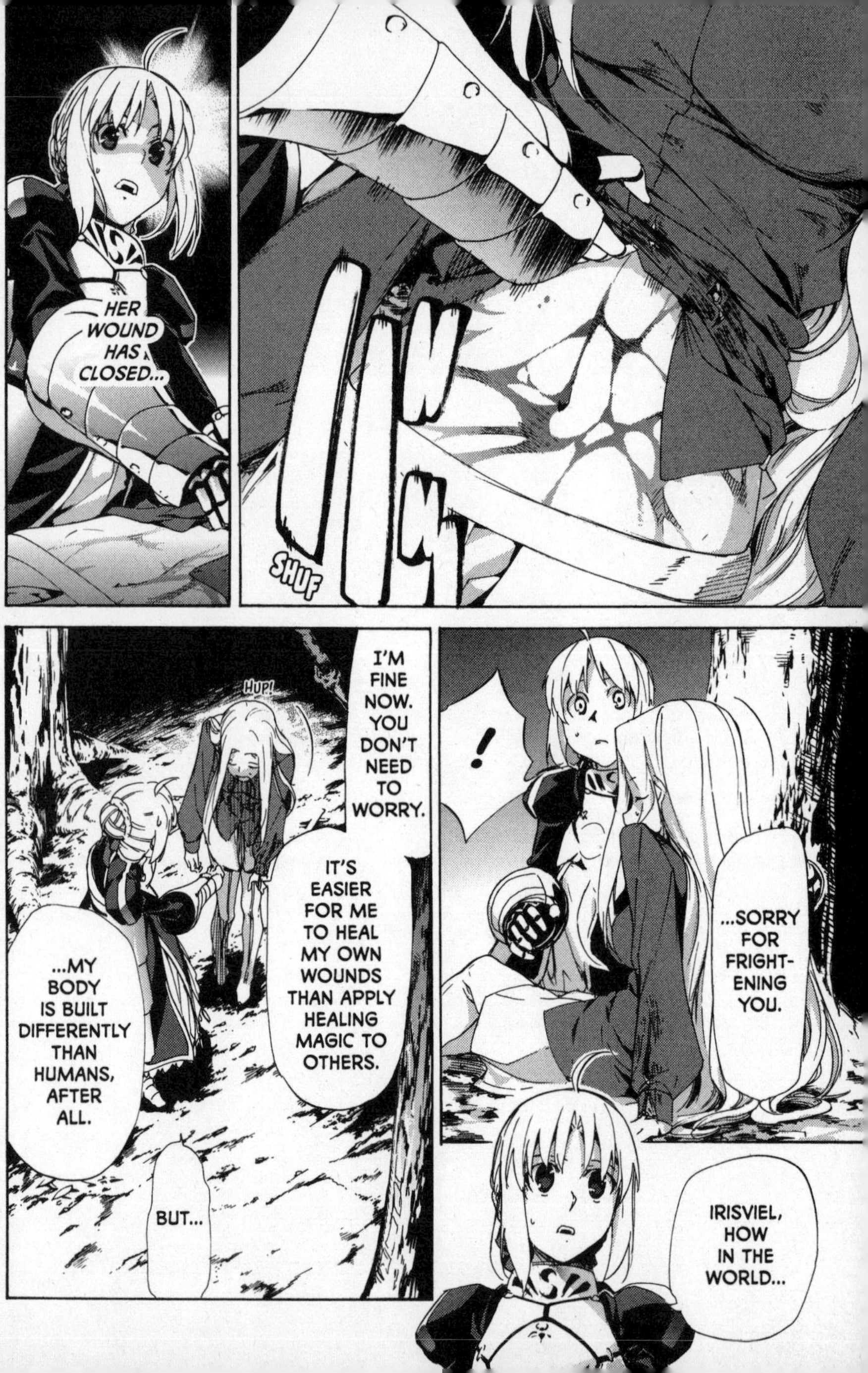
SHUF
HER WOUND HAS CLOSED...
!
...SORRY FOR FRIGHT-ENING YOU.
IRISVIEL, HOW IN THE WORLD...
HUP!
I'M FINE NOW. YOU DON'T NEED TO WORRY.
IT'S EASIER FOR ME TO HEAL MY OWN WOUNDS THAN APPLY HEALING MAGIC TO OTHERS.
...MY BODY IS BUILT DIFFERENTLY THAN HUMANS, AFTER ALL.
BUT...

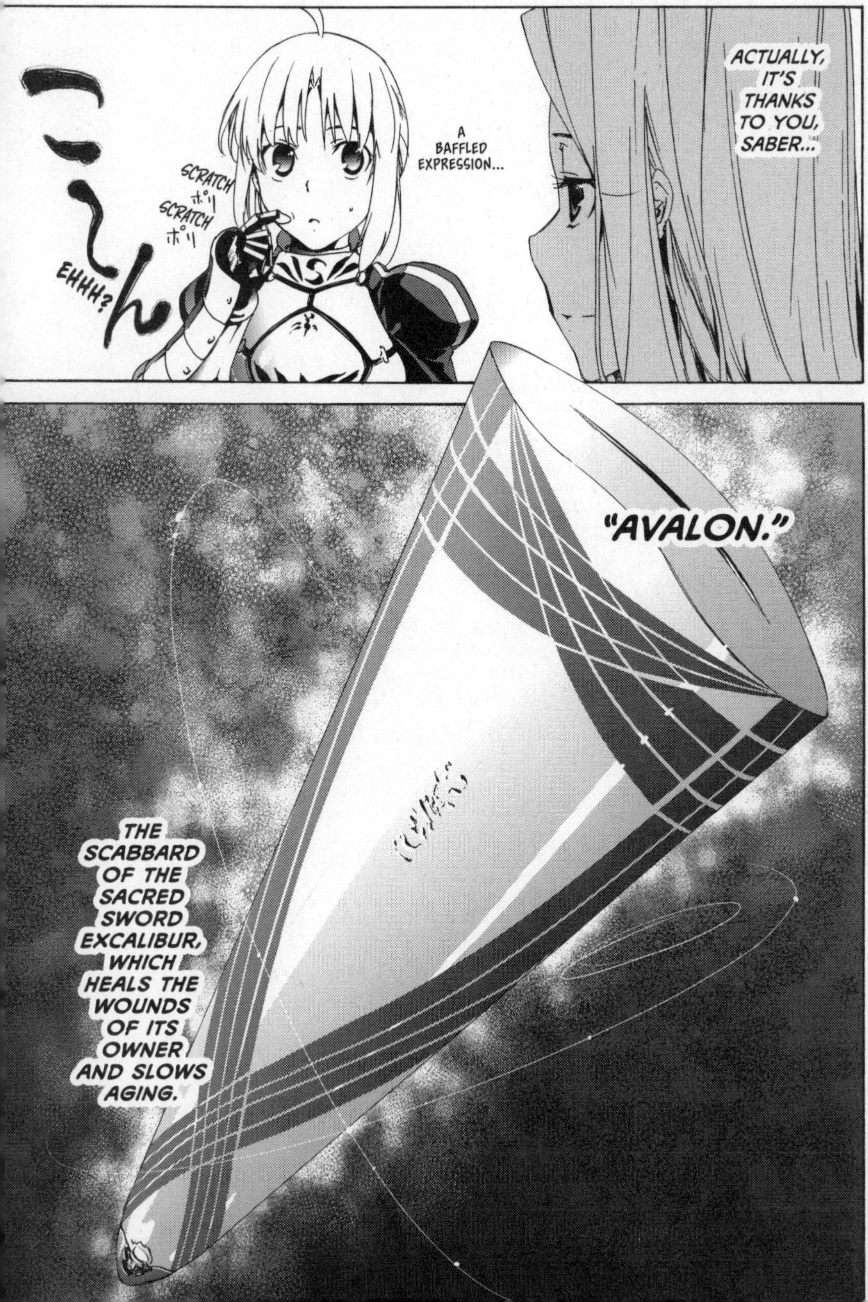
ACTUALLY, IT'S THANKS TO YOU, SABER...
A BAFFLED EXPRESSION...
SCRATCH ポリ
SCRATCH ポリ
EHHH?
"AVALON."
THE SCABBARD OF THE SACRED SWORD EXCALIBUR, WHICH HEALS THE WOUNDS OF ITS OWNER AND SLOWS AGING.

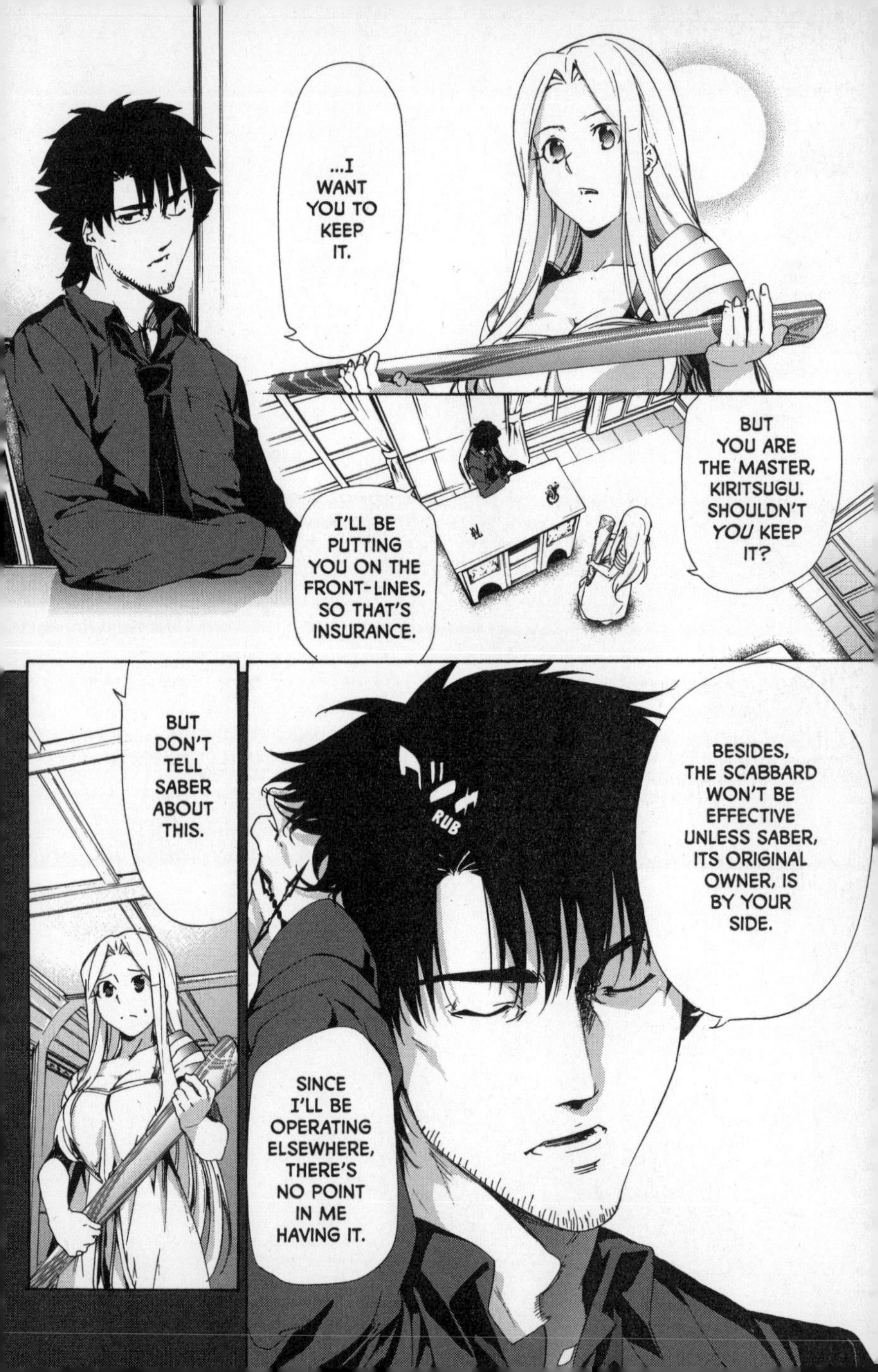
...I WANT YOU TO KEEP IT.
BUT YOU ARE THE MASTER, KIRITSUGU. SHOULDN'T *YOU* KEEP IT?
I'LL BE PUTTING YOU ON THE FRONT-LINES, SO THAT'S INSURANCE.
RUB
BESIDES, THE SCABBARD WON'T BE EFFECTIVE UNLESS SABER, ITS ORIGINAL OWNER, IS BY YOUR SIDE.
SINCE I'LL BE OPERATING ELSEWHERE, THERE'S NO POINT IN ME HAVING IT.
BUT DON'T TELL SABER ABOUT THIS.

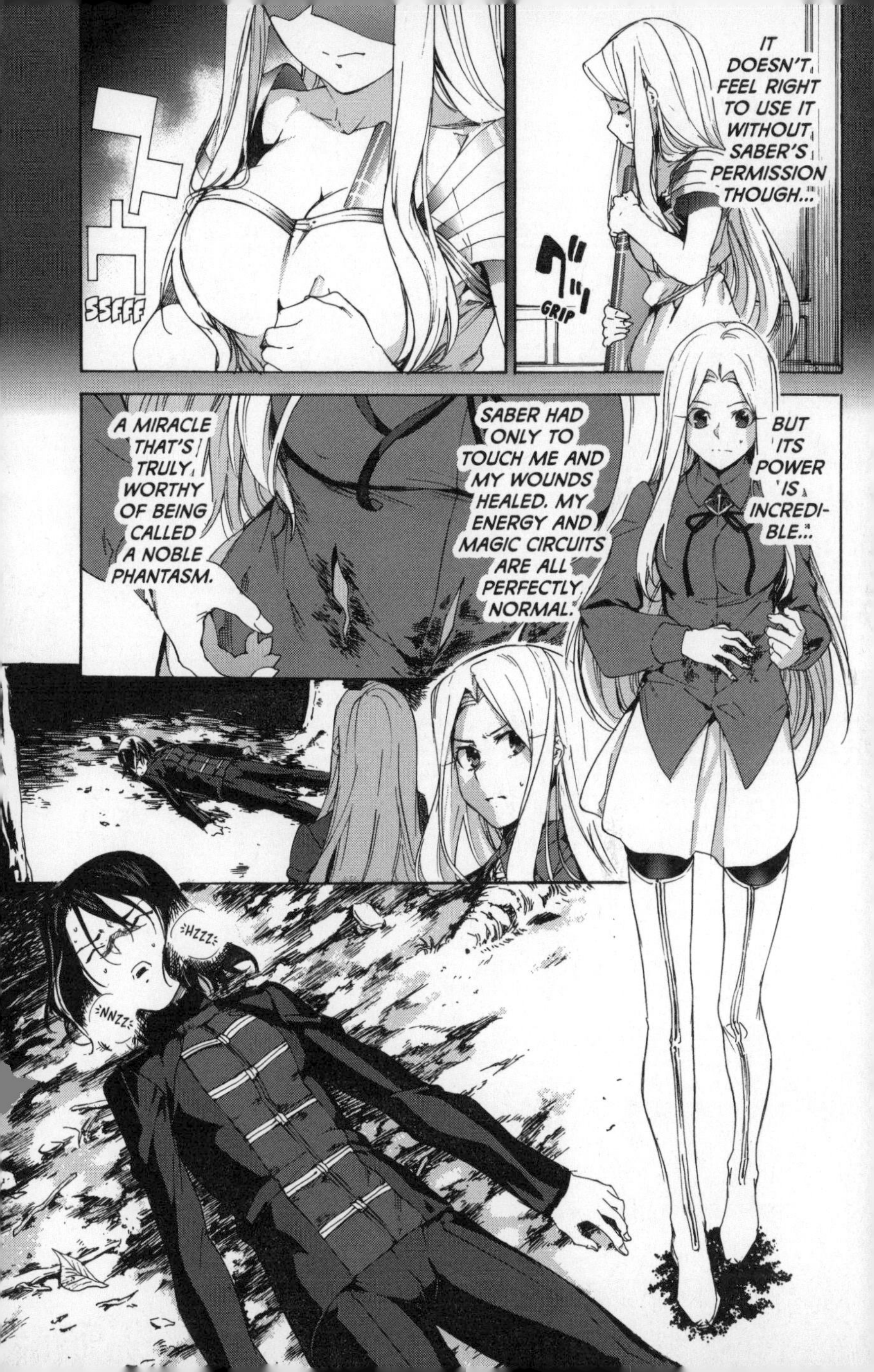
IT DOESN'T FEEL RIGHT TO USE IT WITHOUT SABER'S PERMISSION THOUGH...
GRIP
SSFFF
BUT ITS POWER IS INCREDIBLE...
SABER HAD ONLY TO TOUCH ME AND MY WOUNDS HEALED. MY ENERGY AND MAGIC CIRCUITS ARE ALL PERFECTLY NORMAL.
A MIRACLE THAT'S TRULY WORTHY OF BEING CALLED A NOBLE PHANTASM.
HZZZ
NNZZ

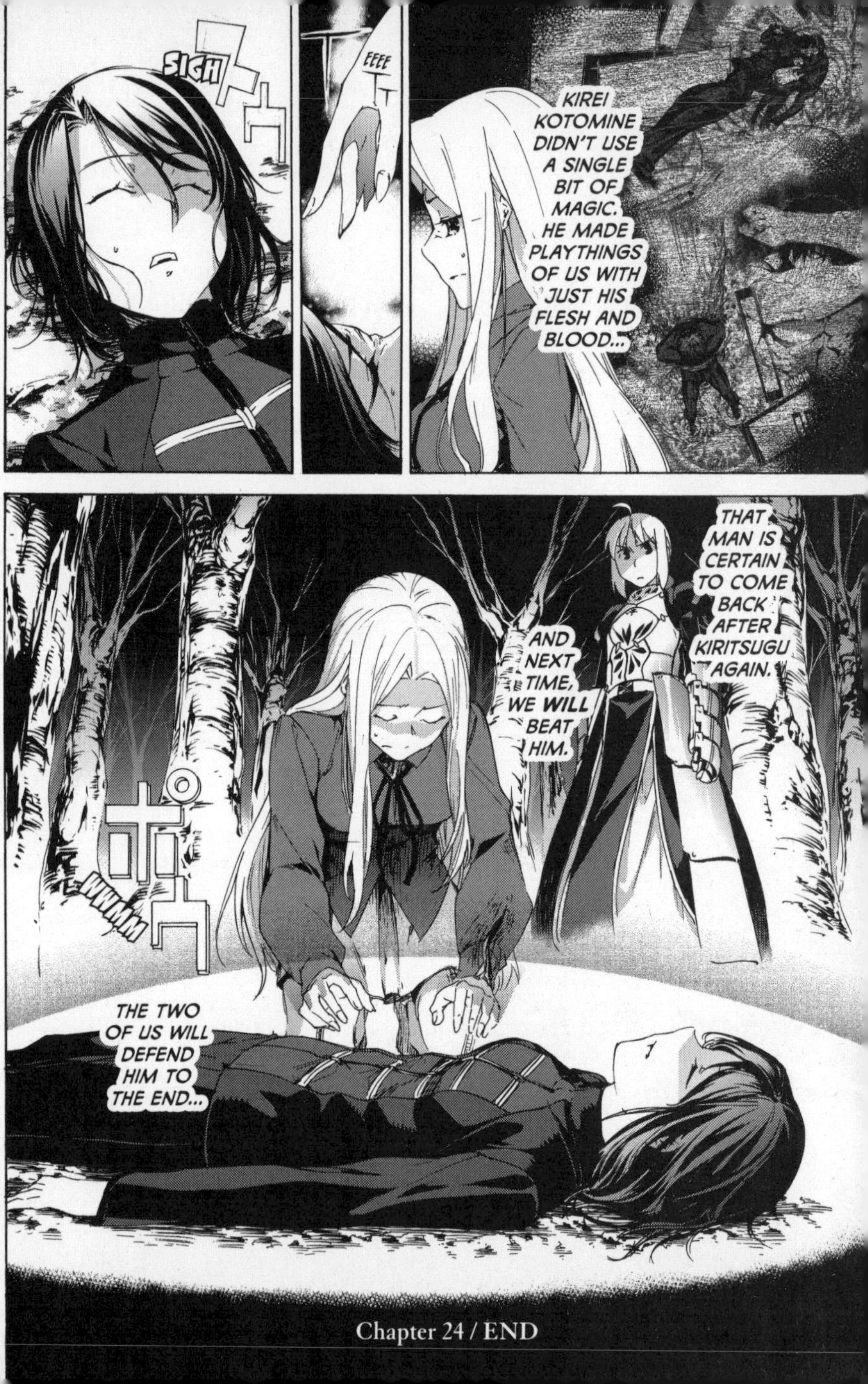
KIREI KOTOMINE DIDN'T USE A SINGLE BIT OF MAGIC. HE MADE PLAYTHINGS OF US WITH JUST HIS FLESH AND BLOOD...
EEEE
SIGH
THAT MAN IS CERTAIN TO COME BACK AFTER KIRITSUGU AGAIN.
AND NEXT TIME, WE **WILL** BEAT HIM.
WWMM
THE TWO OF US WILL DEFEND HIM TO THE END...
Chapter 24 / END

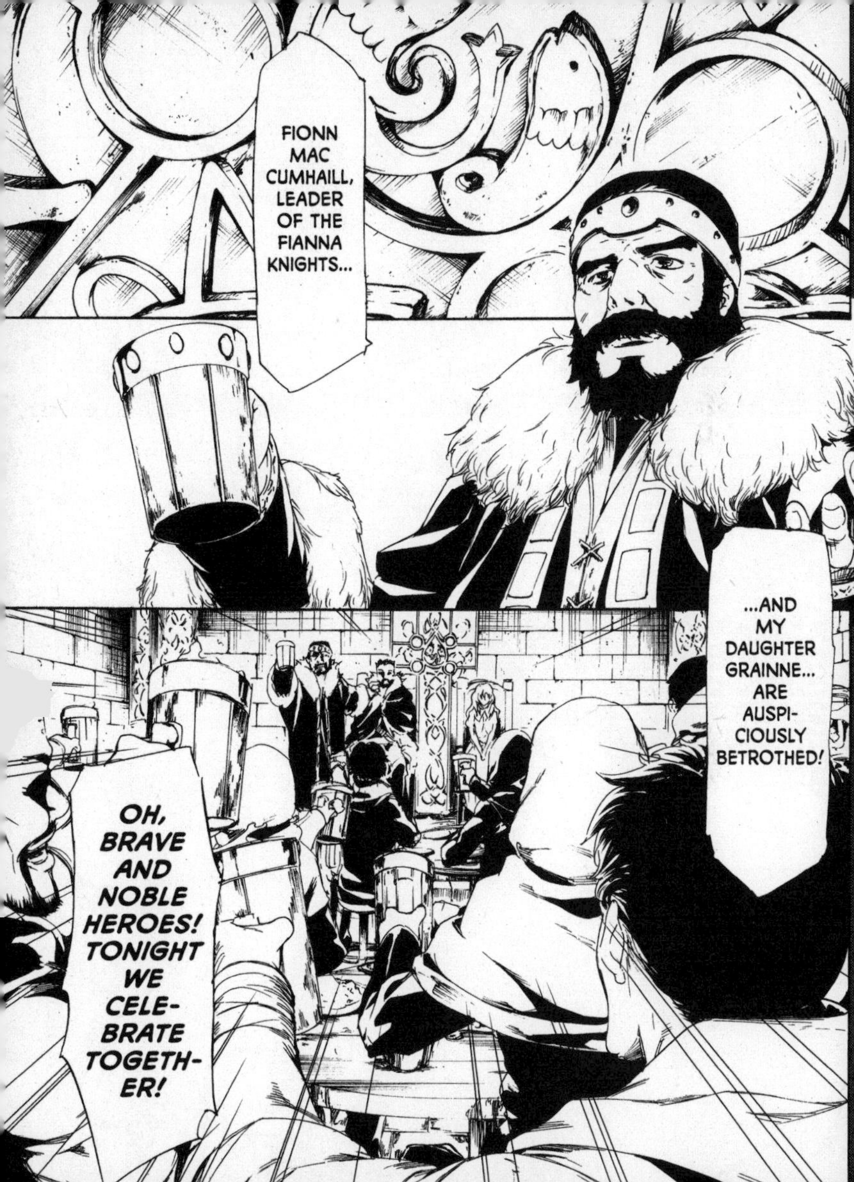
FIONN MAC CUMHAILL, LEADER OF THE FIANNA KNIGHTS...
...AND MY DAUGHTER GRAINNE... ARE AUSPICIOUSLY BETROTHED!
OH, BRAVE AND NOBLE HEROES! TONIGHT WE CELEBRATE TOGETHER!

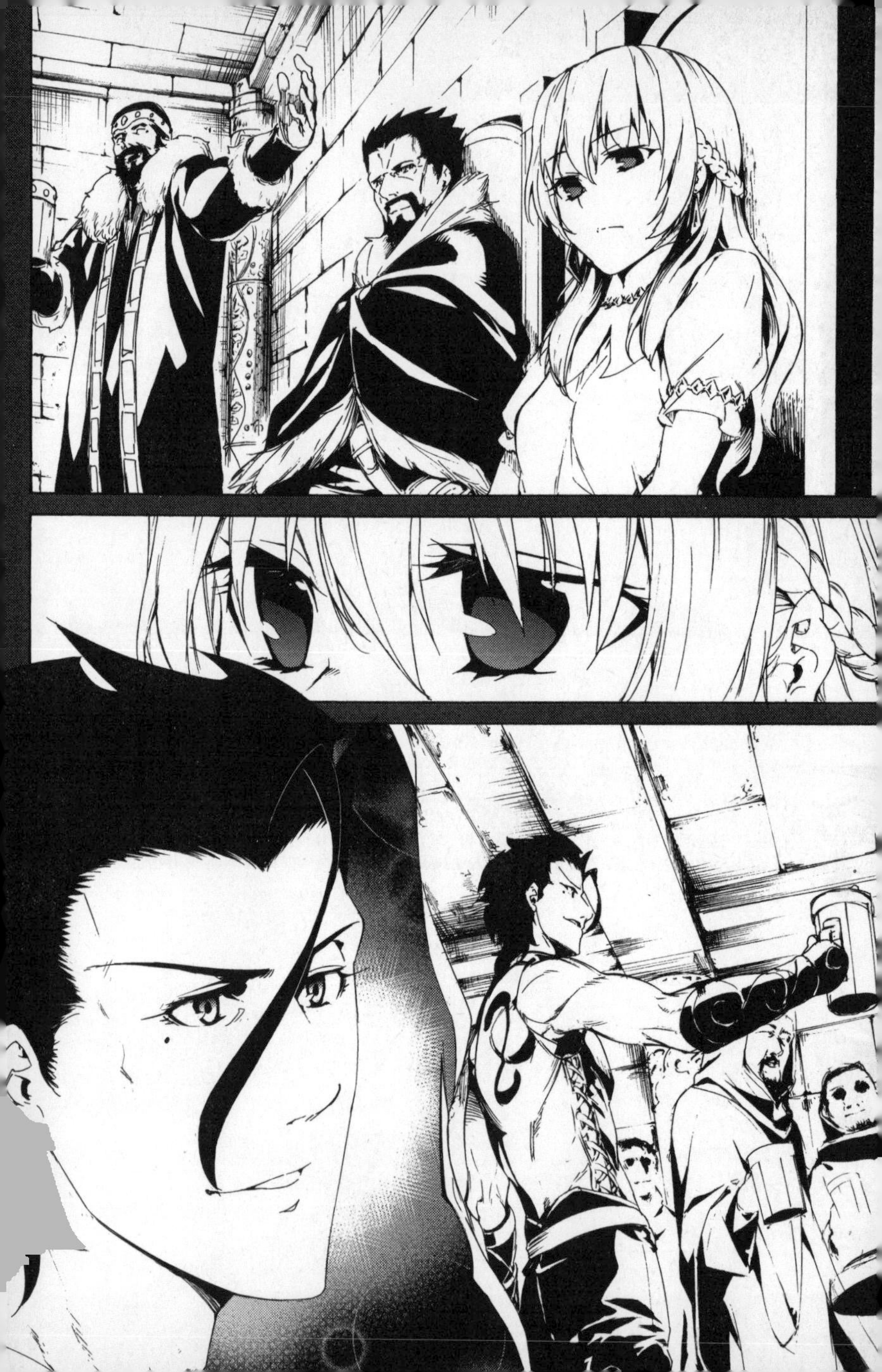

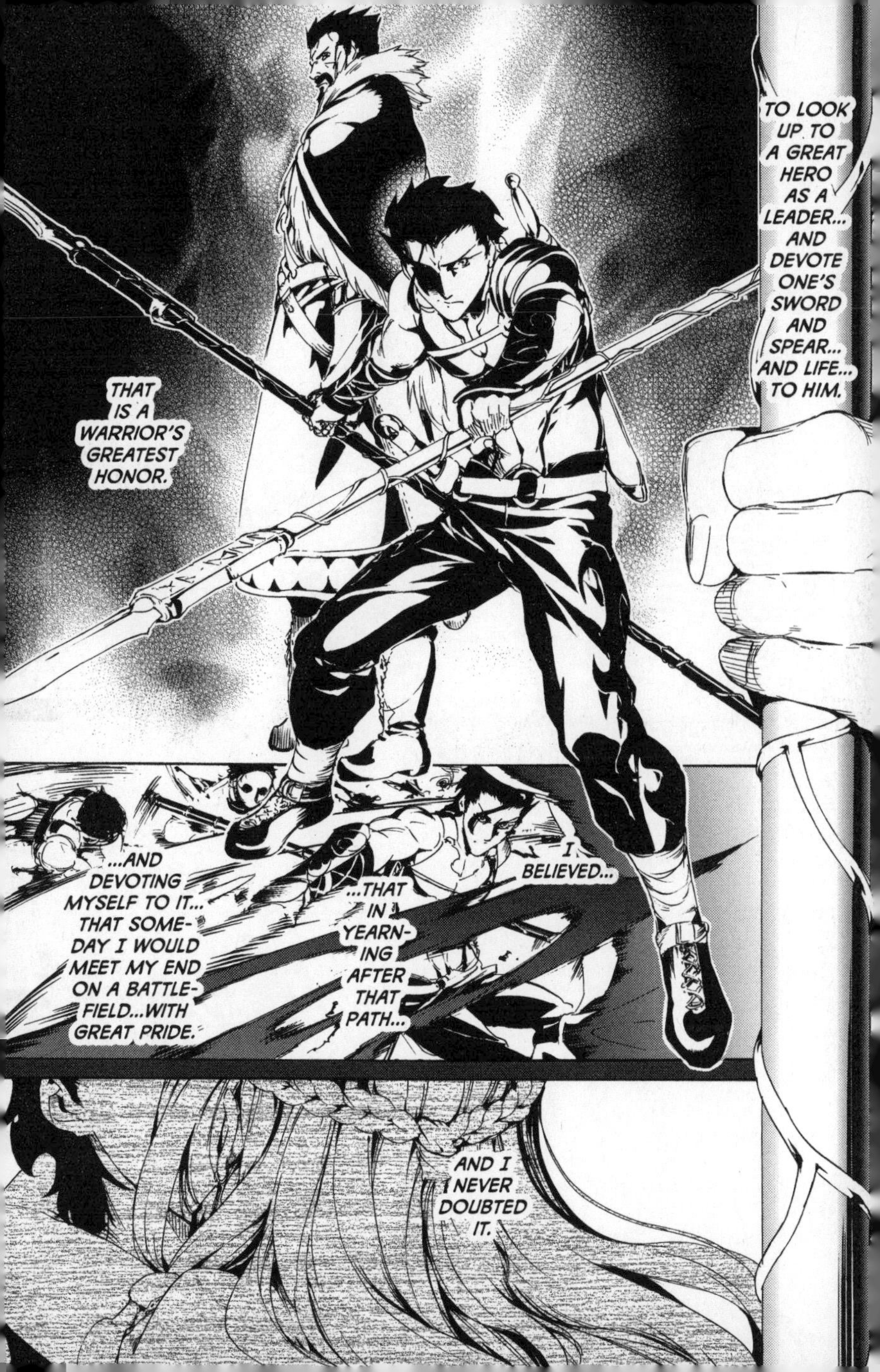
TO LOOK UP TO A GREAT HERO AS A LEADER... AND DEVOTE ONE'S SWORD AND SPEAR... AND LIFE... TO HIM.
THAT IS A WARRIOR'S GREATEST HONOR.
I BELIEVED...
...THAT IN YEARN-ING AFTER THAT PATH...
...AND DEVOTING MYSELF TO IT... THAT SOME-DAY I WOULD MEET MY END ON A BATTLE-FIELD...WITH GREAT PRIDE.
AND I NEVER DOUBTED IT.

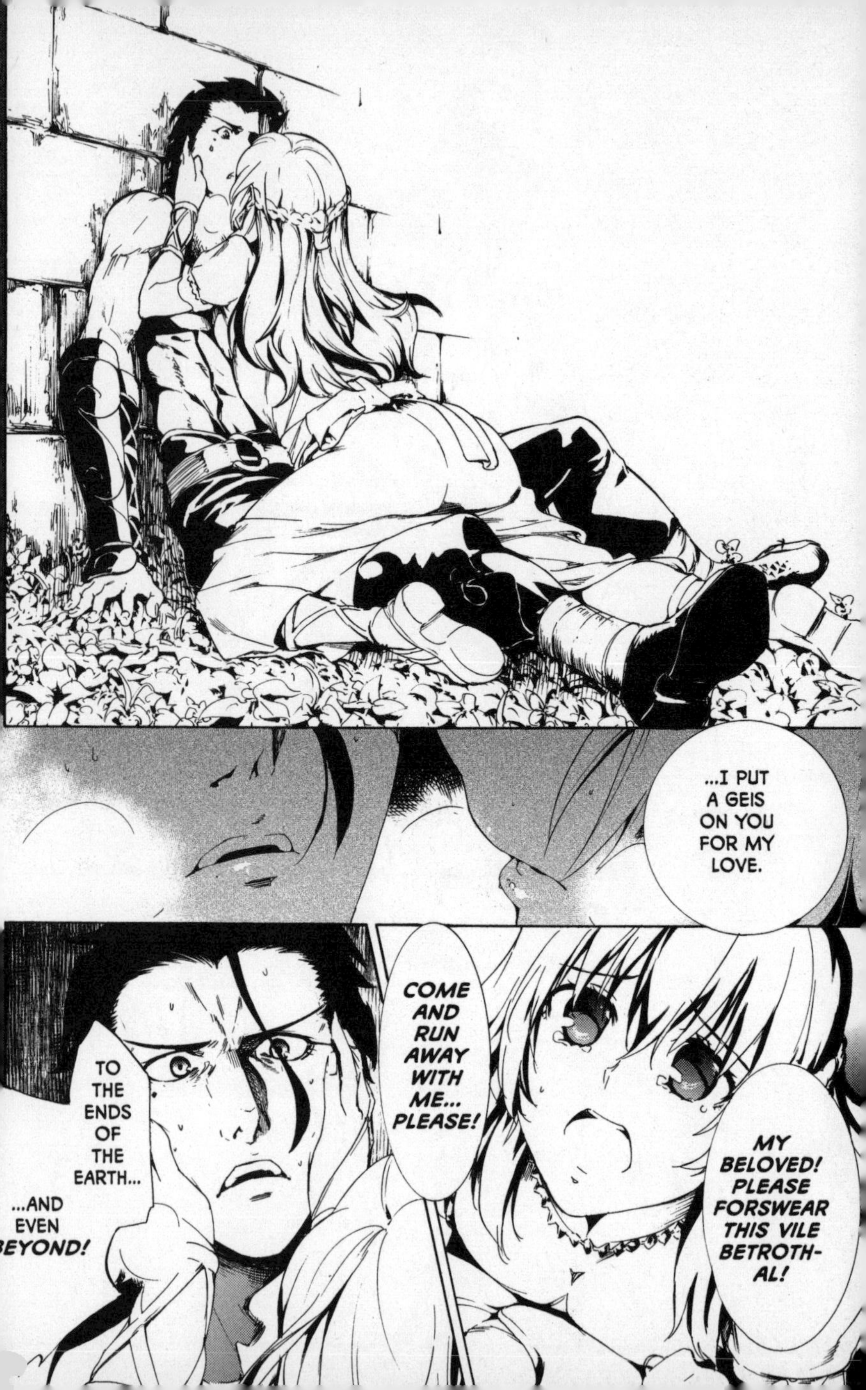
...I PUT A GEIS ON YOU FOR MY LOVE.
MY BELOVED! PLEASE FORSWEAR THIS VILE BETROTH-AL!
COME AND RUN AWAY WITH ME... PLEASE!
TO THE ENDS OF THE EARTH...
...AND EVEN BEYOND!

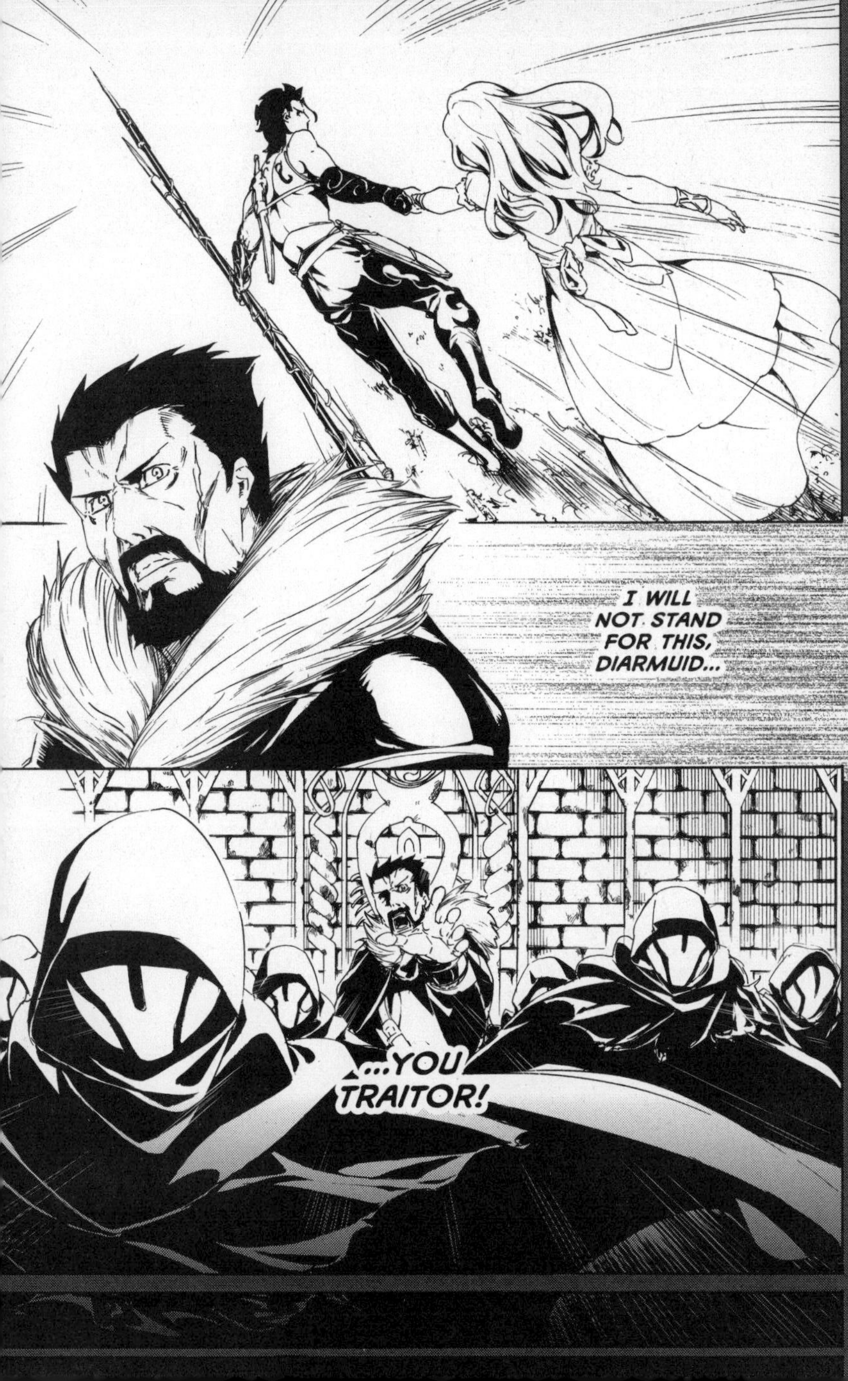
I WILL NOT STAND FOR THIS, DIARMUID...
...YOU TRAITOR!

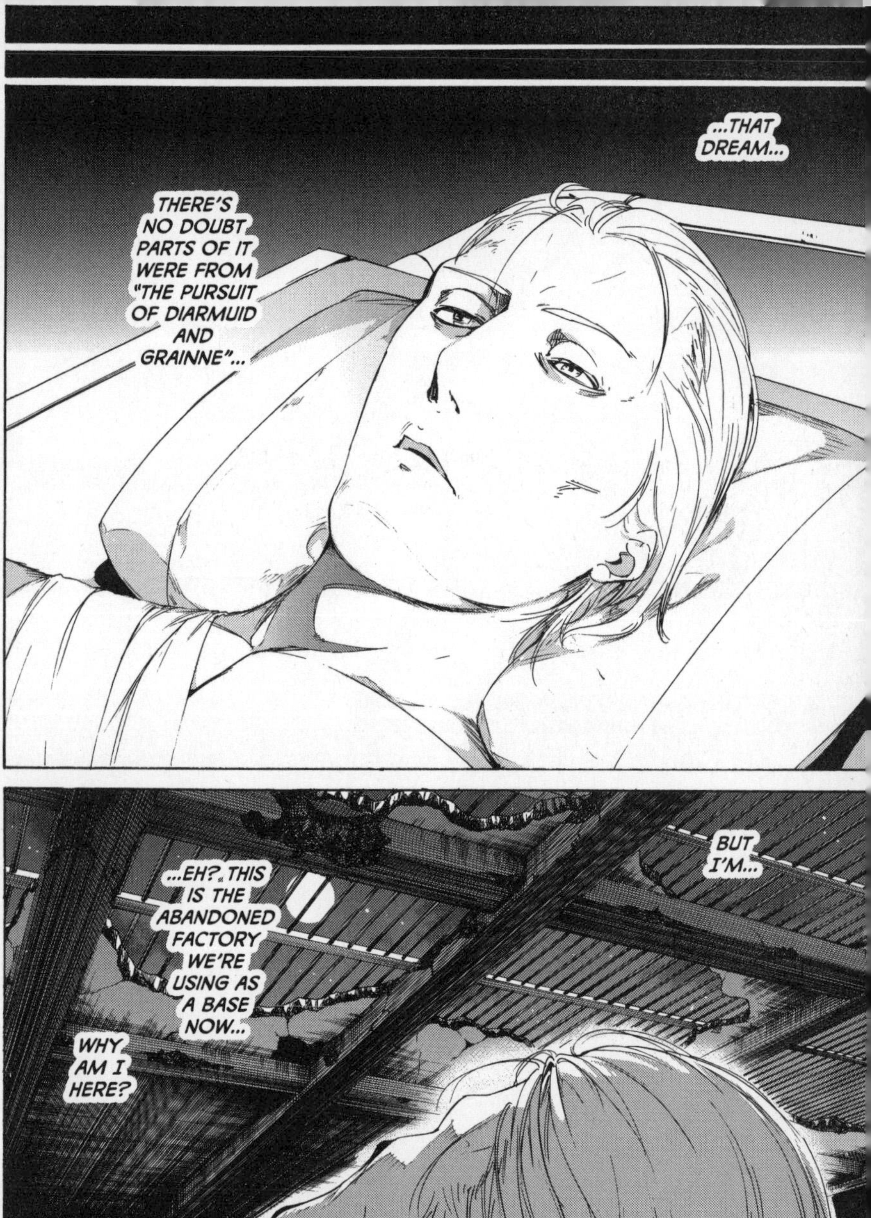
...THAT DREAM...
THERE'S NO DOUBT PARTS OF IT WERE FROM "THE PURSUIT OF DIARMUID AND GRAINNE"...
BUT I'M...
...EH? THIS IS THE ABANDONED FACTORY WE'RE USING AS A BASE NOW...
WHY AM I HERE?

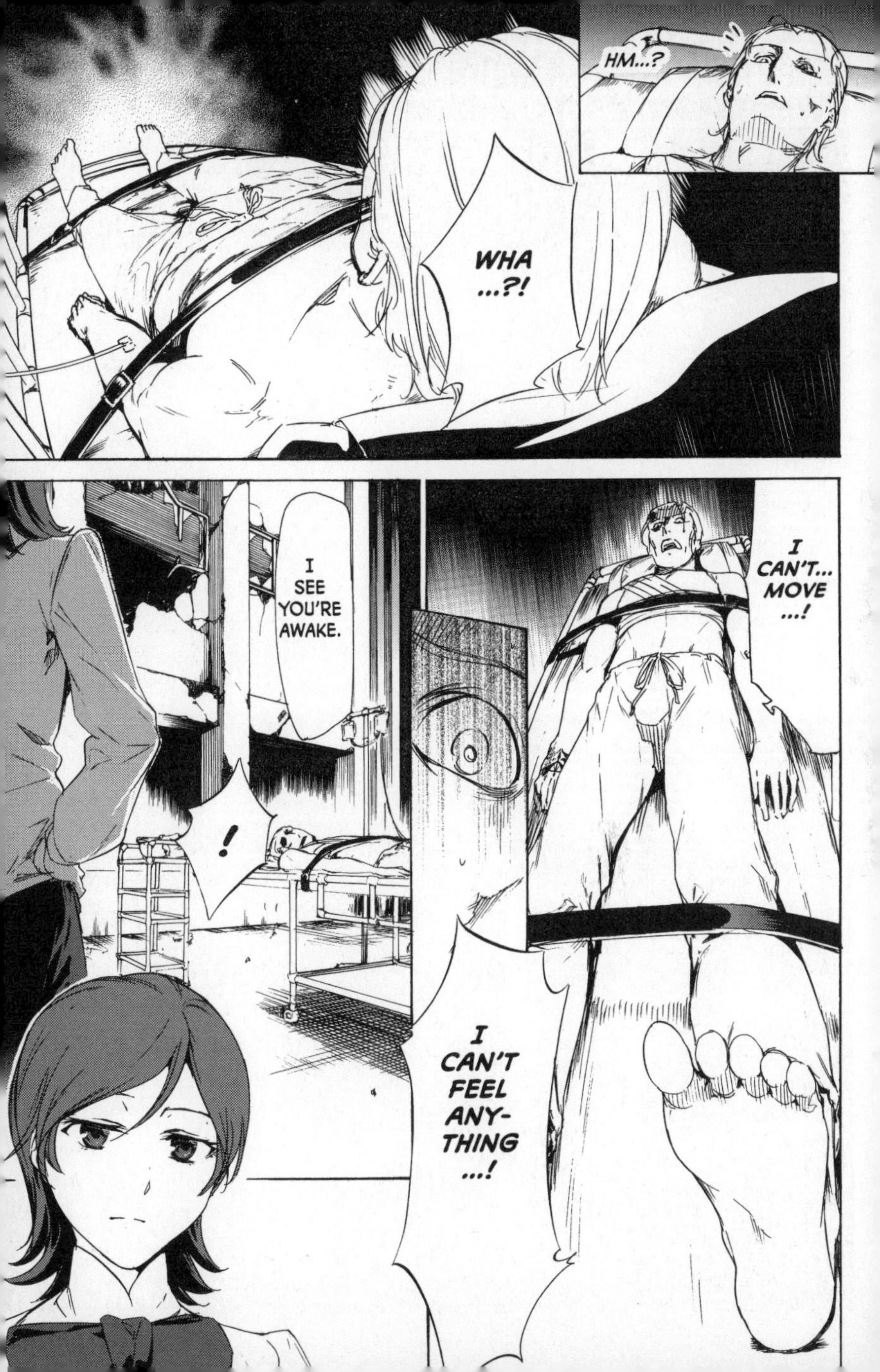
HM...?
WHA ...?!
I CAN'T... MOVE ...!
I CAN'T FEEL ANY-THING ...!
I SEE YOU'RE AWAKE.
!

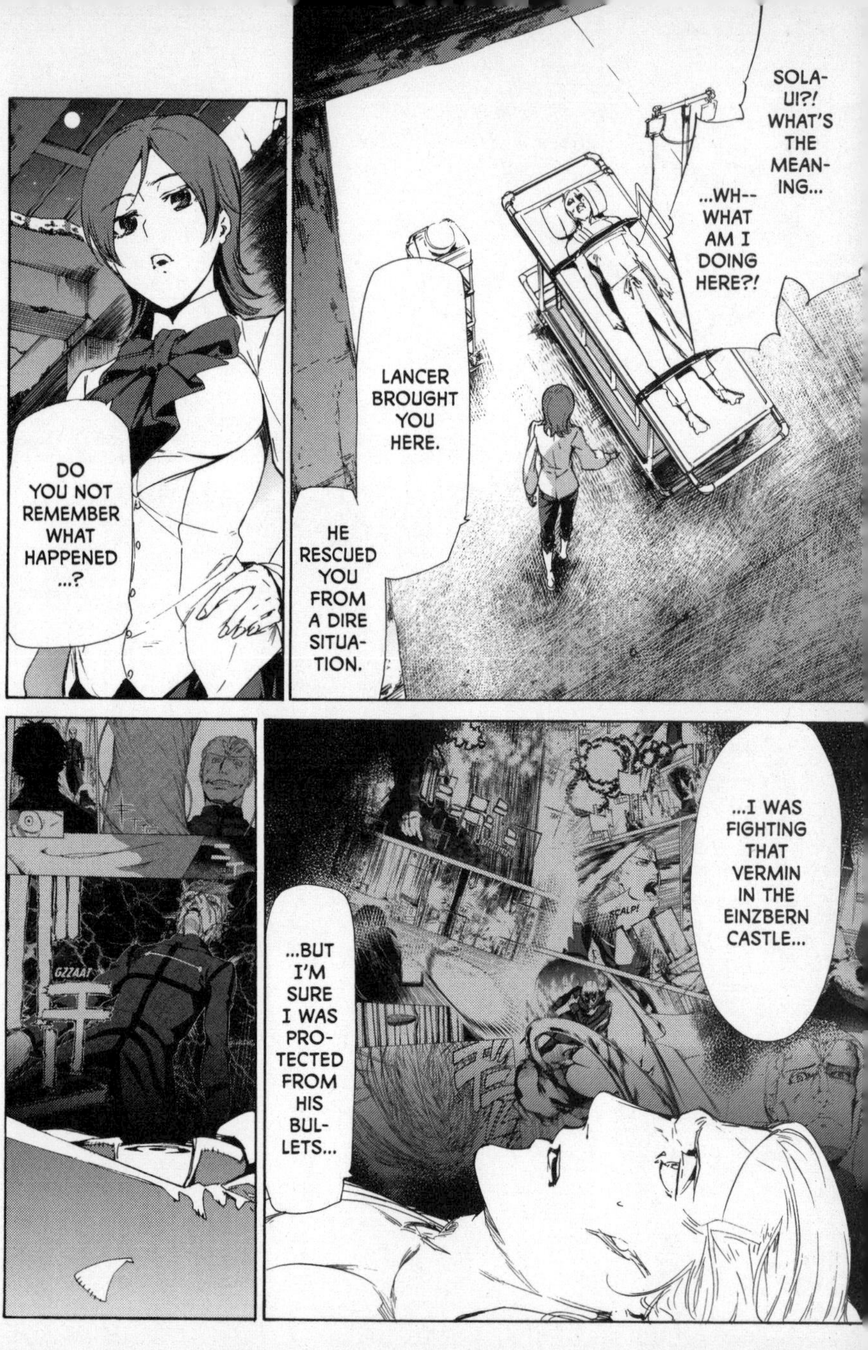
SOLA-UI?! WHAT'S THE MEAN-ING...
...WH-- WHAT AM I DOING HERE?!
LANCER BROUGHT YOU HERE.
HE RESCUED YOU FROM A DIRE SITUA-TION.
DO YOU NOT REMEMBER WHAT HAPPENED ...?
...I WAS FIGHTING THAT VERMIN IN THE EINZBERN CASTLE...
SCALP!
...BUT I'M SURE I WAS PRO-TECTED FROM HIS BUL-LETS...
GZZAAT

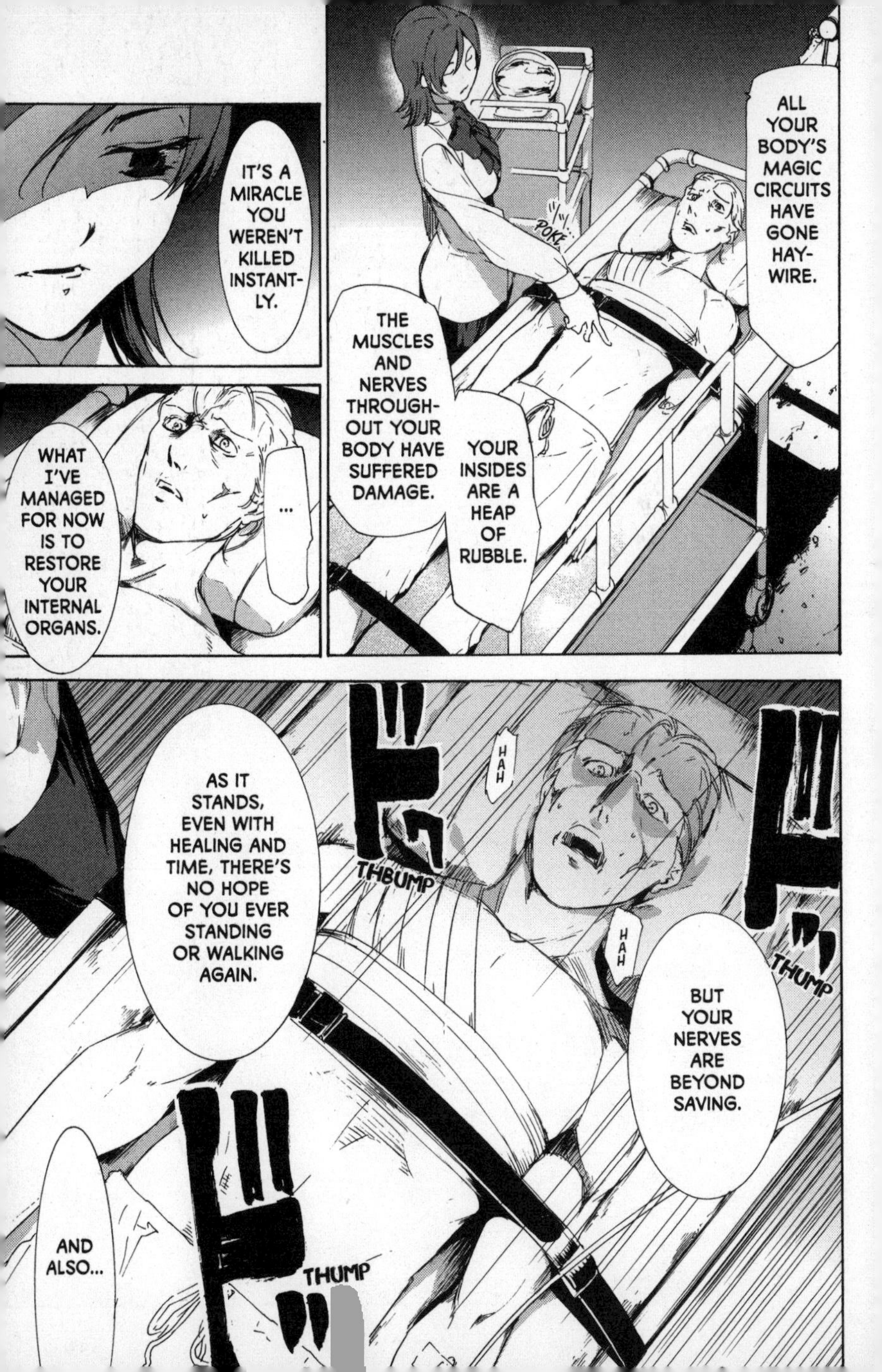
ALL YOUR BODY'S MAGIC CIRCUITS HAVE GONE HAY-WIRE.
POKE
THE MUSCLES AND NERVES THROUGH-OUT YOUR BODY HAVE SUFFERED DAMAGE.
YOUR INSIDES ARE A HEAP OF RUBBLE.
IT'S A MIRACLE YOU WEREN'T KILLED INSTANT-LY.
WHAT I'VE MANAGED FOR NOW IS TO RESTORE YOUR INTERNAL ORGANS.
...
THUMP
HAH
HAH
BUT YOUR NERVES ARE BEYOND SAVING.
THUMP
AS IT STANDS, EVEN WITH HEALING AND TIME, THERE'S NO HOPE OF YOU EVER STANDING OR WALKING AGAIN.
THUMP
AND ALSO...

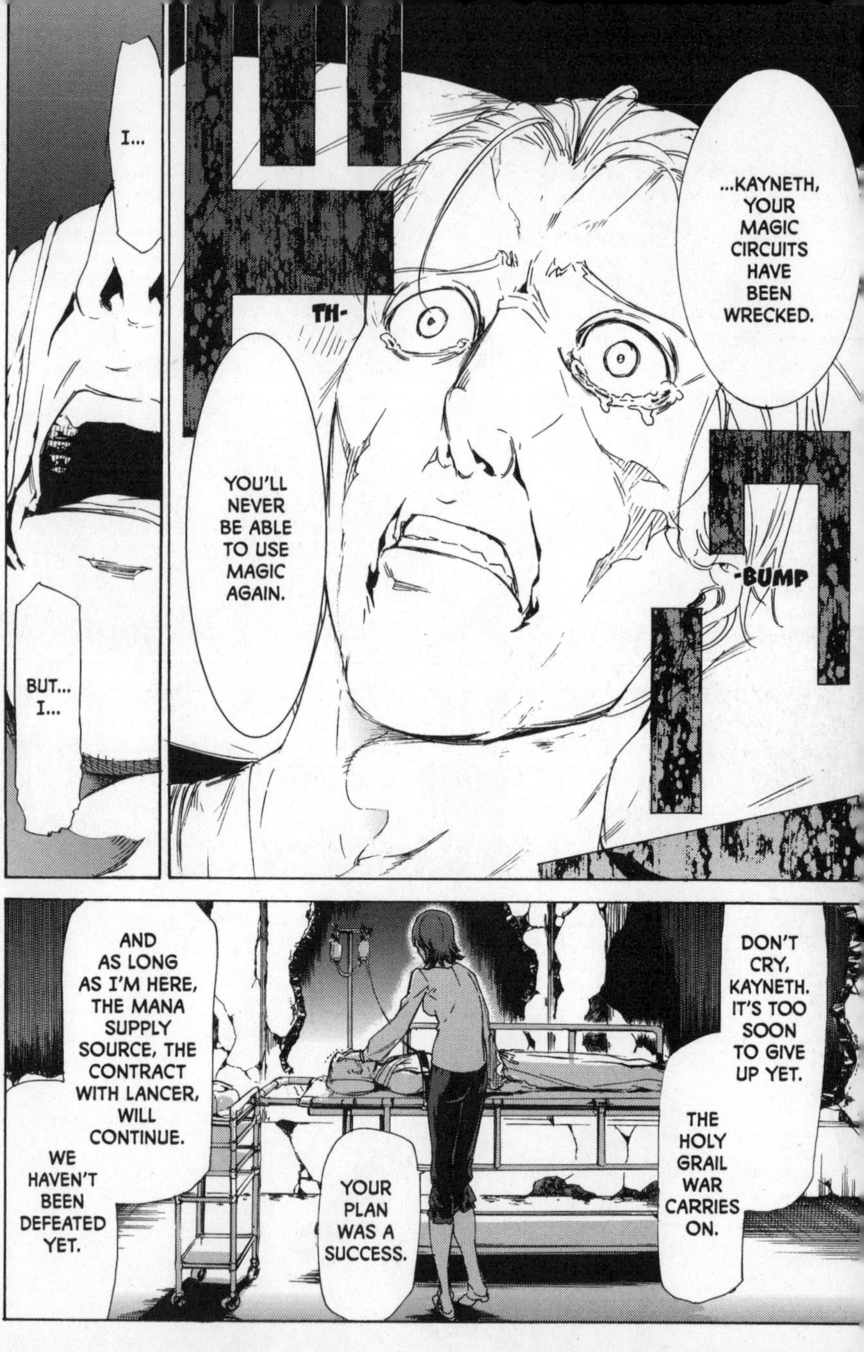
...KAYNETH, YOUR MAGIC CIRCUITS HAVE BEEN WRECKED.
TH-
-BUMP
YOU'LL NEVER BE ABLE TO USE MAGIC AGAIN.
I...
BUT... I...
DON'T CRY, KAYNETH. IT'S TOO SOON TO GIVE UP YET.
THE HOLY GRAIL WAR CARRIES ON.
YOUR PLAN WAS A SUCCESS.
AND AS LONG AS I'M HERE, THE MANA SUPPLY SOURCE, THE CONTRACT WITH LANCER, WILL CONTINUE.
WE HAVEN'T BEEN DEFEATED YET.

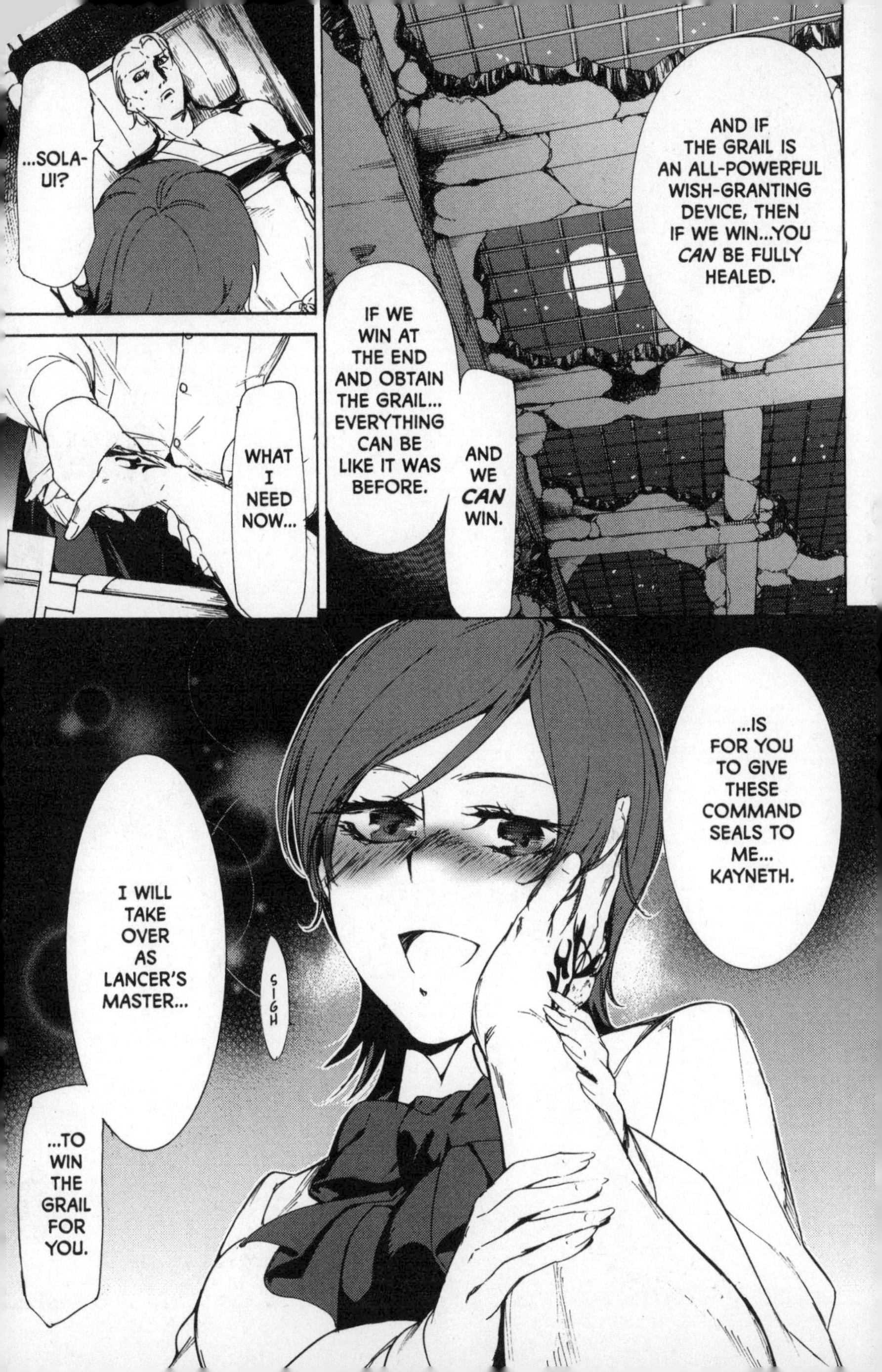
AND IF THE GRAIL IS AN ALL-POWERFUL WISH-GRANTING DEVICE, THEN IF WE WIN...YOU CAN BE FULLY HEALED.
IF WE WIN AT THE END AND OBTAIN THE GRAIL... EVERYTHING CAN BE LIKE IT WAS BEFORE.
AND WE CAN WIN.
...SOLA-UI?
WHAT I NEED NOW...
...IS FOR YOU TO GIVE THESE COMMAND SEALS TO ME... KAYNETH.
SIGH
I WILL TAKE OVER AS LANCER'S MASTER...
...TO WIN THE GRAIL FOR YOU.

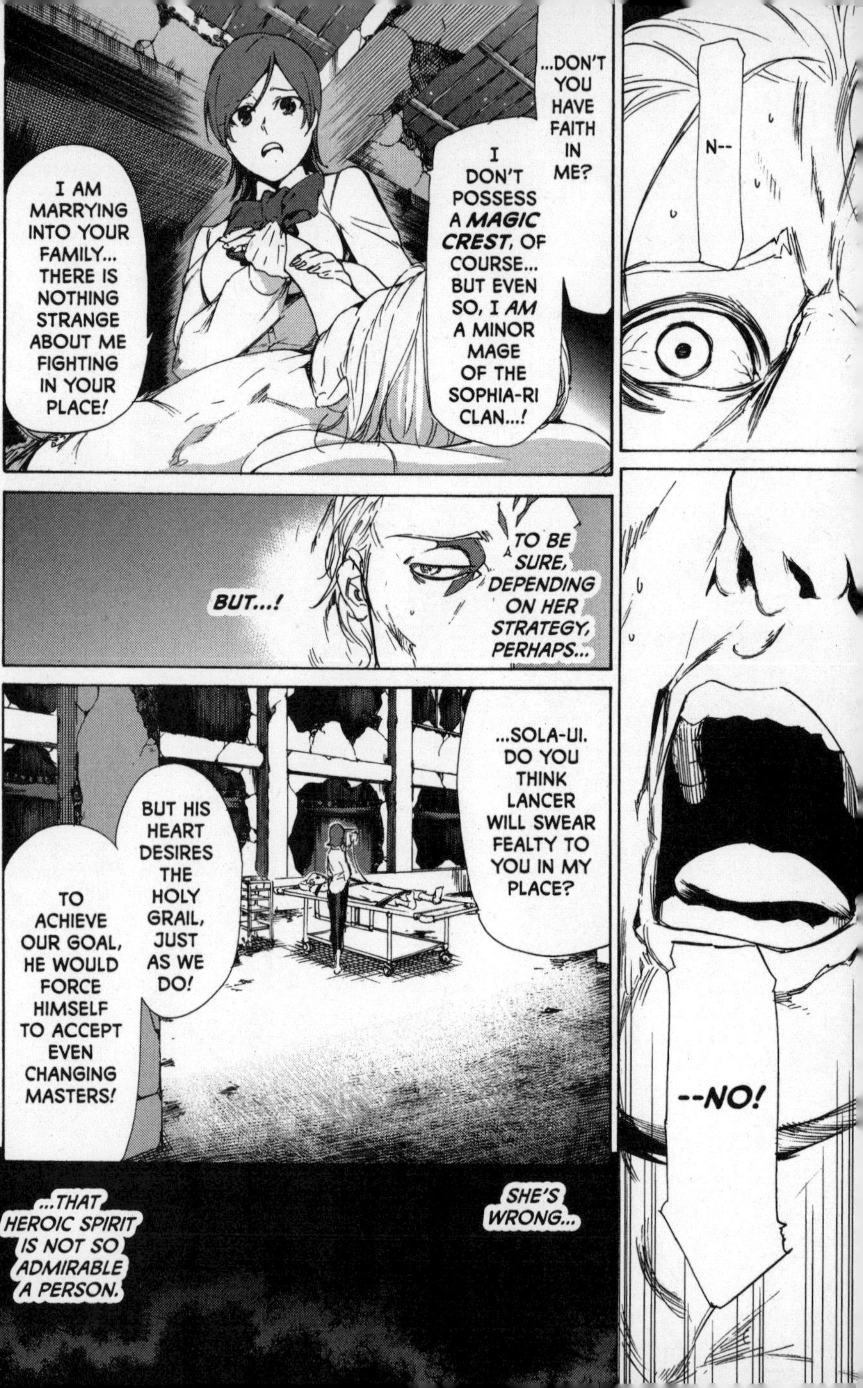
N--
...DON'T YOU HAVE FAITH IN ME?
I DON'T POSSESS A MAGIC CREST, OF COURSE... BUT EVEN SO, I AM A MINOR MAGE OF THE SOPHIA-RI CLAN...!
I AM MARRYING INTO YOUR FAMILY... THERE IS NOTHING STRANGE ABOUT ME FIGHTING IN YOUR PLACE!
--NO!
TO BE SURE, DEPENDING ON HER STRATEGY, PERHAPS...
BUT...!
...SOLA-UI. DO YOU THINK LANCER WILL SWEAR FEALTY TO YOU IN MY PLACE?
BUT HIS HEART DESIRES THE HOLY GRAIL, JUST AS WE DO!
TO ACHIEVE OUR GOAL, HE WOULD FORCE HIMSELF TO ACCEPT EVEN CHANGING MASTERS!
SHE'S WRONG...
...THAT HEROIC SPIRIT IS NOT SO ADMIRABLE A PERSON.

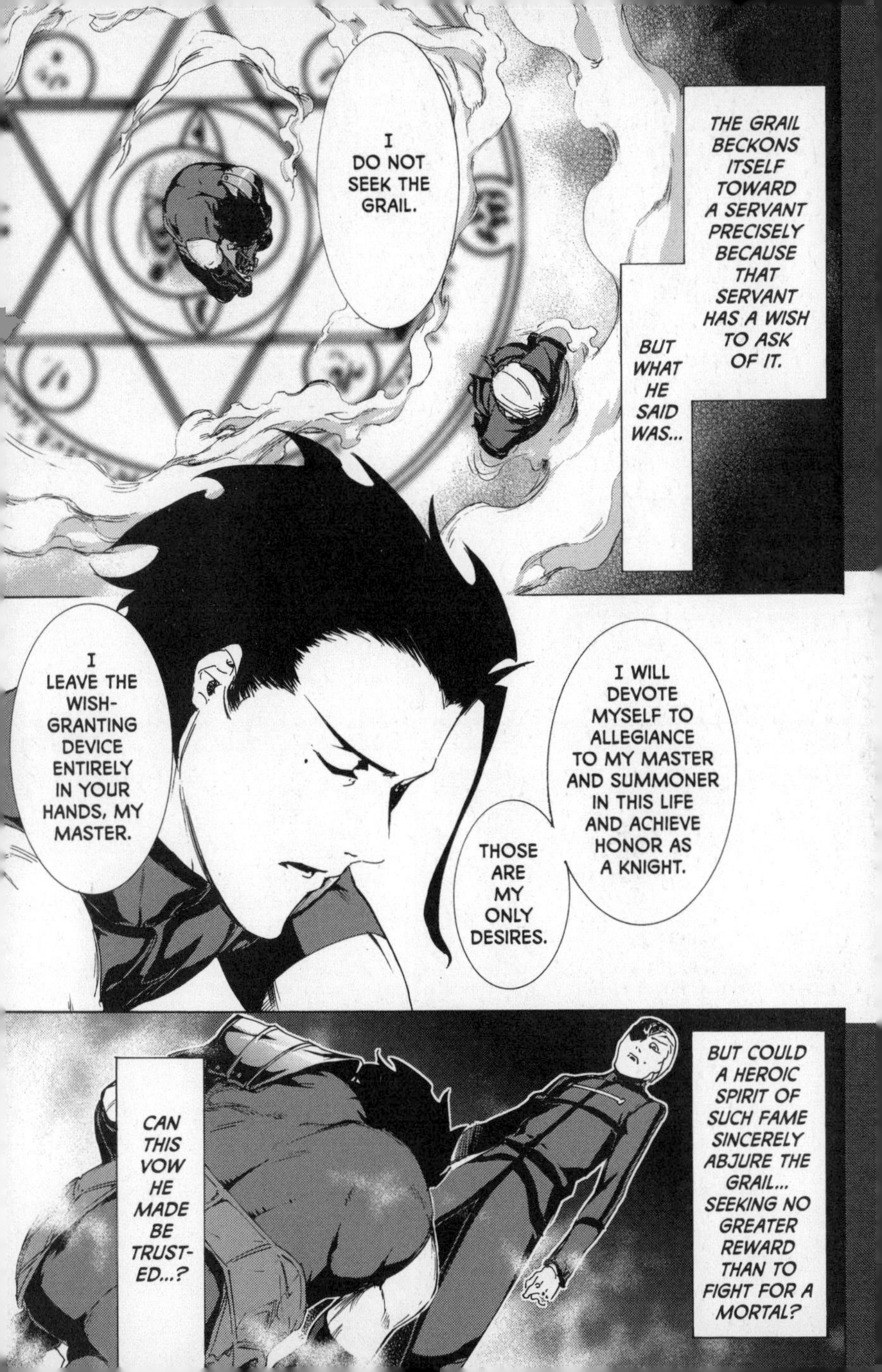
THE GRAIL BECKONS ITSELF TOWARD A SERVANT PRECISELY BECAUSE THAT SERVANT HAS A WISH TO ASK OF IT.
BUT WHAT HE SAID WAS...
I DO NOT SEEK THE GRAIL.
I LEAVE THE WISH-GRANTING DEVICE ENTIRELY IN YOUR HANDS, MY MASTER.
I WILL DEVOTE MYSELF TO ALLEGIANCE TO MY MASTER AND SUMMONER IN THIS LIFE AND ACHIEVE HONOR AS A KNIGHT.
THOSE ARE MY ONLY DESIRES.
BUT COULD A HEROIC SPIRIT OF SUCH FAME SINCERELY ABJURE THE GRAIL... SEEKING NO GREATER REWARD THAN TO FIGHT FOR A MORTAL?
CAN THIS VOW HE MADE BE TRUST-ED...?

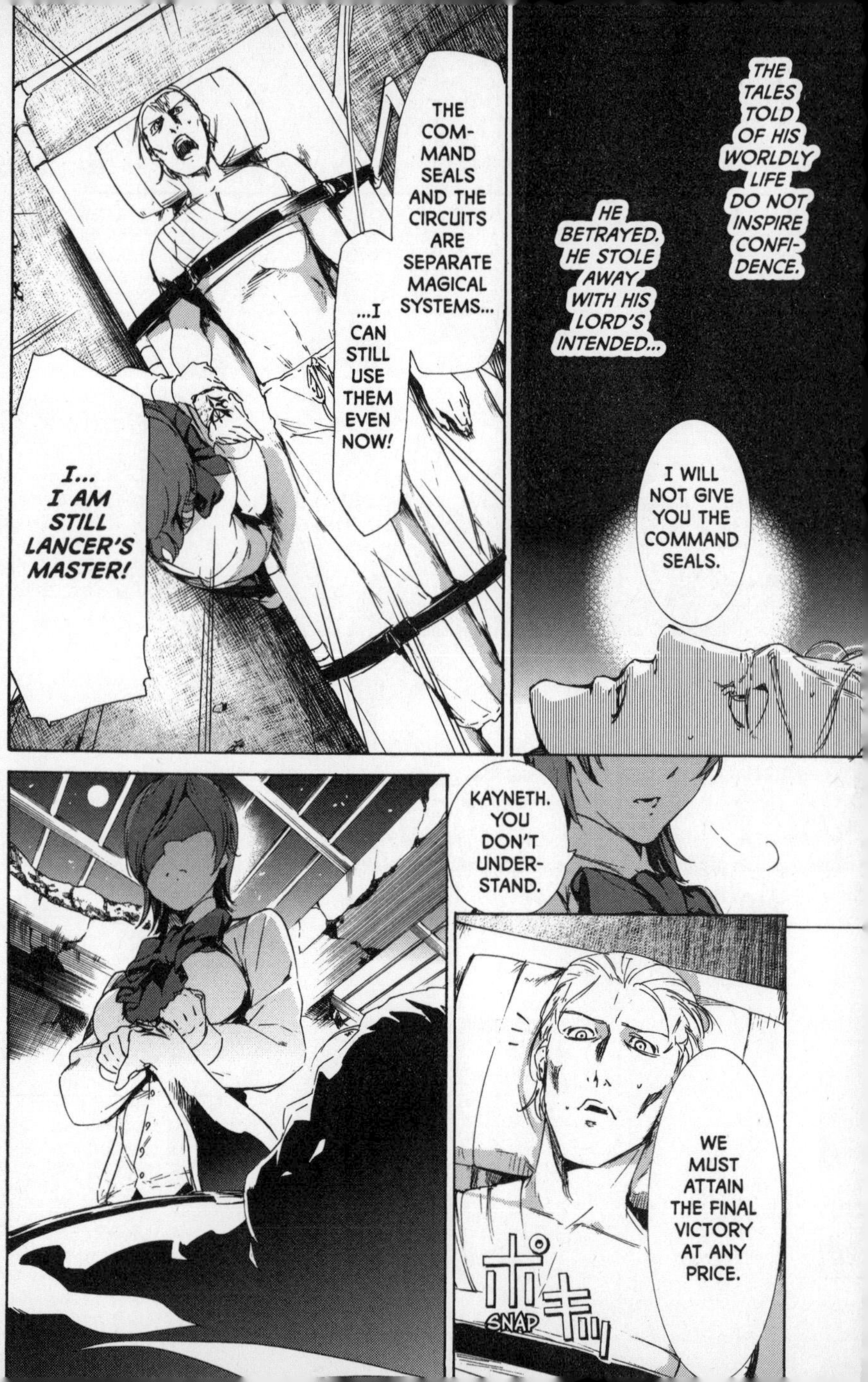
THE TALES TOLD OF HIS WORLDLY LIFE DO NOT INSPIRE CONFIDENCE.
HE BETRAYED. HE STOLE AWAY WITH HIS LORD'S INTENDED...
I WILL NOT GIVE YOU THE COMMAND SEALS.
THE COMMAND SEALS AND THE CIRCUITS ARE SEPARATE MAGICAL SYSTEMS...
...I CAN STILL USE THEM EVEN NOW!
I... I AM STILL LANCER'S MASTER!
KAYNETH. YOU DON'T UNDERSTAND.
WE MUST ATTAIN THE FINAL VICTORY AT ANY PRICE.
ポキッ
SNAP

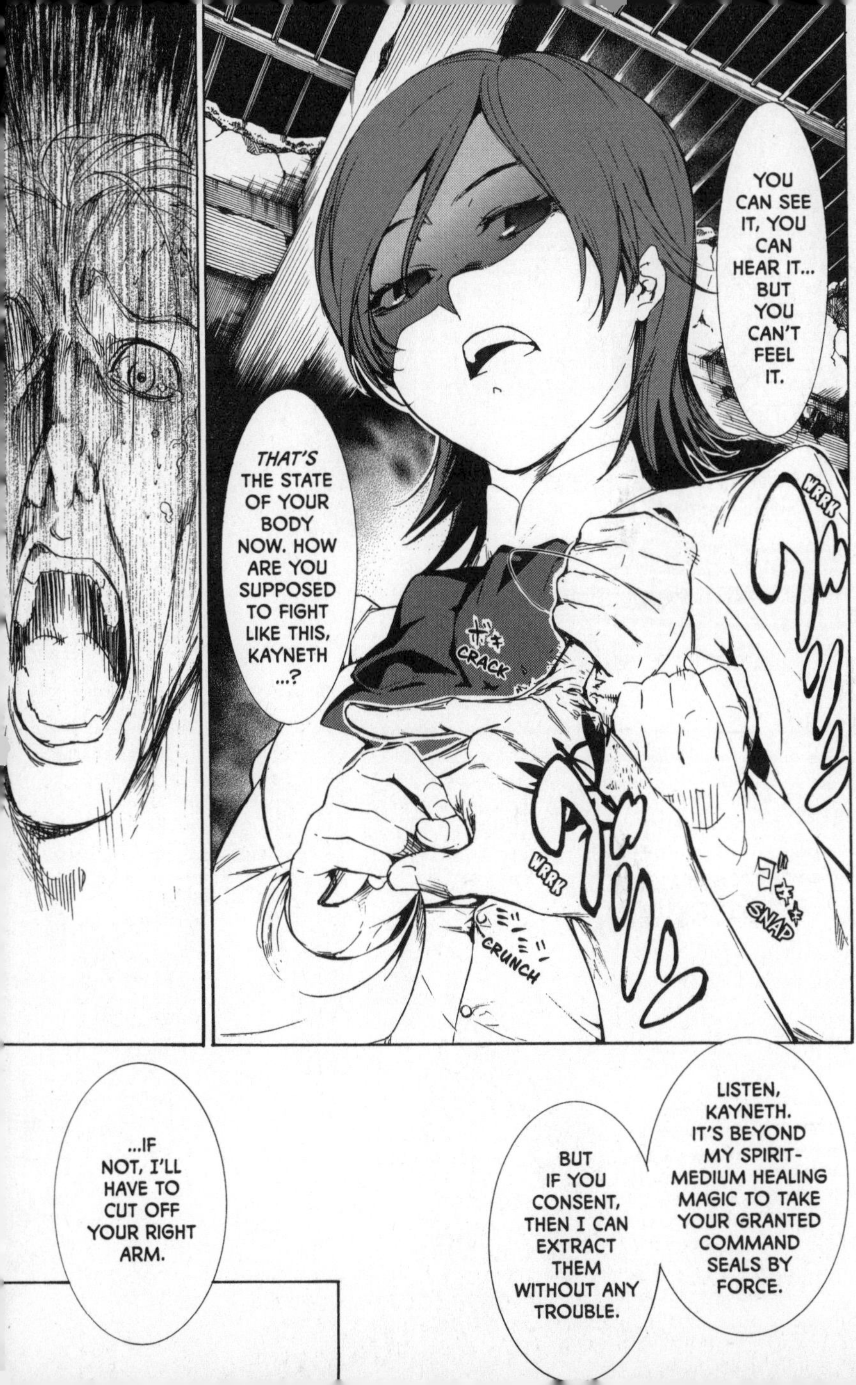
YOU CAN SEE IT, YOU CAN HEAR IT... BUT YOU CAN'T FEEL IT.
THAT'S THE STATE OF YOUR BODY NOW. HOW ARE YOU SUPPOSED TO FIGHT LIKE THIS, KAYNETH ...?
WRRK
CRACK
SNAP
WRRK
CRUNCH
LISTEN, KAYNETH. IT'S BEYOND MY SPIRIT-MEDIUM HEALING MAGIC TO TAKE YOUR GRANTED COMMAND SEALS BY FORCE.
BUT IF YOU CONSENT, THEN I CAN EXTRACT THEM WITHOUT ANY TROUBLE.
...IF NOT, I'LL HAVE TO CUT OFF YOUR RIGHT ARM.

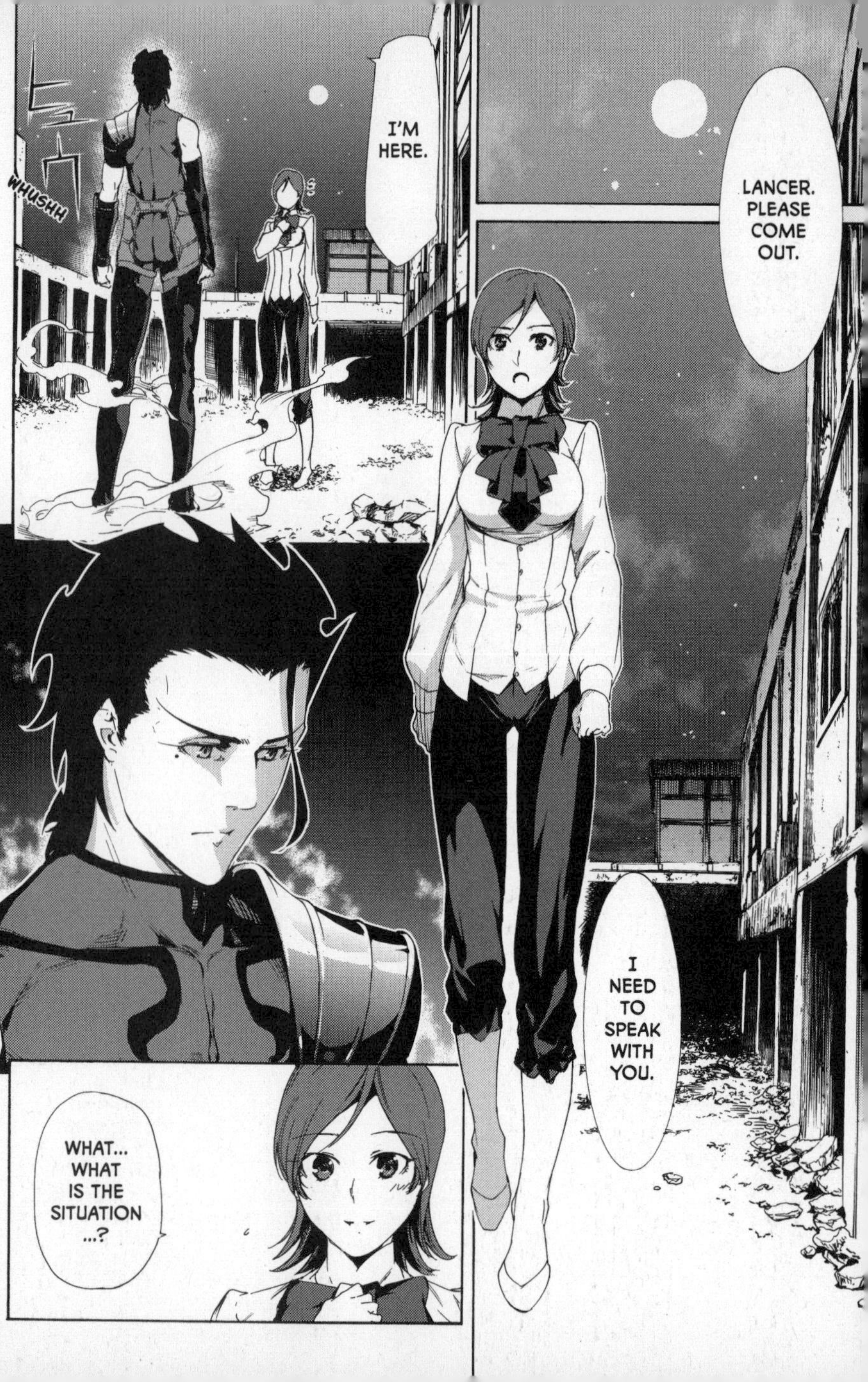
LANCER. PLEASE COME OUT.
I NEED TO SPEAK WITH YOU.
WHUSHH
I'M HERE.
WHAT... WHAT IS THE SITUATION ...?

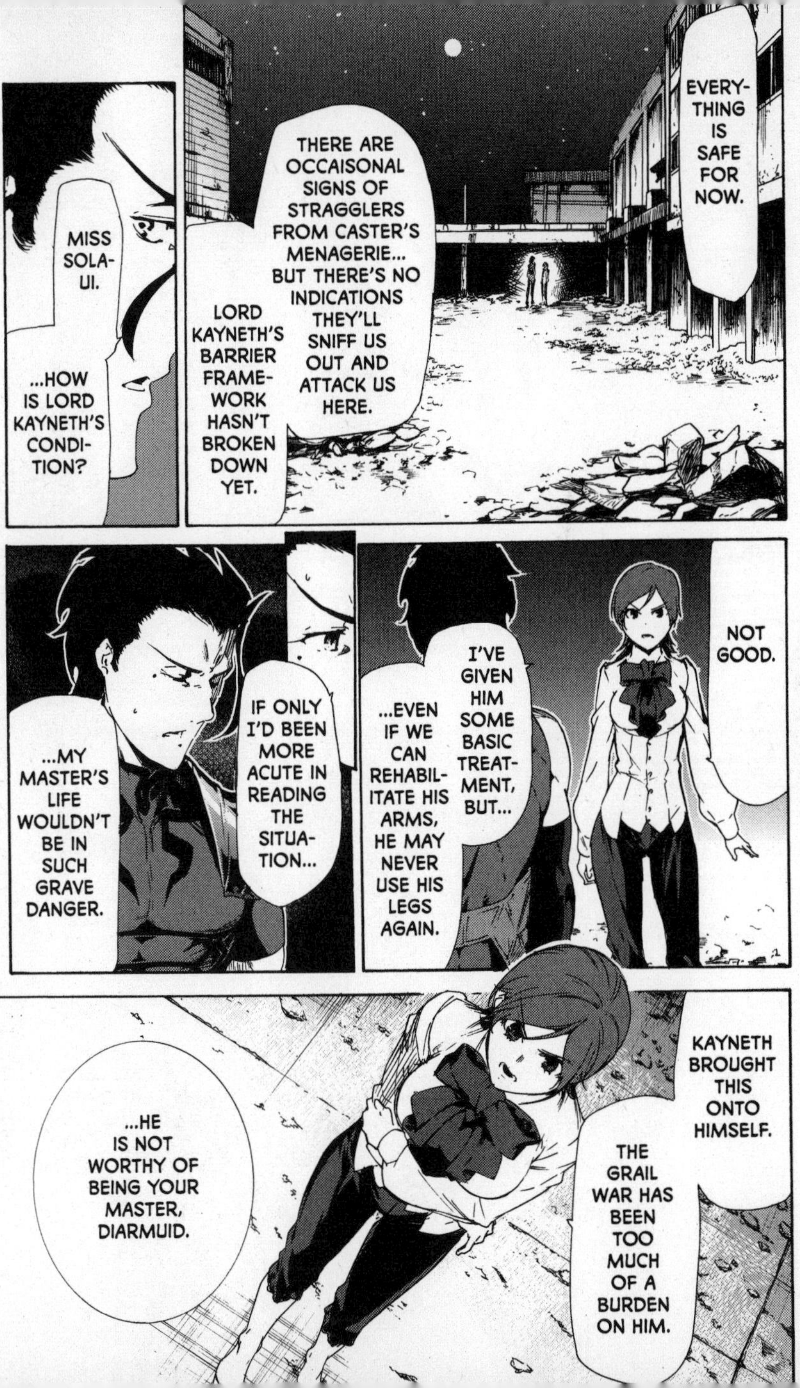
EVERYTHING IS SAFE FOR NOW.
THERE ARE OCCAISONAL SIGNS OF STRAGGLERS FROM CASTER'S MENAGERIE... BUT THERE'S NO INDICATIONS THEY'LL SNIFF US OUT AND ATTACK US HERE.
LORD KAYNETH'S BARRIER FRAMEWORK HASN'T BROKEN DOWN YET.
MISS SOLAUI.
...HOW IS LORD KAYNETH'S CONDITION?
NOT GOOD.
I'VE GIVEN HIM SOME BASIC TREATMENT, BUT...
...EVEN IF WE CAN REHABILITATE HIS ARMS, HE MAY NEVER USE HIS LEGS AGAIN.
IF ONLY I'D BEEN MORE ACUTE IN READING THE SITUATION...
...MY MASTER'S LIFE WOULDN'T BE IN SUCH GRAVE DANGER.
KAYNETH BROUGHT THIS ONTO HIMSELF.
THE GRAIL WAR HAS BEEN TOO MUCH OF A BURDEN ON HIM.
...HE IS NOT WORTHY OF BEING YOUR MASTER, DIARMUID.

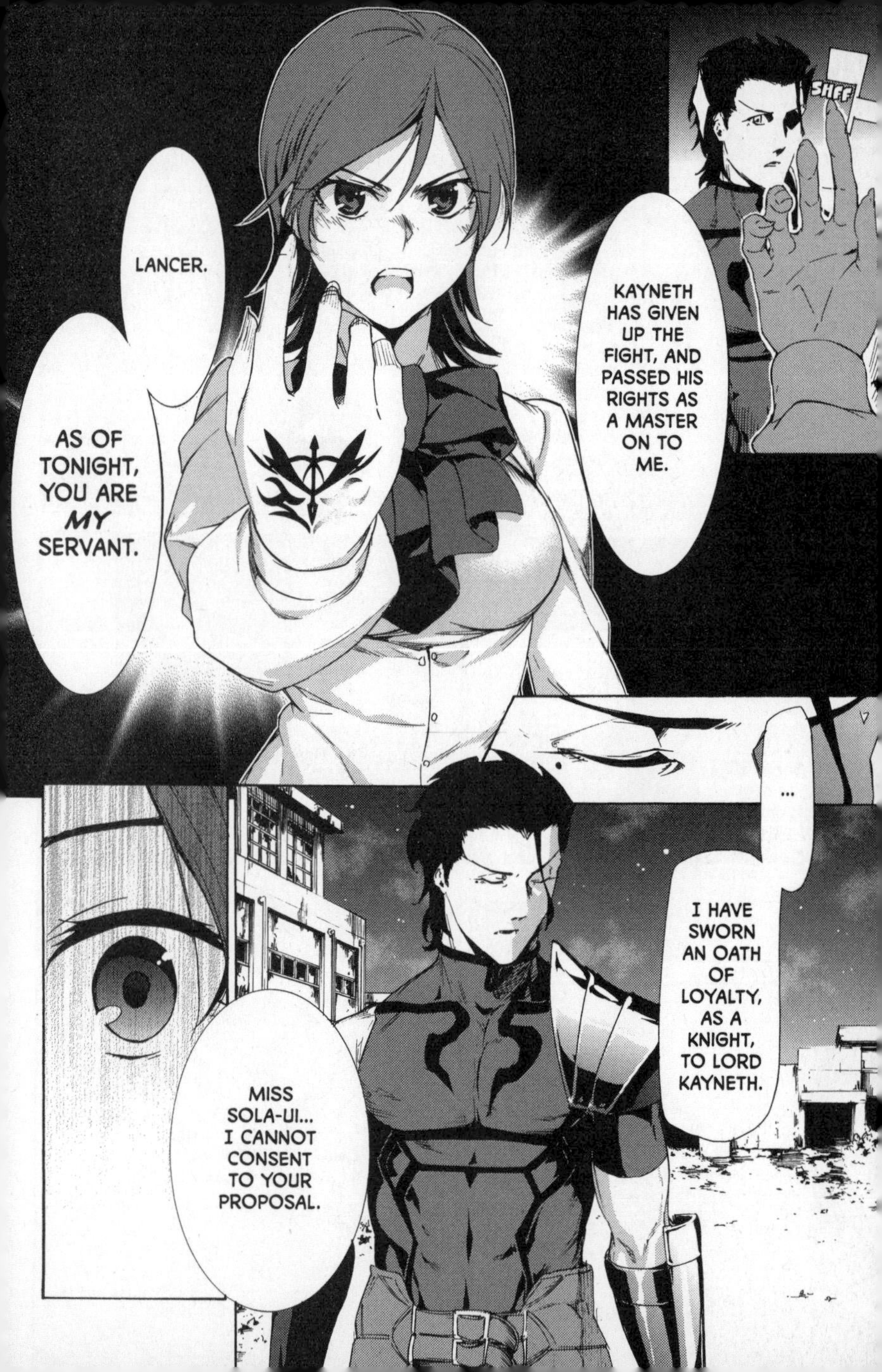
SHFF
LANCER.
KAYNETH HAS GIVEN UP THE FIGHT, AND PASSED HIS RIGHTS AS A MASTER ON TO ME.
AS OF TONIGHT, YOU ARE *MY* SERVANT.
...
I HAVE SWORN AN OATH OF LOYALTY, AS A KNIGHT, TO LORD KAYNETH.
MISS SOLA-UI... I CANNOT CONSENT TO YOUR PROPOSAL.

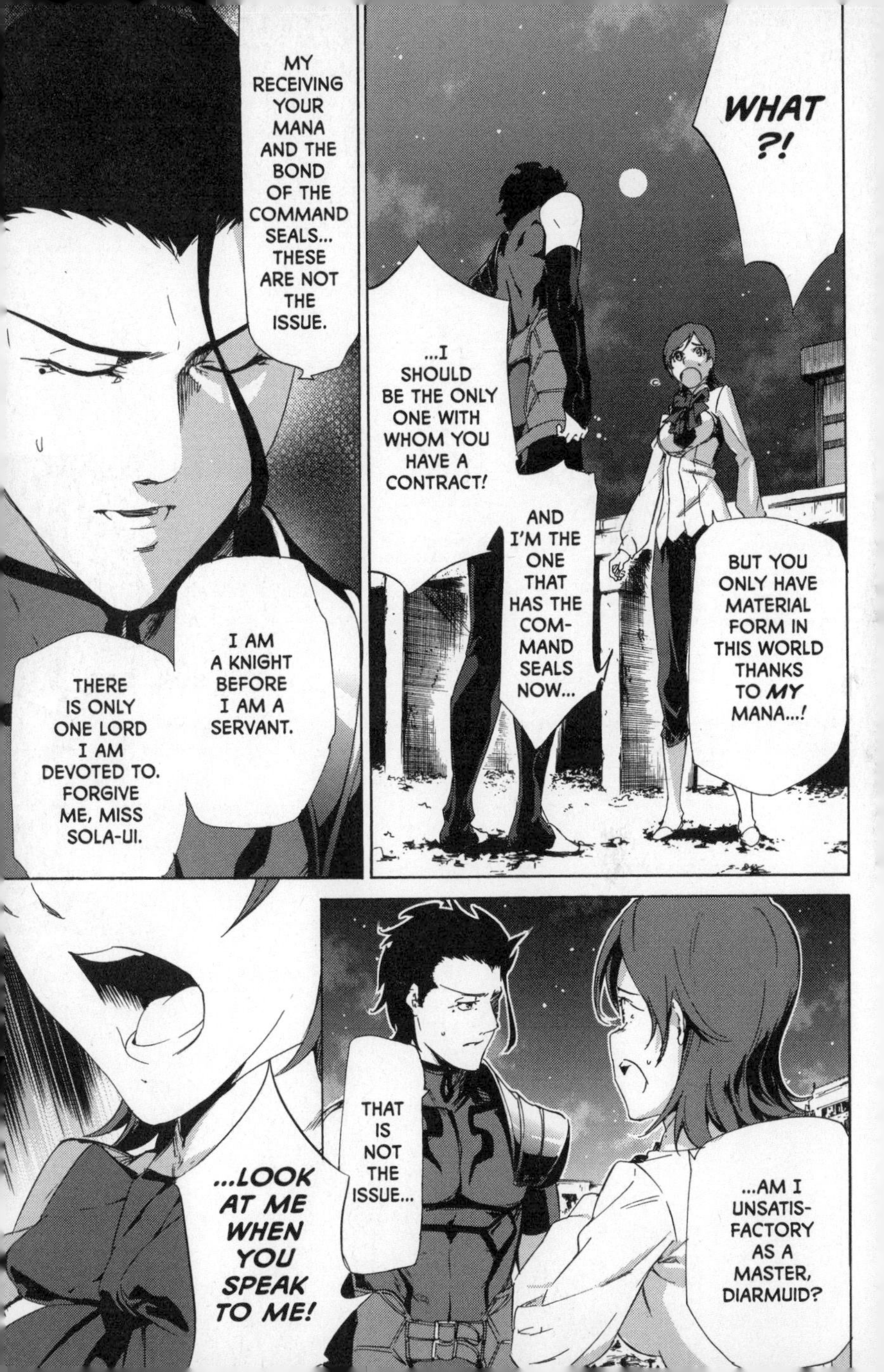
WHAT?!
...I SHOULD BE THE ONLY ONE WITH WHOM YOU HAVE A CONTRACT!
AND I'M THE ONE THAT HAS THE COMMAND SEALS NOW...
BUT YOU ONLY HAVE MATERIAL FORM IN THIS WORLD THANKS TO *MY* MANA...!
MY RECEIVING YOUR MANA AND THE BOND OF THE COMMAND SEALS... THESE ARE NOT THE ISSUE.
I AM A KNIGHT BEFORE I AM A SERVANT.
THERE IS ONLY ONE LORD I AM DEVOTED TO. FORGIVE ME, MISS SOLA-UI.
...AM I UNSATISFACTORY AS A MASTER, DIARMUID?
THAT IS NOT THE ISSUE...
...LOOK AT ME WHEN YOU SPEAK TO ME!

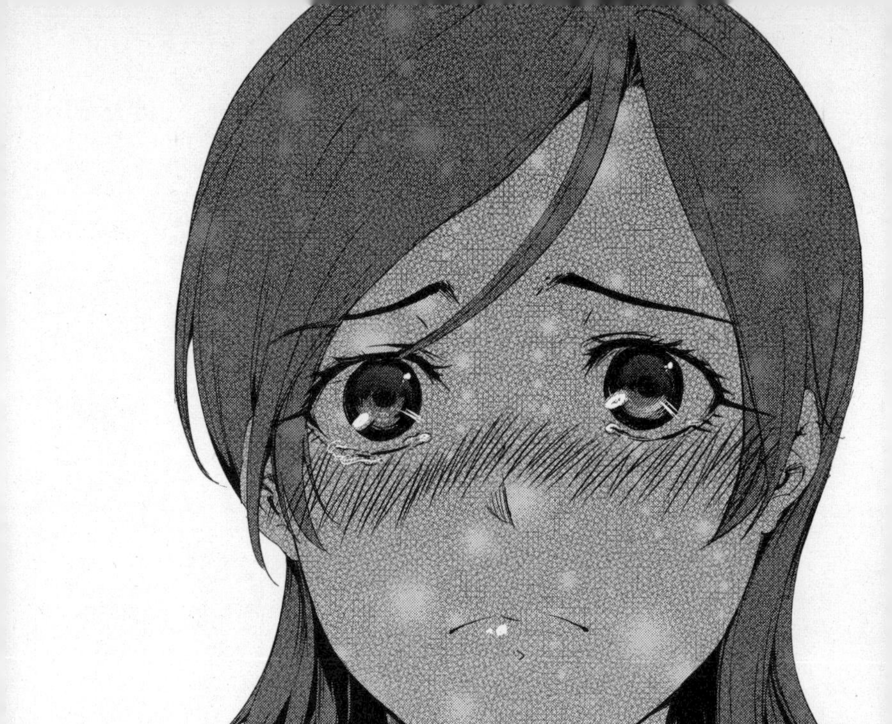
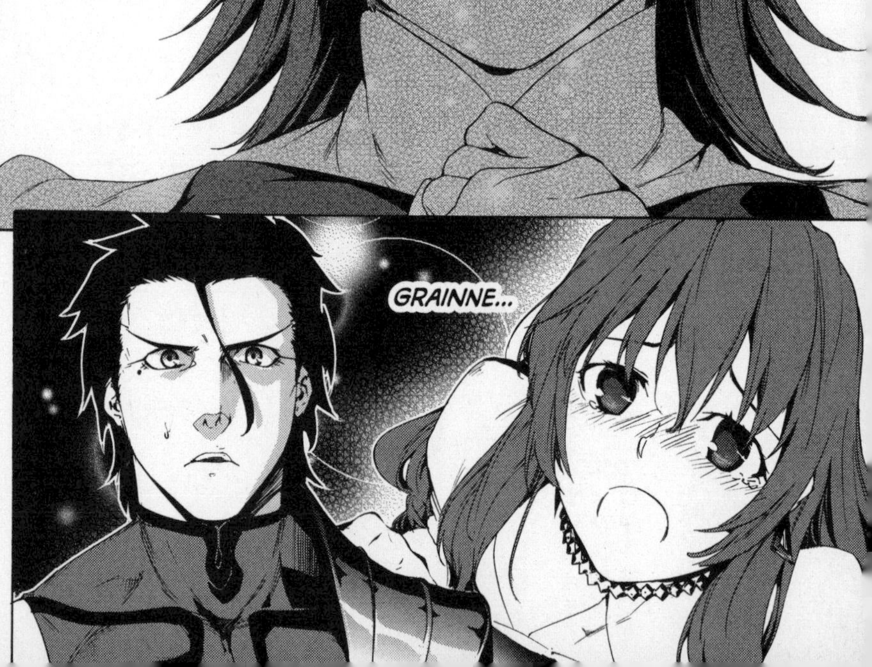
GRAINNE...

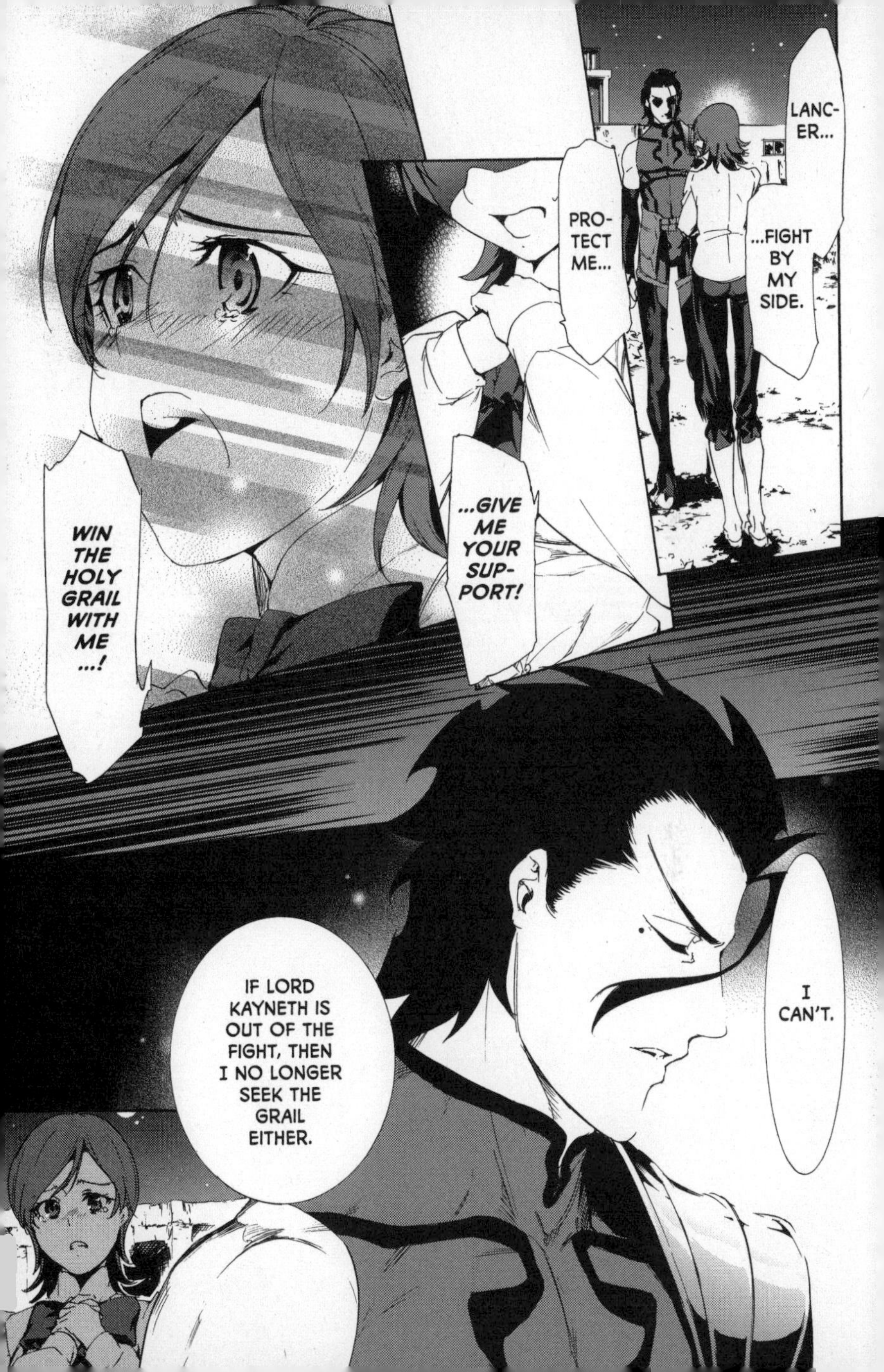
LANCER...
...FIGHT BY MY SIDE.
PROTECT ME...
...GIVE ME YOUR SUPPORT!
WIN THE HOLY GRAIL WITH ME ...!
I CAN'T.
IF LORD KAYNETH IS OUT OF THE FIGHT, THEN I NO LONGER SEEK THE GRAIL EITHER.

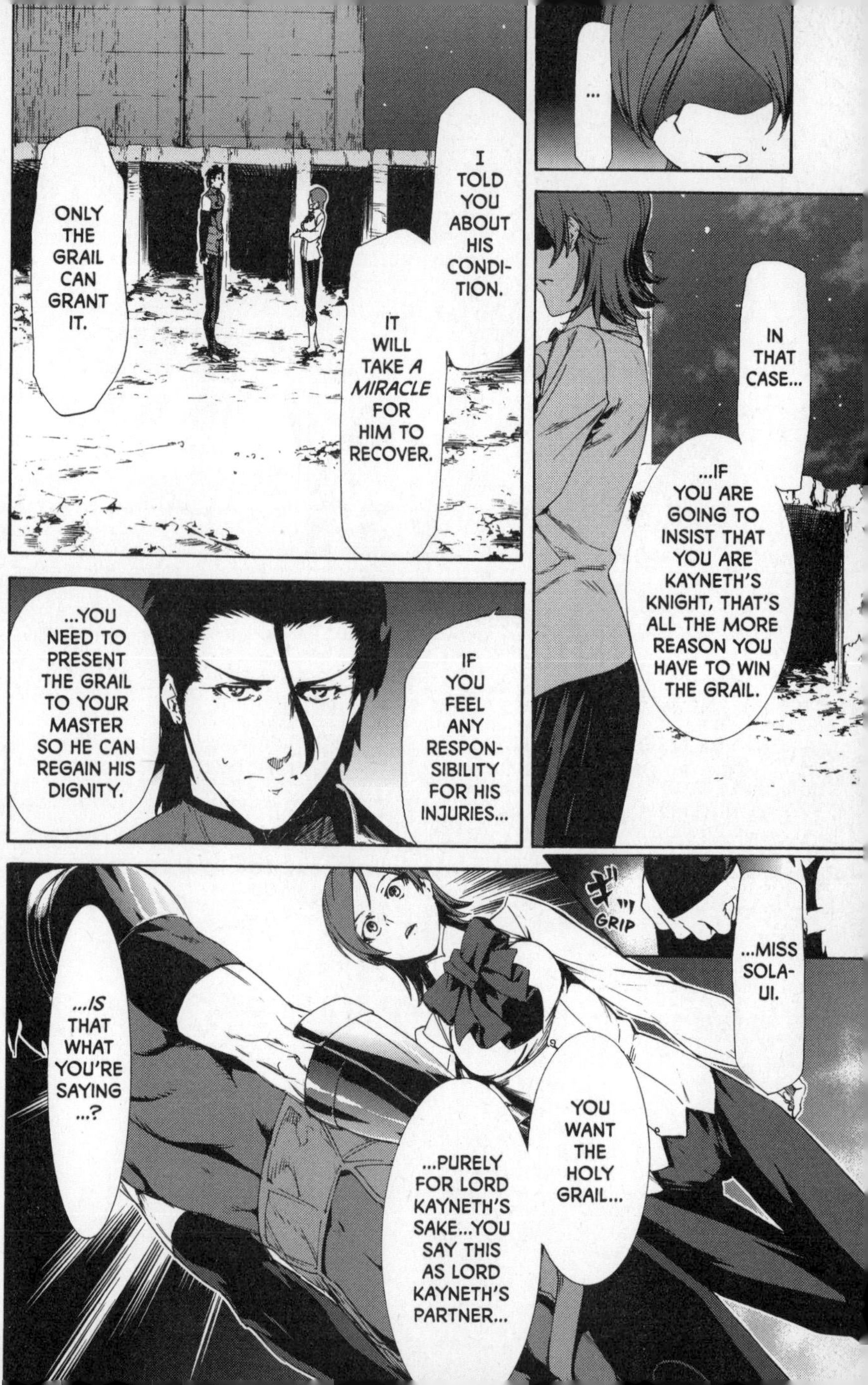
...
I TOLD YOU ABOUT HIS CONDITION.
IT WILL TAKE *A MIRACLE* FOR HIM TO RECOVER.
ONLY THE GRAIL CAN GRANT IT.
IN THAT CASE...
...IF YOU ARE GOING TO INSIST THAT YOU ARE KAYNETH'S KNIGHT, THAT'S ALL THE MORE REASON YOU HAVE TO WIN THE GRAIL.
IF YOU FEEL ANY RESPONSIBILITY FOR HIS INJURIES...
...YOU NEED TO PRESENT THE GRAIL TO YOUR MASTER SO HE CAN REGAIN HIS DIGNITY.
GRIP
...MISS SOLA-UI.
YOU WANT THE HOLY GRAIL...
...PURELY FOR LORD KAYNETH'S SAKE...YOU SAY THIS AS LORD KAYNETH'S PARTNER...
...*IS* THAT WHAT YOU'RE SAYING ...?

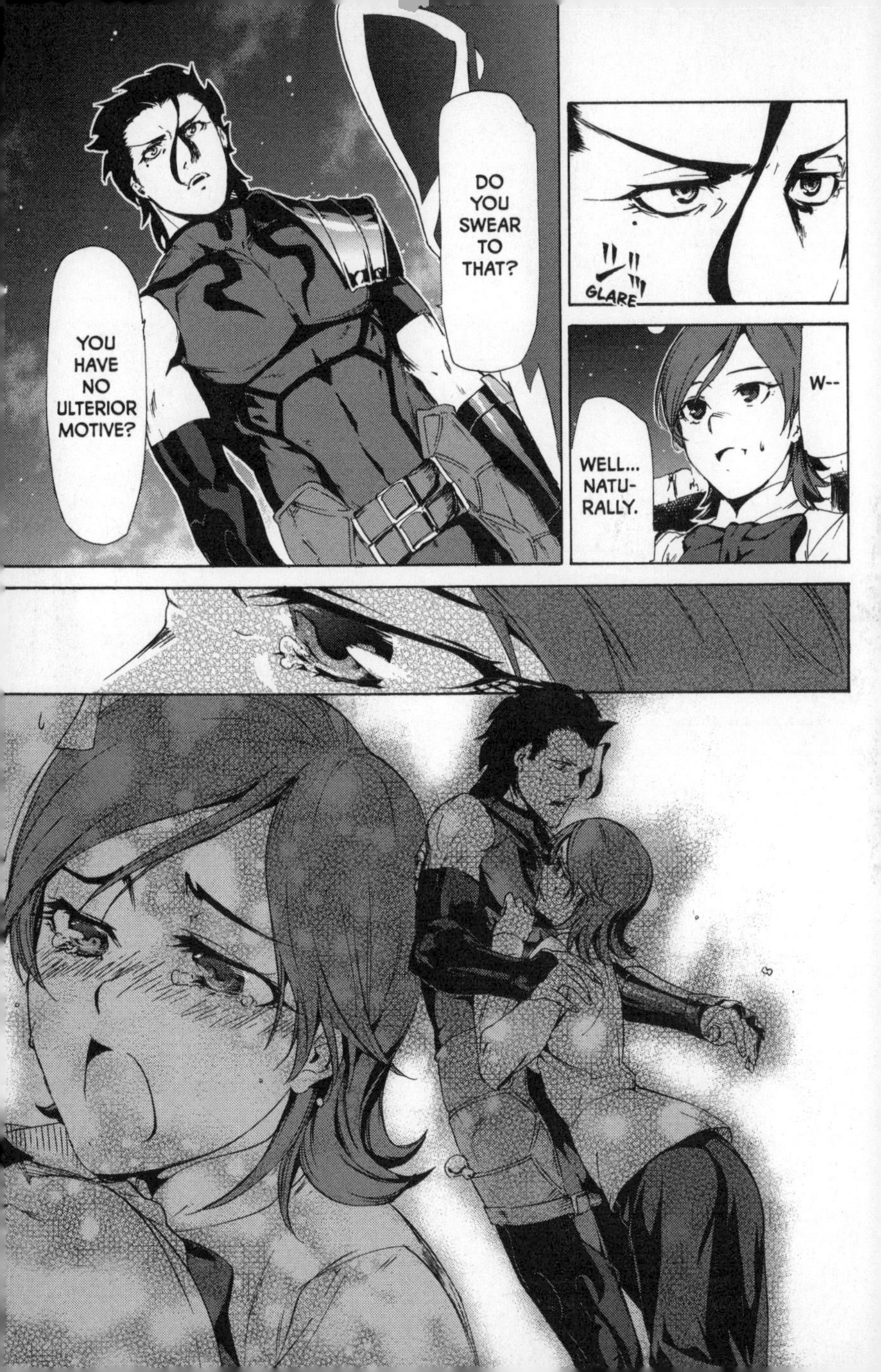
GLARE
W--
WELL... NATU-RALLY.
DO YOU SWEAR TO THAT?
YOU HAVE NO ULTERIOR MOTIVE?

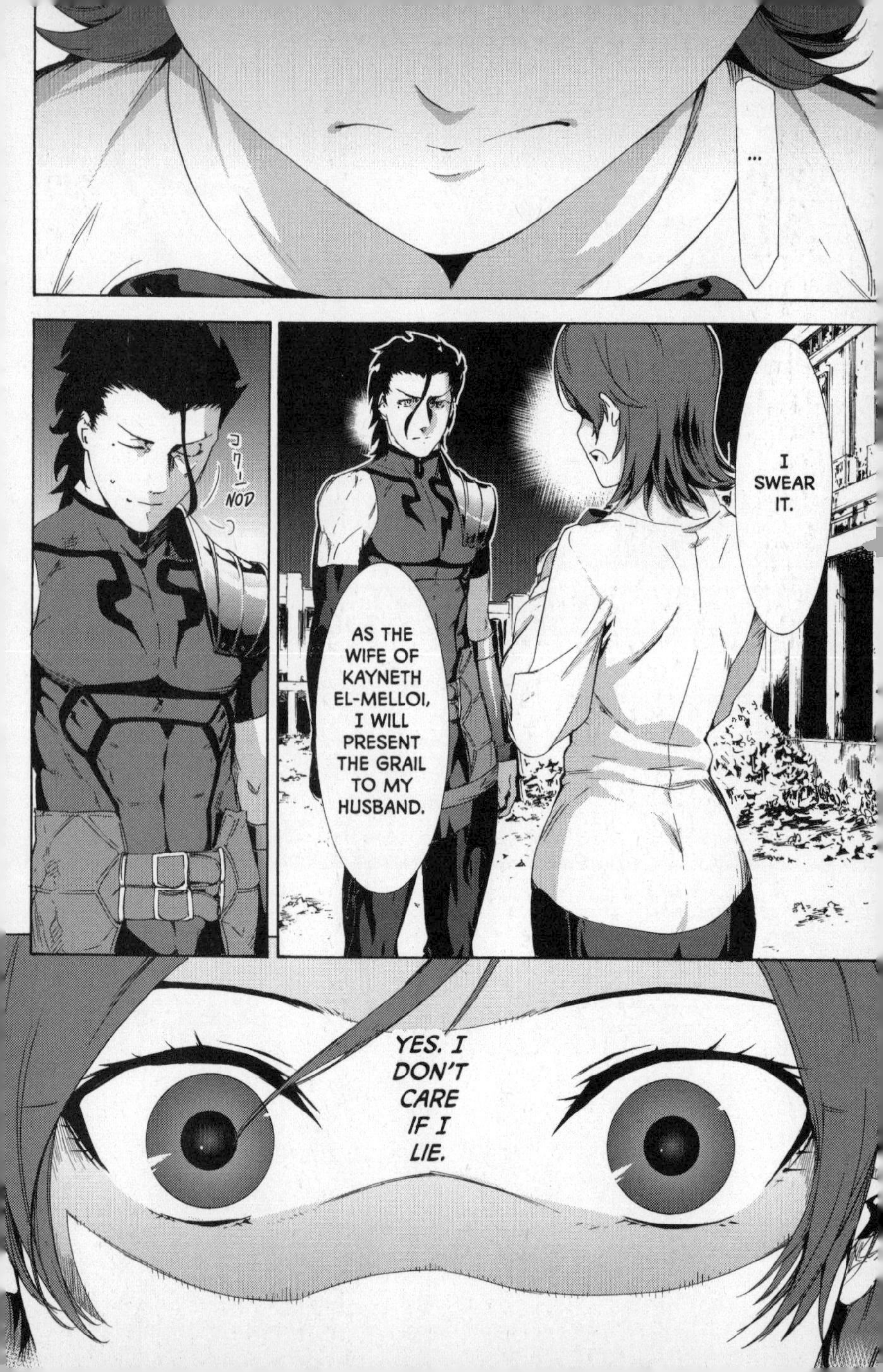
...
I SWEAR IT.
AS THE WIFE OF KAYNETH EL-MELLOI, I WILL PRESENT THE GRAIL TO MY HUSBAND.
NOD
YES. I DON'T CARE IF I LIE.

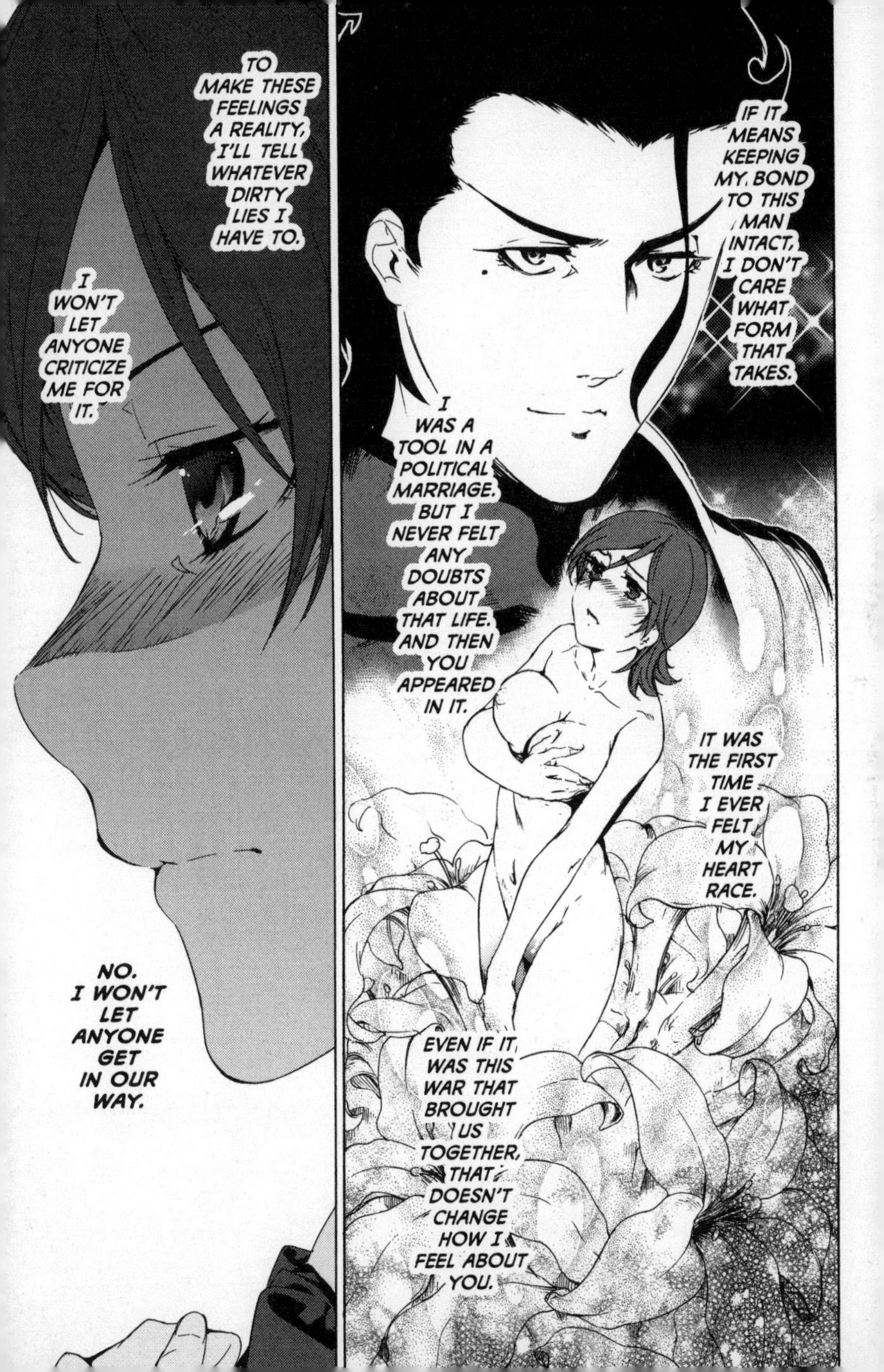
IF IT MEANS KEEPING MY BOND TO THIS MAN INTACT, I DON'T CARE WHAT FORM THAT TAKES.
I WAS A TOOL IN A POLITICAL MARRIAGE. BUT I NEVER FELT ANY DOUBTS ABOUT THAT LIFE. AND THEN YOU APPEARED IN IT.
IT WAS THE FIRST TIME I EVER FELT MY HEART RACE.
EVEN IF IT WAS THIS WAR THAT BROUGHT US TOGETHER, THAT DOESN'T CHANGE HOW I FEEL ABOUT YOU.
TO MAKE THESE FEELINGS A REALITY, I'LL TELL WHATEVER DIRTY LIES I HAVE TO.
I WON'T LET ANYONE CRITICIZE ME FOR IT.
NO. I WON'T LET ANYONE GET IN OUR WAY.

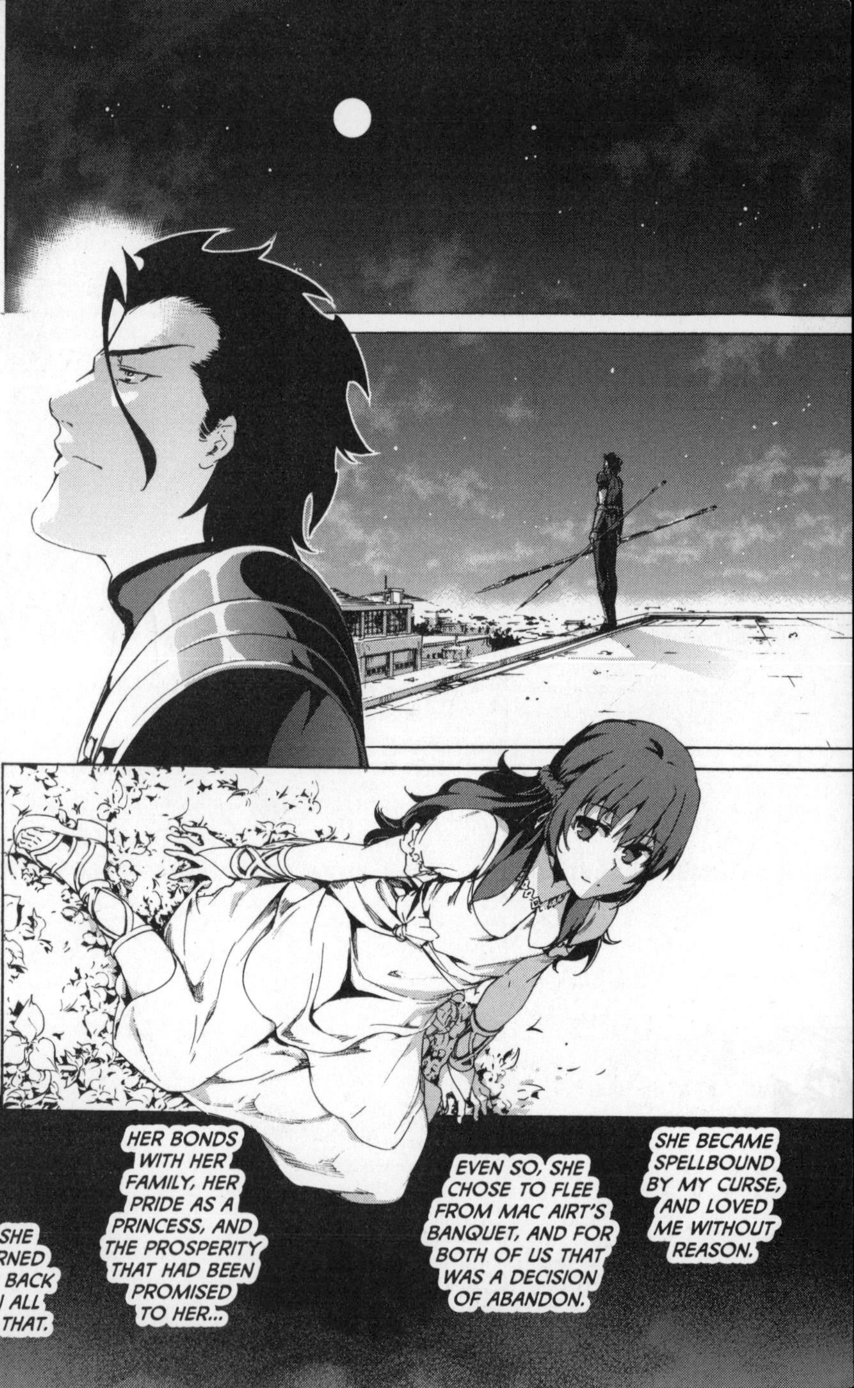
SHE BECAME SPELLBOUND BY MY CURSE, AND LOVED ME WITHOUT REASON.
EVEN SO, SHE CHOSE TO FLEE FROM MAC AIRT'S BANQUET, AND FOR BOTH OF US THAT WAS A DECISION OF ABANDON.
HER BONDS WITH HER FAMILY, HER PRIDE AS A PRINCESS, AND THE PROSPERITY THAT HAD BEEN PROMISED TO HER...
...SHE TURNED HER BACK ON ALL OF THAT.

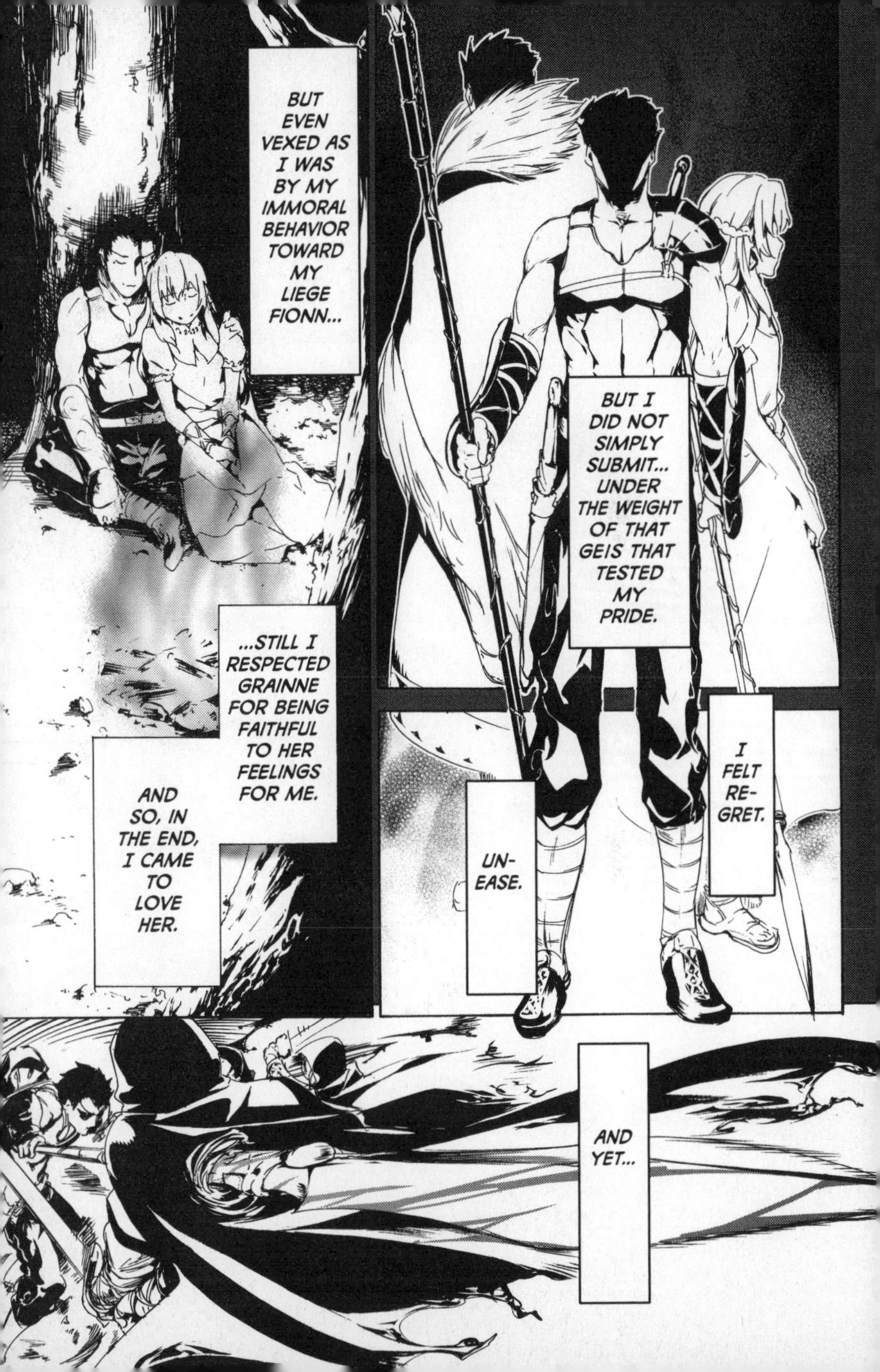
BUT I DID NOT SIMPLY SUBMIT... UNDER THE WEIGHT OF THAT GEIS THAT TESTED MY PRIDE.
I FELT RE-GRET.
UN-EASE.
BUT EVEN VEXED AS I WAS BY MY IMMORAL BEHAVIOR TOWARD MY LIEGE FIONN...
...STILL I RESPECTED GRAINNE FOR BEING FAITHFUL TO HER FEELINGS FOR ME.
AND SO, IN THE END, I CAME TO LOVE HER.
AND YET...

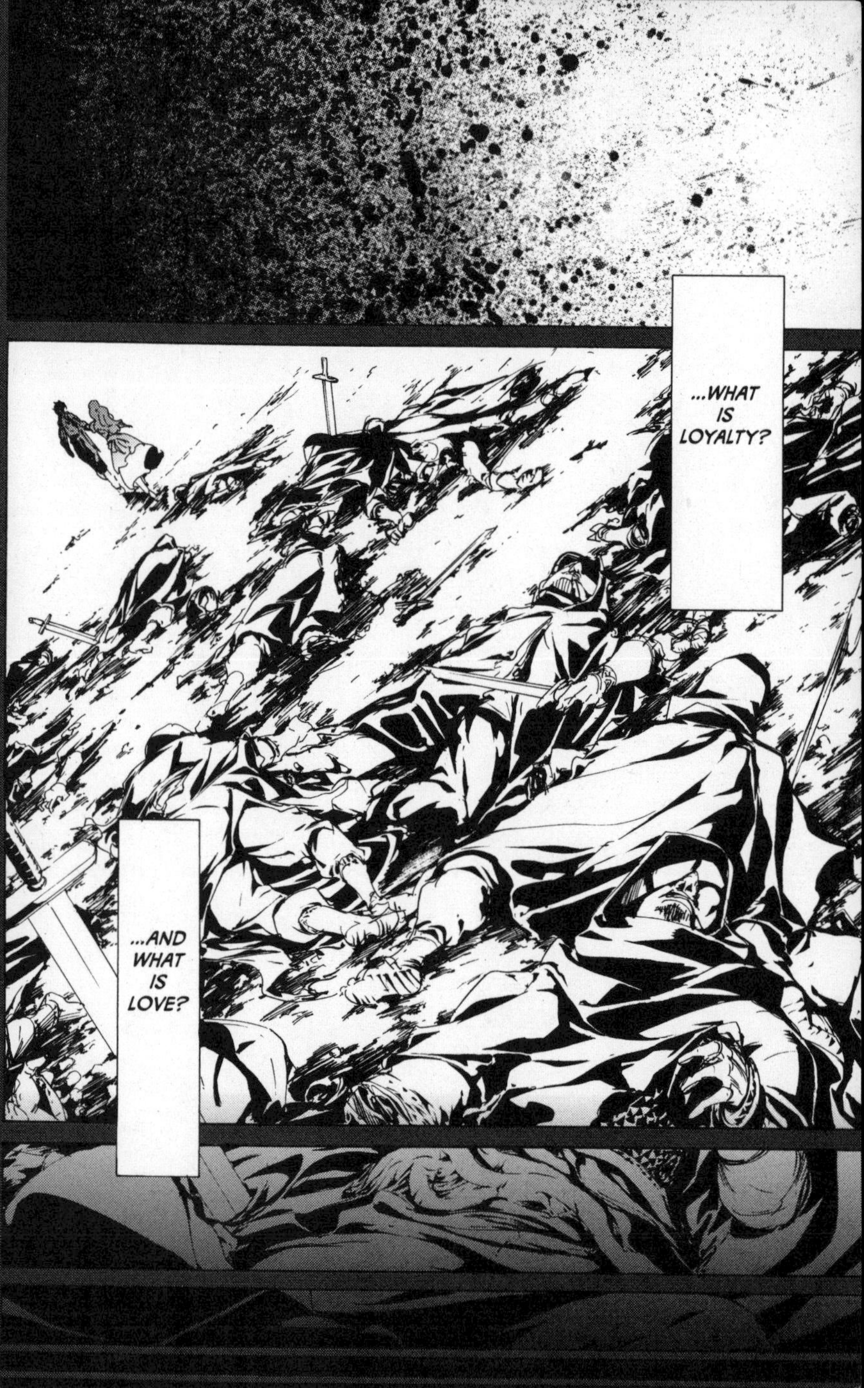
...WHAT IS LOYALTY?
...AND WHAT IS LOVE?

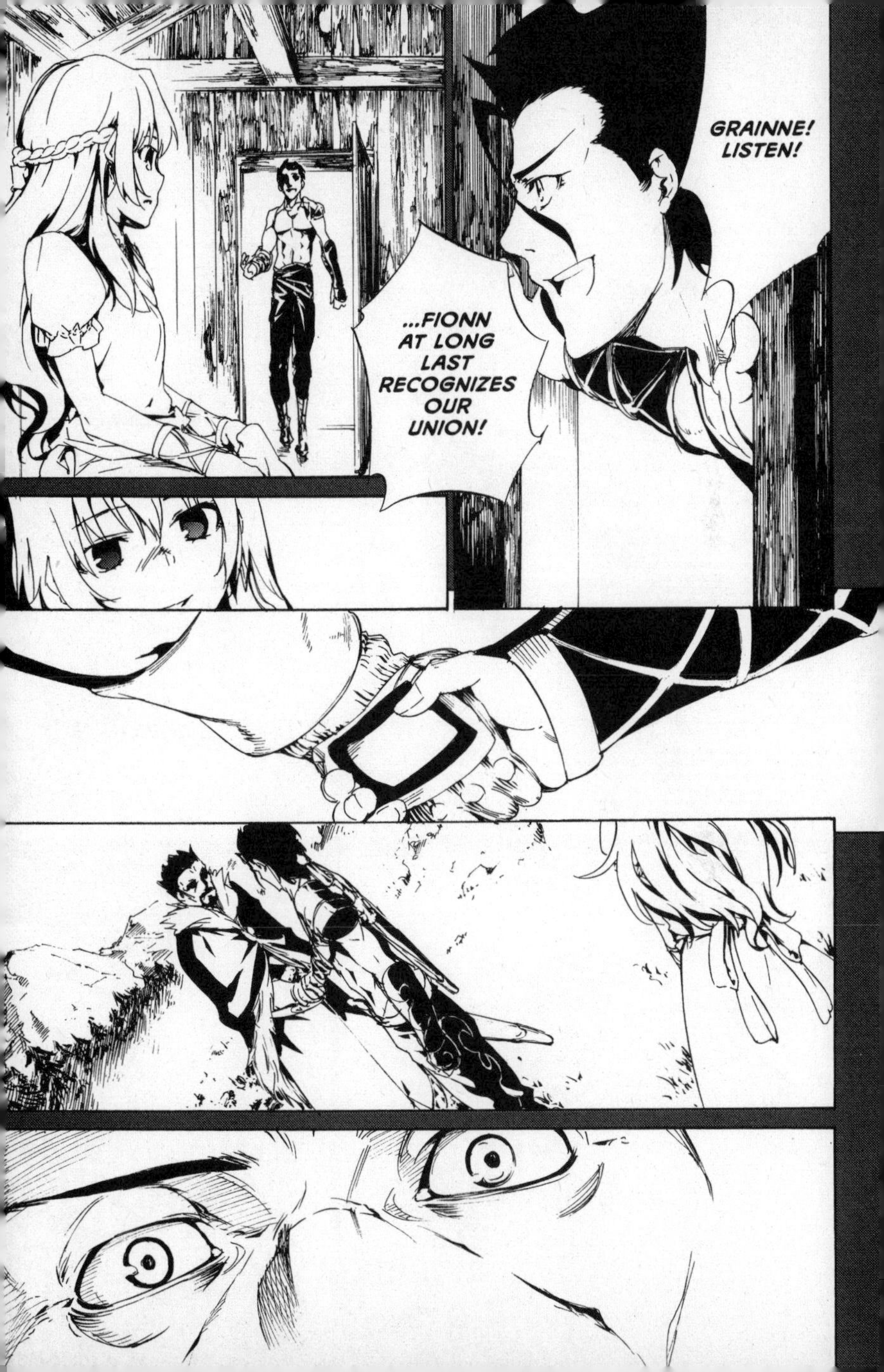
GRAINNE! LISTEN!
...FIONN AT LONG LAST RECOGNIZES OUR UNION!

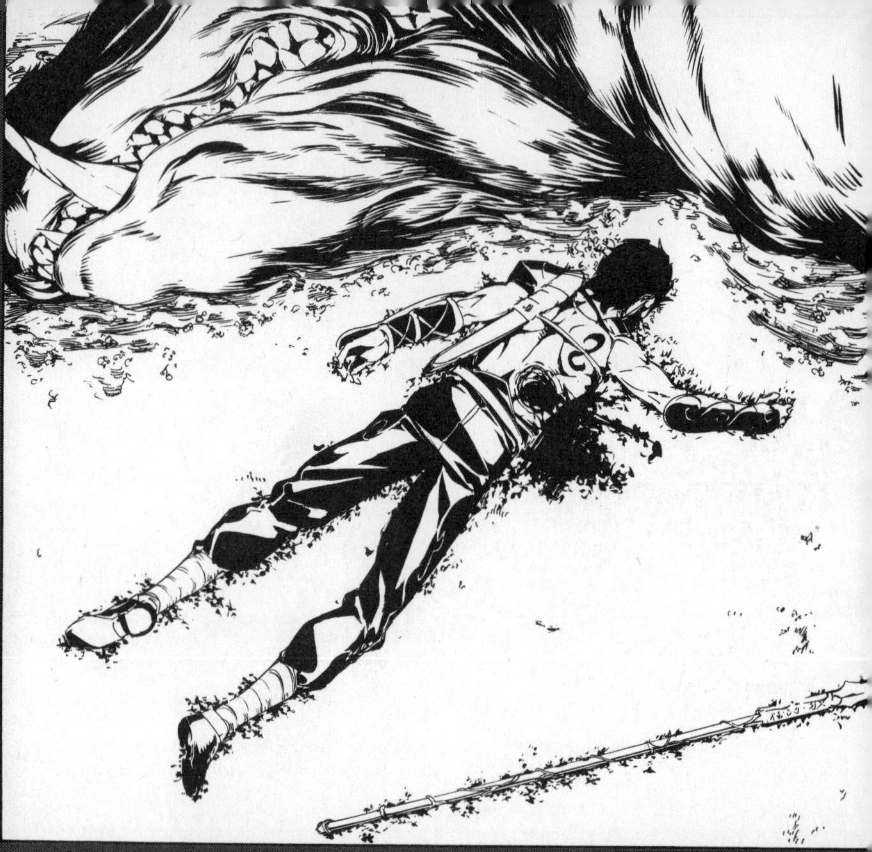
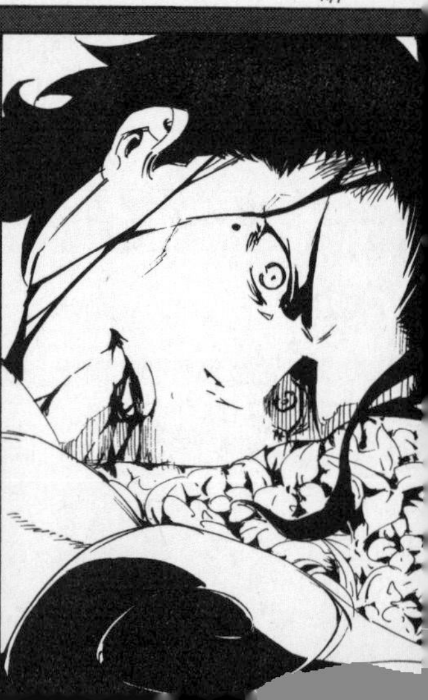
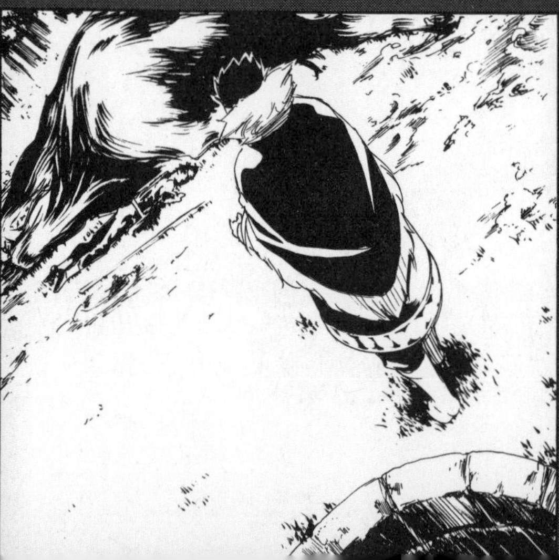

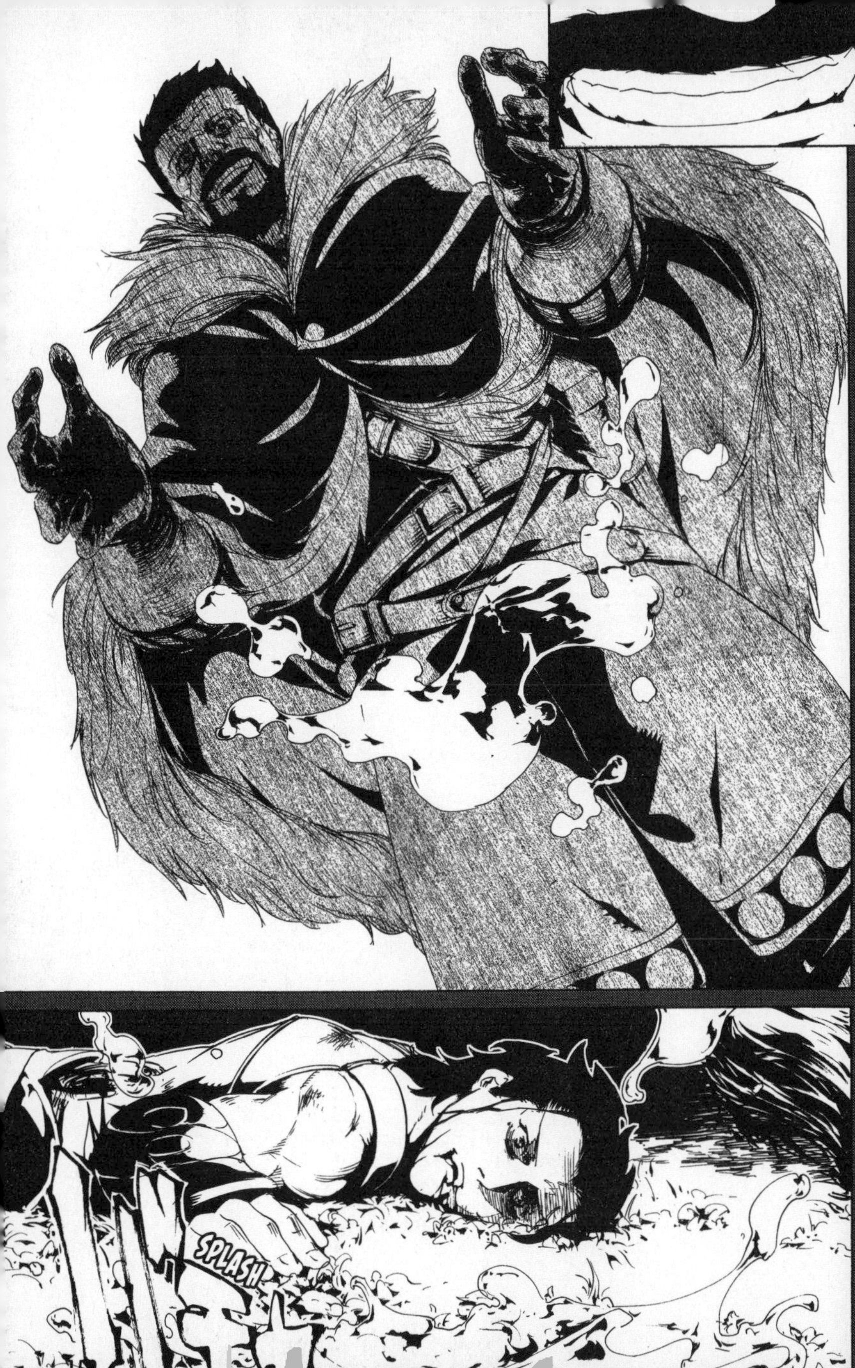
SPLASH

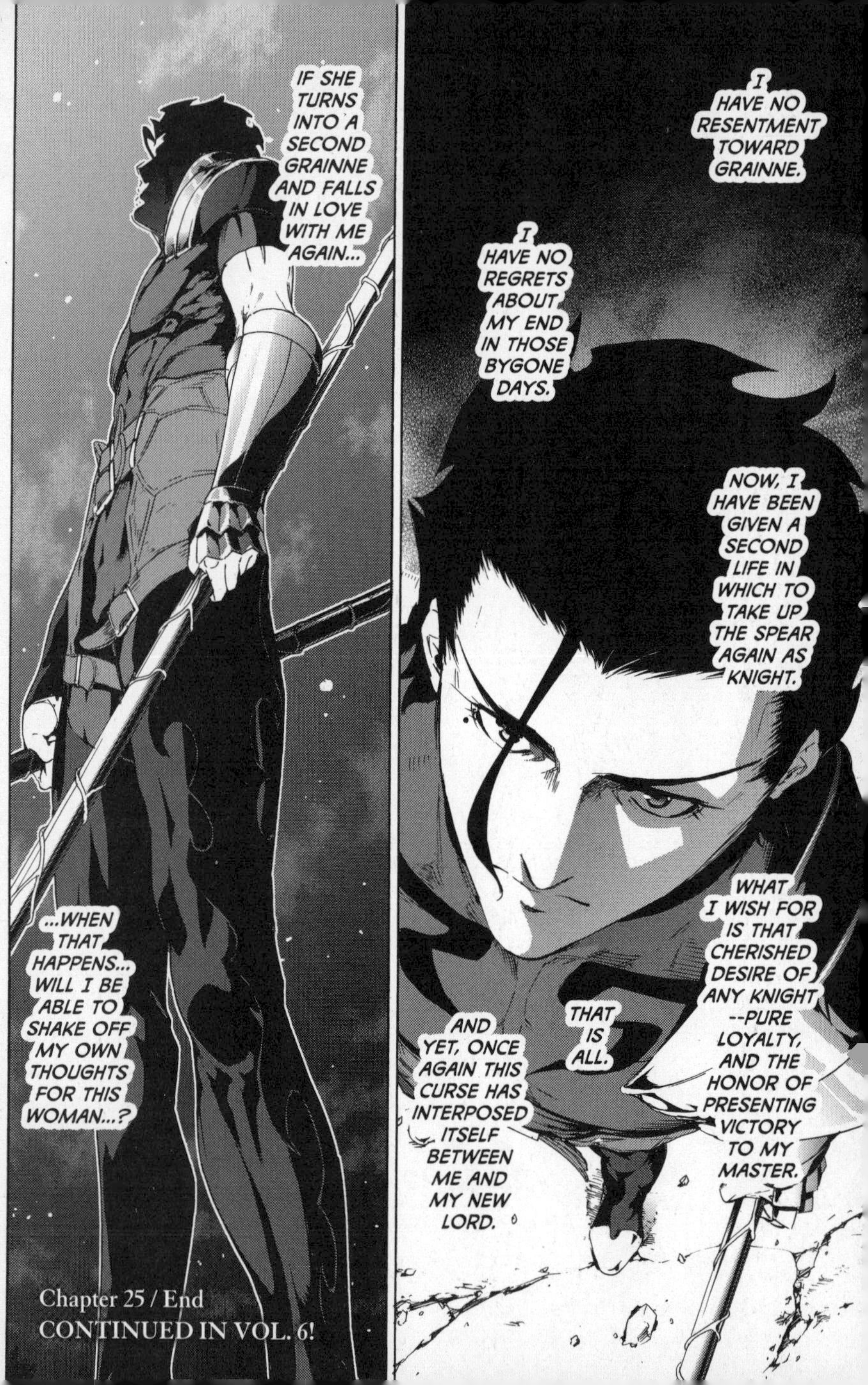
I HAVE NO RESENTMENT TOWARD GRAINNE.
I HAVE NO REGRETS ABOUT MY END IN THOSE BYGONE DAYS.
NOW, I HAVE BEEN GIVEN A SECOND LIFE IN WHICH TO TAKE UP THE SPEAR AGAIN AS KNIGHT.
WHAT I WISH FOR IS THAT CHERISHED DESIRE OF ANY KNIGHT --PURE LOYALTY, AND THE HONOR OF PRESENTING VICTORY TO MY MASTER.
THAT IS ALL.
AND YET, ONCE AGAIN THIS CURSE HAS INTERPOSED ITSELF BETWEEN ME AND MY NEW LORD.
IF SHE TURNS INTO A SECOND GRAINNE AND FALLS IN LOVE WITH ME AGAIN...
...WHEN THAT HAPPENS... WILL I BE ABLE TO SHAKE OFF MY OWN THOUGHTS FOR THIS WOMAN...?
Chapter 25 / End
CONTINUED IN VOL. 6!

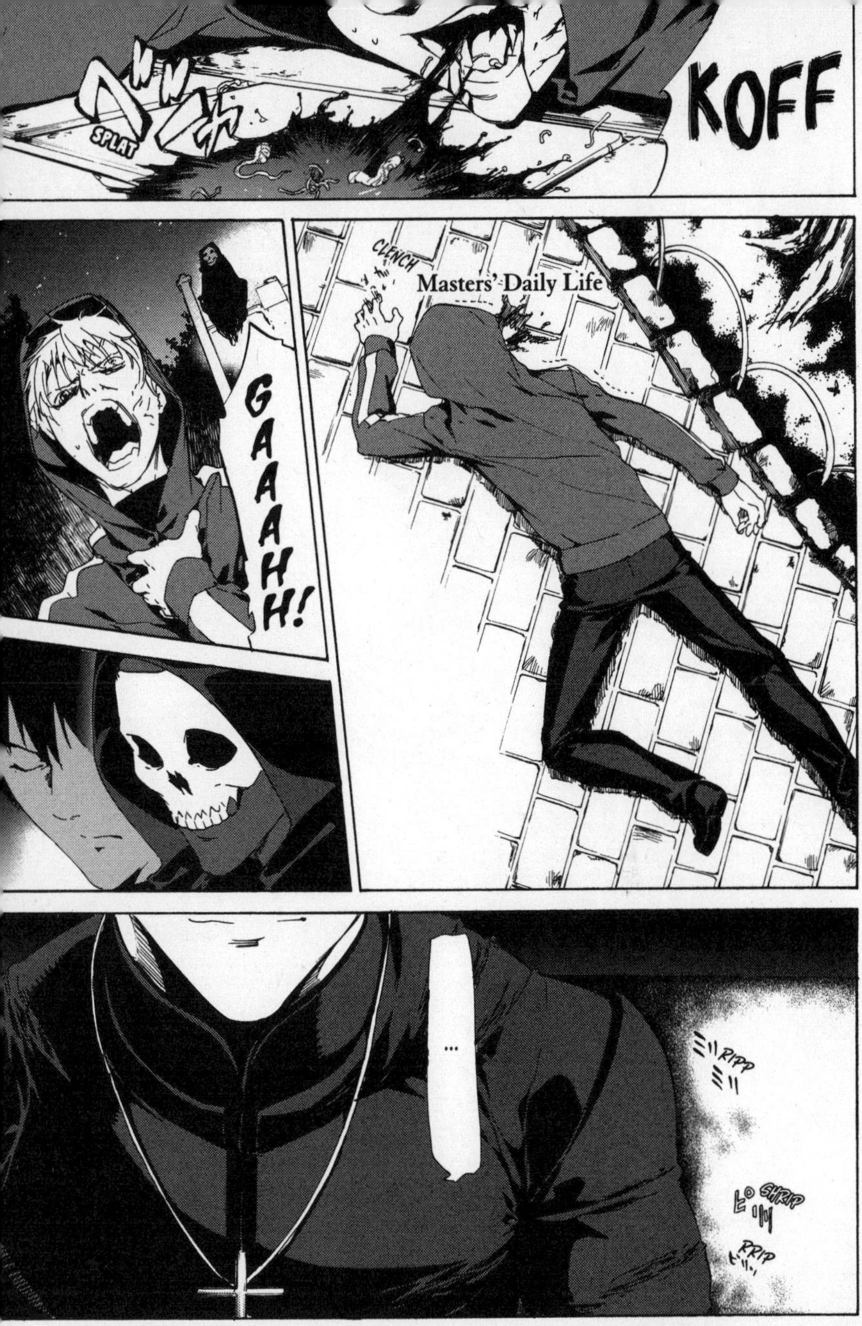
KOFF
SPLAT
CLENCH
Masters' Daily Life
GAAAAHH!
...
RIPP
SHRIP
RRIP

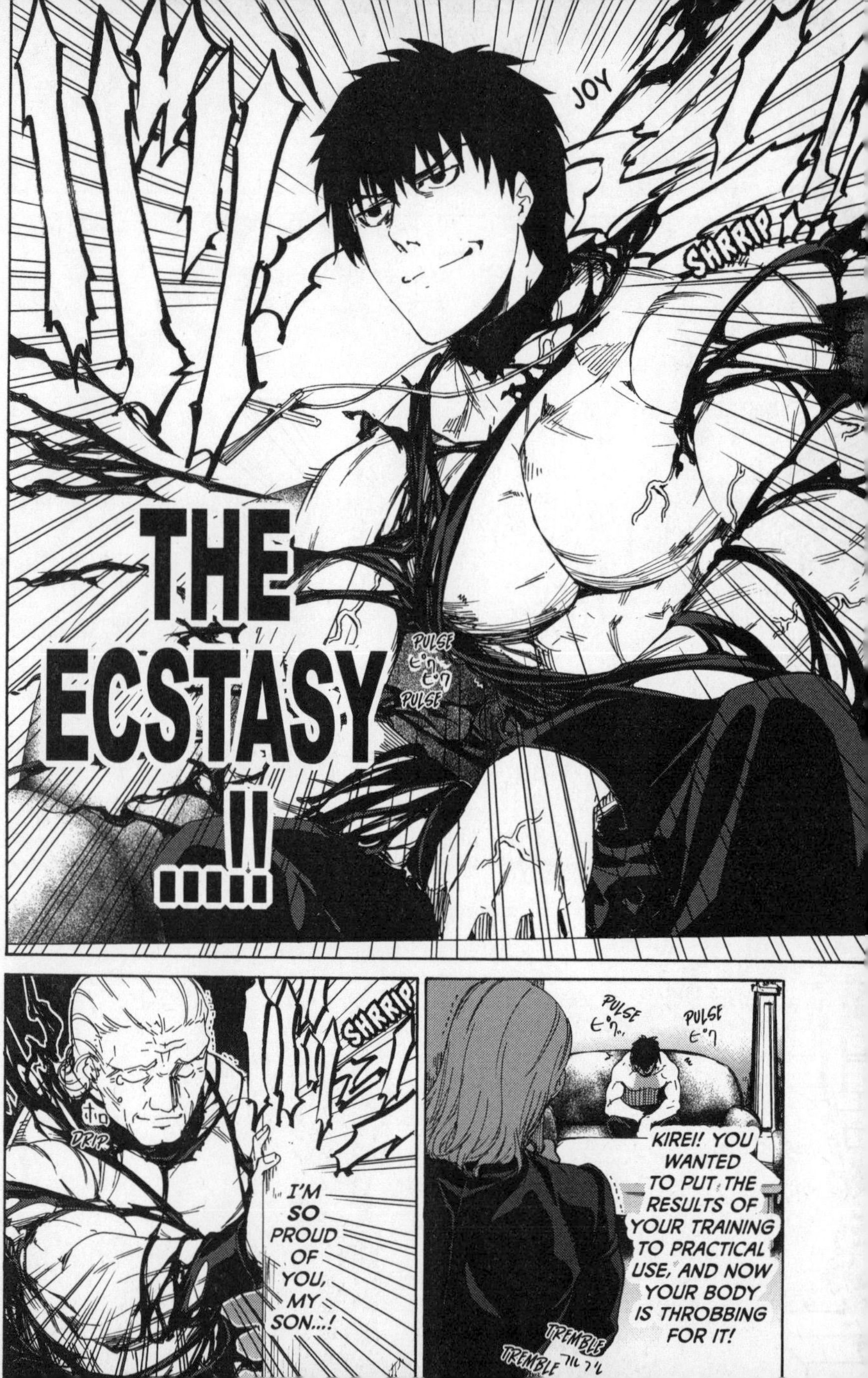
JOY
SHRRIP
THE ECSTASY ....!!
PULSE ピク ピク PULSE
PULSE ピク..
PULSE ピク
KIREI! YOU WANTED TO PUT THE RESULTS OF YOUR TRAINING TO PRACTICAL USE, AND NOW YOUR BODY IS THROBBING FOR IT!
TREMBLE TREMBLE フルフル
SHRRIP
DRIP
I'M SO PROUD OF YOU, MY SON...!

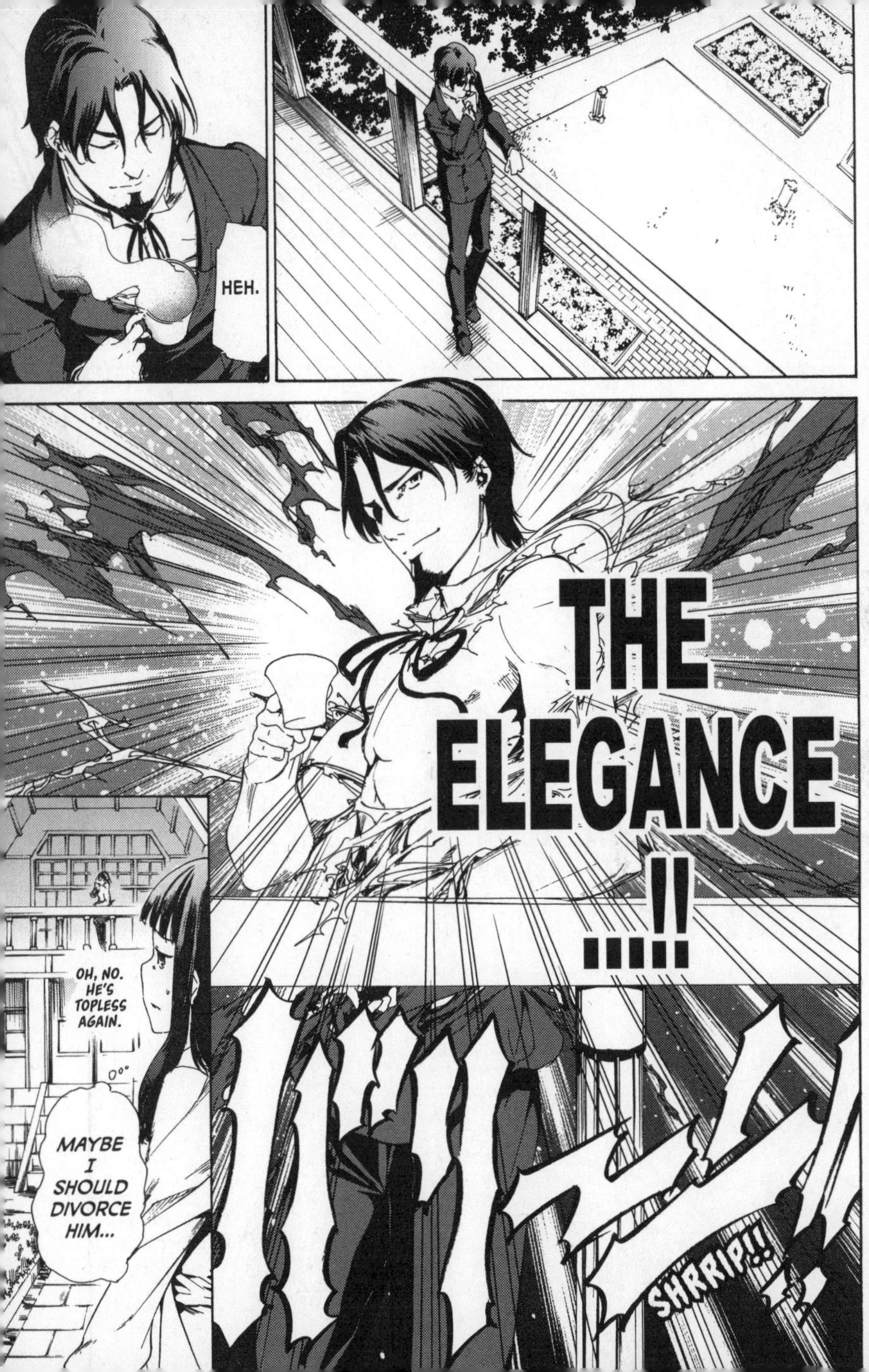
HEH.
THE ELEGANCE ...!!
SHRRIP!!
OH, NO. HE'S TOPLESS AGAIN.
MAYBE I SHOULD DIVORCE HIM...

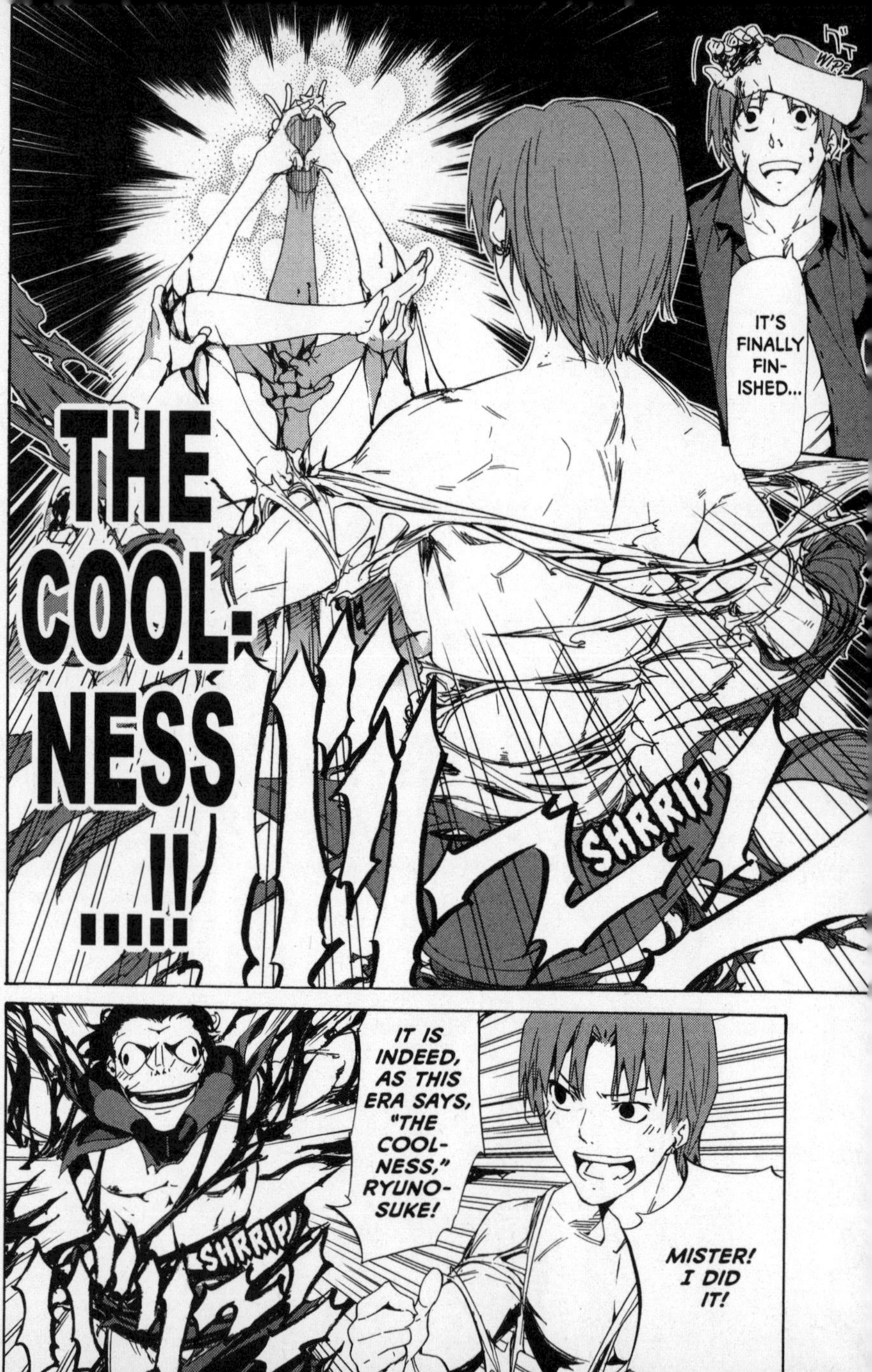
WIPE
IT'S FINALLY FIN-ISHED...
THE COOL-NESS ...!!
SHRRIP
MISTER! I DID IT!
IT IS INDEED, AS THIS ERA SAYS, "THE COOL-NESS," RYUNO-SUKE!
SHRRIP!

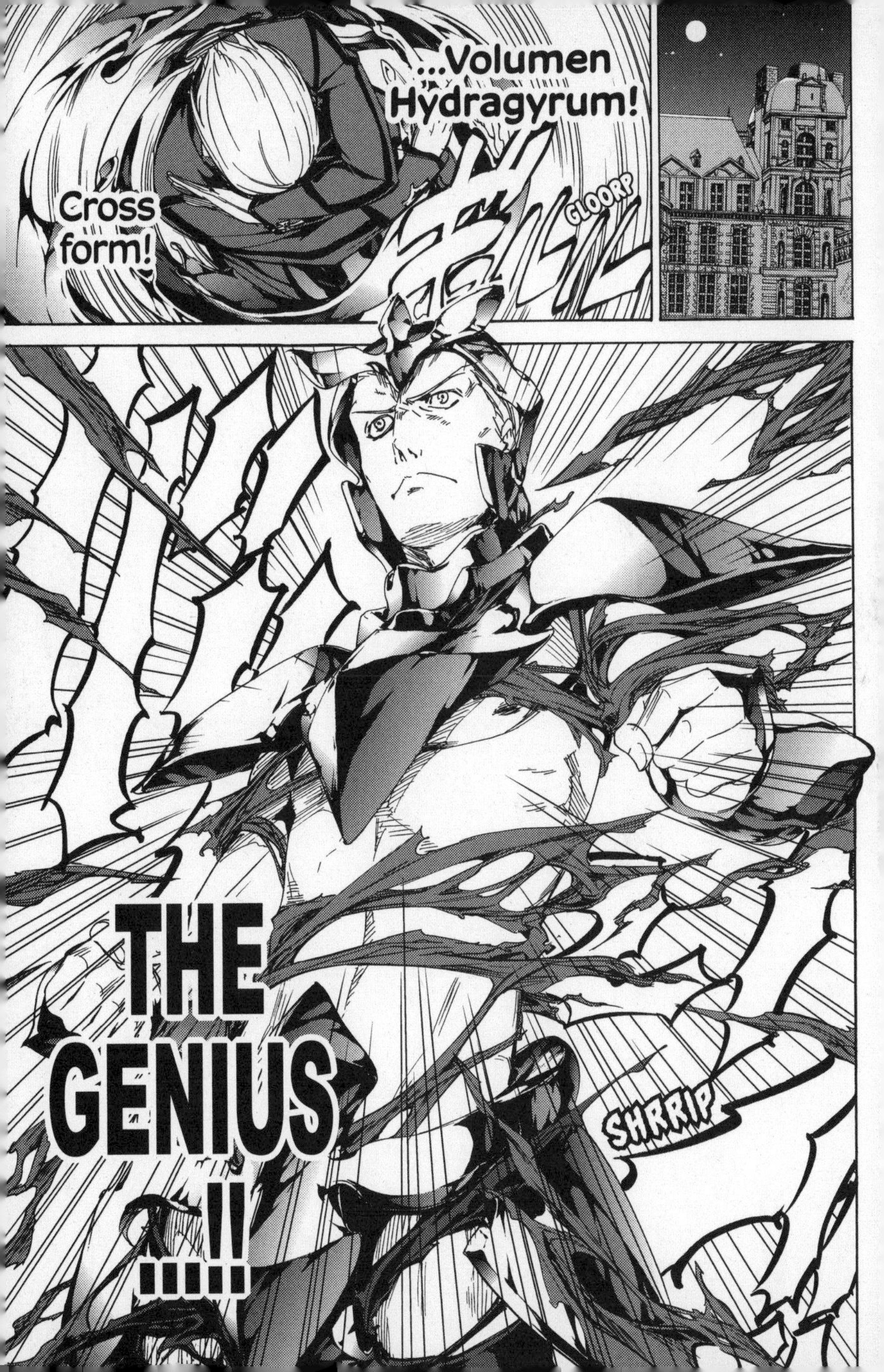
...Volumen Hydragyrum!
GLOORP
Cross form!
SHRRIP
THE GENIUS ...!!

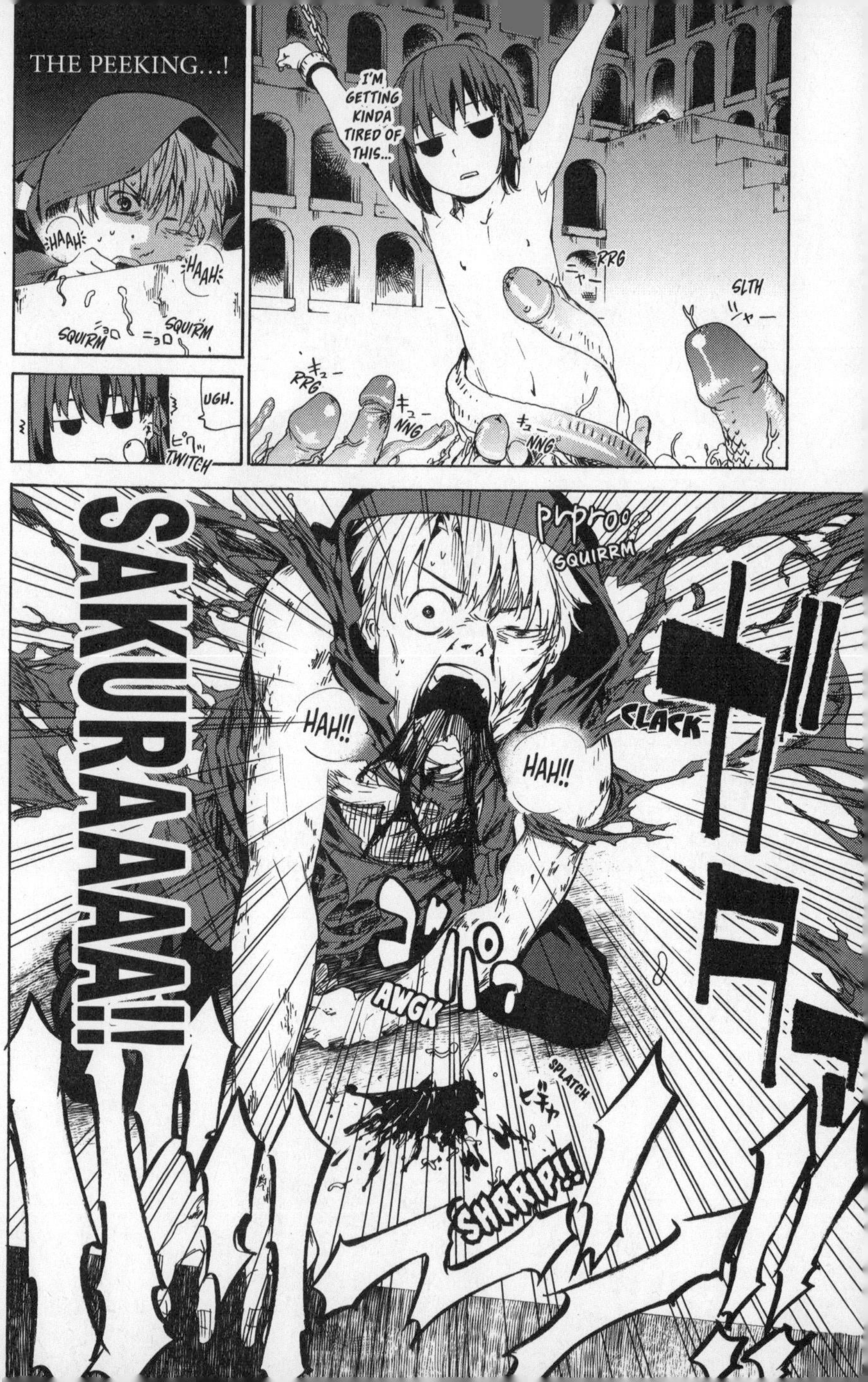
I'M GETTING KINDA TIRED OF THIS...
RRG
SLTH
RRG
NNG
NNG
THE PEEKING...!
HAAAH
HAAAH
SQUIRM
SQUIRM
UGH.
TWITCH
SAKURAAAA!!!
prprooo
SQUIRRM
CLACK
HAH!!
HAH!!
AWGK
SPLATCH
SHRRIP!!

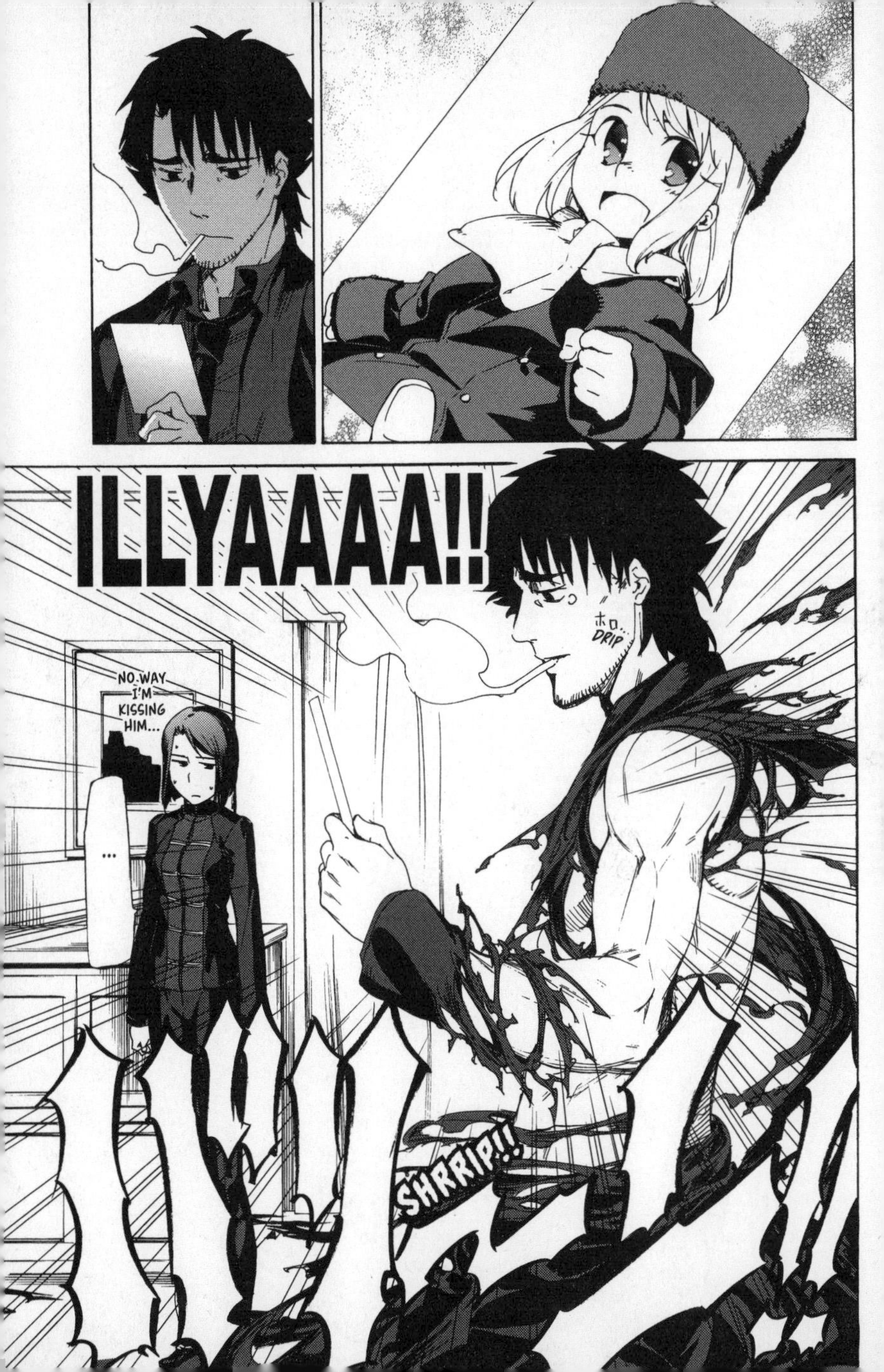
ILLYAAAA!!
ホロ… DRIP
NO WAY I'M KISSING HIM...
...
SHRRIP!!

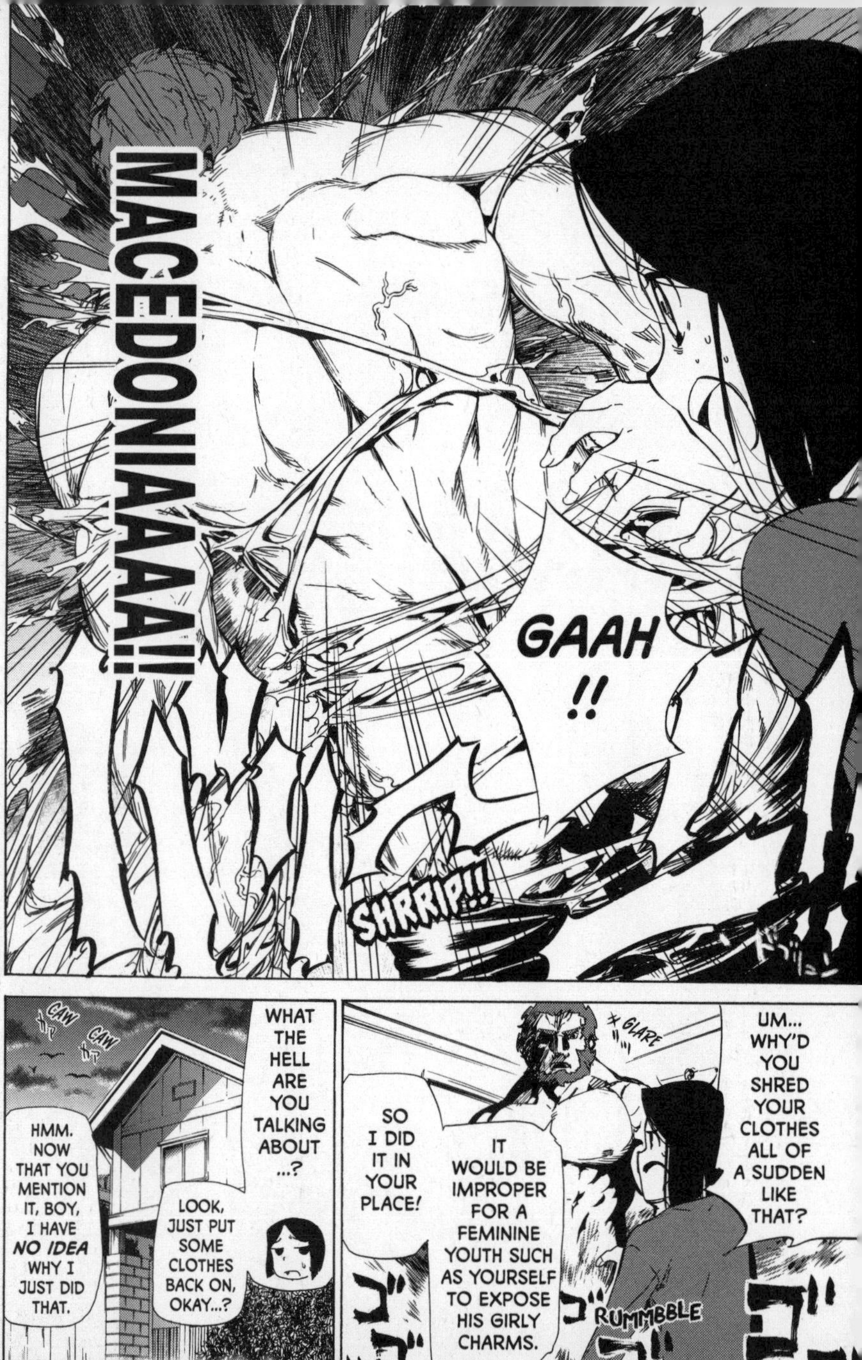
GAAH !!
SHRRIP!!
MACEDONIAAAA!!!
UM... WHY'D YOU SHRED YOUR CLOTHES ALL OF A SUDDEN LIKE THAT?
GLARE
IT WOULD BE IMPROPER FOR A FEMININE YOUTH SUCH AS YOURSELF TO EXPOSE HIS GIRLY CHARMS.
SO I DID IT IN YOUR PLACE!
RUMMBBLE
WHAT THE HELL ARE YOU TALKING ABOUT ...?
CAW
CAW
HMM. NOW THAT YOU MENTION IT, BOY, I HAVE ***NO IDEA*** WHY I JUST DID THAT.
LOOK, JUST PUT SOME CLOTHES BACK ON, OKAY...?
Masters' Daily Life / End

Special thanks to original-edition staff members Ayano Takahiro and Natsume Riku

HATSUNE MIKU: ACUTE

Art and story by Shiori Asahina
Miku, Kaito, and Luka! Once they were all friends making songs—but while Kaito might make a duet with Miku or a duet with Luka, a love song all three of them sing together can only end in sorrow!

ISBN 978-1-50670-341-1
$10.99

HATSUNE MIKU: RIN-CHAN NOW!

Story by Sezu
Art by Hiro Tamura
Miku's sassy blond friend takes center stage in this series that took inspiration from the music video "Rin-chan Now!" The video is now a manga of the same name—written, drawn, and edited by the video creators!

VOLUME 1
978-1-50670-313-8
$10.99

VOLUME 2
978-1-50670-314-5
$10.99

HATSUNE MIKU: MIKUBON

Art and story by Ontama
Hatsune Miku and her friends Rin, Len, and Luka enroll at the St. Diva Academy for Vocaloids! At St. Diva, a wonderland of friendship, determination, and even love unfolds! But can they stay out of trouble, especially when the mad professor of the Hachune Miku Research Lab is nearby . . . ?

ISBN 978-1-50670-231-5
$10.99

UNOFFICIAL HATSUNE MIX

Art and story by KEI
Miku's original illustrator, KEI, produced a best-selling omnibus manga of the musical adventures (and misadventures!) of Miku and her fellow Vocaloids Rin, Len, Luka, and more—in both beautiful black-and-white and charming color!

ISBN 978-1-61655-412-5
$19.99

WHO'S THAT GIRL WITH THE LONG GREEN PONYTAILS YOU'VE BEEN SEEING EVERYWHERE? IT'S HATSUNE MIKU, THE VOCALOID— THE SYNTHESIZER SUPERSTAR WHO'S SINGING YOUR SONG!

AVAILABLE AT YOUR LOCAL COMICS SHOP OR BOOKSTORE

HATSUNE MIKU

TO FIND A COMICS SHOP IN YOUR AREA, CALL 1-888-266-4226. For more information or to order direct:
• On the web: DarkHorse.com • Email: mailorder@darkhorse.com • Phone: 1-800-862-0052 Mon.–Fri. 9 AM to 5 PM Pacific Time.

DRIFTERS

KOHTA HIRANO

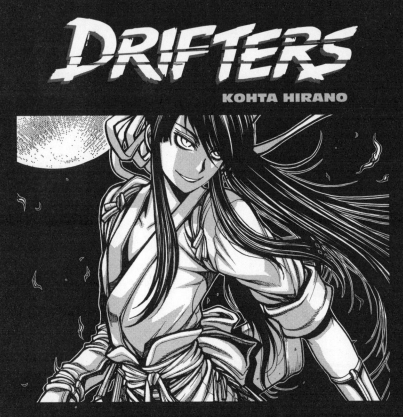

Heroes from Earth's history are deposited in an enchanted land where humans subjugate the nonhuman races. This wild, action-packed series features historical characters such as Joan of Arc, Hannibal, and Rasputin being used as chess pieces in a bloody, endless battle!

From Kohta Hirano, creator of the smash-hit *Hellsing*, *Drifters* is an all-out fantasy slugfest of epic proportion!

VOLUME ONE
978-1-59582-769-2

VOLUME TWO
978-1-59582-933-7

VOLUME THREE
978-1-61655-339-5

$13.99 each

NEON GENESIS EVANGELION

Dark Horse Manga is proud to present new original series based on the wildly popular *Neon Genesis Evangelion* manga and anime! Continuing the rich story lines and complex characters, these new visions of *Neon Genesis Evangelion* provide extra dimensions for understanding one of the greatest series ever made!

NEON GENESIS EVANGELION
Campus Apocalypse

STORY AND ART BY MINGMING

VOLUME 1
ISBN 978-1-59582-530-8 | $10.99

VOLUME 2
ISBN 978-1-59582-661-9 | $10.99

VOLUME 3
ISBN 978-1-59582-680-0 | $10.99

VOLUME 4
ISBN 978-1-59582-689-3 | $10.99

NEON GENESIS EVANGELION
COMIC TRIBUTE

STORY AND ART BY VARIOUS CREATORS

ISBN 978-1-61655-114-8 | $10.99

NEON GENESIS EVANGELION
THE Shinji Ikari Detective Diary

STORY AND ART BY TAKUMI YOSHIMURA

VOLUME 1
ISBN 978-1-61655-225-1 | $9.99

VOLUME 2
ISBN 978-1-61655-418-7 | $9.99

TONY TAKEZAKI'S
NEON GENESIS EVANGELION

STORY AND ART BY TONY TAKEZAKI

ISBN 978-1-61655-736-2 | $12.99

NEON GENESIS EVANGELION
THE SHINJI IKARI RAISING PROJECT

STORY AND ART BY OSAMU TAKAHASHI

VOLUME 1
ISBN 978-1-59582-321-2 | $9.99

VOLUME 2
ISBN 978-1-59582-377-9 | $9.99

VOLUME 3
ISBN 978-1-59582-447-9 | $9.99

VOLUME 4
ISBN 978-1-59582-454-7 | $9.99

VOLUME 5
ISBN 978-1-59582-520-9 | $9.99

VOLUME 6
ISBN 978-1-59582-580-3 | $9.99

VOLUME 7
ISBN 978-1-59582-595-7 | $9.99

VOLUME 8
ISBN 978-1-59582-694-7 | $9.99

VOLUME 9
ISBN 978-1-59582-800-2 | $9.99

VOLUME 10
ISBN 978-1-59582-879-8 | $9.99

VOLUME 11
ISBN 978-1-59582-932-0 | $9.99

VOLUME 12
ISBN 978-1-61655-033-2 | $9.99

VOLUME 13
ISBN 978-1-61655-315-9 | $9.99

VOLUME 14
ISBN 978-1-61655-432-3 | $9.99

VOLUME 15
ISBN 978-1-61655-607-5 | $9.99

VOLUME 16
ISBN 978-1-61655-997-7 | $9.99

VOLUME 17
ISBN 978-1-50670-083-0 | $9.99

Each volume of *Neon Genesis Evangelion* features bonus color pages, your *Evangelion* fan art and letters, and special reader giveaways!

AVAILABLE AT YOUR LOCAL COMICS SHOP OR BOOKSTORE
To find a comics shop in your area, call 1-888-266-4226 • For more information or to order direct: • On the web: darkhorse.com
E-mail: mailorder@darkhorse.com • Phone: 1-800-862-0052 Mon.–Fri. 9 AM to 5 PM Pacific Time.

DarkHorse.com

DARK HORSE MANGA

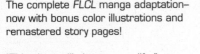

publisher
MIKE RICHARDSON

assistant editor
JEMIAH JEFFERSON

collection designer
SARAH TERRY

digital art technician
CHRIS HORN

Special thanks to Roxy Polk, Michael Gombos, Sandy Tanaka,
Annie Gullion, and Carl Gustav Horn.

Dark Horse Manga, a division of Dark Horse Comics, Inc.
10956 SE Main Street, Milwaukie, OR 97222
DarkHorse.com

To find a comics shop in your area, call the Comic Shop Locator Service toll-free at 1-888-266-4226.

First edition: June 2017
ISBN 978-1-50670-175-2

1 3 5 7 9 10 8 6 4 2
Printed in the United States of America